Rhino for Jewelry

Dana Buscaglia

ISBN#978-0-557-08736-5

INTRODUCTION

OBJECTIVE   The chapters in this book were conceived as step-by-step tutorials to be used for Rhinoceros™ courses for jewelry students and professionals. There was a perceived need for a written text that was jewelry industry specific so that students could review lessons and have a text for reference once the class was over and the real learning curve began.

JEWELRY DESIGNERS   Jewelry designers can use Rhinoceros™ for both the creation of technical drawings/layouts and the building of 3-dimensional models for the purpose of visualization. By using a 3-dimensional modeling approach to design, the designer can participate in the creative process to a greater degree than ever before.

JEWELRY MODEL MAKERS   Jewelry model makers are now able to build jewelry models on the computer, having them "printed" or milled by modern prototyping technology. The ability to model on the computer and to have clients review the rendered images before the actual production of the piece has changed the way jewelry professionals interact with clients. But this is not the only benefit. Models can be partly made on the computer, to be completed by hand after the initial shape has been modeled, "printed" and cast.

CONTENTS This book is divided into two sections:
- **The creation of 2-dimensional drawings and layouts**
  - Basic creation and editing of 2-dimensional objects, such as lines and curves and the creation of technical drawings and layouts.
- **The modeling of 3-dimensional objects**
  - Using knowledge in the first part of the book to create 3-dimension jewelry objects.

SUGGESTED APPROACH
- Go through this book from the beginning and, slowly and thoughtfully, take yourself through the step-by-step chapters. Repeat a chapter if you feel that you had a struggle getting through it. The extra time spent will pay off! Stay calm and understand that everyone goes through this stage!
- Avail yourself of the Help Menu in Rhino. The reader is urged to take advantage of this resource within Rhino. If you see a command described in a tutorial that you may not fully understand, press "F1" and you will be taken to the Help menu *for that command.*
- Take Rhino courses. You will always learn something more with each course that you take.
- Avail yourself of the <u>Rhino Training Manual, Level 1</u> which is included in your Rhino CD in PDF format. The book, <u>Inside Rhinoceros 4</u>, by Ron K.C. Cheng is an excellent reference as well.
- There are many Rhino tutorials on the Internet. If you do a search, you will find free videos on sites like YouTube. Also, check out the Rhino website, **www.rhino3D.com**.
- Understand that most of the learning starts at home, working on your own computer. Don't feel that you have to keep taking courses to continue learning. The hard work is done by you alone, applying commands to your own needs and doing your own problem solving.
- Start using Rhino in your own work. The sooner you do that, the faster you will learn.

CONSIDER RHINOGOLD   RhinoGold™ is an excellent jewelry specific software that operates within Rhino. It makes certain tasks very easy - stones, stone settings, pavé, building and hollowing ring shanks, quick creation of surface textures, excellent photorealistic rendering of models and much more. Check out their website: **www.RhinoGold.com**

Table of Contents

CREATING & EDITING 2-DIMENSIONAL OBJECTS

CREATING & EDITING 3-DIMENSIONAL OBJECTS - next page ➞

CREATING & EDITING 3-DIMENSIONAL OBJECTS

The Rhino Workspace*
A brief tour.

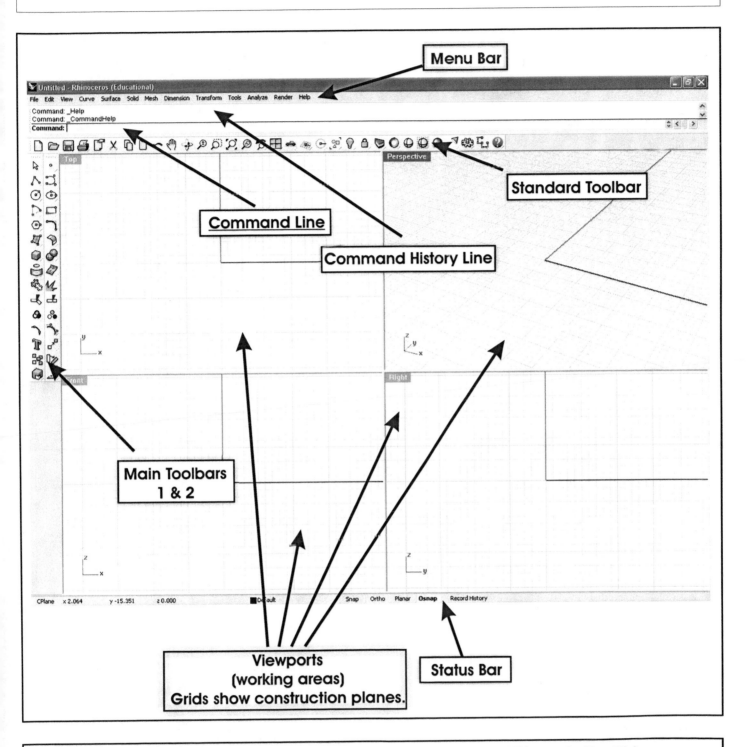

Menu Bar

Standard Toolbar

Command Line

Command History Line

Main Toolbars
1 & 2

Viewports
(working areas)
Grids show construction planes.

Status Bar

* You can also refer to the excellent chapter on the Rhino workspace in the Rhino Training Manual, Level 1.

Viewports

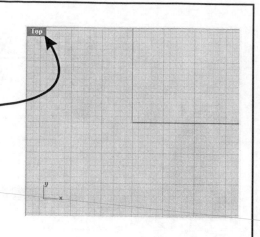

- **Viewports** are the working areas of Rhino. They can be maximized by double clicking on the viewport title or minimized by double clicking again to show more than one view at a time.

- Ordinarily, the **Top** viewport is used for 2D work. The other views come into play when working in 3D space and offer different views of the objects being created.

- The grids shown are on the **Construction Planes**.

- **Construction planes** are the imaginary surfaces upon which objects created are placed by default.

Menus

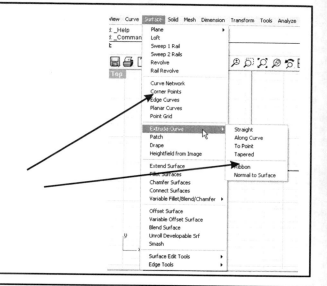

- Just about every Rhino tool and command can be found in the drop-down menus at the top of the workspace.

Toolbars

- Toolbars are sets of buttons that activate various commands when you click on them with the mouse.

- The set of default toolbars in the Rhino space include the **Standard toolbar** and the **Main toolbar 1** and **Main toolbar 2**. This is collectively called the *default toolbar collection*.

- Toolbar collections can be customized. [Ref: Creating a Custom Toolbar Collection - page 433.

Toolbar Flyouts

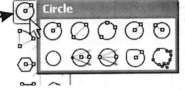
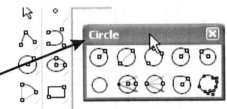

- A little white triangle at the lower right corner of a button means that you can **right click on this button** and another toolbar will appear. This is called a **toolbar flyout**.

- Click and drag the toolbar out into the viewport and it will remain on the screen as a **"floating toolbar"** until you close it by clicking in the upper right corner.

Tooltips

- If you hover the cursor over a single button, a little text box will appear.

- This little text box is called a **tooltip** and it describes the command or commands called up by that button.

- The little black and white symbols to the left of each tooltip are symbols for the left and right mouse buttons.

- In this example, the **left mouse button** accesses the **Control Point Curve** command and the **right mouse button** accesses the **Curve Through Points** command.

Command Line

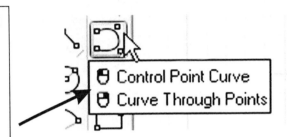

Center of circle (Deformable Vertical 2Point 3Point Tangent AroundCurve FitPoints):

In this example, the **Circle** command is active. The **Command Line** is prompting for the center of the circle.

Within the parentheses are various options in the form of links that can toggle them on or off with a click of the mouse as shown. The hand symbol shown is the form the cursor takes when clicking on one of these options.

- Press the **Esc** key to cancel a command.

- Activate a command from a toolbar button, from the drop-down menu line, or by simply typing in a command.

- Press "enter" or the spacebar to activate the previous command.

Command History Line

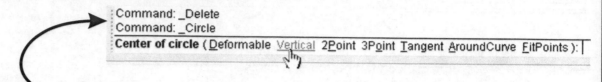

```
Command: _Delete
Command: _Circle
Center of circle (Deformable Vertical 2Point 3Point Tangent AroundCurve FitPoints ):
```

- The **Command History Line** shows the commands that immediately preceded the current command.

- It can also be a source of information, depending on the command.

- You can press the **F2 key** to review the entire command history going back to the start of the file.

- **Right click** in this window for a list of previous commands that you can click on to re-activate.

Rhino Help

Help: Press **F1** and Rhino Help will open up. If you are in a command and press **F1**, Rhino Help will open to the same command in which you are presently working!

Construction Plane

- The two "axes" of the construction plane are called the **X Axis** and the **Y Axis.**

- Where these two axes meet is the center of the grid which is called "0", of "0,0".

- To read more about coordinates of a grid, refer to the Rhino Training Manual, Level 1 for a more extensive description.

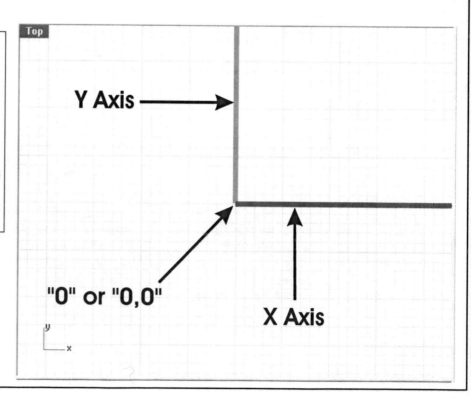

Viewport Navigation for 2D Drawings

- Open Rhino.

- Access the **Open Tutorial Models** command from the **Help** drop-down menu in the **Menu Bar** at the top of the screen as shown.

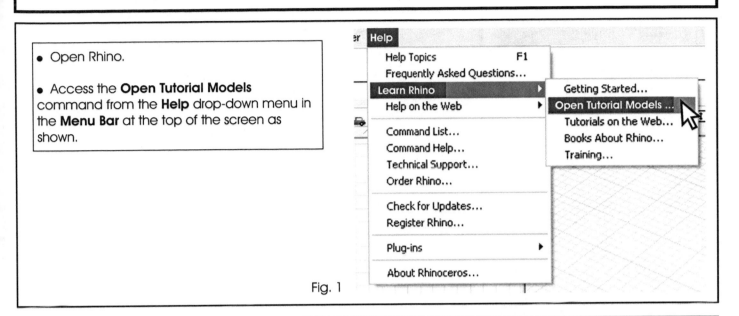

Fig. 1

- Select the **Level 1** folder and click on the "open" button.

- The files in this tutorials folder are practice models that have been provided with the Rhino software.

Fig. 2

- In the **Level 1** folder, click on the file called **Filletex** and click on the "open" button.

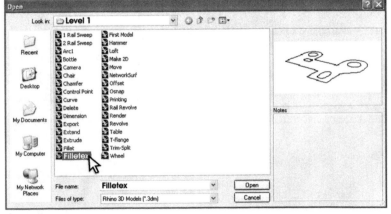

Fig. 3

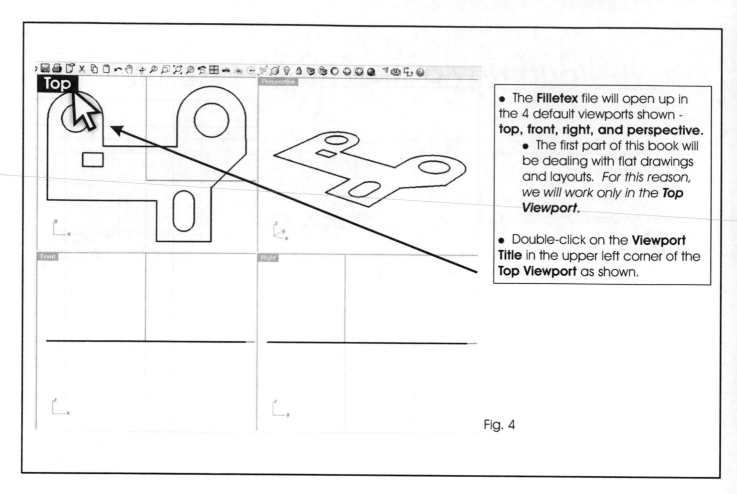

• The **Filletex** file will open up in the 4 default viewports shown - **top, front, right, and perspective.**
  • The first part of this book will be dealing with flat drawings and layouts. *For this reason, we will work only in the Top Viewport.*

• Double-click on the **Viewport Title** in the upper left corner of the **Top Viewport** as shown.

Fig. 4

• The **Top viewport** will "**maximize**" to fill the space formerly occupied by the 4 default viewports.
  • If you double-click on the viewport title again, the view will revert to the 4 default viewports.

• Maximizing the viewport will enable you to see your drawings in more detail.

• Drawings, as flat objects, do not need to be seen in perspective.

• It is advised that you always maximize the viewport when doing 2-dimensional drawings.

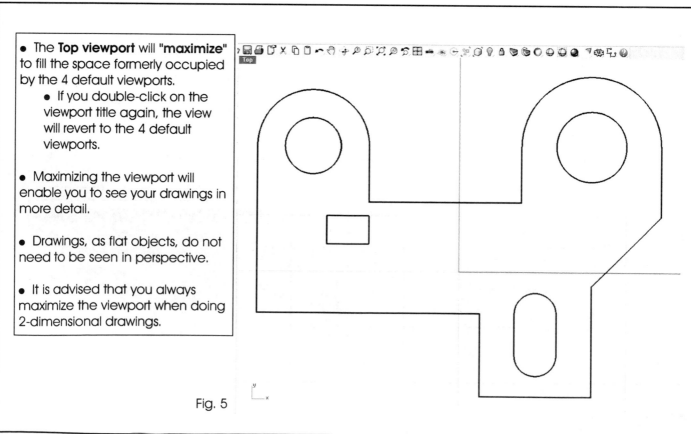

Fig. 5

- Click and drag on the construction plane with the **right mouse button.**

- Note how the view moves with the cursor which has taken on the appearance of a little hand. This is called **Panning.**

- Release the cursor, when the view has moved to the desired position.

- Click and drag as often as necessary, for viewing or during commands to move the view for better visibility.

Fig. 6

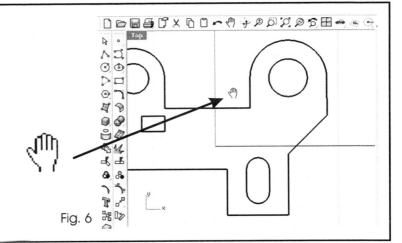

- **Left click** on the **Zoom Extents** command.

- The object is now fully visible again.

- This command will automatically zoom to include anything that is visible in the workspace.

Zoom Extents
command

Fig. 7

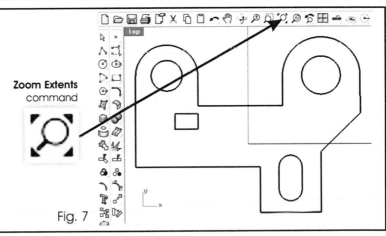

- Turn the scroll wheel on your mouse back and forward that your viewport will zoom in and out.

- This is the easiest way to zoom.

Fig. 8

- Another way to zoom is to click and drag with the **right mouse button** - *while holding down the control key.*
  - When using this method of zooming, the cursor will take on the appearance shown.

Fig. 9

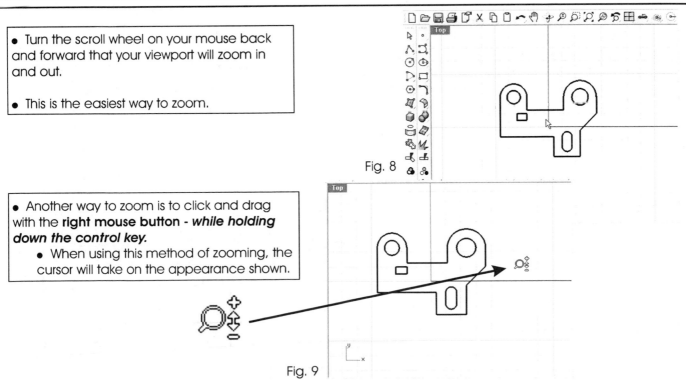

- Zoom in on the portion of the drawing shown.

- Select the circle shown by hovering the cursor over it and **left clicking**.
  - If you click away from this object, it will de-select.

- Click on the **Zoom Selected** command.

Zoom Selected command

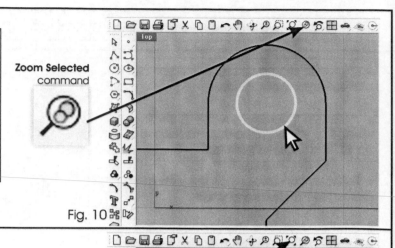

Fig. 10

- You will immediately zoom in on the selected circle which fills the screen.

- **Left click** on the **Undo View Change** command.

Undo View Change command

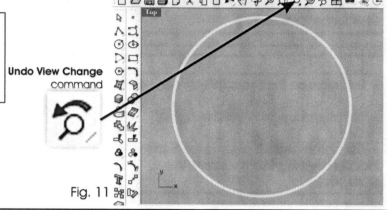

Fig. 11

- The view will revert back to the previous view.

- You can click again to revert back to the view previous to this one.

- **Right click** to revert in the other direction to the view that followed this one.

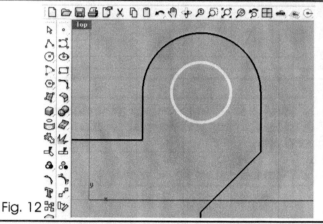

Fig. 12

- Zoom out or click on the **Zoom Extents** command so that you can see the whole drawing once again.

- **Left click** on the **Zoom Window** command.
  - **Drag a window to zoom** prompt: click and drag a window around a section of the drawing as shown. [**click on ❶** then **drag to ❷ and release the button**]

Zoom Window command

Drag a window to zoom (All Dynamic Extents Factor In Out Selected Target 1To1):

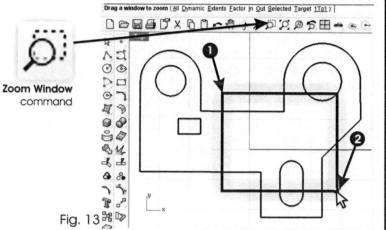

Fig. 13

8

- The view will zoom to the area that you created with the window.

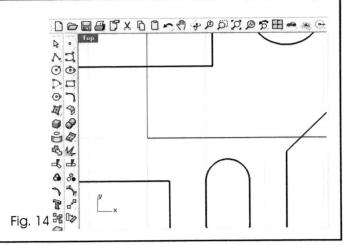

Fig. 14

- Sometimes your viewport will assume a strange aspect. The grid may not look square any more and the drawing may look skewed. Panning with the right mouse button will result in the view tipping and rotating.

- This probably means that you have *inadvertently tipped into 3D space*. This can happen by mistakenly pressing one of the arrow keys or by panning with the **Shift** and **control** keys both being pressed at the same time.

- To quickly get back to the **Top** view, click on the **Top View** command in the **Set View** toolbar flyout as shown.

accesses the
Set View
toolbar flyout

Top View
command

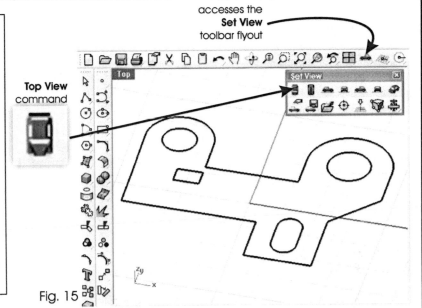

Fig. 15

- The top view will be restored.

- *Important note:* The top view is called a "plan view", or a "parallel view".
  - *This means that you are looking absolutely straight down from a vertical viewpoint onto the construction plane.*
  - *This is the only way that you can get a totally accurate view of your drawing.*

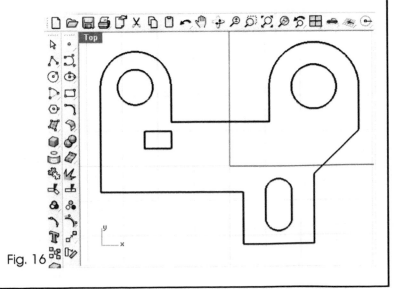

Fig. 16

Anatomy of a Line and a Polyline

- This exercise demonstrates the difference between the creation of a **LINE** and the creation of a **POLYLINE**.

- **LEFT CLICK** refers to the **LEFT MOUSE BUTTON**.

- **RIGHT CLICK** refers to the **RIGHT MOUSE BUTTON**.

Line command

- Access the **Lines** toolbar flyout.

- **LEFT CLICK** on the **Line** command.

accesses
Lines
toolbar flyout

Line
command

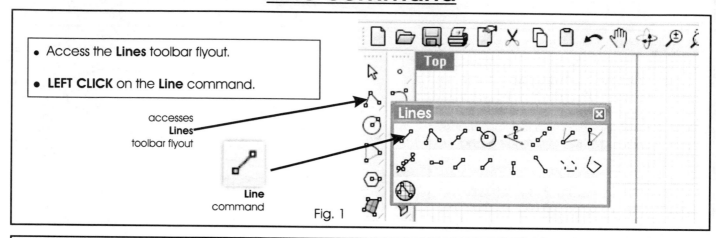

Fig. 1

- **Start of line** prompt: **LEFT CLICK** on a location on the construction plane as shown.
    - This will set the location of the start of the line.

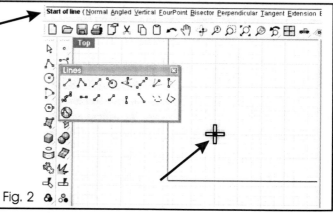

Fig. 2

- **End of Line** prompt: Draw the cursor across the construction plane to arrive at the location for the end of the line.
    - Notice the "rubber band" line preview that now follows the cursor.

end of line

start of line

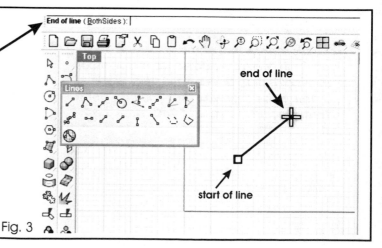

Fig. 3

- **LEFT CLICK** to set the location of the end of the line and the command is finished.

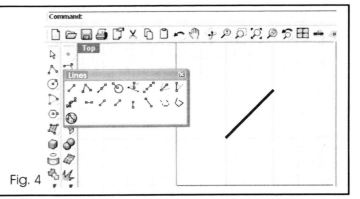

Fig. 4

- Press "enter" or **RIGHT CLICK** to call up the **Line** command once again. You can call up a previous command in this manner, rather than having to click on the button again!

- As before, click on the desired location for the start of the line as shown.
  - Note: Background has been darkened for better visibility for this tutorial.

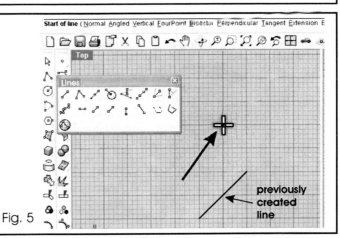

previously created line

Fig. 5

- This time, in order to specify the length of the line you want to create, type **"15"** in the **Command Line** as shown.
- Press "enter" or **RIGHT CLICK.**

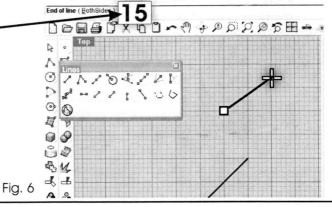

Fig. 6

- The line is now constrained to a 15mm length.
  - The **Command Line** will continue to prompt for the **End of line** until you **left click** to set a location.

- *You can move the cursor in a complete circle but it's length is constrained to 15mm until you type in another number, if you so choose! Then it will be constrained to the new number.*

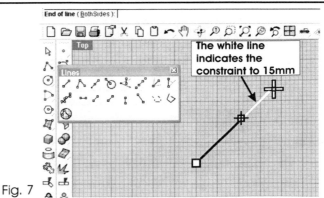

The white line indicates the constraint to 15mm

Fig. 7

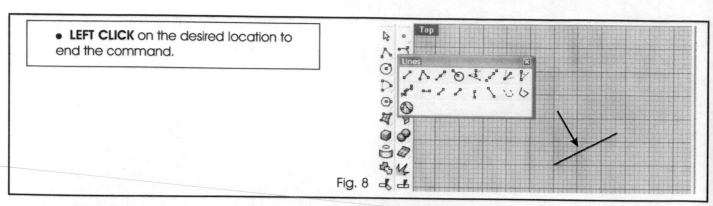

- **LEFT CLICK** on the desired location to end the command.

Fig. 8

Polyline command

- To create a Polyline, which is a line with more than one segment, **LEFT CLICK** on the **Polyline** command in the **Lines** toolbar flyout.

accesses **Lines** toolbar flyout

Polyline command

Fig. 9

- **Start of polyline** prompt: **left click** on the location for the start of the polyline.

Fig. 10

- After clicking on the location for the start of the polyline, you will be prompted for the **Next point of polyline**.
- **LEFT CLICK** on a desired location for the next point of the polyline.

Fig. 11

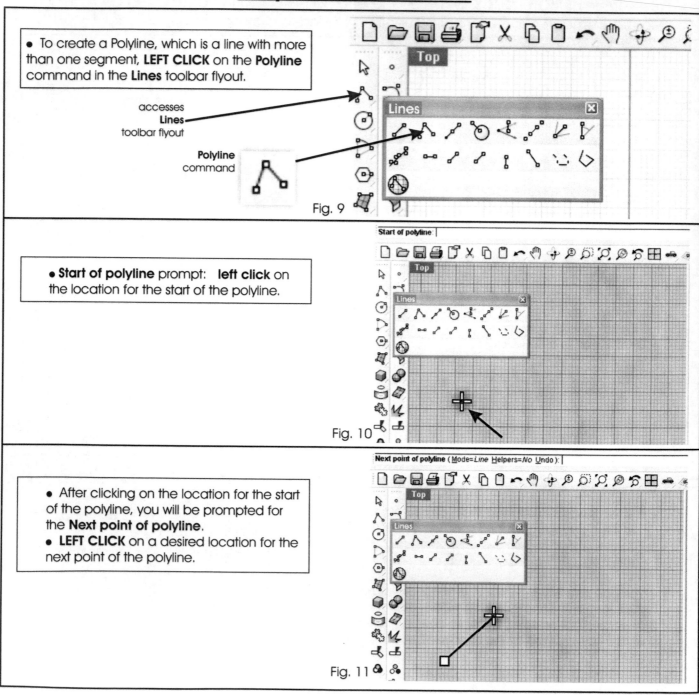

- After clicking on the second point, the **Command Line** will continue to prompt for the **Next point of polyline**.

- *It will also say, **Press Enter when done**. This means that, to end the command when you have enough line segments created, press "enter" to end the command.*

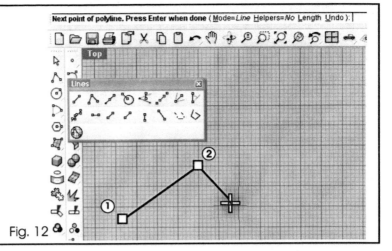

Fig. 12

- A couple of additional segments have been created.
- For the next segment, specify the length by typing "**12.5**" in the **Command Line.**

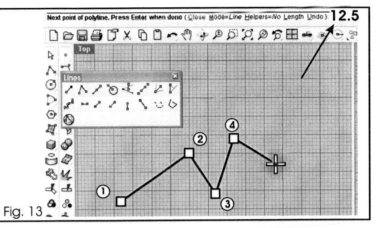

Fig. 13

- Notice that the new line segment is constrained to the specified length of **12.5**.

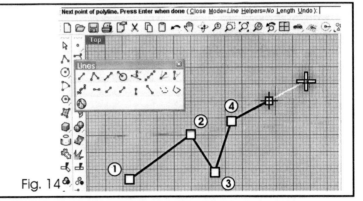

Fig. 14

- A location for the end of the new line has been selected.

- Now, click on the **Undo** option in the **Command Line.**

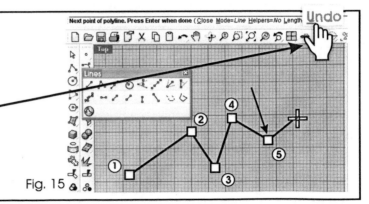

Fig. 15

- The last location point for the polyline has been undone.

- *If you continue to click on the undo link in the **Command Line,** all of the polyline segments will eventually disappear one after another in order.*

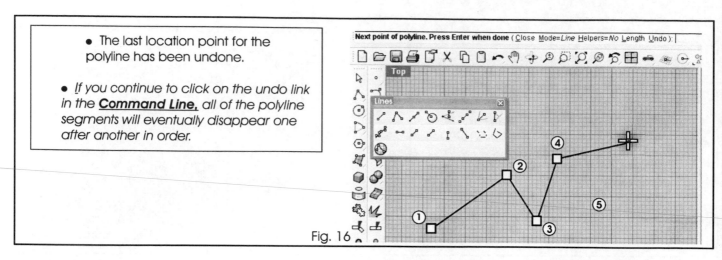

Fig. 16

- Make a few more line segments.
- If you want a closed polyline - all ends touching - click on the **Close** option in the **Command Line.**

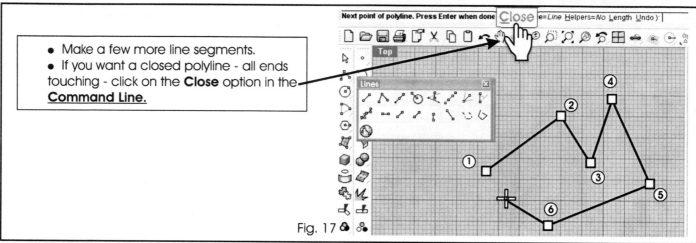

Fig. 17

- *An additional line segment will appear that closes the polyline.*

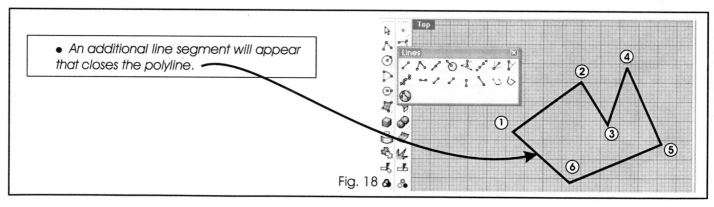

Fig. 18

- If you do not want a closed polyline, just press "enter" and the command is finished.

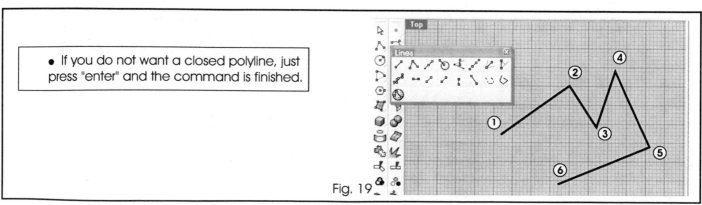

Fig. 19

14

Line and Polyline Distance and Angle Constraints

- **LEFT CLICK** on the **Polyline** command in the **Lines** toolbar flyout.
  - Select a location for the Start of the polygon.

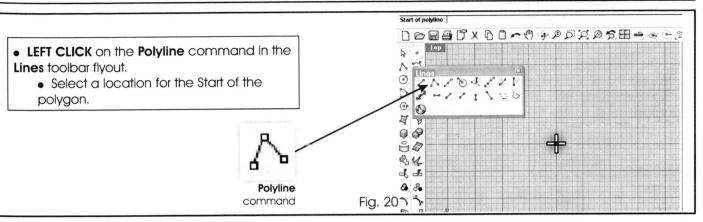

Polyline
command

Fig. 20

- **Next point of polyline** prompt: type "**10**" in the **Command Line** and press "enter".

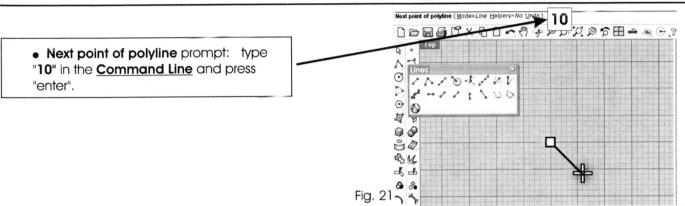

Fig. 21

- Your line will be constrained to a length of 10 units.

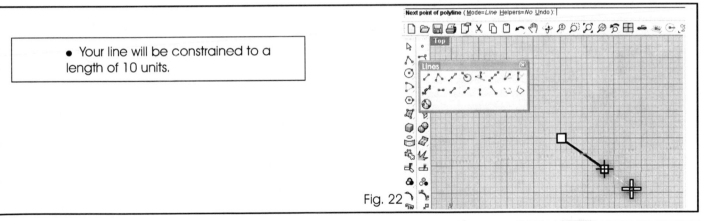

Fig. 22

- Now type "**<45**" in the **Command Line**. [The symbol "**<**" is the upper case for the comma key on your keyboard.]

- Press "enter".

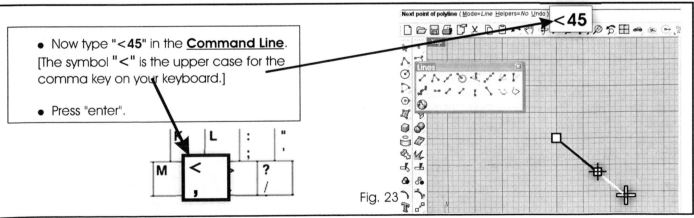

Fig. 23

- *Now the line will not only be constrained to a length of 10 units but it will also be constrained to a 45-degree angle.*

- *You can draw the cursor in a circle around the first point and note that the cursor will snap only to locations in 45-degree increments.*

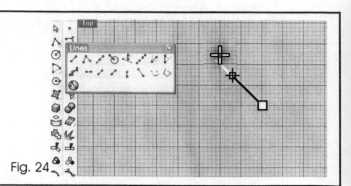

Fig. 24

- Move the cursor around to choose the angle shown by **LEFT CLICKING** to set the location of the end of this line segment.

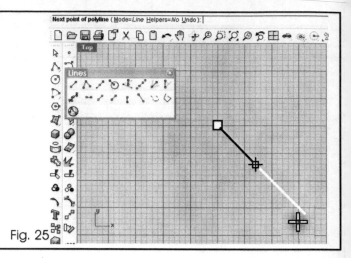

Fig. 25

- Type "**10**" again and press "enter".

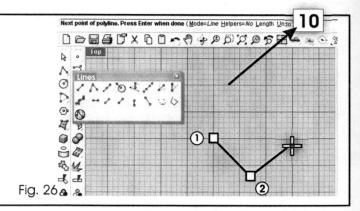

Fig. 26

- Type "**<45**" again and press "enter".

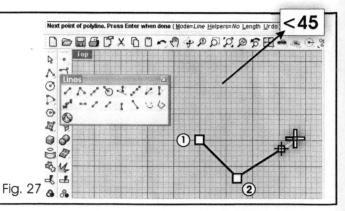

Fig. 27

- Do this a couple of times more and locate the line segments so that they form a square as shown.

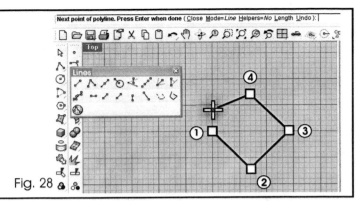
Fig. 28

- You can click on the **Close** option in the **Command Line** to automatically create the final line segment that closes the polyline.

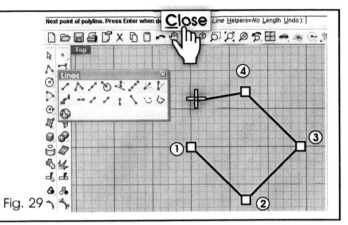
Fig. 29

- The finished closed polyline.

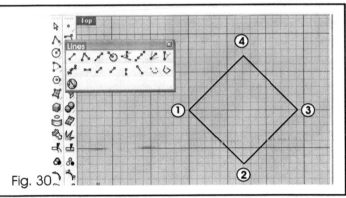
Fig. 30

Anatomy of a Circle
The *Circle: Center Radius* and *Circle: Diameter* commands

Circle: Center, Radius command

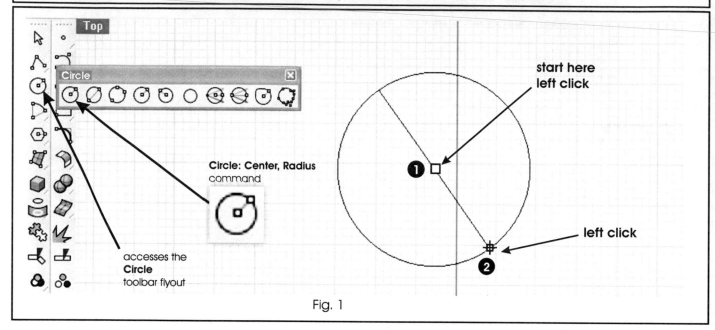

Circle: Center, Radius command

accesses the **Circle** toolbar flyout

start here
left click

left click

Fig. 1

Circle: Diameter command

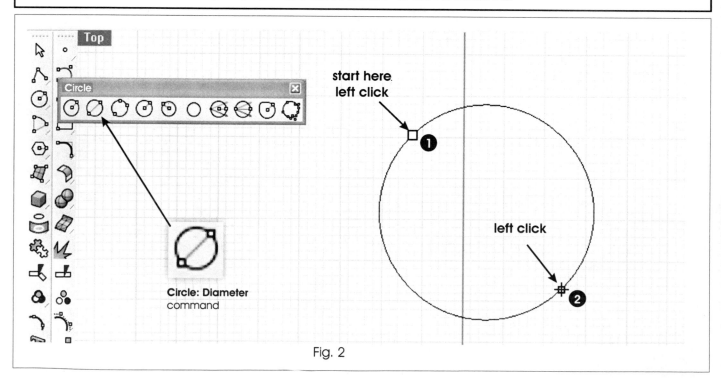

Circle: Diameter command

start here.
left click

left click

Fig. 2

- **Left click** on the **Circle: Center, Radius** command.
  - **Center of circle** prompt: left click on the construction plane at the location where you want the center of the circle.
  - **Radius** prompt: Type "10" in the **Command Line** and press "enter".

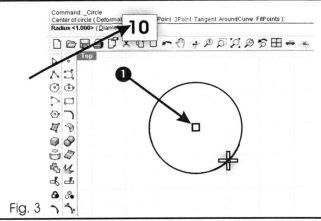

Fig. 3

- A circle with a radius of 10mm will be created around the center point that you designated.

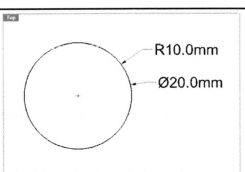

R10.0mm
Ø20.0mm

Fig. 4

- **Left click** on the **Circle: Center, Radius** command.
  - **Center of circle** prompt: type "0" and press "enter".

Circle: Center, Radius command

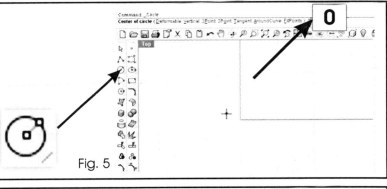

Fig. 5

- The circle is centered on **0,0** which is the best central location around which to work.

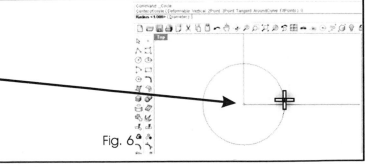

Fig. 6

- The default of this command defines a typed in number as the *radius* of the circle.

- To change that option to **diameter**, click on the **(Diameter)** link in the **Command Line** as shown.

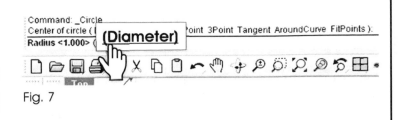

Command: _Circle
Center of circle (**(Diameter)** Point 3Point Tangent AroundCurve FitPoints):
Radius <1.000>

Fig. 7

- Notice that the prompt in the **Command Line** is now for the **diameter**.

- Type "10" and press "enter".

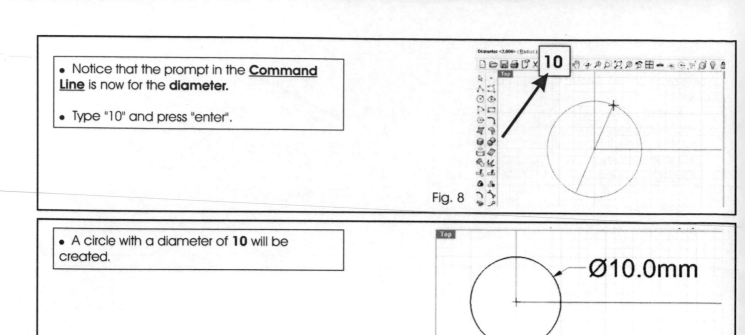

Fig. 8

- A circle with a diameter of **10** will be created.

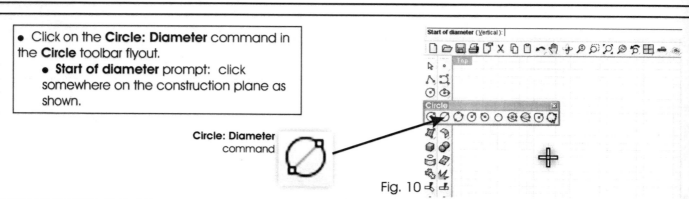

Ø10.0mm

Fig. 9

- Click on the **Circle: Diameter** command in the **Circle** toolbar flyout.
  - **Start of diameter** prompt: click somewhere on the construction plane as shown.

Circle: Diameter command

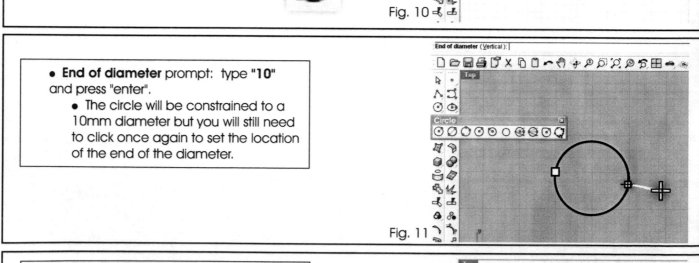

Fig. 10

- **End of diameter** prompt: type **"10"** and press "enter".
  - The circle will be constrained to a 10mm diameter but you will still need to click once again to set the location of the end of the diameter.

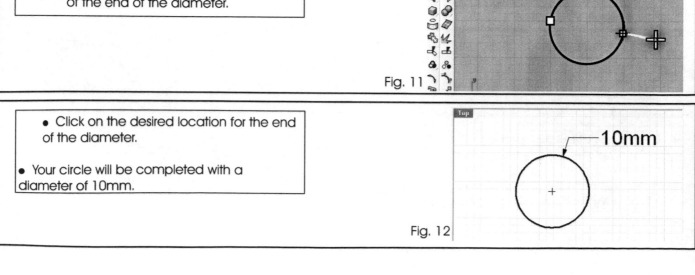

Fig. 11

- Click on the desired location for the end of the diameter.

- Your circle will be completed with a diameter of 10mm.

10mm

Fig. 12

Grid Snap Mode

Constraining the placement of the cursor to the grid of the construction plane.

- At the bottom of the workspace, there is a pane called the **Status Bar.**

- When you click on one of the boxes shown, the text in the bar darkens and the mode it controls is enabled.

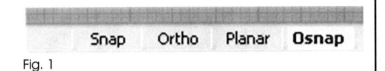

Fig. 1

- Click on the **Snap** button as shown.

- You have enabled a mode called **Grid Snap.**

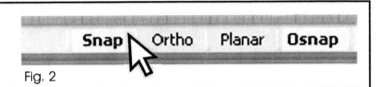

Fig. 2

- Click on the **Polyline Command** and start placing polyline locations on the construction plane.

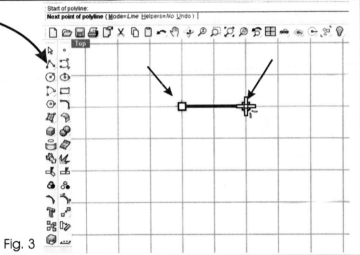

Fig. 3

- Notice that you can only place points at the grid intersections.

- As long as **Grid Snap** is enabled, your locations will be constrained to the grid intersections.

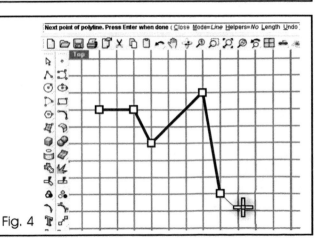

Fig. 4

- After you have placed a number of points, click on the **Snap** button once again. Do this while you are still in the **Polyline** command.

- Notice that when you click on the **Snap** button, the letters will no longer be dark and the background will darken. This means that the **Grid Snap** mode is no longer enabled.

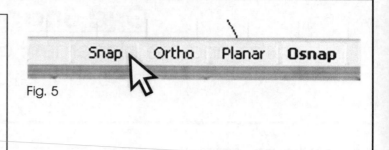

Fig. 5

- Notice that because **Grid Snap** is now disengaged, you can place points anywhere you want.

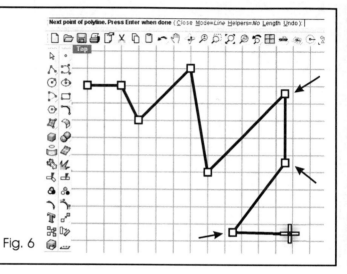

Fig. 6

- **Grid Snap** makes certain tasks very easy.

- The shapes in the illustration were all made in **Grid Snap** mode.

- *NOTE: You can also press the F9 hotkey to toggle GRID SNAP on and off.*

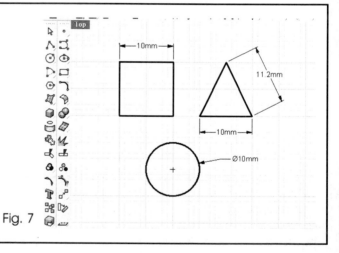

Fig. 7

Ortho Mode
Direction constraint

- On the Status Bar at the bottom of the workspace, in the series of buttons shown, we will be working with the button that says **Ortho**.

Fig. 1

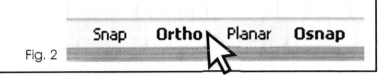

Snap   Ortho   Planar   **Osnap**

- **LEFT CLICK** on the **Ortho** button. The text letters will darken as shown, signifying that the **Ortho** mode is enabled.

Fig. 2

Snap   **Ortho**   Planar   **Osnap**

- Click on the **Polyline** command and start to place locations on the construction plane.

- You will quickly notice that you can only create lines that are either perfectly horizontal or perfectly vertical.

- **Ortho** is constraining the placement of the lines to 90-degree directions.

Fig. 3

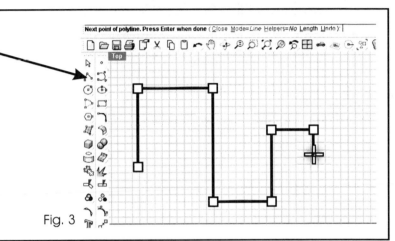

- After you have placed a few points, without exiting the polyline command, click again on the **Ortho** button. The type will lighten up and you will know that you have toggled off **Ortho** mode.

Fig. 4

Snap   Ortho   Planar   **Osnap**

- Place some more locations and you will see that you are no longer constrained by ortho.

- *NOTE: Pressing the SHIFT KEY and holding it down will turn on ORTHO. When you stop holding down the SHIFT KEY, ORTHO will disengage.*

- *The F8 hotkey will also toggle ORTHO on and off.*

Fig. 5

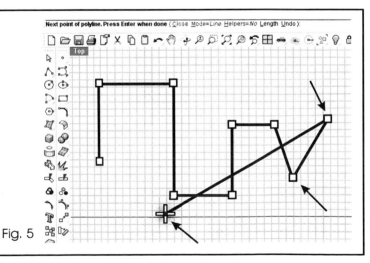

Object Snap "OSNAP"
Ensuring the accurate connection of one object to another

- **OBJECT SNAP ("OSNAP")**: In this exercise, you will learn the various settings that enable you to constrain the mouse cursor to various objects at different points which you can designate.

- **OBJECT SNAP** is one of the most important functions in Rhino and is crucial for accuracy.

- Open Rhino and save your file as **osnap & analysis.3dm**. You will be able to use this file for this exercise and the next one that deals with measuring lines, distances and angles in your work.

- At the bottom of the Rhino screen, click on the **Osnap** button as shown.

- The **Osnap** toolbar will open and dock on the bottom of the screen.

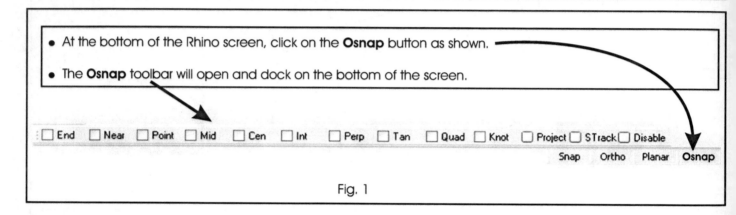

Fig. 1

- Toggle on **snap ("grid snap")** at the bottom of the screen by **left clicking** on it. The button will change to boldface type as shown.

- Use the **Circle** and **Polyline** commands to create the simple circles and squares shown.

- Circles are 10mm in diameter and the squares have 10mm sides and are 5mm apart.

- **Grid snap** will make these shapes quick and easy to create.

- **Toggle off grid snap when done.**

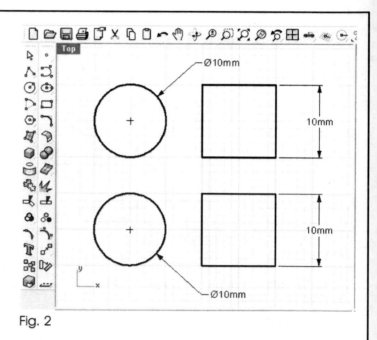

Fig. 2

- Click on the box or text of **End snap** to toggle it on. A little green check will appear in the box as shown.

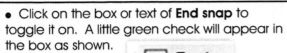

- Use the **Line** command to draw a line from the corners of the two boxes as shown.

- As the cursor is drawn over the corners of the boxes, the cursor will "snap" to them because they are also end points of the lines that make up the squares. Set the start and end of the line at these locations.

  - You will know that you are snapping to these points because a little tooltip will appear saying **"End"** as shown.

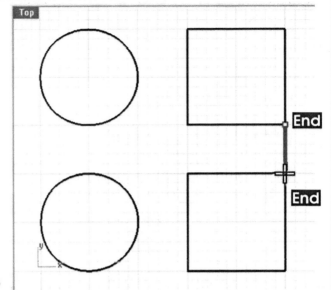

Fig. 3

- Now click on the box or text of **Mid snap** to toggle it on.

- Use the **Line** command to draw a line that connects an endpoint and a midpoint as shown.

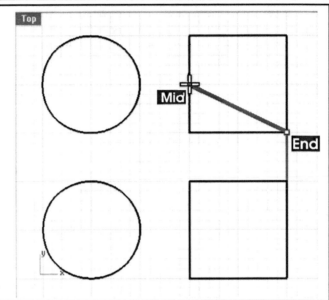

Fig. 4

- Next, click on **Cen osnap (Center osnap)** to toggle it on.

Cen

- Use the **Line** command to draw a line from the center of the lower circle to the center of the lower square.

- To snap to the center of objects, *you must draw the cursor over the outline of the object and snap when the tooltip shows as shown.*

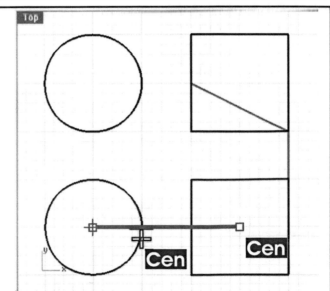

Fig. 5

- Click on all of the enabled osnaps to toggle them off.

- Then toggle on both **Int (Intersection) osnap** and **Tan (Tangent) osnap.**

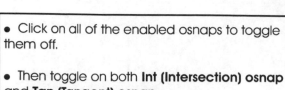

- Create a line that starts at the intersection shown❶ and which ends at the tangent point on the circle shown.❷

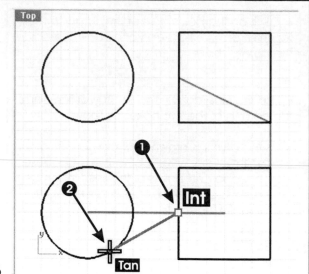

Fig. 6

- If you **right click** on **Quad osnap,** you will simultaneously toggle all other osnaps off and toggle **quad osnap** on.

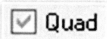

- Create a **Line** that connects the two quad points of the circle at the top.

- The **quad** points are the locations on a circle, oval, or wavy line that are at the furthest extants of the X, Y and Z directions of the grid.

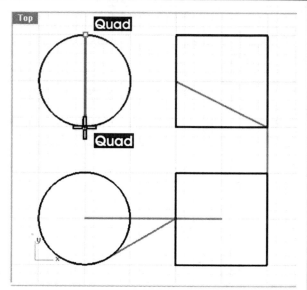

Fig. 7

- Toggle on **Near** and **Perp (Perpendicular)** osnaps.

- Create a **Line** that starts somewhere on the area of the top circle as shown.❶
    - **Near osnap** simply means it touches the line but the exact location is not set until you click on the line.

- The end of the line will snap to a point that creates a perfect perpendicular with it's destination.❷

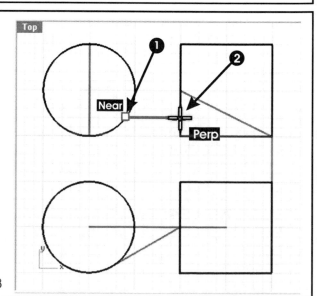

Fig. 8

• **Project:** If **Project** is toggled on, the cursor will snap to objects but will be constrained to the construction plane, even when the points that are snapped to are above or below the construction plane in 3d space.

• **Smart Track:** **Smart Track** attempts to anticipate your needs by trying to set up automatic directions and snaps. It can be a help or a hindrance and it is recommended that you leave it toggled off when beginning to learn Rhino.

• **Disable:** **Disable** shuts off all osnaps, even if they are toggled on. In this way, you can leave your favorite snaps on for later use, disabling them temporarily.

• **Planar:** Constrains commands to a single construction plane elevation in 3D space.

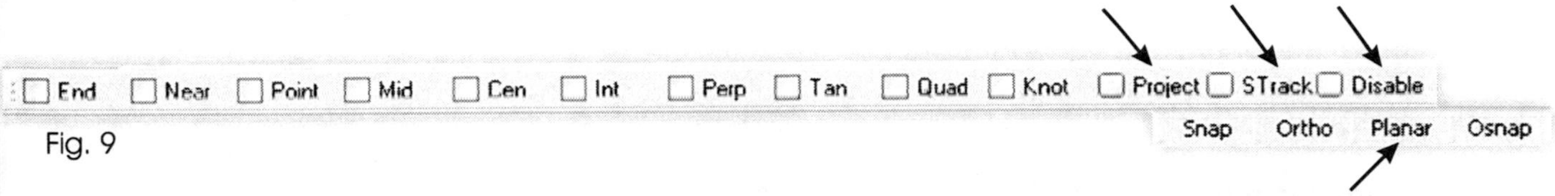

☐ End ☐ Near ☐ Point ☐ Mid ☐ Cen ☐ Int ☐ Perp ☐ Tan ☐ Quad ☐ Knot ☐ Project ☐ STrack ☐ Disable

Fig. 9   Snap   Ortho   Planar   Osnap

27

Analysis Commands
Measuring Length, Distance, Angle, Radius and Diameter

- Open the Rhino file, **osnap & analysis.3dm** from the previous **OSNAP** chapter.

- **To measure the length of a curve or a line, LEFT CLICK** on the **Length** command in the **Analyze** toolbar flyout.

- **Select curves to measure** prompt: select the diagonal line in the upper right square.

accesses the **Analyze** toolbar flyout

Length command

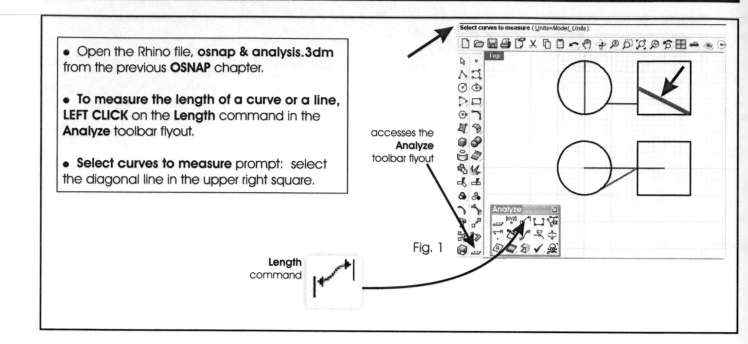

Fig. 1

- You will continue to be prompted to **Select curves to measure.**

- As you only want to measure this one curve, press "enter"

Fig. 2

- The History line will display the exact length of the curve you selected.

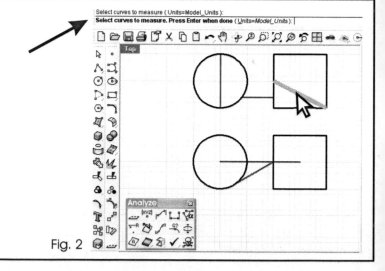

11.180 millimeters 's

Command:

Fig. 3

- **To measure the distance between two points, LEFT CLICK** on the **Distance** command in the **Analyze** toolbar flyout.

  - **First point for distance** prompt: snap to and click on the lower corner of the bottom square as shown. ❶

Distance
command

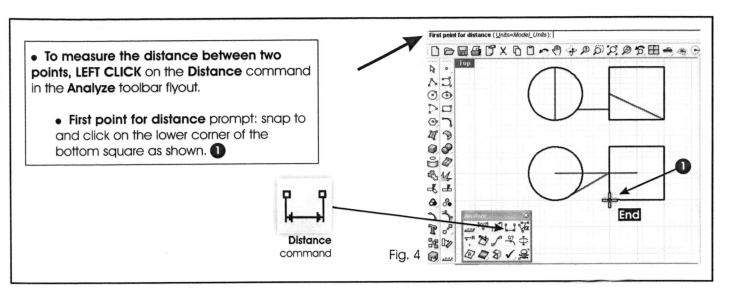

Fig. 4

- **Second point for distance** prompt: click on the the upper right corner of the same box as shown to get a diagonal direction to the measured distance. ❷

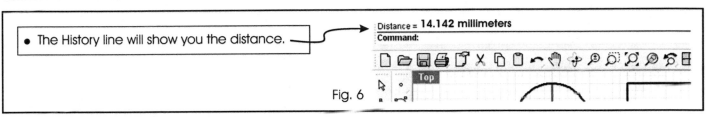

Fig. 5

- The History line will show you the distance.

Distance = **14.142 millimeters**
Command:

Fig. 6

- To measure the **Angle formed by two lines (or any two locations), LEFT CLICK** on the **Angle** command in the **Analyze** toolbar flyout.
  - **Start of first line** prompt: snap to the end point of the diagonal line and click. ❶

Angle
command

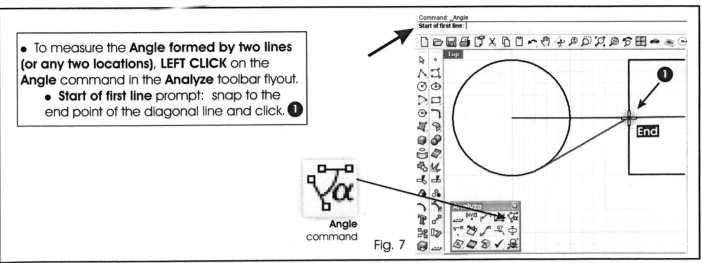

Fig. 7

- **End of first line** prompt: snap to the other end of the diagonal line and click. ❷

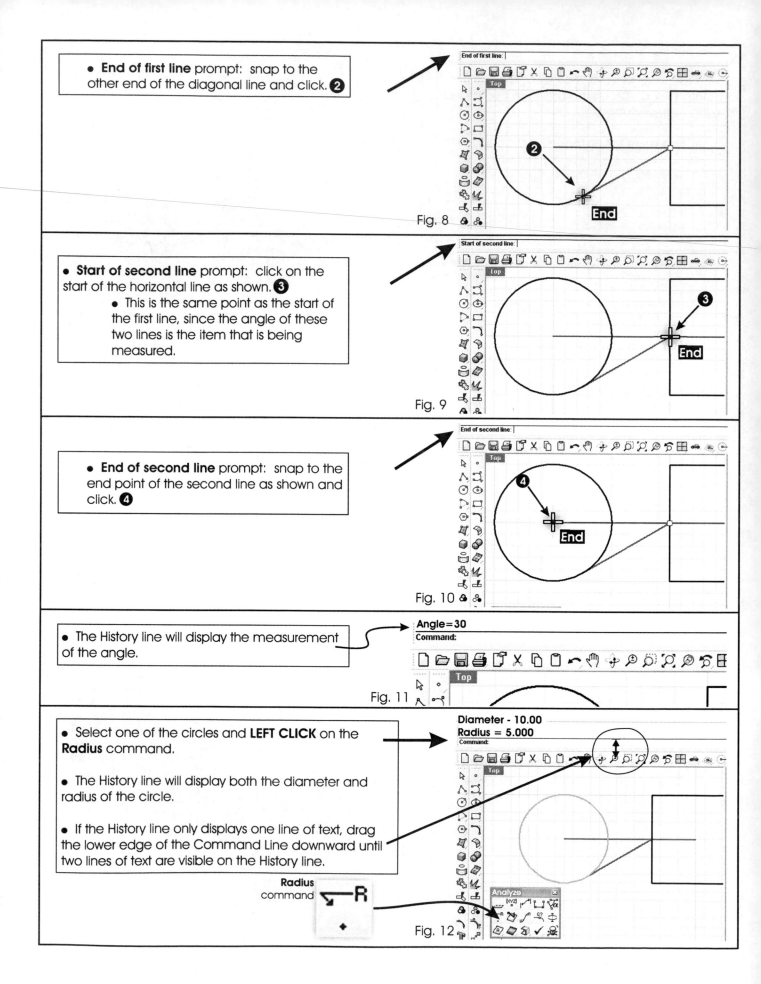

Fig. 8

- **Start of second line** prompt: click on the start of the horizontal line as shown. ❸
  - This is the same point as the start of the first line, since the angle of these two lines is the item that is being measured.

Fig. 9

- **End of second line** prompt: snap to the end point of the second line as shown and click. ❹

Fig. 10

- The History line will display the measurement of the angle.

Angle=30
Command:

Fig. 11

- Select one of the circles and **LEFT CLICK** on the **Radius** command.

- The History line will display both the diameter and radius of the circle.

- If the History line only displays one line of text, drag the lower edge of the Command Line downward until two lines of text are visible on the History line.

Diameter - 10.00
Radius = 5.000
Command:

Radius command

Fig. 12

30

Move & Copy Commands

Drag Command for Simple Move

- Create a circle, using one of the **Circle** commands.

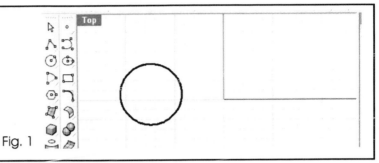

Fig. 1

- Touch the circle with the cursor and **Left click, holding down the left mouse button while you move the cursor.**
    - **[This is also referred to as "click and drag".]**

- A preview circle will move with the cursor as shown.

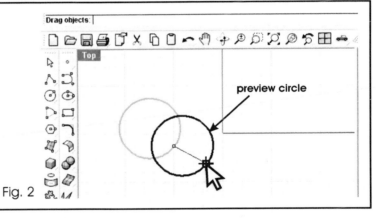

Fig. 2

- Release the **left mouse button** when you are finished moving the circle and the circle will now be in a new location.

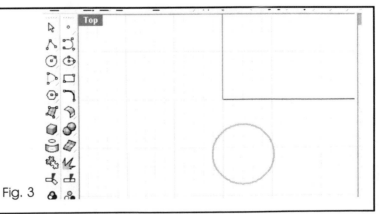

Fig. 3

Move Command

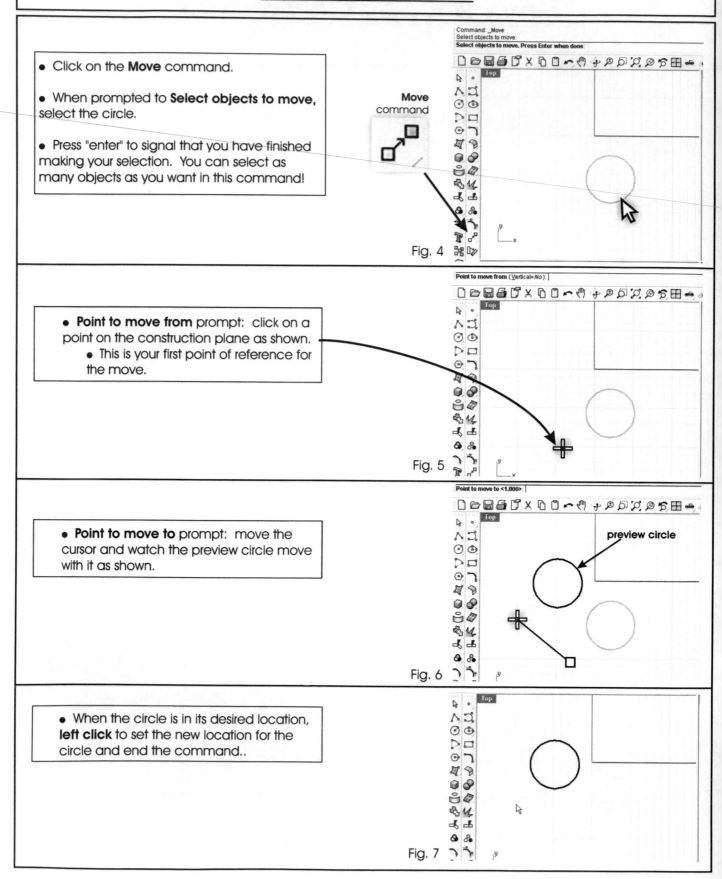

- Click on the **Move** command.

- When prompted to **Select objects to move**, select the circle.

- Press "enter" to signal that you have finished making your selection. You can select as many objects as you want in this command!

Move command

Fig. 4

- **Point to move from** prompt: click on a point on the construction plane as shown.
  - This is your first point of reference for the move.

Fig. 5

- **Point to move to** prompt: move the cursor and watch the preview circle move with it as shown.

preview circle

Fig. 6

- When the circle is in its desired location, **left click** to set the new location for the circle and end the command..

Fig. 7

Moving a Specified Distance

- Click on the **Move** command and select the circle as before.

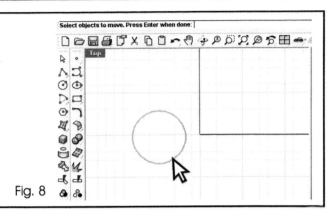

Fig. 8

- **Point to move from** prompt: click on the construction plane for a first point of reference as you did before.
- When prompted for the **Point to move to,** type **"10"** in the **Command Line** and press "enter".

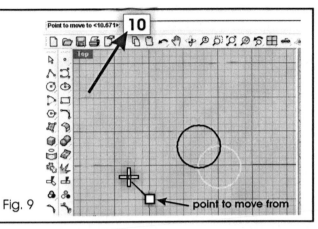

Fig. 9

- Draw the cursor out and notice that the line from the first point is constrained to **10mm**.
  - Also notice the white elastic line that stretches between the end of the line and the cursor. This line signifies some type of constraint. In this case, it is a distance constraint.

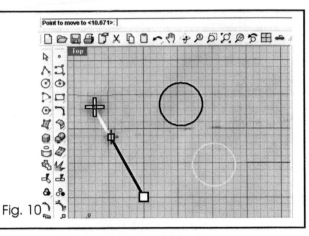

Fig. 10

- **Left click** to set the new location and the command is ended.

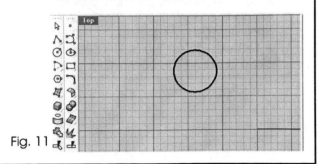

Fig. 11

33

- Use the **Polyline** command to create a line with 3 segments similar to the one shown. Specified lengths and angles are not needed here.

Fig. 12

- **Left click** on the **Move** command.
  - **Select objects to move** prompt: select the circle and press "enter".

Select objects to move. Press Enter when done

Fig. 13

- **Point to move from** prompt: Use **center osnap** to snap to the center of the circle and **left click**.

- *Reminder: for Center Osnap to work, the cursor has to be touching the perimeter of the circle, not the center.*

Point to move from (Vertical=No):

Cen

Fig. 14

- **Point to move to** prompt: use **end osnap** to snap to the end point of the nearby polyline as shown.
  - **Left click** to set the new location for the circle and end the command.

Point to move to <8.699>:

End

Fig. 15

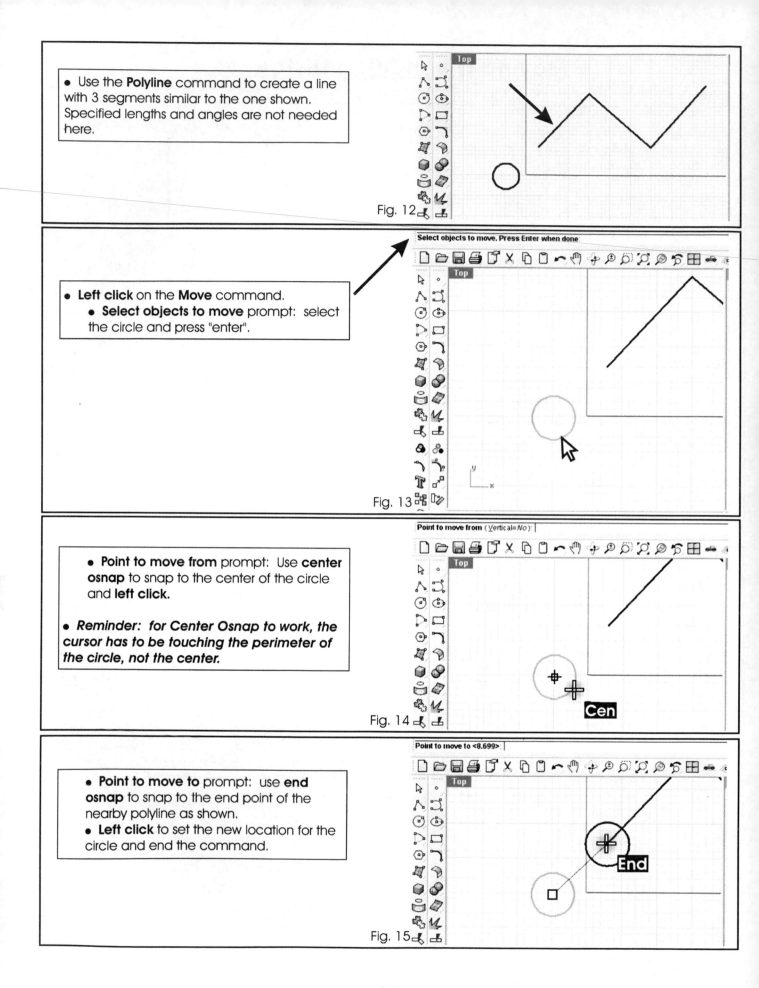

- The circle has been moved to a new location with it's center on the endpoint of the polyline.

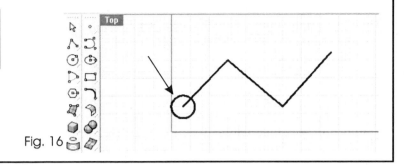

Fig. 16

Copy Command

- **Left click** on the **Copy** command.
  - **Select objects to copy** prompt: select the circle and press "enter".

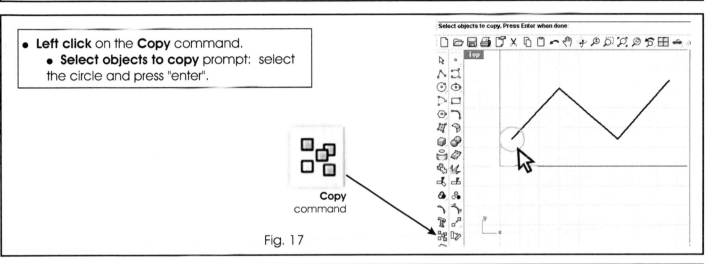

Copy
command

Fig. 17

- **Point to copy from** prompt: use **center osnap** to snap to the center of the circle and click to set the location.

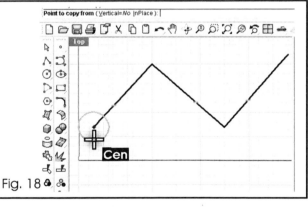

Fig. 18

- **Point to copy to** prompt: use **end osnap** to snap to the next end point on the polyline and **left click** to set the location for the first copy.

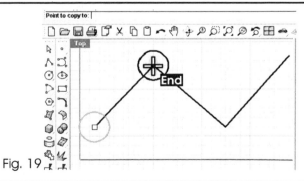

Fig. 19

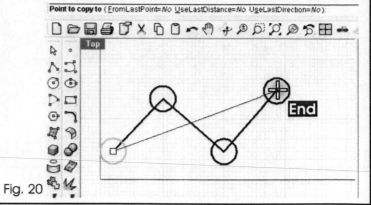

- Snap to the rest of the endpoints on the line and left click to set the locations of new copies.
- Press "enter" to end the command when all of the copies have been made as shown.

Fig. 20

- The finished copies.

Fig. 21

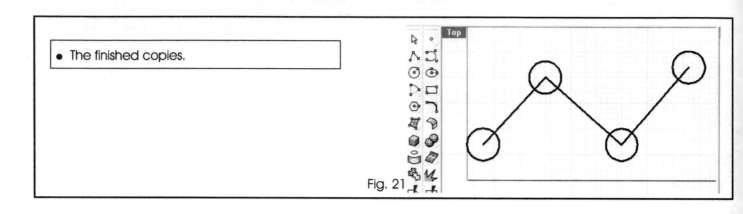

36

Picture Frame Command
Placing and Scaling a Design image.
Tracing with Freeform Curves.

• Open Rhino and save the file as **leaf design.3dm.** It will be used in the following chapter for the **Rotate** and **Mirror** commands.

• On the next page, you will find a full page image of the stylized leaf sketch shown here. Scan this image - or have it scanned - and save the image file as **leaf drawing.jpg.**
   • **You can also save it in the following formats: .bmp, .tga, .jpg, .jpeg, .pcx, .png, .tif, and .tiff**

• **200dpi is a good resolution for this purpose. Image size does not matter.**

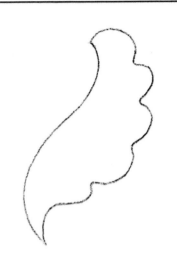

Fig. 1

• Access the **Plane** toolbar flyout as shown.

• Note that the Plane toolbar flyout is found in the **Surface Toolbar Flyout.**

• **Left click** on the **Picture Frame** command.

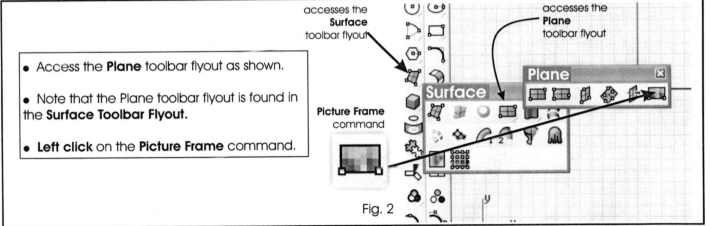

accesses the **Surface** toolbar flyout

accesses the **Plane** toolbar flyout

Plane

Surface

Picture Frame command

Fig. 2

• The **Open Bitmap** dialog box will open.
• Navigate to the folder in your computer that holds the scanned image and select that image as shown.
• Click on the "Open" button.

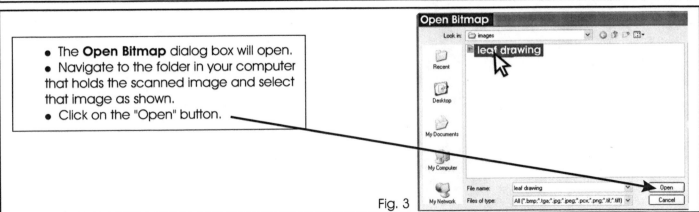

Fig. 3

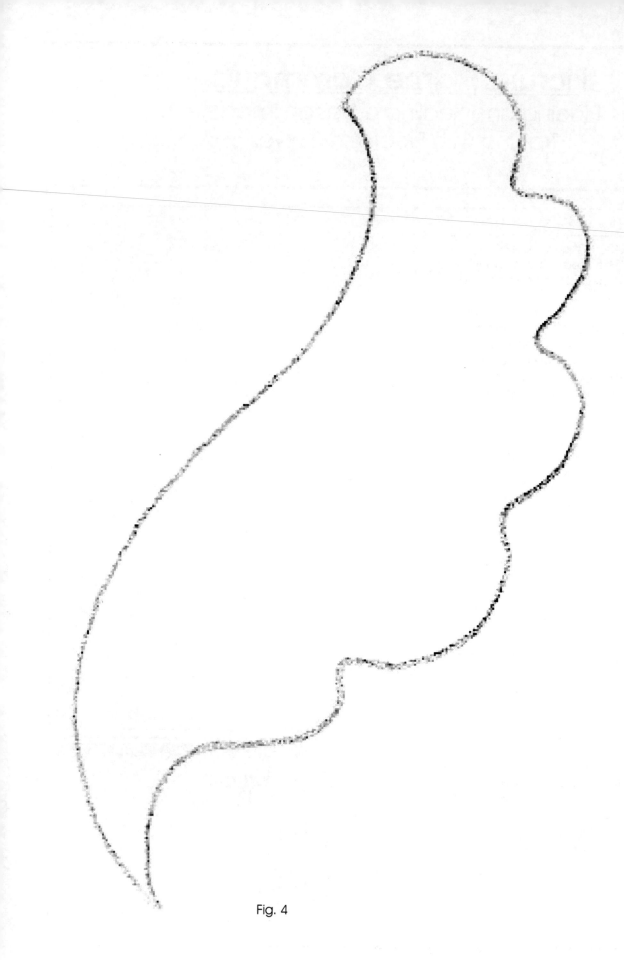

Fig. 4

- **First corner of picture frame** prompt: **LEFT CLICK** somewhere in the lower left hand part of the top viewport as shown. **❶**

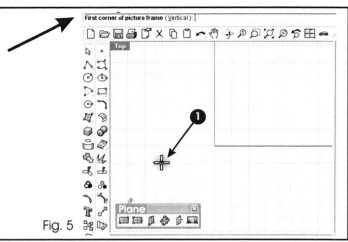

Fig. 5

- **Length of picture frame** prompt: Drag the cursor horizontally across to the opposite side of the viewport.
  - Use **Ortho** for horizontal accuracy. Otherwise your image will be tipped, rather than straight.
  - A preview outline of the bitmap you are placing will form as shown. **❷**

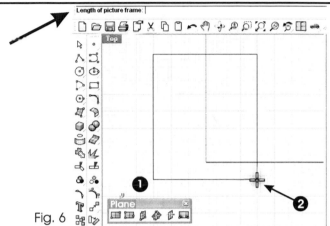

Fig. 6

- **LEFT CLICK** to set the location of the second corner and the image of the bitmap will appear.

- The viewport in this tutorial is set so that the construction Plane is white. That is why the sketch is shown against a white background

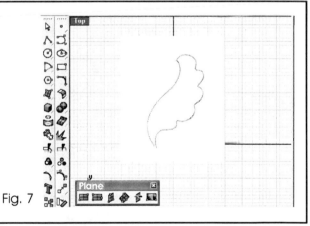

Fig. 7

- This illustration shows how the bitmap will look against the default grey of the Construction Plane color.

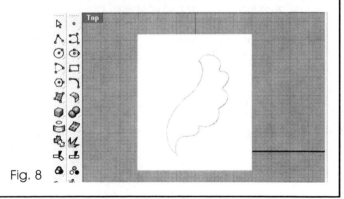

Fig. 8

- Select the bitmap image you have just brought in to Rhino.

- Notice that a series of lines will "light up".

- These lines signify that a **surface** has been selected.

- The rectangular border lines are the **edges of the surface**. The crossing lines going through the middle of the surface are called **isocurves** and are a feature of all surfaces.

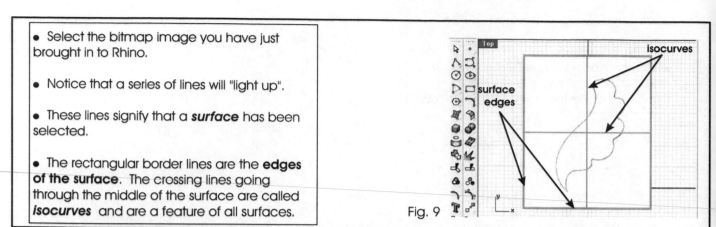

Fig. 9

- The 2 elements of a **Picture Frame:**
  - The **surface**
  - The **texture map**, which is the image that has been applied to the surface.

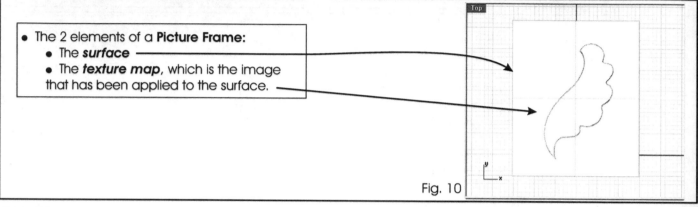

Fig. 10

- Select the **Picture Frame** and press the **F3** hotkey at the top of your keyboard. [You can also click on the **Object Properties** button in the standard toolbar.

Object Properties
command

- The **Properties** dialog box will appear.

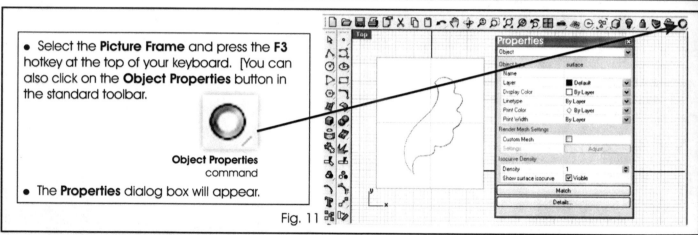

Fig. 11

- Locate and click on the **Material** category in the drop-down list at the top of the **Properties** box as shown.

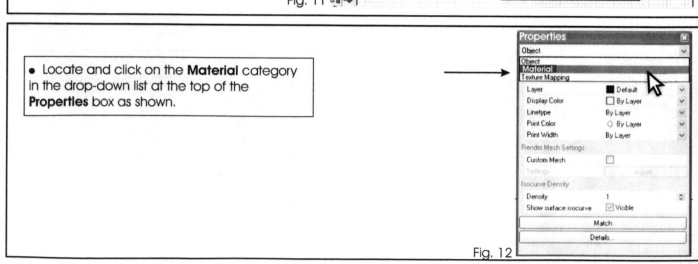

Fig. 12

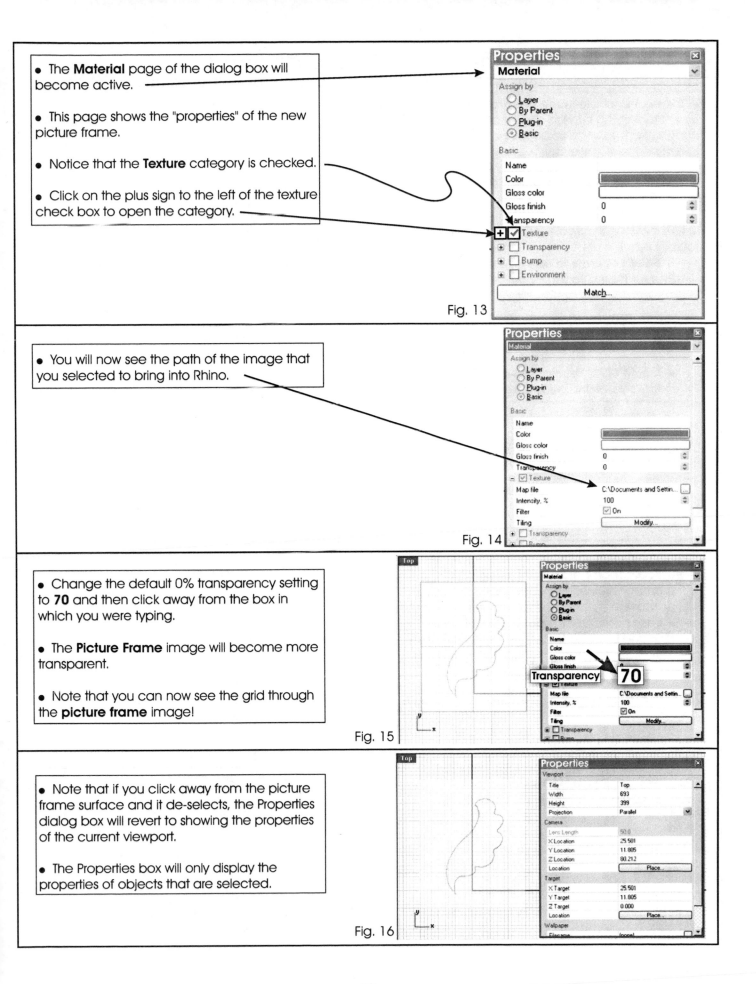

- The **Material** page of the dialog box will become active.

- This page shows the "properties" of the new picture frame.

- Notice that the **Texture** category is checked.

- Click on the plus sign to the left of the texture check box to open the category.

Fig. 13

- You will now see the path of the image that you selected to bring into Rhino.

Fig. 14

- Change the default 0% transparency setting to **70** and then click away from the box in which you were typing.

- The **Picture Frame** image will become more transparent.

- Note that you can now see the grid through the **picture frame** image!

Fig. 15

- Note that if you click away from the picture frame surface and it de-selects, the Properties dialog box will revert to showing the properties of the current viewport.

- The Properties box will only display the properties of objects that are selected.

Fig. 16

Scaling The Picture Frame Image

- The next step is to **scale the drawing to its desired size.** Placing this bitmap image on the workspace is not an exact science so scaling is always necessary if specified size is important.

- **The desired size of the drawing is 20mm from tip to tip of the leaf image.**

- **Left click** on the **Scale 2-D** command in the **Scale** toolbar flyout.
  - **Select objects to scale** prompt: select the **Picture Frame** surface and press "enter".

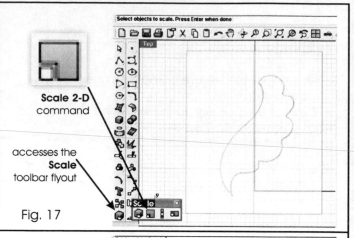

Scale 2-D command

accesses the **Scale** toolbar flyout

Fig. 17

- **Origin point** prompt: click on the bottom tip of the leaf drawing as shown.

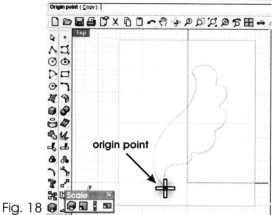

origin point

Fig. 18

- **Scale factor or first reference point** prompt: click on the upper tip of the leaf as shown.
- **Second reference point** prompt: type **"20"** and press "enter".

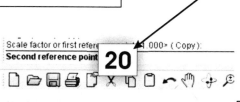

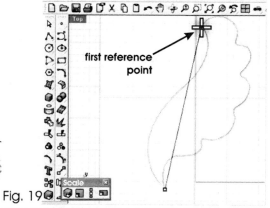

first reference point

Fig. 19

- The image will now be scaled so that it measures **20mm** from one tip of the leaf to another.

- The **picture frame** can be moved, rotated, dragged, copied, arrayed, mirrored and point edited. You can also bring more than one picture frame into your Rhino workspace for multiple images and in different viewports if you wish.

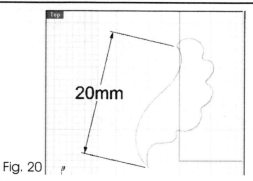

20mm

Fig. 20

• Select the picture frame surface and **left click** on the **Lock** command shown to "lock" the picture frame surface so that it can not be selected by mistake but it still visible for tracing reference.

*[To **Unlock**, just **right click** on the lock command button to release the surface again.]*

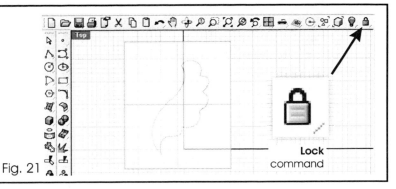

Fig. 21

Lock command

• The next step is to use one of Rhino's freeform curve commands to start to trace the image of the leaf.

• **LEFT CLICK** on the **Control Point Curve** command in the **Curve** toolbar flyout.
   • **Start of curve** prompt: Position the cursor at the bottom tip of the leaf as shown and **LEFT CLICK** to set the location of the start of the curve.

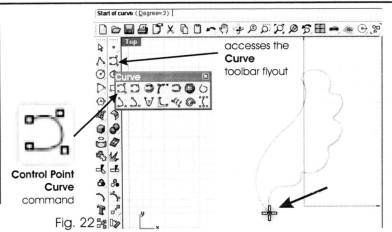

accesses the **Curve** toolbar flyout

Control Point Curve command

Fig. 22

• Draw the cursor out and notice the "rubber band" effect of the line that now is attached to it.
• **LEFT CLICK** again at the approximate location shown.

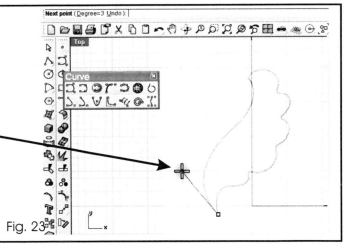

Fig. 23

• Draw the cursor along the direction of the line to be traced and click a couple more times as shown.

• **NOTE: Your line will not follow the line to be traced exactly. Do not worry about this. Make as few clicks as possible for a smooth line. You will edit this line later with control point manipulation.**

   • Click at the top of the curve and press "enter" to end the command.

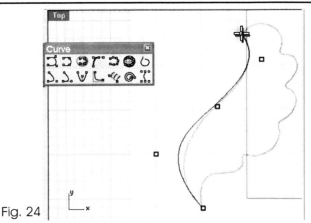

Fig. 24

- The finished curve will be graceful but will probably not exactly follow the line in the sketch to be traced..

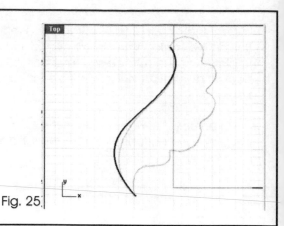

Fig. 25.

- Select the curve you have just created and **LEFT CLICK** on the **Control Points On** command.

- A series of points separated by dotted lines will appear in the same locations on which you clicked when creating this line.

- *Note: There are very few control points here which makes for a very graceful line.*

Control Points On command

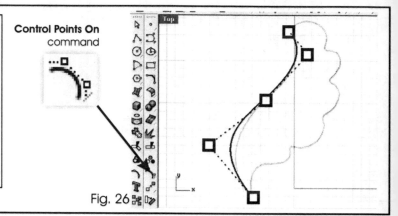

Fig. 26

- **Drag** one of the control points and notice that a preview curve moves along with it.

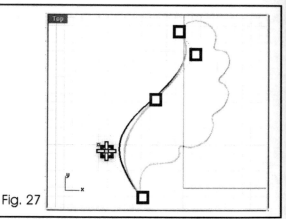

Fig. 27

- A couple of points have been dragged here but now it is necessary to add a control point in order to move the middle section of the line so that it follows more closely the leaf design.

- **LEFT CLICK** on the **Insert Knot** command in the **Point Editing** toolbar as shown.
    - This command will add a new control point to the line where you specify.

Insert Knot command

accesses the **Point Editing** toolbar flyout

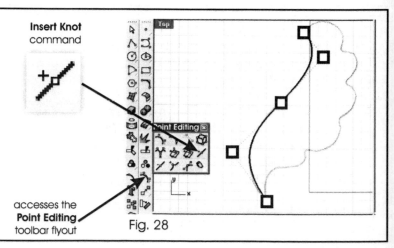

Fig. 28

- **Select curve or surface for knot insertion** prompt: click on the curve to select it.

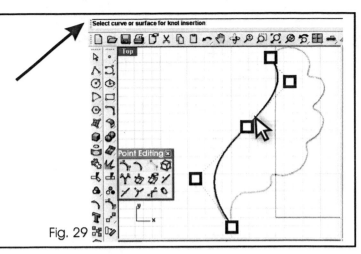

Fig. 29

- **Point on curve to add knot** prompt: click on the parts of the curve that need added control points as shown.

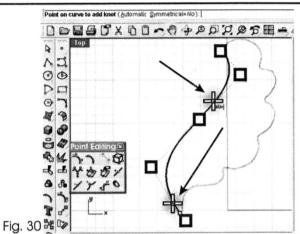

Fig. 30

- Press "enter" to end the command and notice that a new control point has been added.

- *Notice that the point was not exactly where you clicked and another knot may have been moved. Rhino is trying to keep a uniform curve.*

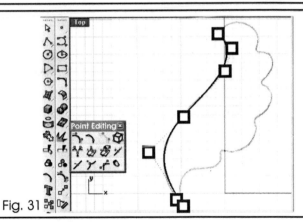

Fig. 31

- Some additional editing of the control points and the curve follows the line of the design more closely.

- **RIGHT CLICK** on the **Points Off** command to toggle off control points.

- Pressing the **Esc** key will toggle off control points as well. (If one or more control points are selected, you must press the **Esc** key twice.

Points Off
command
[right click]

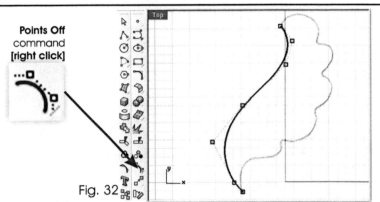

Fig. 32

45

- **LEFT CLICK** on the **Curve: Interpolate Points** command in the **Curves** toolbar flyout as shown.

- Toggle on **End Osnap** and snap to the end point of the lower end of the curve just created as shown. Notice that zooming in lets you work with greater visibility and accuracy.

- **LEFT CLICK** to set locations of control points as before.

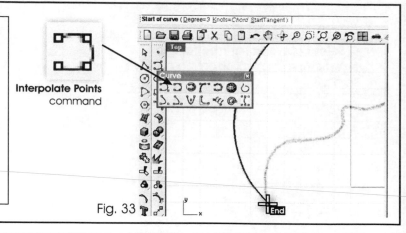

Interpolate Points
command

Fig. 33

- You will notice that, unlike in the **Control Point Curve** command, the curve being created continues to pass through the points as they are being placed as shown.

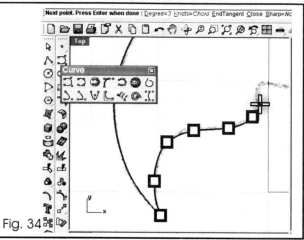

Fig. 34

- As you continue to place points, you will see the need to place more points at sharper parts of curves and less points at more relaxed areas.

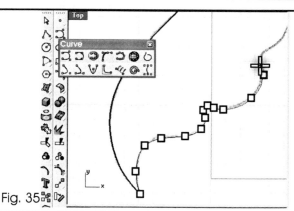

Fig. 35

- When you reach the top of the leaf design, snap to the end point of the previous line as you did at the bottom. Press "enter".

- Turn on control points for the curve you have just created and drag control points to refine the shape.

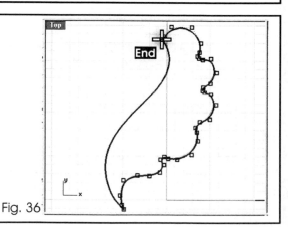

Fig. 36

46

- You can **Delete** control points to refine a shape.

- Select the control point you want to delete.

- Press the "**Delete**" key on your keyboard.

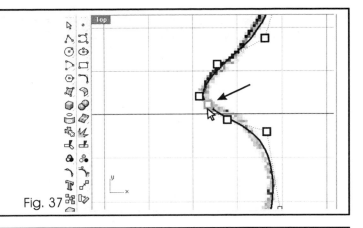

Fig. 37

- The unwanted control point is removed and the curve has become more graceful at that point.

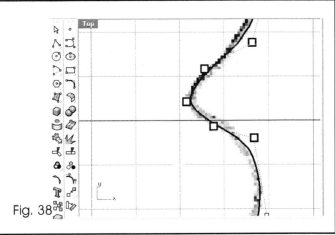

Fig. 38

- **Right click** on the **Lock** button to unlock the **Picture frame** surface. Then select the **Picture Frame** surface and **left click** on the **Hide** button next to the **Lock** button.

[Note: You can **RIGHT CLICK** on the same button to toggle the **picture frame** back on.

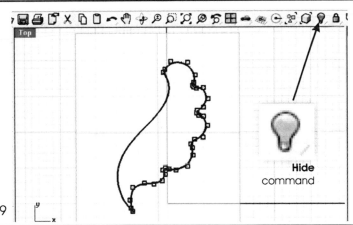

Hide
command

Fig. 39

- With the background image hidden, further refinements can be made to the design.

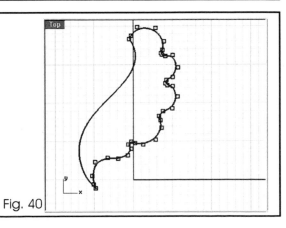

Fig. 40

Migrating your Picture Frame image to another computer.

• If you need to open your Rhino file on another computer, your picture frame surface will look blank as shown.

• This is because the placement of the design image is path specific which means that it needs to be re-introduced to the Rhino file in the new computer. *(This issue may be addressed in Rhino 5.0).*

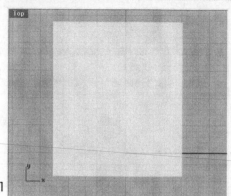

Fig. 41

• Select the **picture frame** surface and press the **F3** hotkey to open the **Properties** dialog box.

• Access the **Material** page as before, using the drop-down menu at the top.

• Open up the **Texture** category as before.

• Note that the name of the map file that you originally selected for your image is still in place - *but this needs to be updated anyway.*

• Delete this entry and click on the browse button to the right of the name of the map file.

Fig. 42

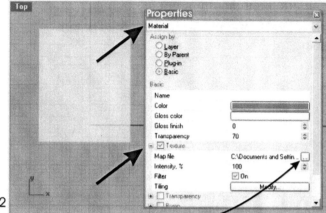

• Find your bitmap image in the **Open Bitmap** dialog box that opens up.

• Highlight your choice and click on the "open" button.

Fig. 43

• The image will appear on the **picture frame** surface.

• If you had already scaled your image, the new image will already be scaled as it will take on the size of the picture frame surface.

Fig. 44

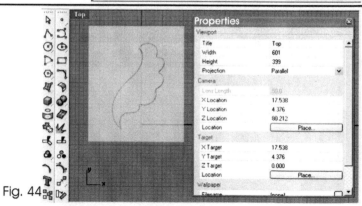

Mirror and Rotate Commands
Creating a Design with the Leaf Motif

• Open the Rhino file, **leaf design.3dm** that you created in the previous tutorial.

• Select the **picture frame** surface and click on the **Hide** command as shown.

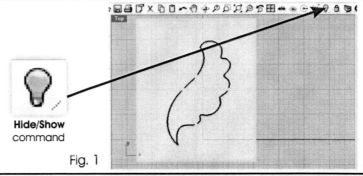

Hide/Show command

Fig. 1

• The picture frame will be hidden.

• You can **right-click** on this command when you want to **Show** the hidden object again.

• Keep it hidden for this exercise.

Fig. 2

• Select the leaf and click on the **Move** command.
   • **Point to move from** prompt: snap to the **end** of the curves at the bottom of the leaf and click to set this location.
   • **Point to move to** prompt: type "**0**" in the **Command Line** and press "enter".

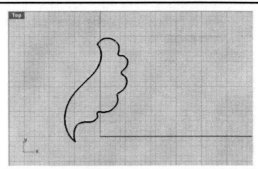

Move command

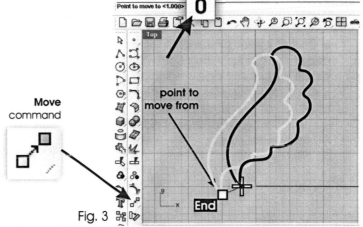

point to move from

End

Fig. 3

• The leaf will move so that its bottom tip will sit right on "**0**".

• The coordinate of this location is expressed as **0,0**" but Rhino lets you type merely "**0**" to specify it as a location designation in its commands.

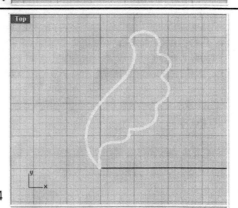

Fig. 4

49

- Click on the **Record History** button at the bottom of the workspace.

Fig. 5

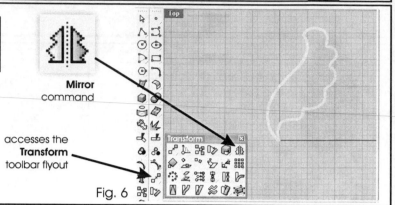

- Keep the leaf selected and click on the **Mirror** command in the **Transform** toolbar flyout.

Mirror command

accesses the **Transform** toolbar flyout

Fig. 6

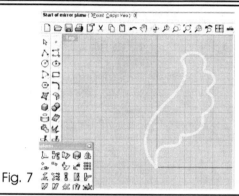

- **Start of mirror plane** prompt: type "**0**" and press "enter".

Fig. 7

- **End of mirror plane** prompt: draw the cursor straight up, using **ORTHO** so that the plane is perfectly perpendicular.
- Click anywhere on this plane to set the direction of the mirror plane.
  - Entering a number or coordinate is not necessary.

end of mirror plane

start of mirror plane

Fig. 8

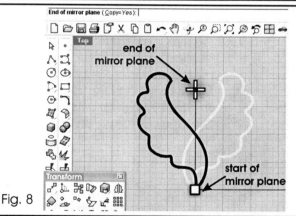

- A perfect mirror image copy of the leaf has been created. Both original and copy are equal distances from the mirror plane.

- Make sure that the original leaf is still selected.

- Click on the **Rotate** command.

Rotate command

Fig. 9

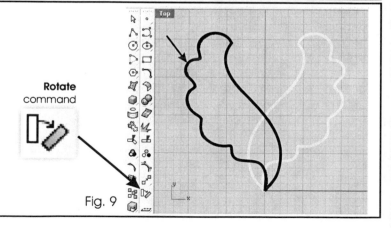

- **Center of rotation** prompt: snap to the **end** of the curves at the bottom of the leaf and click to set this location.

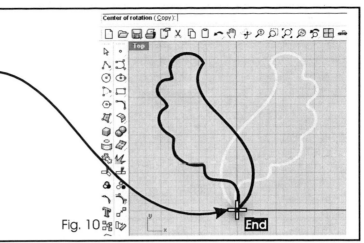

Fig. 10

- Draw the cursor upward and notice the "rubber band" line that stretches between It and the point designated as the center of rotation.

- Also, notice the white circle that surrounds the center of rotation and follows the cursor.

- **Angle or first reference point** prompt: click on the construction plane in the general area as the cursor shown. ❶

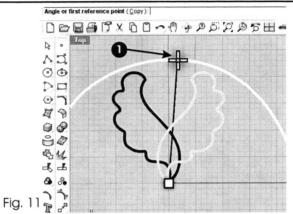

Fig. 11

- **Second reference point** prompt: draw the cursor clockwise until the preview of the new location is in a position that you choose. ❷
- Click to set this new location.

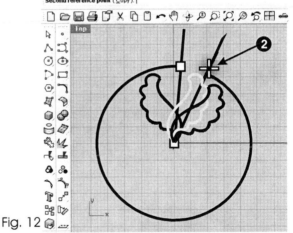

Fig. 12

- The selected leaf shape is now be rotated into a new position.

- Note: The mirror image leaf *updates to still mirror the original leaf.*

- Because **History** was toggled on [Fig. 5] for this command, the original leaf is the **Parent** and the mirrored copy is the **Child.**

- **The child will always update when the parent is edited.**

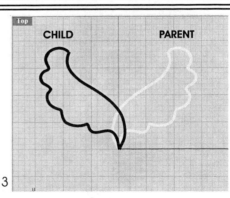

Fig. 13

- **Drag** the parent object to the right so that it is entirely to the right of the perpendicular "Y" axis as shown.

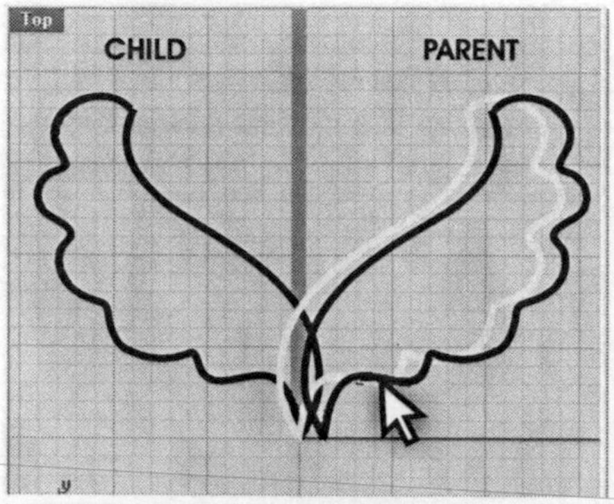

Fig. 14

- The **Child** updates as shown..

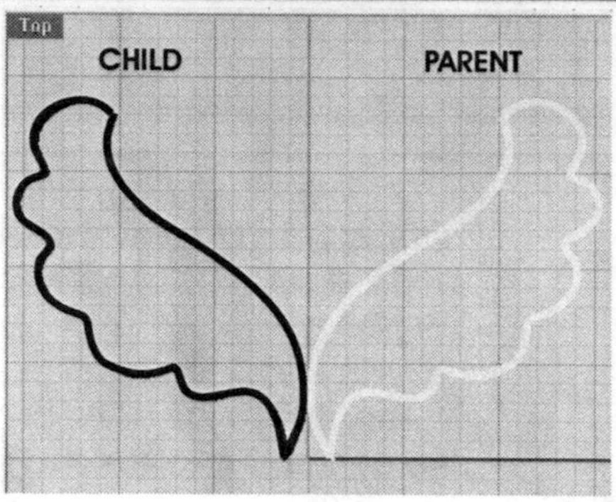

Fig. 15

- Click on the **Record History** button at the bottom of the workspace.

| Snap | Ortho | Planar | **Osnap** | **Record History** |

Fig. 16

- Select both **Parent** and **Child** and **Mirror** them vertically, designating the mirror axis shown.

- Note: The upper left leaf is now **both a CHILD and a PARENT**. This is because it is being mirrored with History toggled on.
    - It is the **PARENT** of the mirrored copy directly under it.

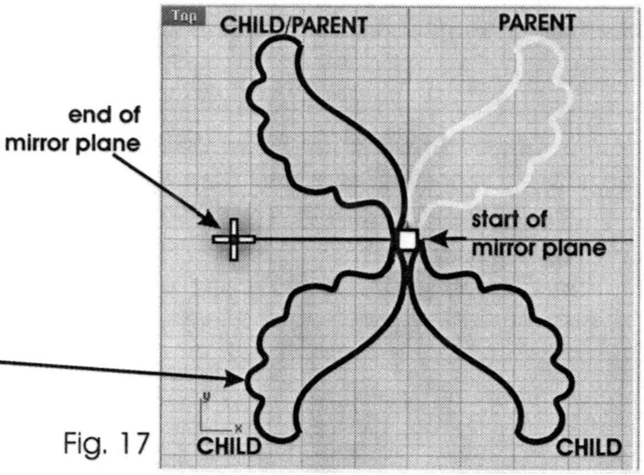

CHILD/PARENT   PARENT

end of mirror plane

start of mirror plane

CHILD   CHILD

Fig. 17

- **Rotate** the original parent with **center of rotation** and **First reference point** as shown.

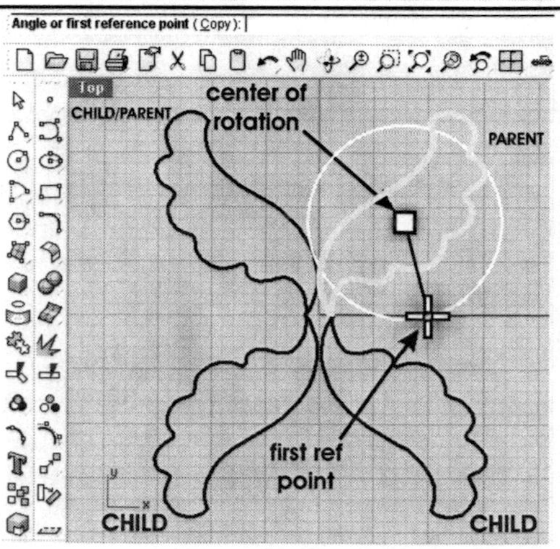

Angle or first reference point (Copy):

CHILD/PARENT   center of rotation   PARENT

first ref point

CHILD   CHILD

Fig. 18

- Rotate until the leaf is in the approximate position shown and click to set the location.

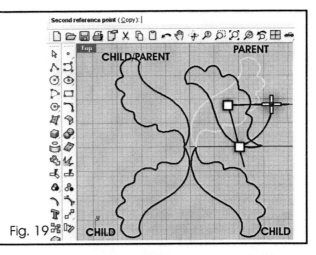

Fig. 19

- All four **Children** will update.

- Editing of the parent object will update the rest of the pieces.

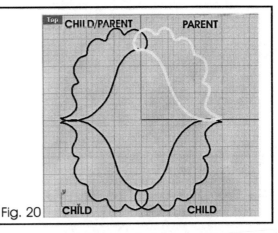

Fig. 20

- See if you can make these designs....

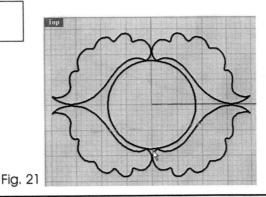

Fig. 21

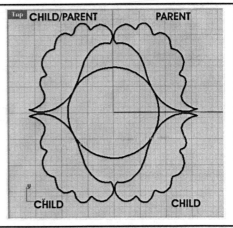

- If you try to move or edit one of the child objects, the **History Warning** dialog box will appear with the warning shown.

- If you want to keep the History relationship between child and parent, Undo this step.

Fig. 22

History Warning

Dragging broke history on 1 object.

To restore history and undo your changes, run the Undo command.

☐ Don't show this message again

OK

Trim & Split commands

Trim Command

- Create three circles, each with a single line passing through it as shown.

- Measurements are not important here.

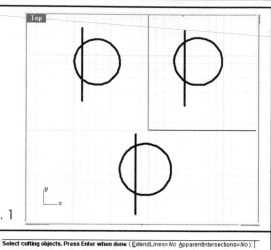

Fig. 1

- Zoom in on one of the circle/line combinations as shown.

- **Left click** on the **Trim** command.
  - **Select cutting objects** prompt: select the circle as shown.
  - Press "enter".

Trim
command

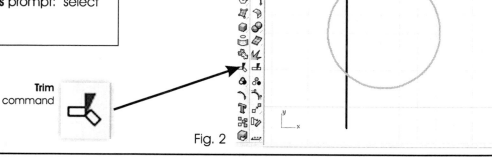

Fig. 2

- **Select object to trim** prompt: click on the end of the line at the approximate position shown.

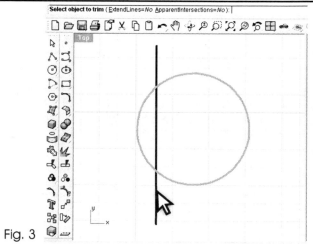

Fig. 3

- The end of the line that you selected will be "trimmed off" at the point where it intersects the designated cutting object which was the circle.

Fig. 4

- Click on the other end of the line to trim that end off as well.

Fig. 5

- Press "enter" to indicate that you are finished with the trim command.

- Your end result is as shown.

Fig. 6

- Pan over to another circle and try trimming it as shown!

Fig. 7

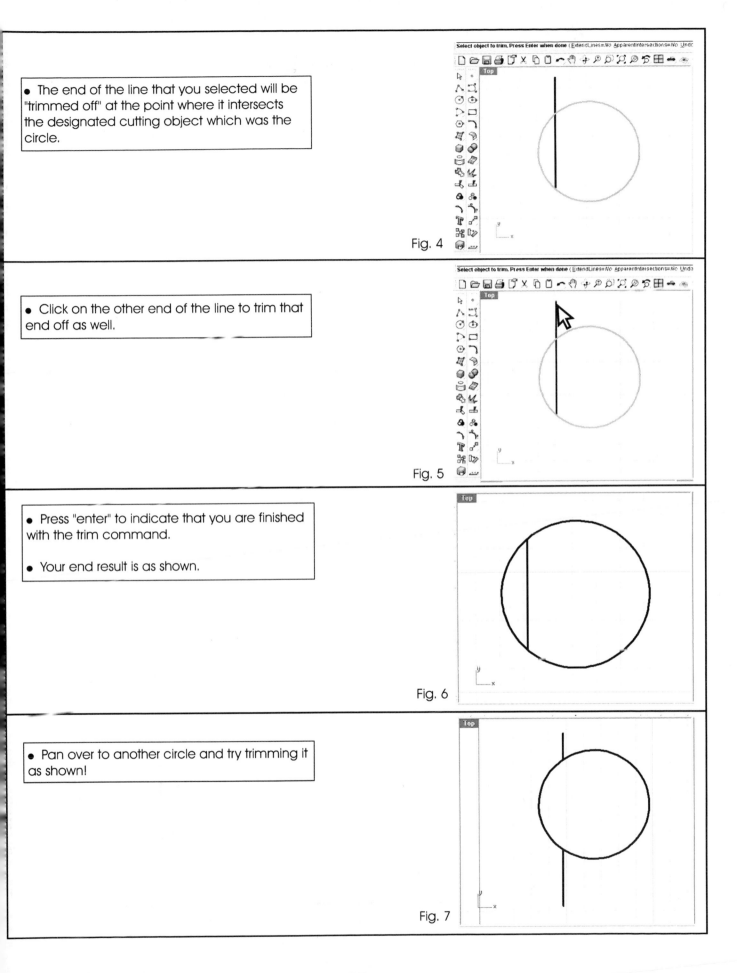

Split Command

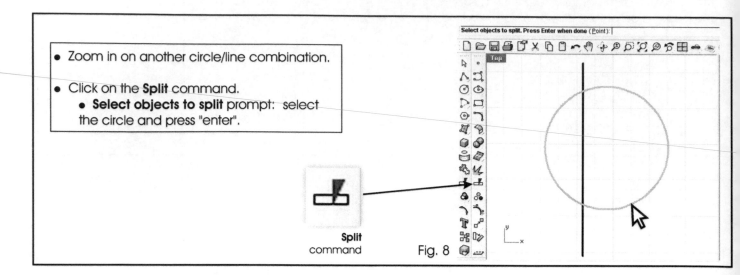

- Zoom in on another circle/line combination.

- Click on the **Split** command.
  - **Select objects to split** prompt: select the circle and press "enter".

Split
command

Fig. 8

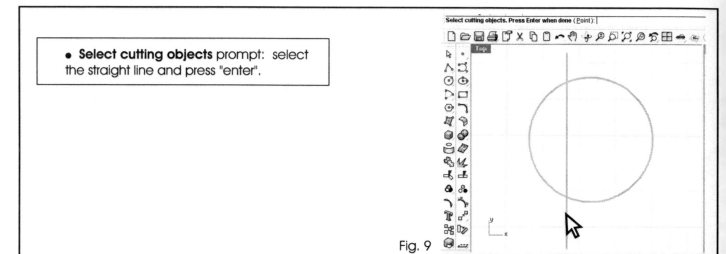

- **Select cutting objects** prompt: select the straight line and press "enter".

Fig. 9

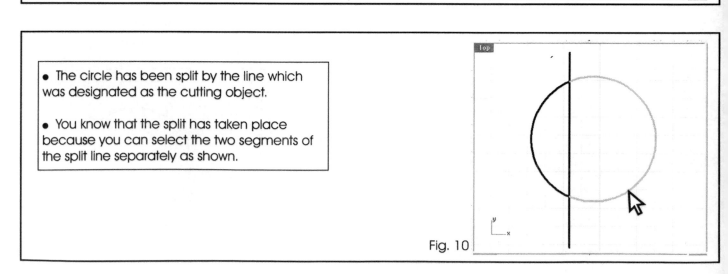

- The circle has been split by the line which was designated as the cutting object.

- You know that the split has taken place because you can select the two segments of the split line separately as shown.

Fig. 10

- Click on the **Join** command.
  - **Select object for join** prompt: select first one segment of the circle and then the other.

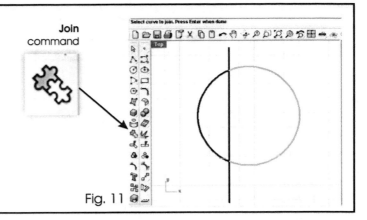

Join command

Fig. 11

- The two curve segments will be joined into one closed curve.

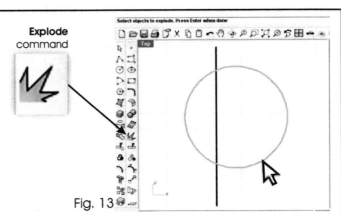

Fig. 12

- Click on the **Explode** command.
  - **Select objects to explode** prompt: select the circle that you just joined together and press "enter".

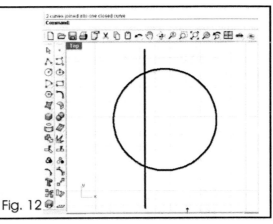

Explode command

Fig. 13

- The circle will once again be in two pieces.

- *Once you split an object, it will always be in pieces and will have to be joined to be one piece again. But it will still be able to be exploded unless it is rebuilt, in which case it will be a single line again.*

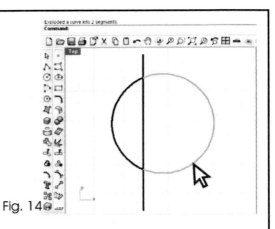

Fig. 14

Simple Stones and Prongs - Creating with Circles

Tangent-Tangent-Radius and Tangent to 3 Curves commands

- Open Rhino and save this file off as **simple stones & prongs.3dm**. You will use this file for this exercise and the next.

- Use the **Circle: Center, Radius** command to create a **10mm diameter** circle around **0,0** as shown.

Circle: Center, Radius command

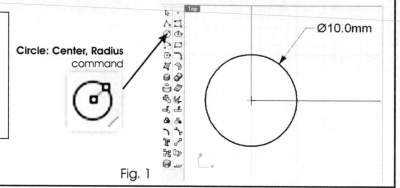

Fig. 1

- Use the **Circle: Diameter** command to create a **6mm diameter circle** from the right quad point of the first circle.

- Use **Quad osnap**.

- Use **ortho**.

Circle: Diameter command

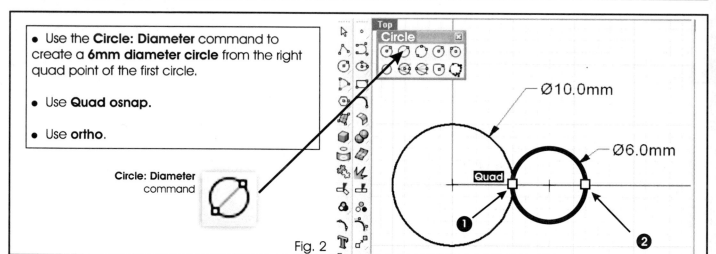

Fig. 2

- Create two more circles, each inside the original two circles as shown.

  - **9mm circle**: created around **0,0**.

  - **5.4mm diameter circle**: Use **Center Osnap** to snap to the center of the 6mm circle in order to set the center of this smaller circle.

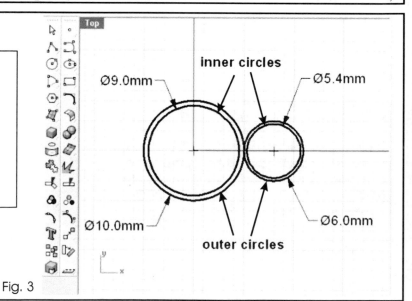

Fig. 3

58

- Click on the **Circle: Tangent, Tangent, Radius** command in the **Circle** toolbar flyout.

  - **First tangent curve** prompt: Drag the cursor over the **inner circle** on the right as shown.
    - Notice that a white constraint line appears as the cursor touches the circle.
  - Click on the approximate location shown to set this curve as one of the curves to which the circle you are creating will be tangent. **1**

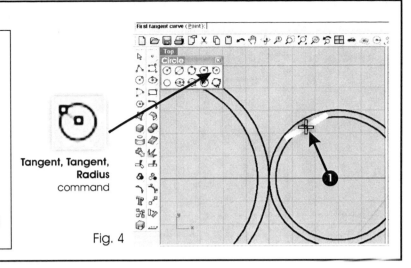

Tangent, Tangent, Radius
command

Fig. 4

- At you start to draw the cursor toward the second circle, notice that a preview circle is present.
- **Second tangent curve or radius** prompt: type the number "**.75**" and press "enter".

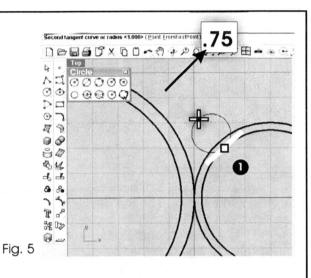

Fig. 5

- Drag the cursor over **inner circle** on the left as shown.
  - A white constraint line will appear as before.
- Click on this location. **2**

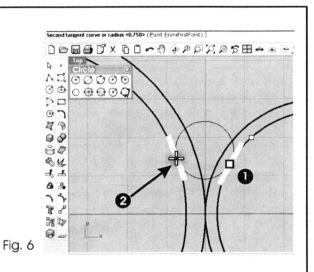

Fig. 6

- The resulting circle will be tangent to both specified curves and will measure **1.5mm in diameter because of the specified radius of .75mm.**

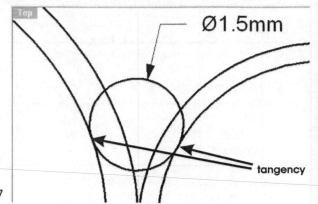

Fig. 7

- **Mirror** the circle you just created vertically with the **mirror plane on the X Axis** create the lower prong as shown.

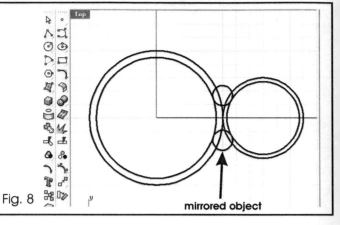

Fig. 8

- At another location on the construction plane, creat two concentric circles as shown.
  - The **Circle: Center, Radius** command probably works best for this combined with the use of **Center osnap.**
  - Use **Grid snap** to center the circles.

- The outer circle is **10mm** in diameter and the inner circle, **9mm.**

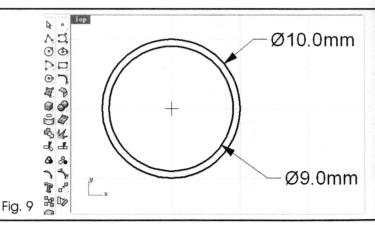

Fig. 9

- Leave **Grid Snap** on and create a polyline that creates a square enclosing the circles.

- **Grid Snap** will make this an easy task.

- **NOW TURN OFF GRID SNAP. The following command will not work with it turned on.**

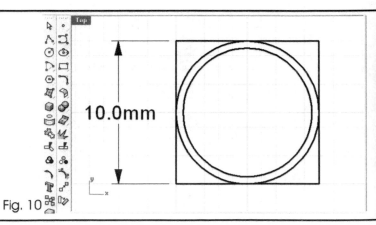

Fig. 10

- Click on the **Circle: Tangent to 3 curves** command in the **Circle** toolbar flyout.
  - **First tangent curve** prompt: drag the cursor over the inside circle as shown. ❶
    - Notice the white constraint line that indicates that the cursor is snapping to that curve.

- Click to set this curve as one of the three tangent curves.

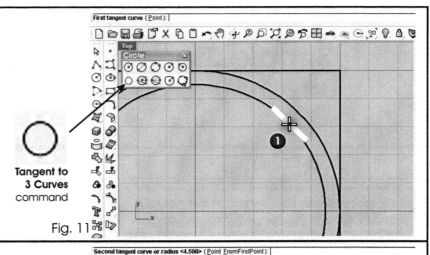

Tangent to 3 Curves command

Fig. 11

- **Second tangent curve or radius** prompt: drag the cursor over to the wall of the surrounding square as shown.
  - Click to set this line as the second tangent curve. ❷

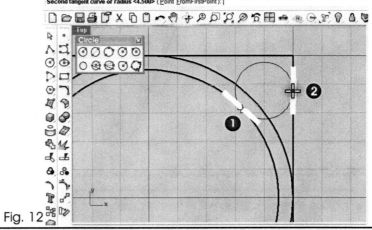

Fig. 12

- **Third tangent curve** prompt: drag the cursor over the top line of the square as shown and click to assign this curve as the third tangent. ❸

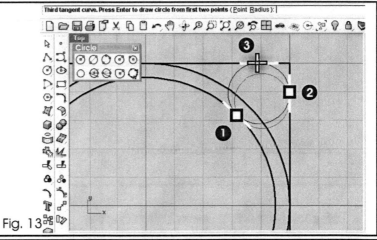

Fig. 13

- Practice this command by doing the other three corners as shown.

- Save this file or continue on to the next section of this exercise.

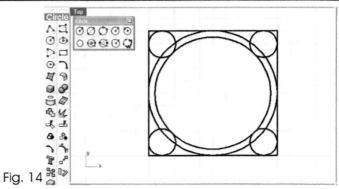

Fig. 14

Simple Stones and Prongs - Layers
Using the Layers functions to organize your work.

- Open the Rhino file created in the previous exercise, **Simple Stones and Prongs.3dm**

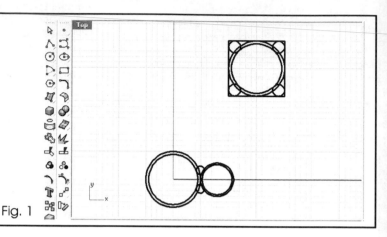

Fig. 1

- Notice that all lines are the same color.

- Zoom in on the square configuration shown.

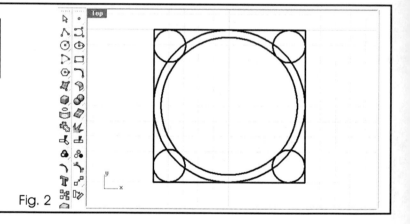

Fig. 2

- **Left click** on the **Edit Layers** button and the **Layers** box will open and dock on the right as shown.

- If the Layers box is not automatically docked, you can drag is over the right and dock it manually.

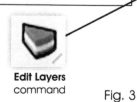

Edit Layers
command

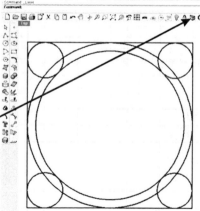
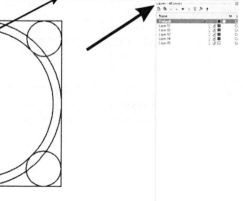

Fig. 3

- The **Layers** dialog box is shown here.

- The layers you see here is the default configuration.

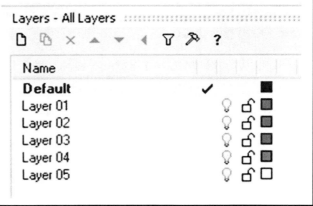

Fig. 4

- **Right click** on the word "Default" in the colum with the word "Name" at the head.

- A drop-down context menu will appear.

- Slide the cursor down to the words, **Rename Layer** and **left click** to select that option.

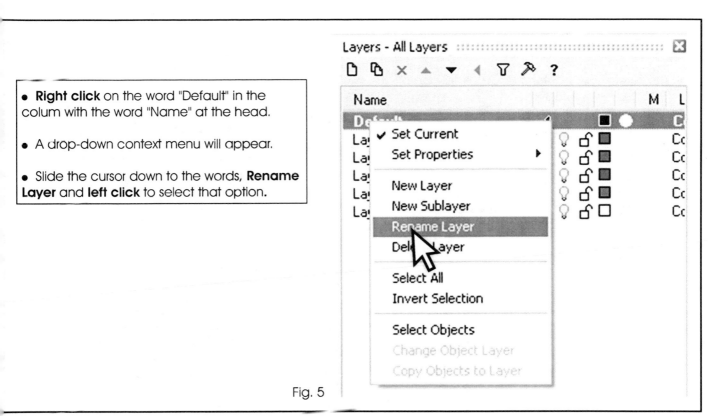

Fig. 5

- You will be invited to rename that layer as shown.

- You can also rename a layer by slowly left clicking twice on the layer title and then typing in a new name.

- Name this layer **STONES**.

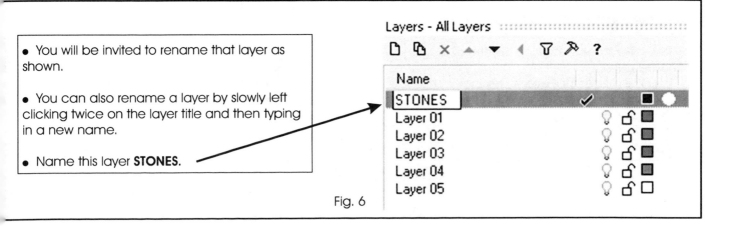

Fig. 6

- Use the same procedure to name the rest of the layers as shown.

- Notice that some layer names are in upper case and some in lower.

- This is a simple system that allows you to quickly see what layers show jewelry elements and which layers have construction lines, or reference geometry. This is a suggested way to organize the layers box for quick and easy use.

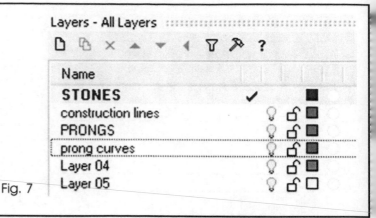

Fig. 7

- Click on the little color box on the PRONGS line as shown.

- The **Select Layer Color** dialog box will open.

- Click on the **DarkGreen** color in the list on the left as shown.

- Click the OK button at the bottom of the dialog box.

- The color of the PRONGS layer will be changed to Dark Green.

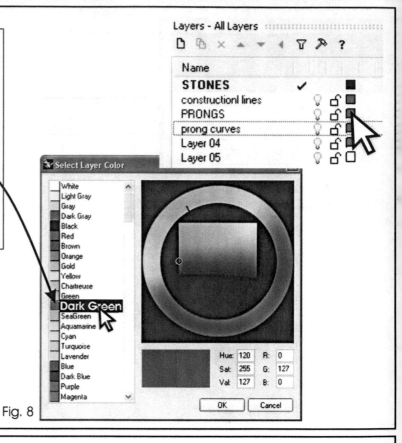

Fig. 8

- Apply this procedure to the other layers.

- Note the "check" mark on the line of the **STONES** layer.
    - This means that everything that you create will be on this layer.
    - You can change current layers by checking on the line of another layer in the same column - the check will move to that line and that layer will be current.

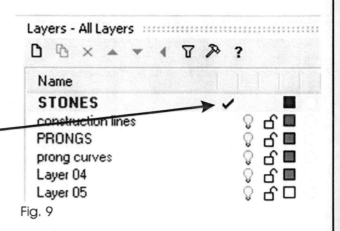

Fig. 9

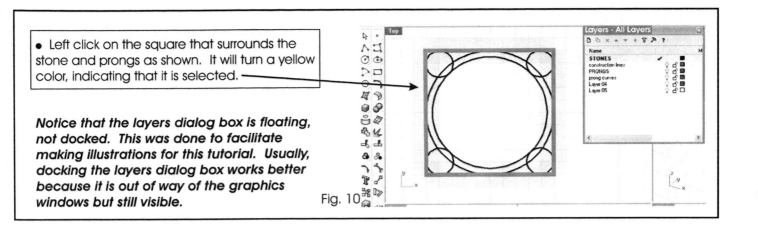

- Left click on the square that surrounds the stone and prongs as shown. It will turn a yellow color, indicating that it is selected.

Notice that the layers dialog box is floating, not docked. This was done to facilitate making illustrations for this tutorial. Usually, docking the layers dialog box works better because it is out of way of the graphics windows but still visible.

Fig. 10

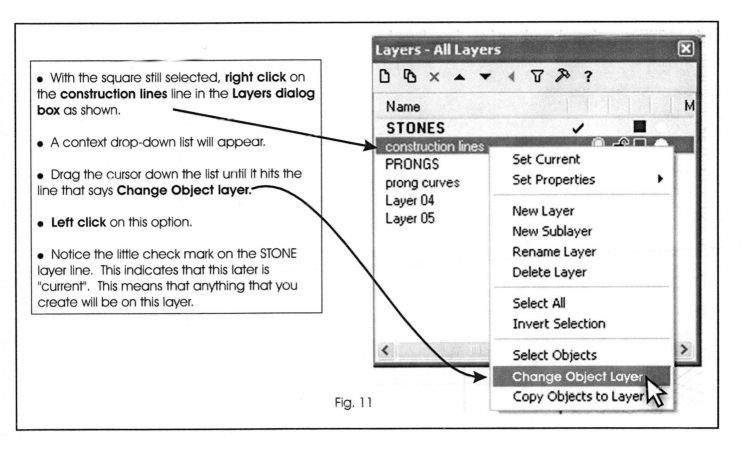

- With the square still selected, **right click** on the **construction lines** line in the **Layers dialog box** as shown.

- A context drop-down list will appear.

- Drag the cursor down the list until It hits the line that says **Change Object layer.**

- **Left click** on this option.

- Notice the little check mark on the STONE layer line. This indicates that this later is "current". This means that anything that you create will be on this layer.

Fig. 11

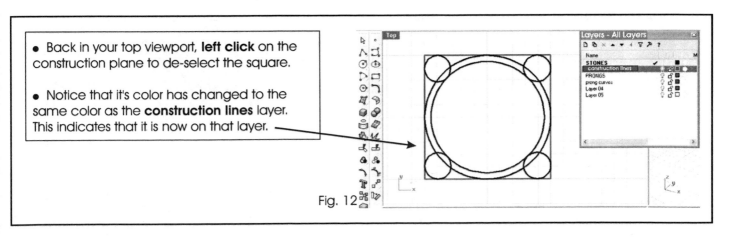

- Back in your top viewport, **left click** on the construction plane to de-select the square.

- Notice that it's color has changed to the same color as the **construction lines** layer. This indicates that it is now on that layer.

Fig. 12

- Click on the little yellow light bulb on the **construction lines** layer line. It will darken in color, looking like it has been "turned off".

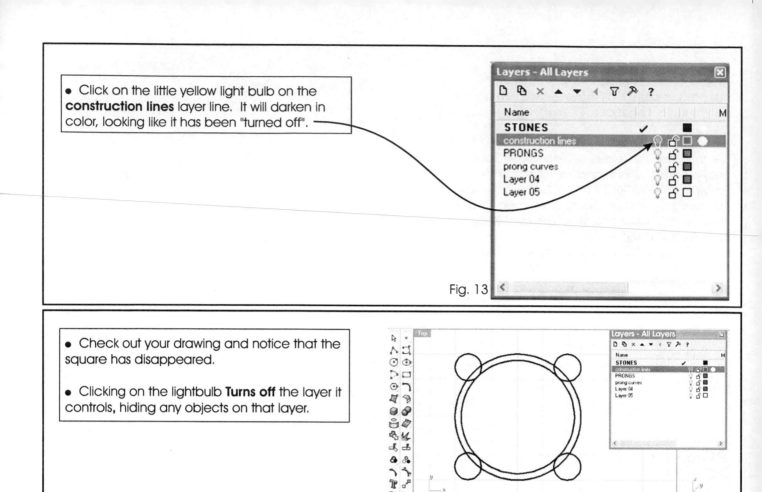

Fig. 13

- Check out your drawing and notice that the square has disappeared.

- Clicking on the lightbulb **Turns off** the layer it controls, hiding any objects on that layer.

Fig. 14

- Click the lightbulb a second time and it turns yellow once again. Layer visibility is toggled back on.

Fig. 15

- Change the layers of the rest of the objects as shown.

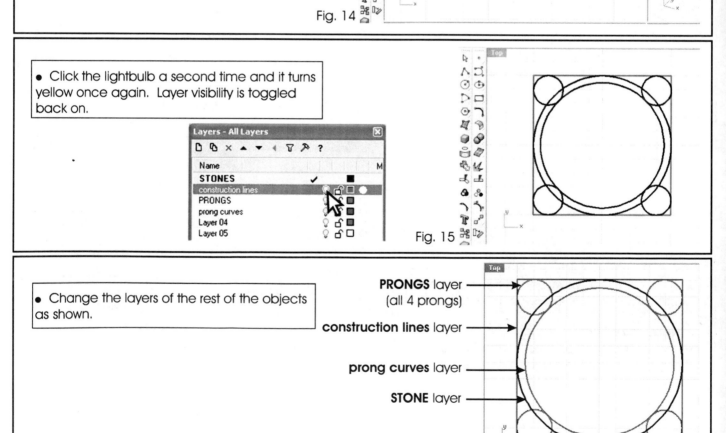

PRONGS layer
(all 4 prongs)

construction lines layer

prong curves layer

STONE layer

Fig. 16

- Click off the light bulbs for the **construction lines** layer and for the **prong curves** layer.

- The light bulbs turn dark and you can see that the two layers are now turned off and you can only see the **STONES** layer and the **PRONGS** layer.

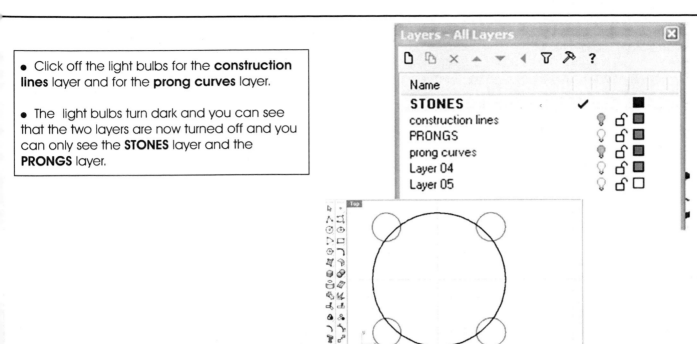

Fig. 17

- **Left click** on the **Trim** command.
  - **Select cutting objects** prompt: select all 4 prong circles as shown.
  - Press "enter".

Trim
command

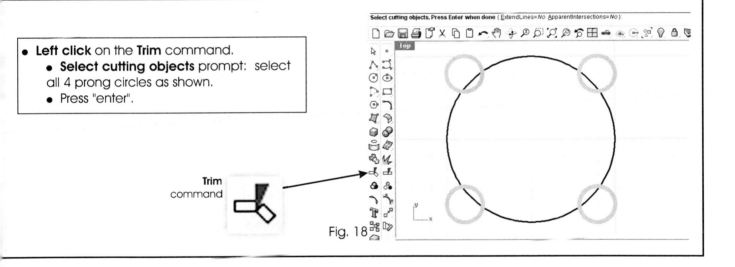

Fig. 18

- **Select object to trim** prompt: click on the line that intersects the little selected prong circles.
  - When you select them, the parts of the line that you selected will be trimmed out - it will go away as shown with the prong on the right.
- Press "enter" when you have trimmed out all 4 prong circles.

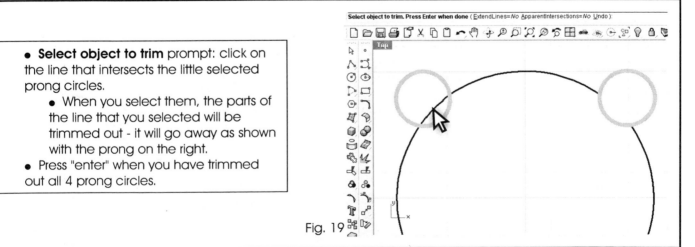

Fig. 19

- The trimmed drawing.

- Prongs now look like they sit on top of the stone as they should.

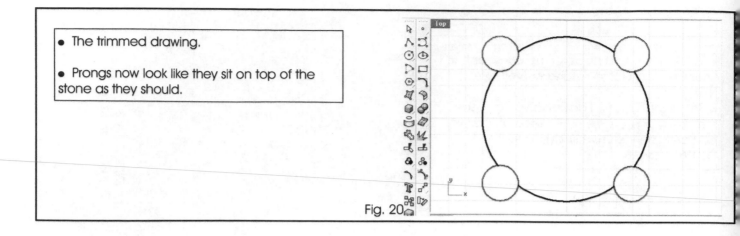

Fig. 20

- Zoom in on the other drawing and assign layers to the elements as shown.

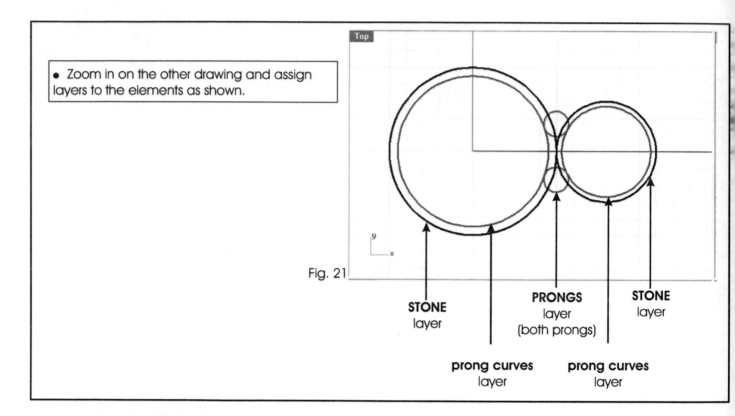

Fig. 21

STONE
layer

PRONGS
layer
(both prongs)

STONE
layer

prong curves
layer

prong curves
layer

- Turn off the **construction lines** layer and the **prong curves** layers.

- **Trim** out inside the prongs as before.

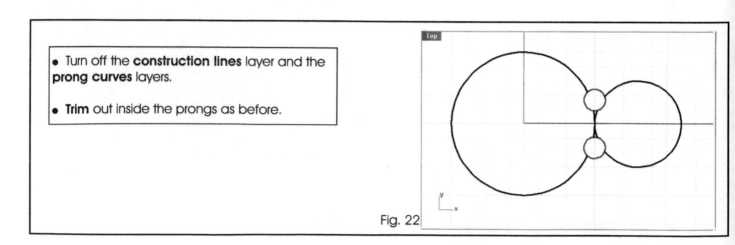

Fig. 22

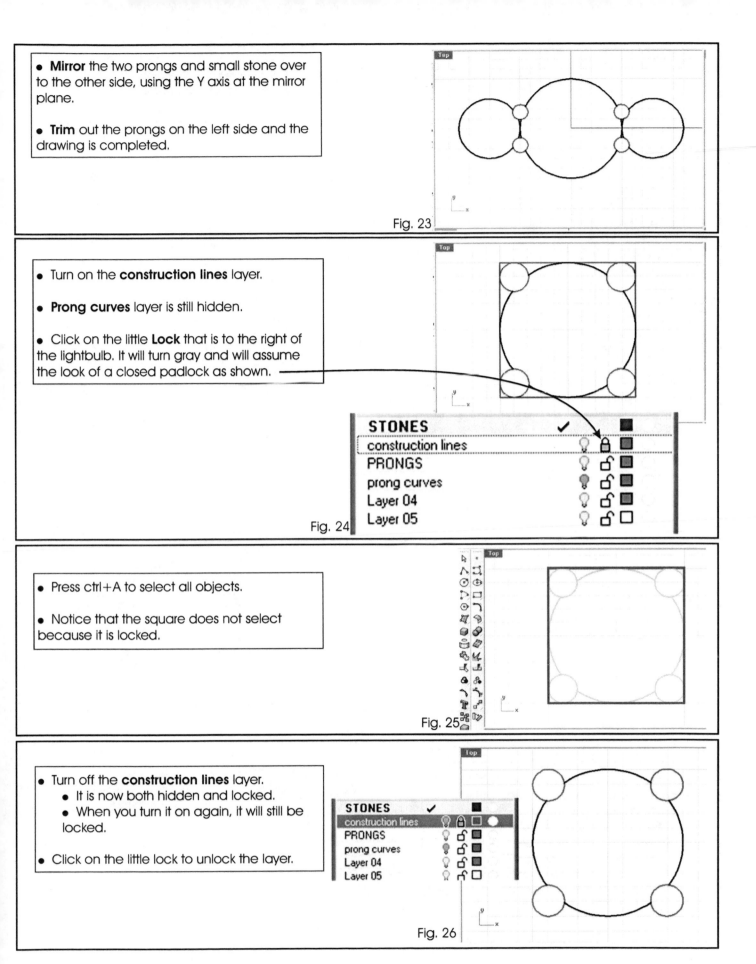

- **Mirror** the two prongs and small stone over to the other side, using the Y axis at the mirror plane.

- **Trim** out the prongs on the left side and the drawing is completed.

Fig. 23

- Turn on the **construction lines** layer.

- **Prong curves** layer is still hidden.

- Click on the little **Lock** that is to the right of the lightbulb. It will turn gray and will assume the look of a closed padlock as shown.

STONES ✓
construction lines
PRONGS
prong curves
Layer 04
Layer 05

Fig. 24

- Press ctrl+A to select all objects.

- Notice that the square does not select because it is locked.

Fig. 25

- Turn off the **construction lines** layer.
  - It is now both hidden and locked.
  - When you turn it on again, it will still be locked.

- Click on the little lock to unlock the layer.

STONES ✓
construction lines
PRONGS
prong curves
Layer 04
Layer 05

Fig. 26

Technical Drawing - Pearl Ring

- Open Rhino and save the file as **pearl ring.3dm**. **We will use this file again.**

- Make the **TECH LINES** layer "current" by clicking in the column to the right of the layer name.
  - **A check mark will appear, designating this layer as the "current" layer - anything created will be on this layer.**
  - **Click in this column on the line of another layer, and that layer becomes "current".**

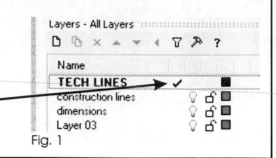

Fig. 1

- **Top viewport.** Double-click on the viewport title to maximize it.

- Create a circle with its center at "**0,0**". Type "**17**" when prompted for the diameter in the **Command Line** to make the diameter of the circle 17mm.

- *Make sure you check in the **Command Line** to make sure that you are specifying 17 as the diameter, not the radius!*

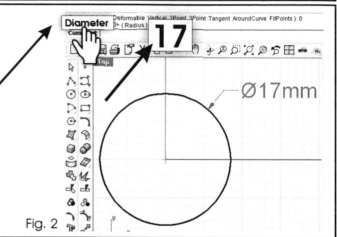

Ø17mm

Fig. 2

- Repeat the **Circle** command, creating another circle with it's center at "**0,0**".

- The diameter for this circle is **21mm**.

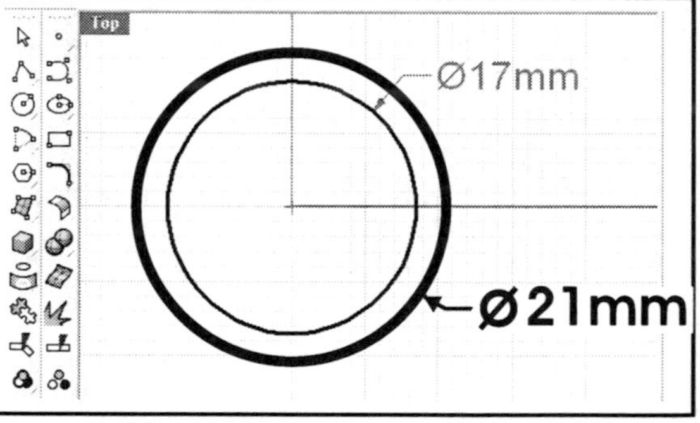

Ø17mm

Ø21mm

Fig. 3

- Click on the **Circle: Diameter** command to create a circle at the top of the ring as shown.
  - **Start of Diameter** prompt: using **quad osnap**, click on the top quad of the outer circle as shown. ❶
  - **End of Diameter** prompt: type "**6**" in the **Command Line** and press "enter".
    - **Left click** directly perpendicular to the first point, using **Ortho** to set the location of the end of the diameter. ❷

accesses the **Circle** toolbar flyout

Circle: diameter command

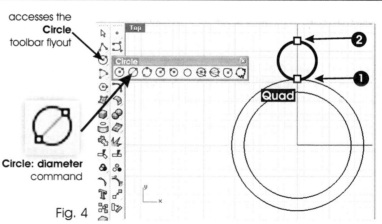

Fig. 4

70

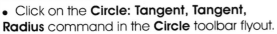
First tangent curve (Point):

- Click on the **Circle: Tangent, Tangent, Radius** command in the **Circle** toolbar flyout.
  - **First tangent curve** prompt: draw the cursor over the large center circle where shown.
  - A white constraint line will appear, signifying that the cursor is in contact with this line. **1**
  - Left click.

Circle: Tangent, Tangent, Radius command

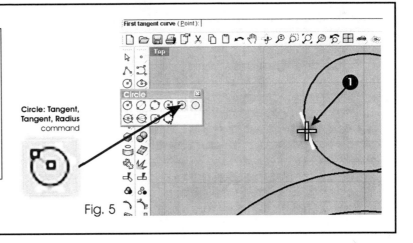

Fig. 5

- **Second tangent curve or radius** prompt: type "**2**" and press "enter".

Second tangent curve or radius <2.000> (Point FromFirs **2**

Fig. 6

- **Second tangent curve or radius** prompt: draw the cursor over the ring band curve and click when the white constraint line appears as shown. **2**
  - Notice that a preview circle will move with the cursor.

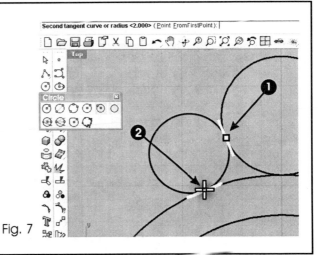
Second tangent curve or radius <2.000> (Point FromFirstPoint):

Fig. 7

- A circle will be created that is 4mm in diameter and which is tangent to the two curves designated as shown.

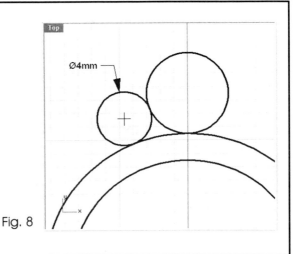

Ø4mm

Fig. 8

- **construction lines** layer current.

- Toggle on **Grid Snap**. | Snap | Ortho |

- Using the **Line: from Midpoint** command, create a horizontal line that is about 25mm above the front view of the ring as shown.. **This will be the center line of your TOP ring elevation.**
  - Create this line on a darker grid line for easy visual reference.
    - Use **Ortho** to ensure that this center line is perfectly horizontal.

Line: from Midpoint command

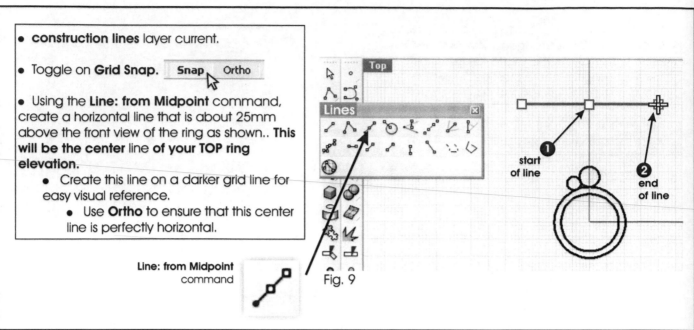

Fig. 9

- **Construction lines layer.**

- Using the **Line** command, draw vertical construction lines from the **quad points of the circles** upward as shown.
  - Line length is not important, just so the lines cross the center line of the top elevation.
    - Use **Quad Osnap** and **ortho**.

- Draw an additional vertical center line from "**0**" that crosses the center line of the top elevation as shown.

Line command

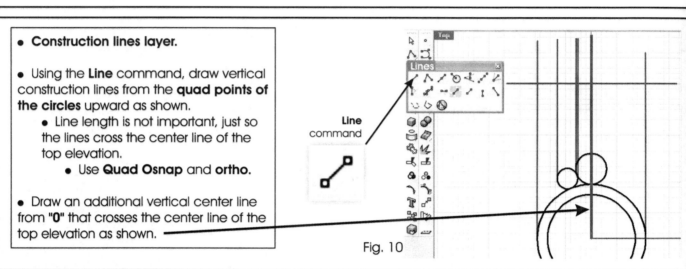

Fig. 10

- **TECH LINES LAYER.**

- Select the horizontal TOP center line and click on the **Offset** command in the **Curve Tools** toolbar flyout.
  - **Side to Offset** prompt: type **"1.5"** and press "enter".
  - Click on the **BothSides** option in the **Command Line** and offsets will appear on both sides of the line as shown.
  - **Left click** to complete the command.

accesses the **Curve Tools** toolbar flyout

Select curve to offset (Distance=1.5 Corner=Sharp

BothSides | 1.5 |

line to be offset

Offset command

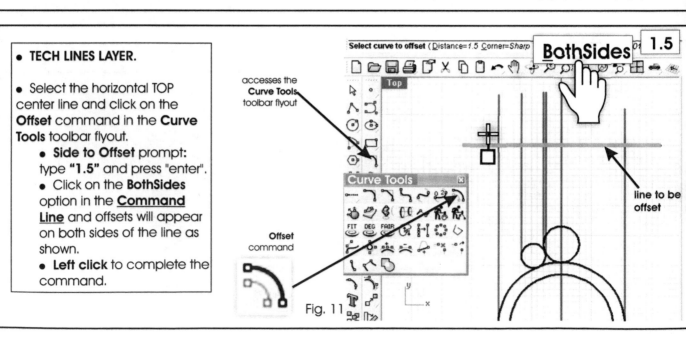

Fig. 11

- The offsets are completed on both sides of the center line of the top elevation as shown.

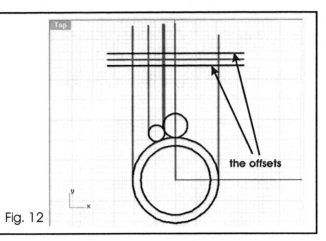

the offsets

Fig. 12

- The next step will start to create the round curvature of the ring shank top elevation.

- Zoom in on the left side of the top elevation.

- Click on the **Circle: Tangent to 3 Curves** command in the **Circle** toolbar flyout.
    - **First tangent curve** prompt: draw the cursor over the top offset line as shown.
        - Click when a white constraint line appears. **1**

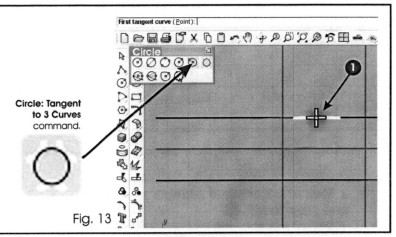

Circle: Tangent to 3 Curves command.

First tangent curve (Point):

Fig. 13

- **Second tangent curve** prompt: draw the cursor over the vertical construction line shown.
    - Click when a white constraint line appears. **2**
    - Notice that the first constraint line **1** moves to adjust the tangency of the new circle being created.

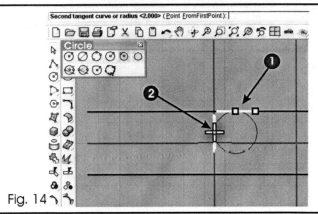

Second tangent curve or radius <2.000> (Point FromFirstPoint):

Fig. 14

- **Third tangent curve** prompt: draw the cursor over the lower offset curve.
    - Click when a white constraint line appears. **3**

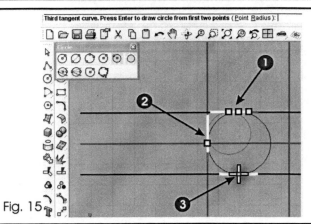

Third tangent curve. Press Enter to draw circle from first two points (Point Radius):

Fig. 15

- A circle has been created that touches all three designated curves.

- This is the first step to defining the roundness of the ring shank in the top elevation.

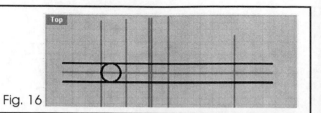
Fig. 16

- Select the two circles shown and click on the **Mirror** command in the **Transform** toolbar flyout.

Mirror command

accesses the **Transform** toolbar flyout

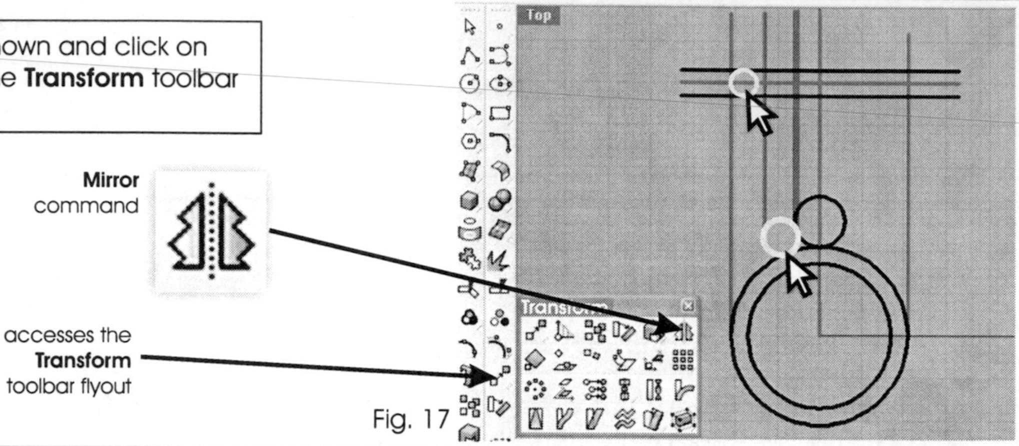

Fig. 17

- **Start of mirror plane** prompt: type "0" and press "enter". ❶
- **End of mirror plane** prompt: use **ortho** when drawing the cursor straight up to define the direction of the mirror plane. ❷
- Click to set location. ❷

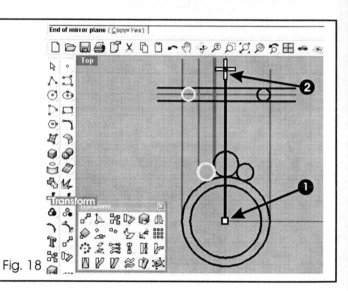
Fig. 18

- The two circles have been mirrored over to the right side of the drawing.

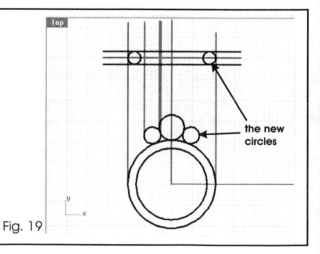

the new circles

Fig. 19

- Select the offsets and two circles of the top elevation as shown and click on the **Trim** command.
  - **Select object to trim** prompt: click on the lines and curves at the locations shown.

- *Note: It is advised to lock the **construction lines** layer for this step to avoid selecting or trimming them away by mistake.*

Trim
command

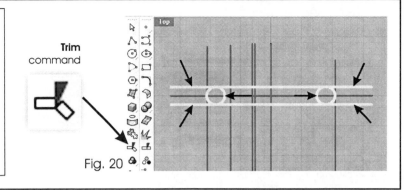

Fig. 20

- Press "enter" to end the command when the shape seen here is achieved.

- Select the trimmed curves and click on the **Join** command.

Join
command

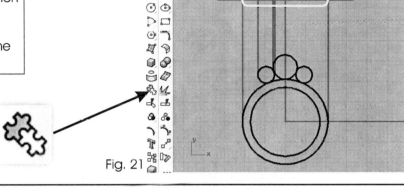

Fig. 21

- Select the top view of the ring band and it's center line and click on the **Rotate** command.
  - **Center of rotation** prompt: be sure to click on the **Copy** option in the **Command Line.**
  - **Center of rotation** prompt: type "0" and press "enter".
  - **Angle or first reference point** prompt: type "-90" to indicate that you want to rotate *"minus 90-degrees"*.
    - ***The reason for the "minus" sign is that this rotation will be in a clockwise direction, which is a "minus" direction when measuring degrees.***

Rotate
command

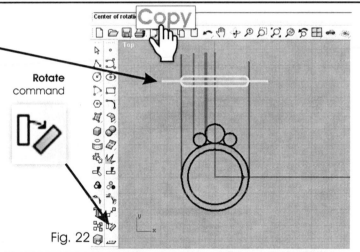

Fig. 22

- A rotated copy of the ring shank, along with it's center line has been rotation copied to the right of the front view.
  - Because the center of rotation was "0", the new side elevation shank is the same distance from "0" as the top elevation shank.

- This is the first step of creating the side elevation of the ring technical.

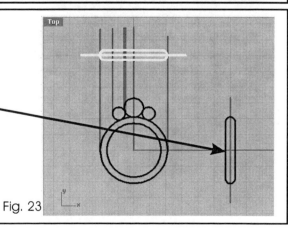

Fig. 23

- Toggle on the **Center** and the **Perp** osnaps.

- Select the large center circle and click on the **Copy** command.
  - **Point to copy from** prompt: snap to the center of the large circle and click.
  - **Point to copy to** prompt: draw the cursor up and use **perp osnap** to snap to the center line of the top elevation as shown.
  - Press "enter" to end the command.

Copy command

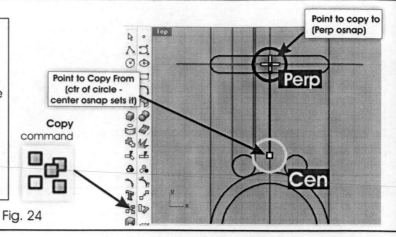

Fig. 24

- **Copy** the smaller circle up to the top elevation the same way.

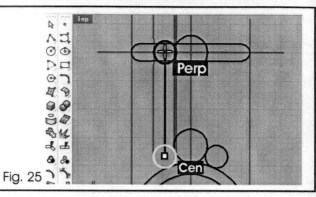

Fig. 25

- Select the newly copied little circle and click on the **Mirror** command.
  - **Start of mirror plane** prompt: snap to the **intersection** of construction lines as shown. **1**
  - **End of mirror plane** prompt: with **ortho** engaged, draw the cursor straight up and click to set the location. **2**

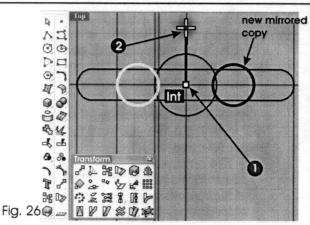

Fig. 26

- **Copy** the large and small circles over to the side elevation, using **Center** and **Perp** osnaps as you did when copying these circles up to the top elevation.

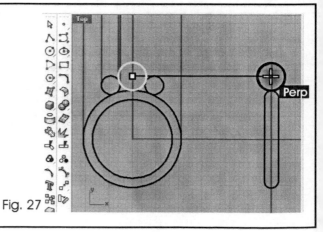

Fig. 27

- Both large and small stones are copied over to the side elevation.

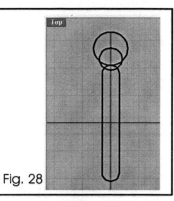

Fig. 28

- Turn off the **construction lines** layer.

- Carefully **Trim** out both top and side elevations.

Trim
command

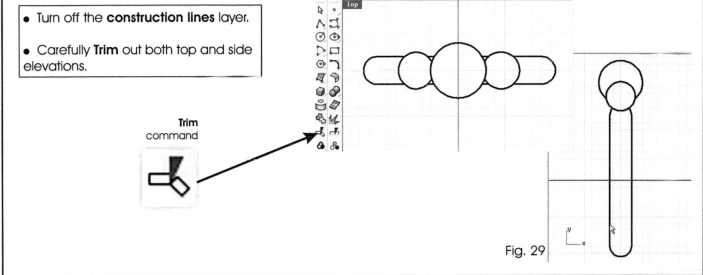

Fig. 29

- Using the **Dimension** toolbar flyout, put dimensions on the drawing.

- **Note: To get correct dimensions, osnaps are essential!**
  - For this example, **Quad Osnap** and **Center Osnap** are needed.

Horizontal Dimension
command

Vertical Dimension
command

Diameter Dimension
command

accesses the **Dimensions** toolbar flyout

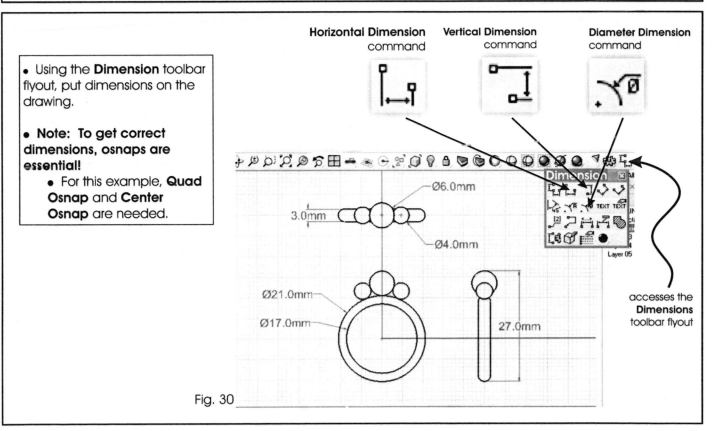

Ø6.0mm

3.0mm

Ø4.0mm

Ø21.0mm

Ø17.0mm

27.0mm

Fig. 30

Polygon - Rectangle
Simple Ring Bands

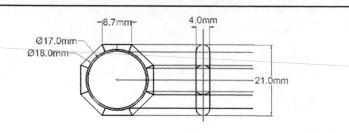

- **8-Sided Polygon shape for basic band.**

- Create layers as shown.
- Make the **TECH LINES** layer current.

Name		
TECH LINES	✓	■
construction lines	💡 🔓	■

Fig. 1

- Create two circles around **0,0**.
- Diameters should be **17mm** and **18mm** as shown.

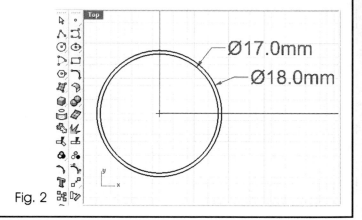

Ø17.0mm
Ø18.0mm

Fig. 2

- **construction lines** layer.
- Create a 2mm perpendicular line from the upper quad point of the inner circle.

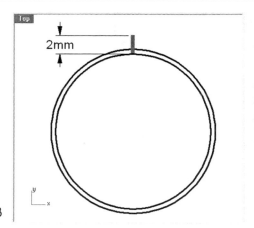

2mm

Fig. 3

- Click on the **Circumscribed Polygon: Center, Radius** command in the **Polygon** toolbar flyout.
  - **Center of inscribed polygon** prompt: type **"0"** and press "enter".
    - Click on the **NumSides** option in the **Command Line** as shown.

accesses the **Polygon** toolbar flyout

Circumscribed Polygon: Center, Radius command

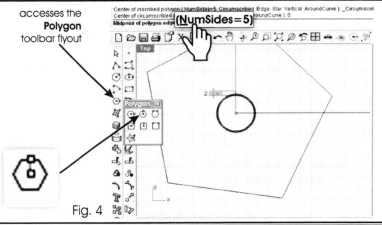

Fig. 4

- **Number of sides** prompt, type **"8"** and press "enter".
  - the number of sides will be set at 8.

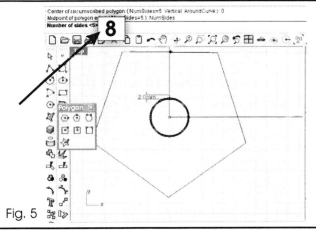

Fig. 5

- **Midpoint of polygon edge** prompt: To set the orientation and radius of the polygon, snap to the **End** point of the little perpendicular construction line at the top of the circle as shown.
  - Click on this location to end the command.
    - This will ensure that the ring band will be 2mm wide at its narrowest

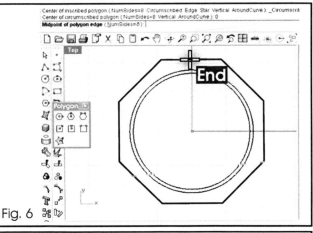

Fig. 6

- Create a single line from one of the angles of the polygon in to the outer circle line.

- Use **end osnap** to start the line.❶

- Use **Perpendicular osnap** to place the end of the line the touches the circle.❷

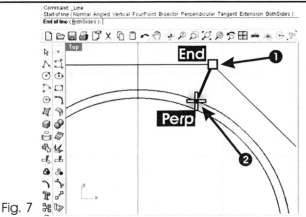

Fig. 7

- Use the **Polar Array** command in the **Transform** toolbar flyout to array the line just created around the ring.

- Select the line just created and click on the **Polar Array** command.
  - **Center of polar array** prompt: Type "0" and press "enter".
  - **Number of objects** prompt: type **"8"** and press "enter".
  - **Angle to fill** prompt: press "enter" to accept the default value of **360**

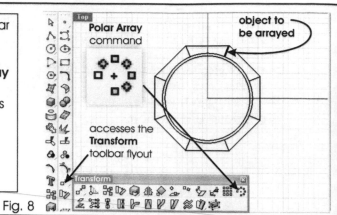

Polar Array command

object to be arrayed

accesses the **Transform** toolbar flyout

Fig. 8

- **construction lines** layer.

- Create lines from the endpoints of the ring as shown. Also, create a line from the center of the center circle as shown. These must be perfectly horizontal. Use **Ortho mode** to ensure accuracy.

- Engage **grid snap** to create the perpendicular line shown so that it will rest on a major grid line.

Fig. 9

- Click on the **Rounded Rectangle** command in the **Rectangle** toolbar flyout as shown.
  - **First corner of rectangle** prompt: Click on the **Center** option in the **Command Line.**
    - The rectangle will be formed from a center, rather than from a corner point.

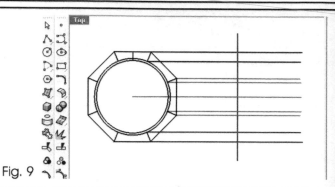

accesses the **Rectangle** toolbar flyout

Rounded Rectangle command

First corner of rectangle (3Point Vertical Center Rounded): Rounded
First corner of rectangle (3Point Vert
First corner of rectangle (3Point Ve

Center

Fig. 10

- **Center of rectangle** prompt: snap to the **intersection** of the two construction lines shown and click to set this location for the center of the rectangle.

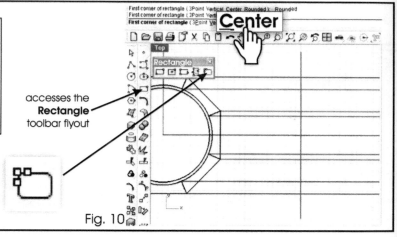

First corner of rectangle (3Point Vertical Center): Center
Center of rectangle: _Pause
Center of rectangle:

Int

Fig. 11

- **Other corner or length** prompt: type "4" and press "enter".
  - This number refers to the measurement of the rectangle in the X direction.

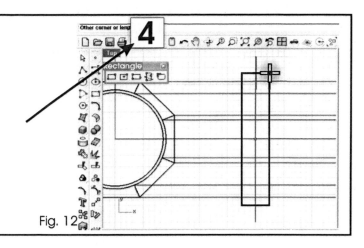

Fig. 12

- **Width** prompt: use **Near osnap** to snap to the highest horizontal line as shown.
  - Click to set this location.

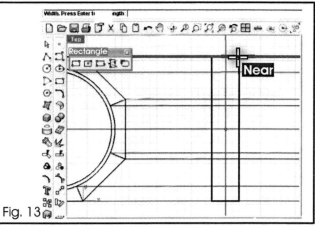

Fig. 13

- **Radius or point for rounded corner to pass through** prompt: snap to the **Intersection** shown and click to set the radius of the rounded corners.

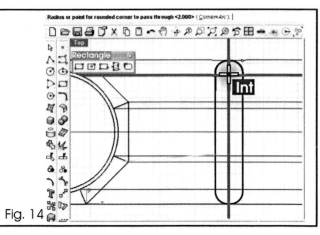

Fig. 14

- The finished rounded rectangle defines the side view of the ring, showing the rounded top of the ring.

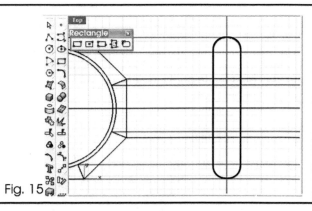

Fig. 15

- Use the **Arc: Start, End, Point on Arc** command to create the arc for the side view as shown.

- Use **Intersection osnap** for all three points on the arc.

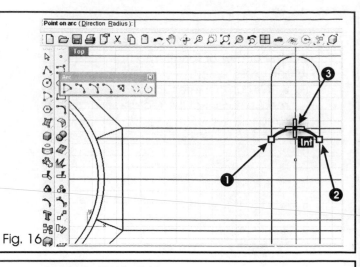

Fig. 16

- **Mirror** the arc just created down to the lower half of the ring as shown.
  - Make the Mirror plane start at **"0"**, ❶ drawing the cursor straight to the side, using **ortho,** and clicking for the end of the mirror plane. ❷

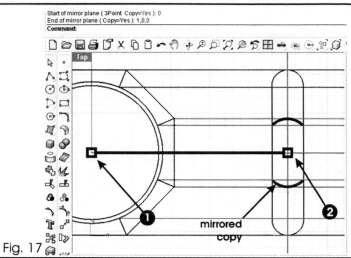

Fig. 17

- The finished technical drawing.

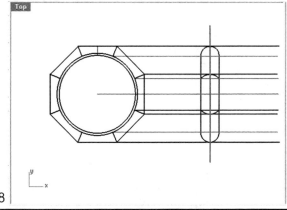

Fig. 18

- The finished technical drawing with dimensions added.

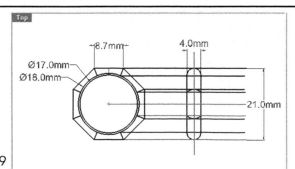

Fig. 19

Soft Rectangle shape with "Conic" corners for simple band ring.

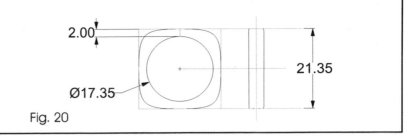

2.00

Ø17.35

21.35

Fig. 20

- Create layers shown.

- Make the **TECH LINES** layer current.

Fig. 21

Name			
TECH LINES	✓		■
construction lines		💡 🔓	■

- Create a circle with a diameter of **17.35mm** around **0,0**.

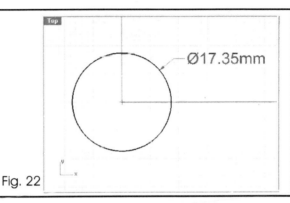

Ø17.35mm

Fig. 22

- **construction lines** layer.

- Create a perpendicular line from the top quad point of the circle.
    - Use **Quad osnap** and **ortho** for accuracy.

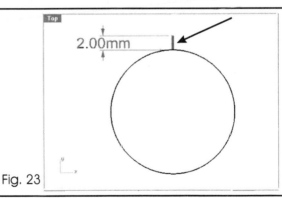

2.00mm

Fig. 23

- Click on the **Circumscribed Square: Center, Radius** command in the **Polygon** toolbar flyout.
    - **Center of circumscribed polygon:** type "**0**" and press "enter".
    - **Midpoint of polygon edge** prompt: snap to the end of the little construction line at the top of the ring as shown.
    - Click to set location.

Circumscribed Square: Center, Radius
command

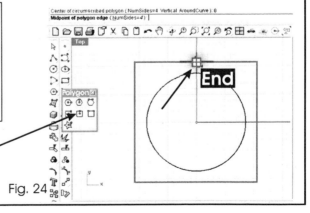

Fig. 24

83

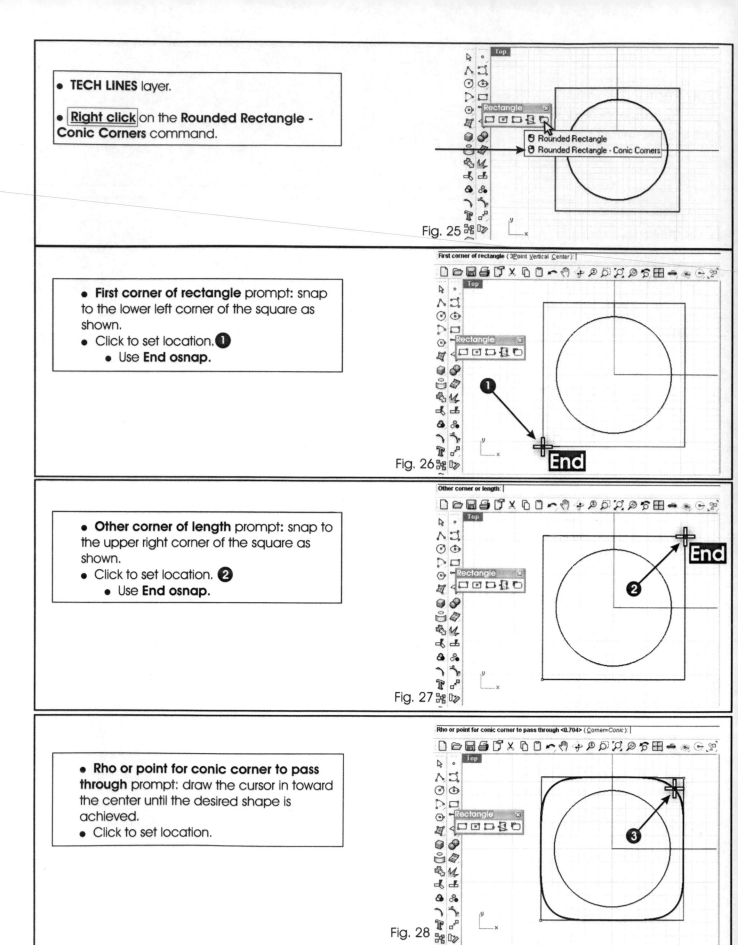

- **TECH LINES** layer.

- Right click on the **Rounded Rectangle - Conic Corners** command.

Fig. 25

- **First corner of rectangle** prompt: snap to the lower left corner of the square as shown.
  - Click to set location. **1**
    - Use **End osnap.**

Fig. 26

- **Other corner of length** prompt: snap to the upper right corner of the square as shown.
  - Click to set location. **2**
    - Use **End osnap.**

Fig. 27

- **Rho or point for conic corner to pass through** prompt: draw the cursor in toward the center until the desired shape is achieved.
  - Click to set location.

Fig. 28

- The front view of the ring is finished.

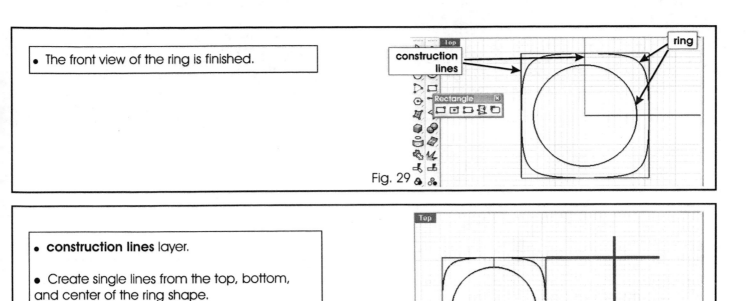

Fig. 29

- **construction lines** layer.

- Create single lines from the top, bottom, and center of the ring shape.
    - Use **End osnap** and **ortho.**

- Engage **grid snap** and create a vertical line along a major grid line.

Fig. 30

- Click on the **Rectangle: Center, Corner** command in the **Rectangle** toolbar flyout.
    - **Center of rectangle** prompt: snap to the intersection shown and click to set the location of the center of the rectangle.

Rectangle: Center, Corner command

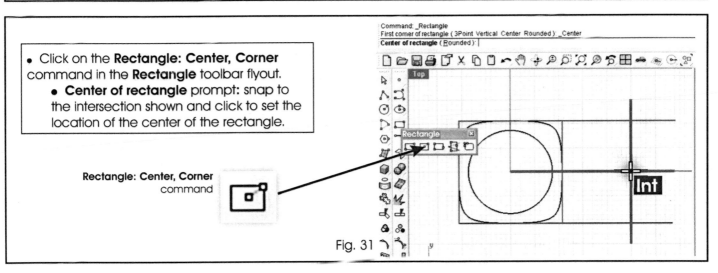

Fig. 31

- **Other corner or length** prompt: type **"5"** and press "enter".

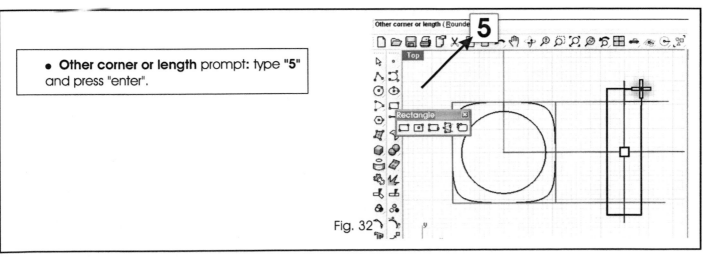

Fig. 32

- **Width** prompt: use **near osnap** to snap to the upper horizontal line as shown.
- Press "enter".

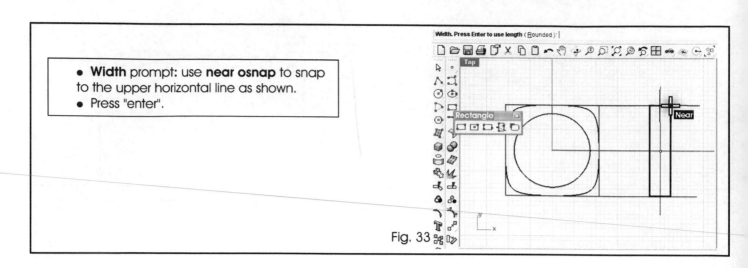

Fig. 33

- The finished drawing. Notice that certain construction lines have been hidden.

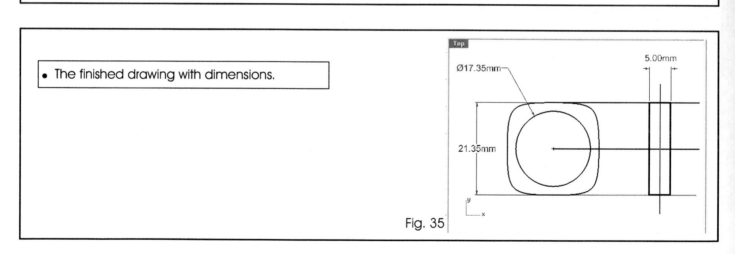

Fig. 34

- The finished drawing with dimensions.

Ø17.35mm

5.00mm

21.35mm

Fig. 35

The Star
Drawing stars in Rhino.

• Click on the **Polygon: Star** command in the **Polygon** toolbar flyout.

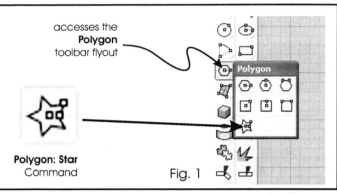

accesses the **Polygon** toolbar flyout

Polygon: Star
Command

Fig. 1

• **Center of star** prompt: click somewhere on the Construction Plane.
  • You can type **"0"** if you want the star centered on 0.

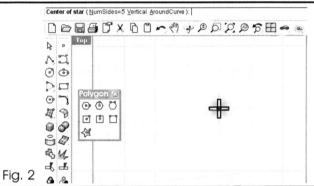

Fig. 2

• **Corner of star** prompt: draw your cursor out to the desired size of the star, clicking on the desired radius by eye or by entering a number.

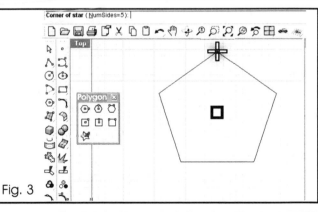

Fig. 3

• **Second star radius** prompt: press "enter" which will result in a star whose line segments will be in alignment with each other.

• This will give you a classic star shape as shown.

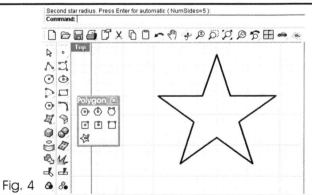

Fig. 4

- The two additional stars shown, demonstrate how the star will look if you don't elect to press **"enter"**, opting to set the second radius by eye.

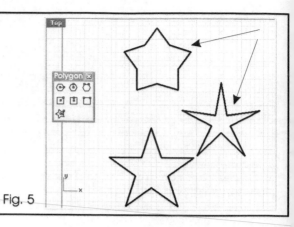

Fig. 5

- Activate the command once again and click to place the center of the star as before.

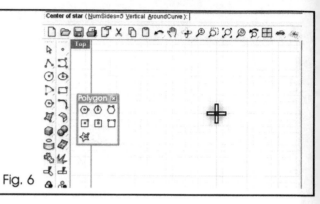

Fig. 6

- Click on the **NumSides-5** link in the **Command Line.**
- **Number of sides** prompt: type the number **"12"** in the **Command Line** and press "enter".

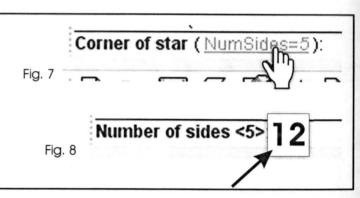

Fig. 7

Corner of star (NumSides=5):

Fig. 8

Number of sides <5> **12**

- **Corner of star** prompt: this time type the number **"15"** in the **Command Line** and press "enter".
  - The outer radius of the star will be constrained to 15mm.
  - Now click to set the location of the corner of the star. Use **ORTHO** if you want the cursor's point of the star to be perpendicular as shown.

Fig. 9

Corner of star (NumSides=12) **15**

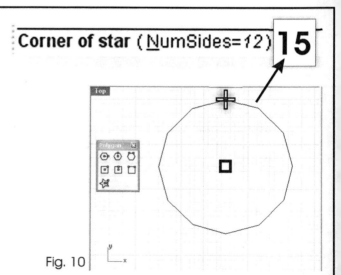

Fig. 10

88

- **Second star radius,** type "**6**" and press "enter".

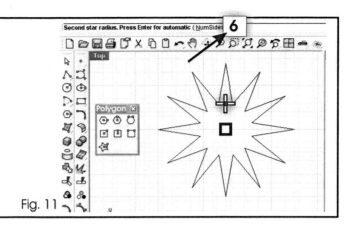

Fig. 11

- Your star will be complete.

- If you draw two circles out with their centers snapped to the center of the star (use **Center osnap**) and their diameter locations snapped to the inner and outer endpoints of the star's rays, you will notice that the radii of these two circles corresponds to the two radii that you assigned to the star when you were creating it.

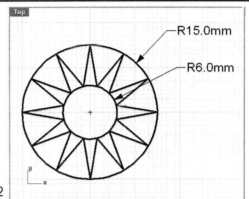

R15.0mm
R6.0mm

Fig. 12

- You can turn control points on for editing of this star.

- In this example, **Scale 2D** is being used to vary the length of every other ray.
  - Ref: 1-Dimensional and 2-Dimensional Scaling - page 111.

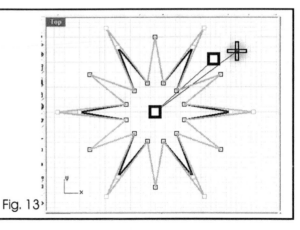

Fig. 13

- The finished star.

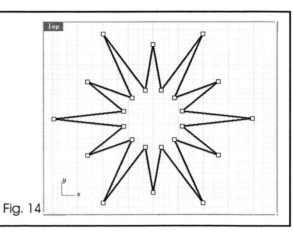

Fig. 14

Flat Spiral

• **RIGHT CLICK** on the **Flat Spiral** command in the **Curve** toolbar flyout.

accesses the **Curve** toolbar flyout

Spiral/Flat Spiral command

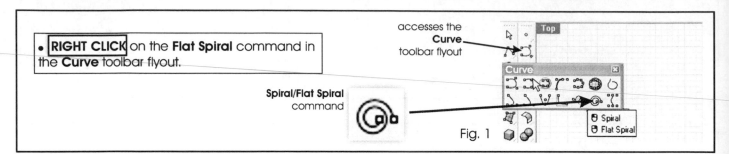

Fig. 1

• **Spiral center** prompt: type **"0"** and press "enter".
• **First Radius and start point** prompt: type **"10"** and press "enter"
   • **Left click** on the point that defines the first radius of the spiral.
   • In this case, use **Ortho** to set this point directly above the start point.

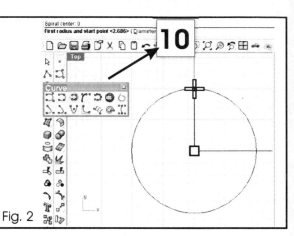

Fig. 2

• **Second Radius** prompt: accept the default of **"0"** by pressing "enter".

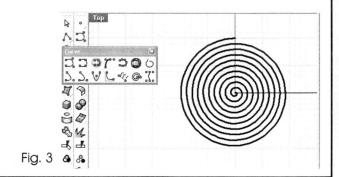

Fig. 3

• The spiral is completed.

• With the **Second radius** being **0**, the center of the spiral end point of the inside of the spiral are the same.

• In the next exercise, this end point will not be in the center of the spiral, but at a specified radius that is not in the center.

• Drag this spiral out of the way to the left.

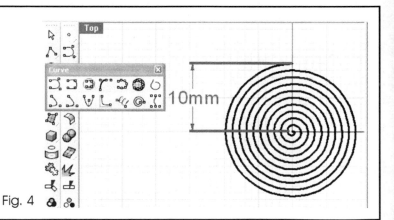

Fig. 4

- This spiral starts out the same way as the previous example.

- **Right click** on the **Flat Spiral** command once again.
  - **Start of axis** prompt: type **"0"** and press "enter".
  - **First Radius and start point** prompt: type **"10"** and press "enter"
  - **Left click** on the point that defines the first radius of the spiral. In this case, use **Ortho** to start the spiral line perfectly perpendicular to the start point.

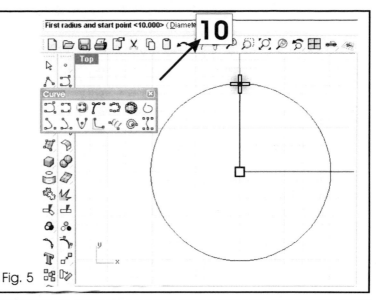

Fig. 5

- Toggle on the **Mode=Turns** option in the **Command Line.**
- Click on the **Turns=10** option in the **Command Line.**
- **Number of Turns** prompt: type **"2"** and press "enter".

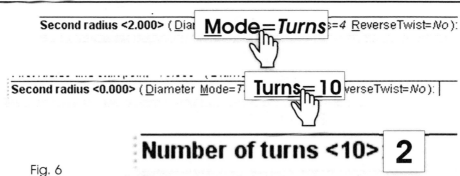

Fig. 6

- **Second radius** prompt: type **"2"** and press "enter".

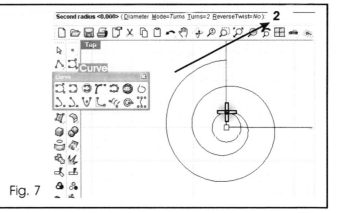

Fig. 7

- The spiral is completed.

- Notice that the inner end of this spiral is not in the same location at the center of the spiral.
  - It is 2mm away from the center.

- Notice that the number of turns has been adjusted to 2 instead of 10.

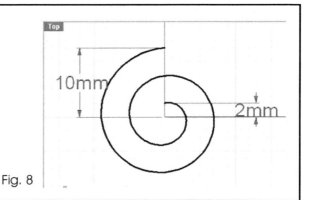

Fig. 8

- This spiral starts out the same way as the previous example.

- **Right click** on the **Flat Spiral** command once again.
    - **Start of axis** prompt: type "0" and press "enter".
    - **First Radius and start point** prompt: type **"10"** and press "enter"
    - **Left click** on the point that defines the first radius of the spiral. In this case, use **Ortho** to start the spiral line perfectly perpendicular to the start point.

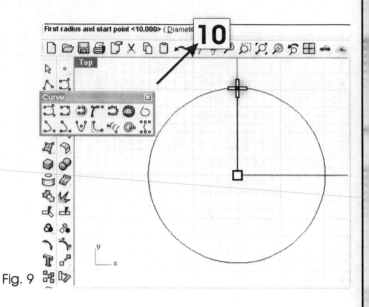

Fig. 9

- Toggle on the *Mode=Pitch* option in the **Command Line.**
- Click on the *Pitch=0.75* option in the **Command Line.**
- **Pitch** prompt: type **"5"** and press "enter".

Second radius <0.129> (Dia *Mode=Pitch* .75 ReverseTwist=*No*):

Second radius <0.129> (Diameter Mode=*Pi* *Pitch=0.75* Twist=*No*):

Pitch <5>: **5**

Fig. 10

- **Second radius** prompt: type **"0"** and press "enter".

- Setting the **Pitch** means that you are setting the distance between turns of the spiral.

- The spiral you have just done has a pitch of 5mm.

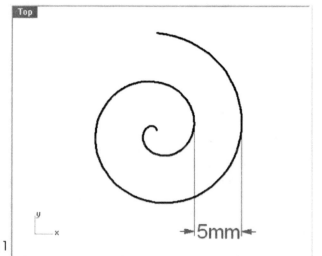

Fig. 11

Polar Array Command with History
Designing a Circular Pattern

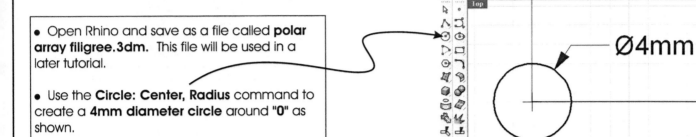

- Open Rhino and save as a file called **polar array filigree.3dm**. This file will be used in a later tutorial.

- Use the **Circle: Center, Radius** command to create a **4mm diameter circle** around "0" as shown.

Ø4mm

Fig. 1

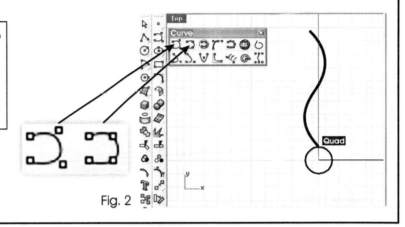

- Use one of the freeform curve commands to create an "S" shaped curve from the top **quad point** of the circle as shown.

- Use **quad osnap** to start the curve touching the top of the circle as shown.

Fig. 2

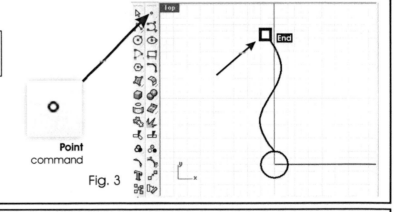

- Use the **Point** command to create a point on the end of the line as shown.

Point command

Fig. 3

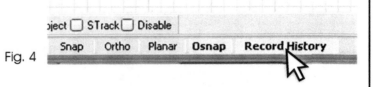

- Click on the **Record History** button at the bottom of the workspace as shown.

- The button will become brighter which will signify that **History Mode** is toggled on.

Fig. 4

93

- Click on the **Polar Array** command in the **Transform** toolbar flyout.
  - **Object to Array** prompt: select the "S" curve and press "enter"
  - **Center of Array** prompt: type **"0"** and press "enter"
  - **Number of items** prompt: type **"20"** and press "enter".
  - **Angle to fill**: accept the default of 360-degrees by pressing "enter".

Polar Array command

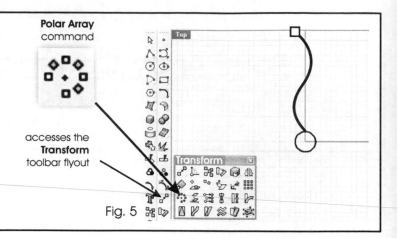

accesses the **Transform** toolbar flyout

Fig. 5

- 20 copies of the "S" curve have been copied around 0 in the circular pattern shown.

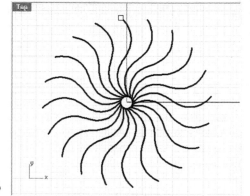

Fig. 6

- Turn on the control points of the original "S" curve as shown.

- **Move** or **Drag** one of the control points as shown..

- Notice how the point you placed on the original curve in the previous step now makes it easy to identify from the other copies which have been created in the Array.

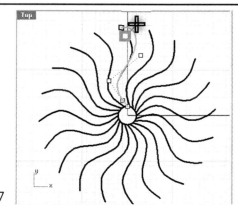

Fig. 7

- After you finish moving or dragging a control point, the rest of the curves will update to the exact shape of the original curve.

- The original curve is called the **Parent.**

- The rest of the arrayed curves are called the **Children.**

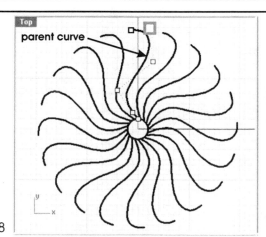

parent curve

Fig. 8

94

- Move another control point on the **Parent curve** as shown.

- Notice the use of **Near osnap** makes it possible for the end point of the parent curve to be dragged over to touch the curve to the left.

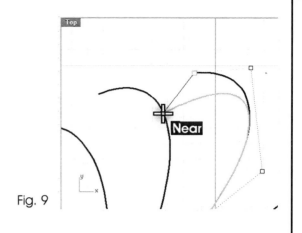

Fig. 9

- The **Children** will again update to the exact shape of the **Parent.**

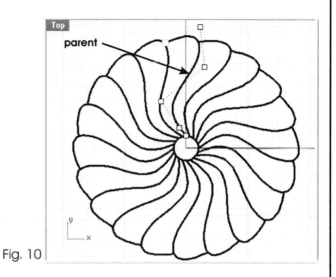

parent

Fig. 10

- **Select** the **Parent curve** and click on the **Rebuild** command in the **Curve Tools** toolbar flyout.
  - When the **Rebuild Curve** dialog box appears, assign the number "**8**" in the white point count box.
    - The number in parentheses before this box indicates the *present* number of control points in the selected curve.
  - Click the OK button.

- The curve will be "Rebuilt" to contain 8 control points instead of 6.

- The **Children** will rebuild as well.

accesses **Curve Tools** toolbar flyout

Rebuild command

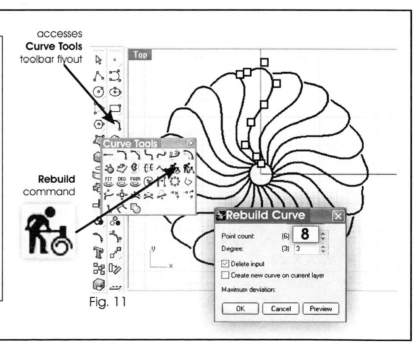

Fig. 11

- Continue to move or drag control points to further develop the design.

- If **osnap** conflicts with smooth pont editing, disable it temporarily by holding down the **Alt** key.

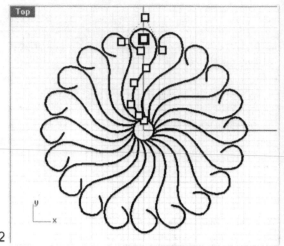

Fig. 12

- Turn on the control points of one of the **Children** and drag it as shown.

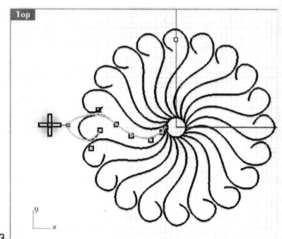

Fig. 13

- The **History Warning** dialog box will appear.

- If you edit or move one of the **Children**, this will "break history". This means that it will be a child no longer and will not update with the rest of the children when the parent is edited or moved.

- If you want to break History, click OK.

- If you do not want to break History, click OK and then click **Undo.**

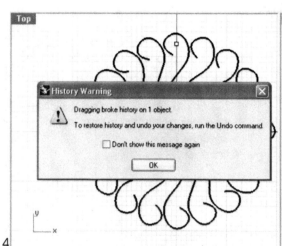

Fig. 14

Polar Array Command
Arraying Circles around a Square

- Create the layers illustrated in Fig. 1.

- Make the **TECH LINES** layer current.

- Maximize the **Top Viewport**.

Fig. 1

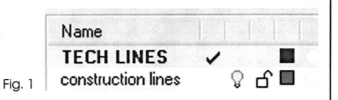

- **Left click** on the **Circumscribed Square: Center, Radius** on the **Polygon** toolbar.
  - **Center of Circumscribed polygon** prompt: type **"0"** and press **"enter"**.
  - **Midpoint of polygon edge** prompt: type **"5"** and press **"enter"**.
  - **Left click** at the top of the square to set the end of the line.
    - Use **mid osnap** for accuracy.

Circumscribed Square: Center Radius
command

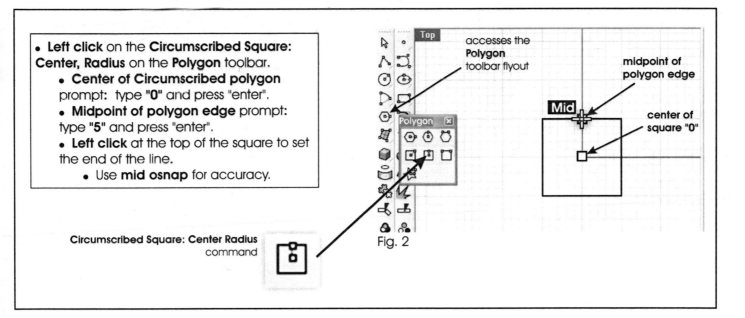

accesses the **Polygon** toolbar flyout

midpoint of polygon edge

center of square "0"

Fig. 2

- **construction lines** layer.

- Select the square and click on the **Offset** command in the **Curve Tools** toolbar flyout.
  - **Side to offset** prompt: type **".75"** and press **"enter"**.
  - **Side to offset** prompt: draw the cursor to the outside of the square and click to set the offset location.

- Use the **Explode** command to break the offset created into 4 separate line segments.

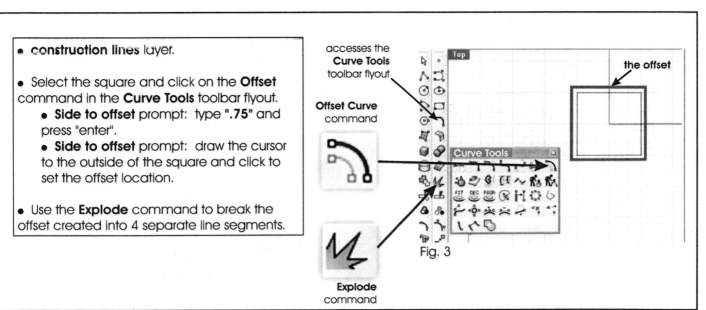

accesses the **Curve Tools** toolbar flyout

Offset Curve command

the offset

Explode command

Fig. 3

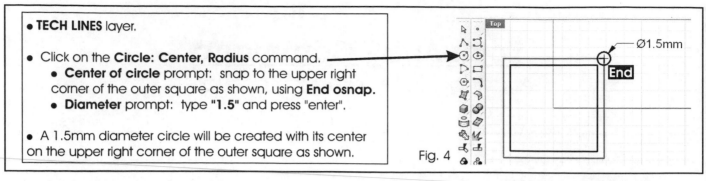

- **TECH LINES** layer.

- Click on the **Circle: Center, Radius** command.
  - **Center of circle** prompt: snap to the upper right corner of the outer square as shown, using **End osnap**.
  - **Diameter** prompt: type **"1.5"** and press "enter".

- A 1.5mm diameter circle will be created with its center on the upper right corner of the outer square as shown.

Ø1.5mm

End

Fig. 4

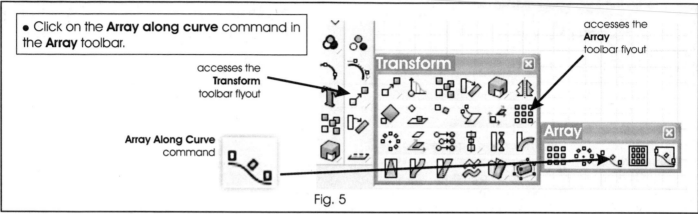

- Click on the **Array along curve** command in the **Array** toolbar.

accesses the **Transform** toolbar flyout

accesses the **Array** toolbar flyout

Array Along Curve command

Fig. 5

- **Select objects to array** prompt: select the circle you just created and press "enter".
- **Select path curve** prompt: select the offset curve at the top of the square. Select just this top line segment.

path curve

object to array

Fig. 6

- As soon as the path curve is selected, the **Array Along Curve Options** dialog box will appear.
  - Type the number **"8"** in the line for **Number of Items.**
- Click on the OK button to exit the dialog box.

Select path curve (Basepoint):

Top

Array Along Curve Options

Method
- Number of Items: **8**
- Distance between items

Orientation
- No rotation
- Freeform
- Roadlike

OK   Cancel   Help

Transform

Array

Fig. 7

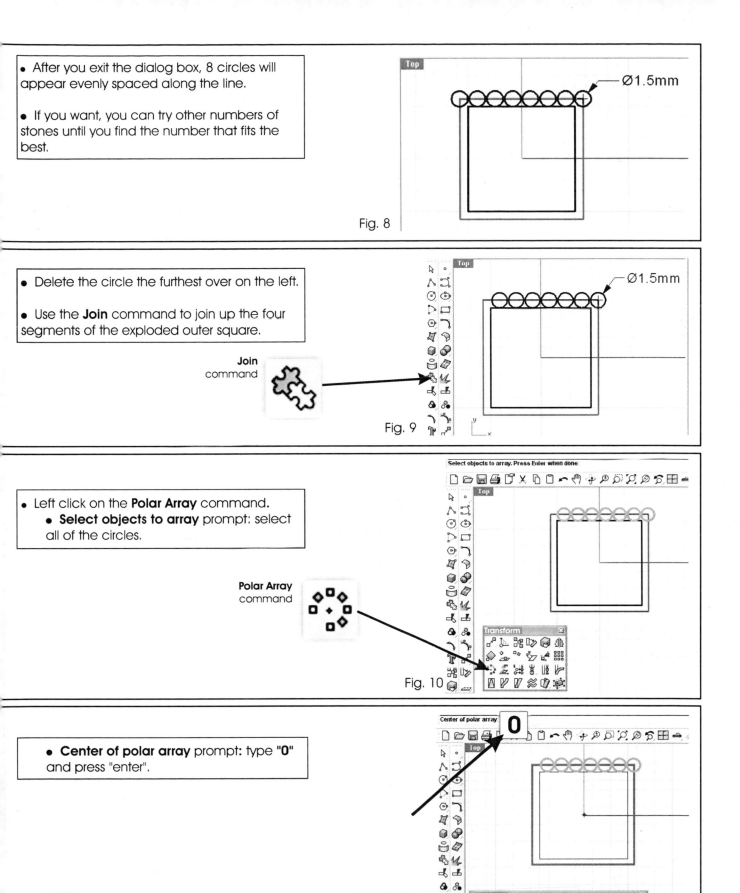

- After you exit the dialog box, 8 circles will appear evenly spaced along the line.

- If you want, you can try other numbers of stones until you find the number that fits the best.

Ø1.5mm

Fig. 8

- Delete the circle the furthest over on the left.

- Use the **Join** command to join up the four segments of the exploded outer square.

Join
command

Ø1.5mm

Fig. 9

- Left click on the **Polar Array** command.
  - **Select objects to array** prompt: select all of the circles.

Polar Array
command

Select objects to array. Press Enter when done:

Fig. 10

- **Center of polar array** prompt: type "0" and press "enter".

Center of polar array: **0**

Transform

Array

Fig. 11

- **Number of items** prompt: type "**4**" and press "enter".

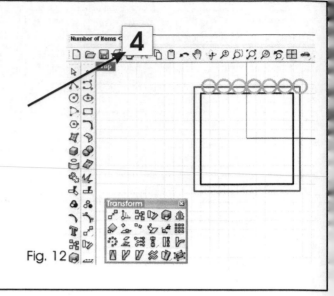

Fig. 12

- **Angle to fill** prompt: press "enter" to accept the default angle of 360-degrees .

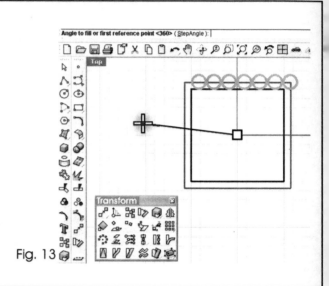

Fig. 13

- The circles will be arrayed around the center of the square which is also "0"..

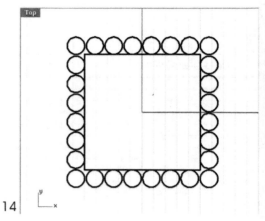

Fig. 14

Array Along a Curve Command
Arraying Stones Around an Oval

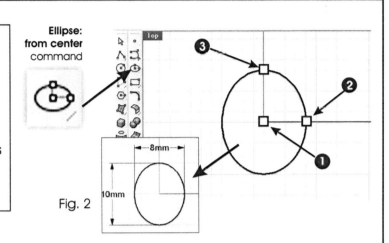

- Create the layers shown in the illustration. Make the **OVAL** layer current.

Name		M	Linetype
OVAL	✓ ☐ ⬤		**Continuous**
construction lines	💡 🔓 ⬛		Continuous
STONES	💡 🔓 ⬛		Continuous
PRONGS	💡 🔓 ⬛		Continuous
Layer 04	💡 🔓 ⬛		Continuous

Fig. 1

- Click on the **Ellipse: from center** command.
  - **Ellipse Center** prompt: type "**0**", press "enter".
  - **End of first axis** prompt: type "**4**", press "enter".❶
    - Draw the cursor over to the right, and click to set location. ❷ Use **ortho**.
  - **End of second axis** prompt: type "**5**", press "enter". ❸
    - Draw the cursor straight up and click to set the location of the top of the ellipse.

Ellipse: from center command

Fig. 2

8mm
10mm

- **STONES** layer.

- Click on the **Circle: Diameter** command.
  - **Start of diameter** prompt: snap to the **Quad** point at the top of the oval and click to set location. ❶
  - **End of diameter** prompt: type "**2**" and press "enter".
    - Draw the cursor up, using **ortho,** and click to set the location of the end of the diameter. ❷

Circle: Diameter command

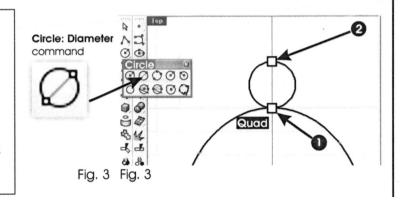

Quad

Fig. 3 Fig. 3

- **Construction lines** layer.

- Click on the **Offset** command in the **Curve Tools** toolbar flyout.
  - **Select curve to offset** prompt: select the little 2mm diameter circle just created.
  - **Side to offset:** type "**.2**" and press "enter".
  - **Side to offset:** draw the cursor inside the circle and click to set the new offset curve inside the circle as shown.

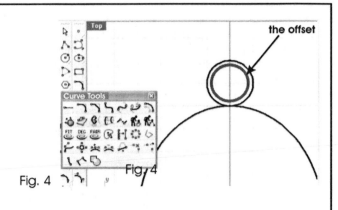

the offset

Curve Tools

Fig. 4

- **PRONGS** layer.

- Using the **Circle: diameter** command again, create a **.7mm diameter** circle on top of the **offset curve** just created, using **quad osnap** to sit the circle on top of the offset circle as shown.

- Check the diameter dimensions of all three curves.

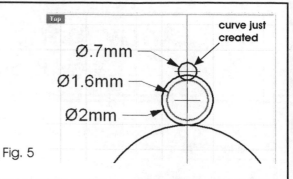

Ø.7mm
Ø1.6mm
Ø2mm

curve just created

Fig. 5

- Click on the **Array Along Curve** command in the **Array** toolbar flyout.
    - **Objects to array** prompt: select the three small circles at the top of the stone.
    - **Path curve** prompt: select the 8 x 10mm oval.
    - The **Array Along Curve Options** dialog box will appear.
        - **Number of items to array** prompt: type "**16**" in the **Array Along Curve Options** dialog box as shown and click OK.

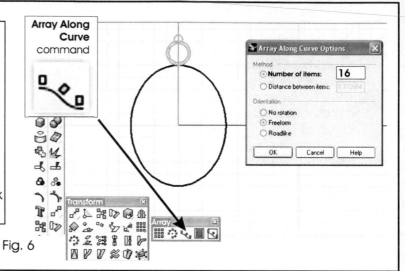

Array Along Curve command

Fig. 6

- Notice that the stones do not array evenly. This is because of the oval shape of the path curve.

- **Undo** the array.

Fig. 7

- **construction lines** layer.

- Select the oval and click on the **Offset Curve** command.
    - Select the **ThroughPoint** option in the command line.

Offset command

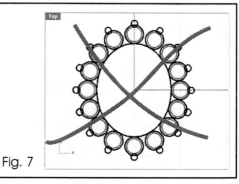

Fig. 8

102

- Toggle on **Center osnap.**
- **Through point** prompt: Draw the offset out until it snaps to the center of the circle at the top of the oval.
  - **Center Osnap** is necessary to accurately place the through point.

- The top part of the offset curve just created now runs exactly through the center of the "diamond" on top of the center stone.

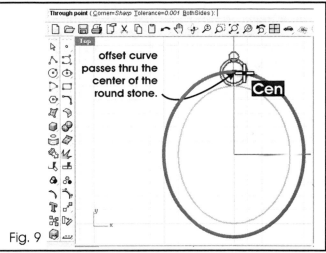

offset curve passes thru the center of the round stone.

Fig. 9

- Use the **Array Along Curve** again to array the little circles as before.

- This time use the new offset as the **path curve.**

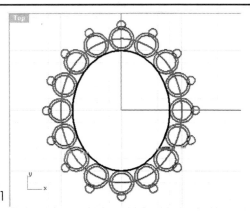

path curve

Fig. 10

- This time the **Path Curve** curve just created with the new offset passes through the center of the arrayed stones.

- Notice how much better this solution is for getting an even spread around the center stone.

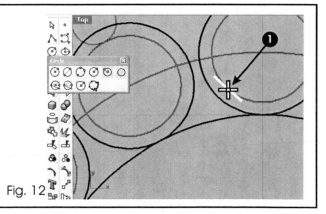

Fig. 11

- Zoom in on the top stone and it's neighbor to the left as shown.

- Click on the **Circle: Tangent to 3 curves** command in the **Circle** toolbar flyout.
  - **First tangent curve** prompt: draw the cursor over the prong curve shown.
  - Click to set this first location when the white constraint line appear as shown. **1**

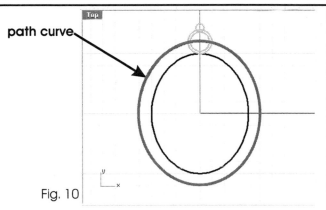

Fig. 12

- **Second tangent curve** prompt: draw the cursor across the neighboring circle as shown.
  - Click when the white constraint line appears as before.❷

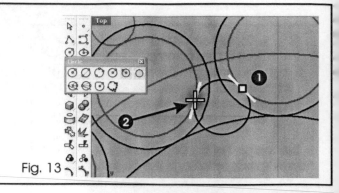

Fig. 13

- **Third tangent curve** prompt: draw the cursor over the large oval curve as shown.
  - Click when the white constraint line appears as before. ❸

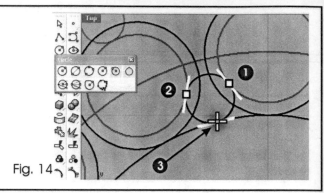

Fig. 14

- The new prong curve is tangent to both prong curves inside the stones and the large oval of the center stone.

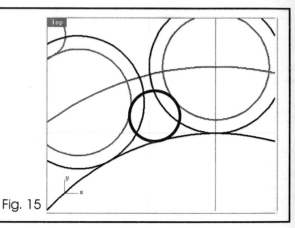

Fig. 15

- Create 3 more prongs, using the same technique as shown.

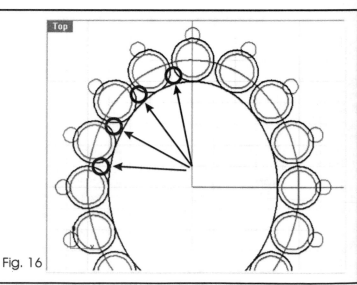

Fig. 16

- Select the prong curves shown and click on the **Trim** command.

Trim
command

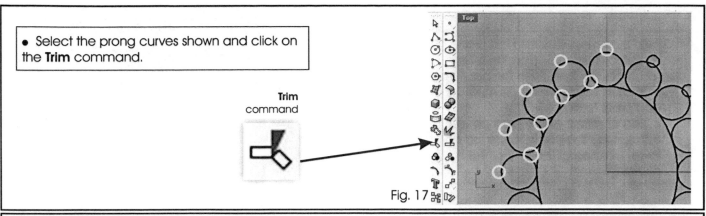

Fig. 17

- **Select object to trim** prompt: zoom in the click on the lines that are crossing inside the prong circles as shown.

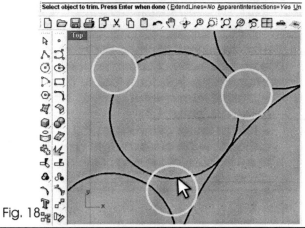

Fig. 18

- If you mistakenly trim the wrong line, as shown, click on the **Undo** option in the **Command Line** and the mistake will undo.

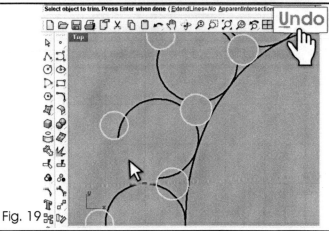

Fig. 19

- Press "enter" when all the selected prongs have been trimmed out as shown.

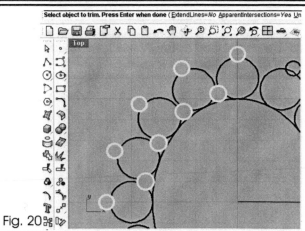

Fig. 20

- Select the lowest trimmed-out prong on the inside as shown and click on the **Mirror** command in the **Transform** toolbar flyout.
  - **Start of mirror plane** prompt: type "**0**" and press "enter". ❶
  - **End of mirror plane** prompt: using **ortho**, draw the cursor to the left and click to set location of the end of the mirror plane. ❷

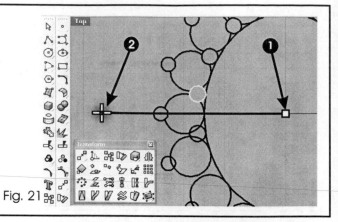

Fig. 21

- Select the highest trimmed-out prong on the inside as shown and click on the **Mirror** command in the **Transform** toolbar flyout.
  - **Start of mirror plane** prompt: type "**0**" and press "enter". ❶
  - **End of mirror plane** prompt: using **ortho**, draw the cursor straight up and click to set location of the end of the mirror plane. ❷

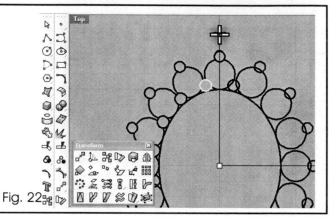

Fig. 22

- Select the trim out the new new prongs.

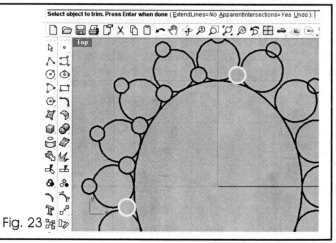

Fig. 23

- Zoom out and carefully window select one half of the objects as shown.

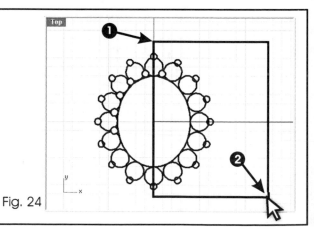

Fig. 24

106

- Press the "delete" key to delete the selected curves.

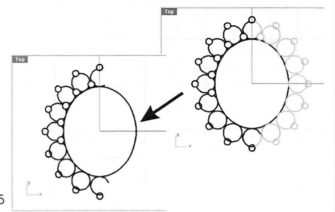

Fig. 25

- Window select the lower prong and stone curves as shown.

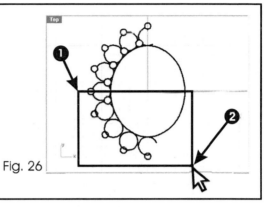

Fig. 26

- Once again, press the "delete" key to deleted the selected curves.

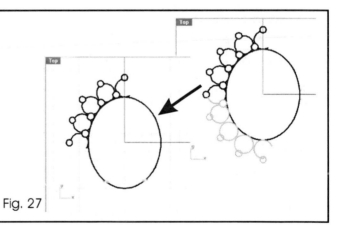

Fig. 27

- Turn off the **OVAL STONE** layer.

- Create two lines, one vertical and one horizontal.

- Start both lines at **"0"** and use **ortho** to ensure that these lines are accurately vertical and horizontal.

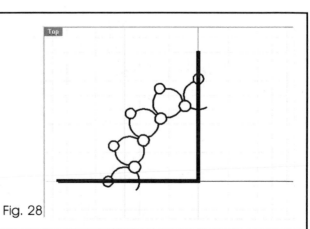

Fig. 28

- Select the new lines and click on the **Trim** command.
  - **Select object to trim** command: trim off all lines that cross the new lines as shown.

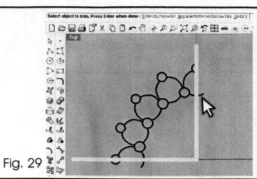

Fig. 29

- Press"enter" when all lines have been trimmed as shown.

- Delete the two lines that were used as cutting objects.

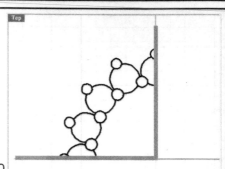

Fig. 30

- Select the remaining curves and click on the **Mirror** command.
  - **Start of mirror plane** command: type "0" and press "enter". ❶
  - **End of mirror plane** command: draw the cursor straight upward and click to set location. ❷

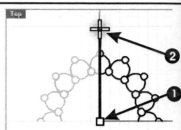

Fig. 31

- Select all of the curves and click on the **Mirror** command.
  - **Start of mirror plane** command: type "0" and press "enter". ❶
  - **End of mirror plane** command: draw the cursor horizontally and click to set location. ❷

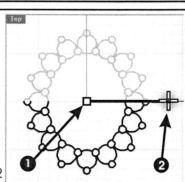

Fig. 32

- Turn the **OVAL STONE** layer to view the finished drawing.

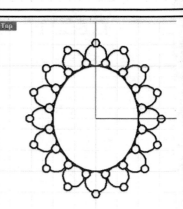

Fig. 33

Arraying Along a Freeform Curve
Using a freeform curve for the array path.

- Create the two layers shown.

- Make the **PATH CURVE** layer current.

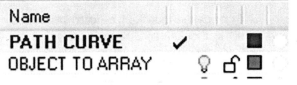

Fig. 1

- Create an "S" curve as shown. Use one of the Freeform curve commands for this.

- Avoid sharp turns in this curve for this exercise.

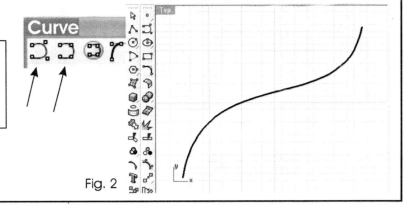

Fig. 2

- Switch to the **OBJECT TO ARRAY** layer.

- Create a short line from an end point of the "S" curve as shown. Use **End osnap.**

- Try to create this line at a similar angle relative to the "S" curve as shown for this exercise.

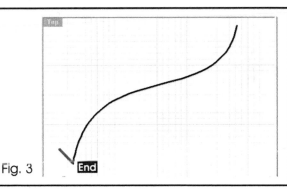

Fig. 3

- Click on the **Array along Curve** command in the **Array** toolbar flyout as shown.

Array Along Curve
command

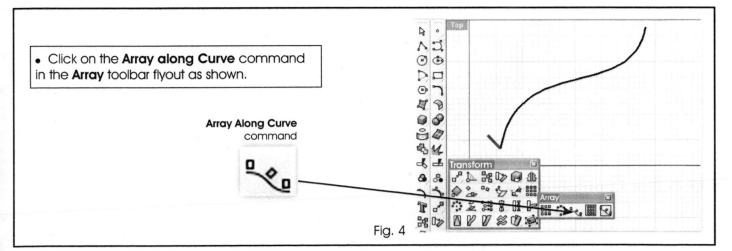

Fig. 4

- **Select object to array** prompt: select the little line as shown and press "enter".
- **Select path curve** prompt: select the "S" curve.
- Upon selection of the **path curve,** the **Array Along Curve Options** dialog box will open.
   - Type **"50"** in the **Number of Items** box.
- Accept the default **freeform** option among the **Orientation** options.
- Click OK.

Array Along Curve
command

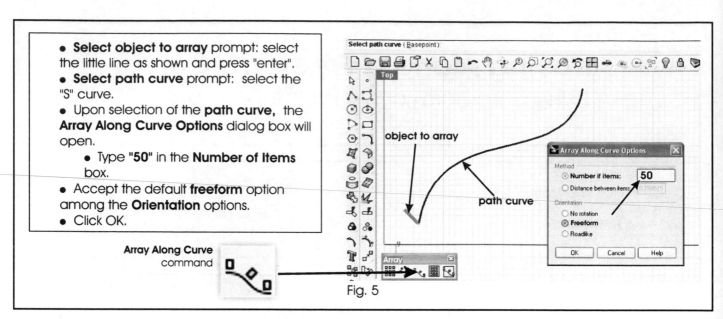

Fig. 5

- The selected **object to array** will be arrayed along the curve 50 times along the length of the **path curve** as shown.

- Using the **freeform option,** will create 50 new objects, *all at the same angle in relation to the path curve.*

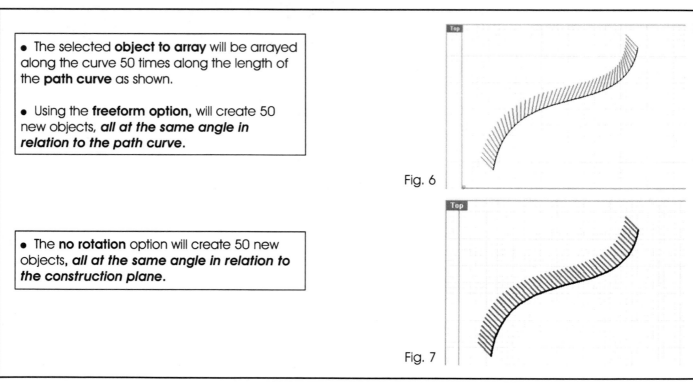

Fig. 6

- The **no rotation** option will create 50 new objects, *all at the same angle in relation to the construction plane.*

Fig. 7

- Start to experiment!

- In this illustration, another **object to array** was added on the other side of the **path curve** and was then arrayed for "50" items like the first time.

- Try other numbers of items. Try different shapes of path curves. Try other shapes of items to array.

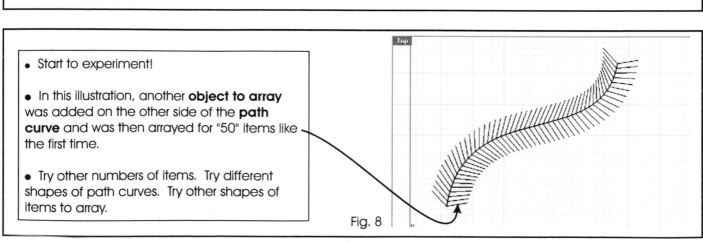

Fig. 8

1-Dimensional and 2-Dimensional Scaling
2-dimensional Scaling applications

- The Rhino <u>Scale</u> commands enable you to reduce or enlarge objects in 3-dimensional, 2-dimensional, or 1-dimensional directions.

  - In this exercise, we will deal with Scaling in the 1- and 2-dimensional directions.

- Create the squares and circles shown. Assign the same measurements as shown. (Dimensions are not necessary.)

- Use **Grid Snap** to quickly make these simple objects.

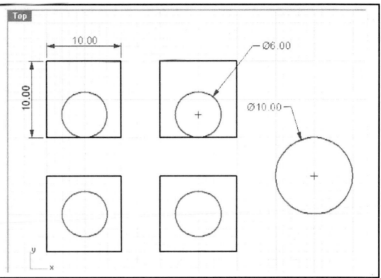

Fig. 1

1-Dimensional Scaling

- Zoom in on the square in the upper left corner.

- Click on the **Scale 1-D** command.

Scale 1-D command

accesses the **Scale** flyout toolbar

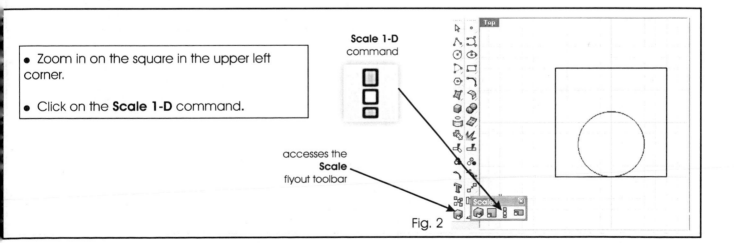

Fig. 2

- **Select objects to scale** prompt: Select the circle and press "enter".

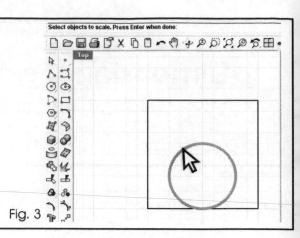

Fig. 3

- **Origin Point** prompt: Left click on the middle of the bottom line of the circle. **1**
  - **Mid osnap** will ensure proper placement of this location.

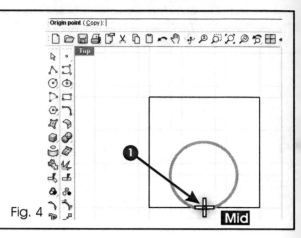

Fig. 4

- **Scale factor or first reference point** prompt: Drag the cursor up to the top of the circle and select it as shown. **2**
  - **QUAD OSNAP** will help you accurately place this point.
  - Notice the preview line as the circle is being scaled.
- **Second reference point** prompt: Snap to the **midpoint** of the top of the square and left click to set the location. **3**

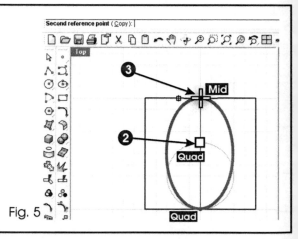

Fig. 5

- The circle has been scaled in 1 direction to form a different shape.

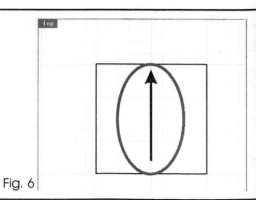

Fig. 6

112

- Zoom in on the square in the lower left corner.

- Click on the **Scale 1-D** command.
  - **Select objects to scale** prompt: select the circle and press "enter".

Scale 1-D
command

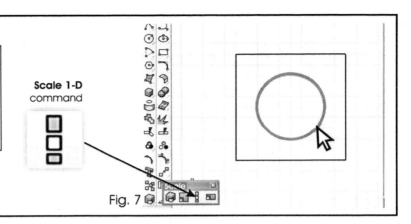

Fig. 7

- **Origin Point** prompt: Snap to the **center** of the circle and click to set location. ❶
  - Use **Cen Osnap** to select the origin point as shown.

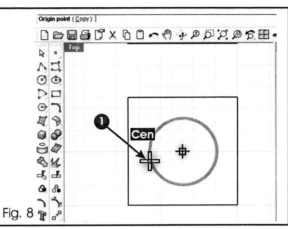

Fig. 8

- **Scale factor or first reference point** prompt: Drag the cursor up to the top of the circle and use **Quad Osnap** to snap to the upper quad point of the circle. ❷
  - Click to set location.

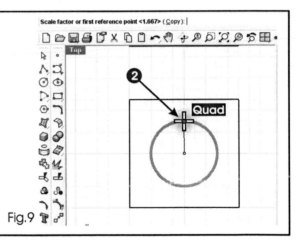

Fig.9

- **Second Reference Point** prompt: Drag the cursor up to the top of the square and snap to the **midpoint** of the top of the square as shown. ❸
  - Click to set location.
    - As you are dragging the cursor up, notice the preview of the finished scale as well as the still yellow shape of the original circle.

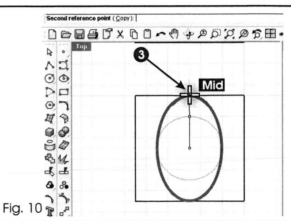

Fig. 10

- With the circle starting out in the center of the square and the origin point in the center of the circle, the 1-D scaling moved in 2 directions but with the same result as before.

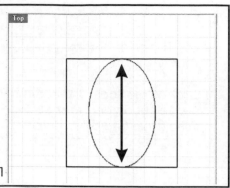

Fig. 11

2-Dimensional Scaling

- Zoom out so that you can see the two sets in the top row.

- Click on the **Scale 2-D** command.

Scale 2-D command

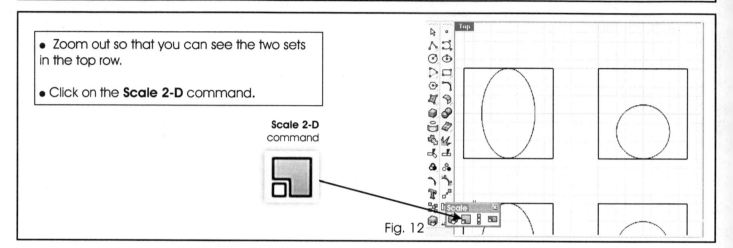

Fig. 12

- **Select objects to scale** prompt: Select the circle and press "enter".

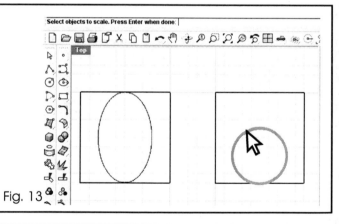

Fig. 13

- **Origin point** prompt: Left click at the bottom of the selected circle as shown. **1**
  - **Mid osnap** will be essential to pick this location with accuracy.

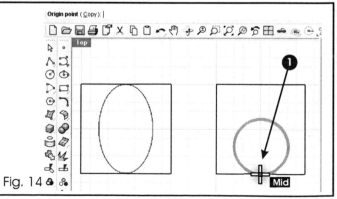

Fig. 14

114

- **Scale factor or first reference point**
prompt: Drag the cursor up to the top of
the circle and use **Quad Osnap** to snap to
the upper quad point of the circle as
shown. ❷
  - Click to set location.

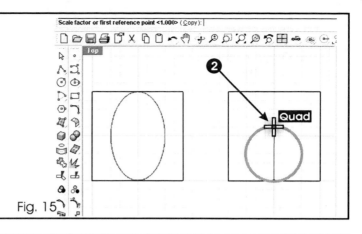

Fig. 15

- **Second reference point** prompt: Drag
the cursor up to the top of the square and
snap to the **mid point** of the top line of the
square as shown.
  - Click to set location.

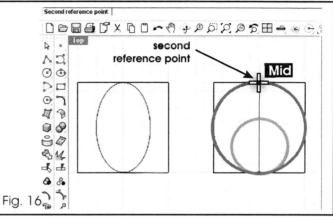

Fig. 16

- The scaled circle fills the surrounding square
- **Scale 2D** has caused the circle to scale in all
directions from the **Origin Point.**

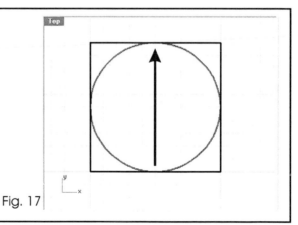

Fig. 17

- Pan downward so that you can see the
square and circle directly below the circle you
have just scaled.

- Click on the **Scale 2-D** command.
  - **Select objects to scale** prompt: Select
the circle and press "enter".

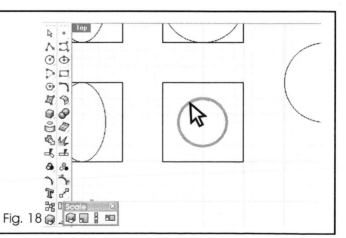

Fig. 18

115

- **Origin point** prompt: Use **Cen Osnap** to snap to the center of the circle as shown.❶
- Click to set location.

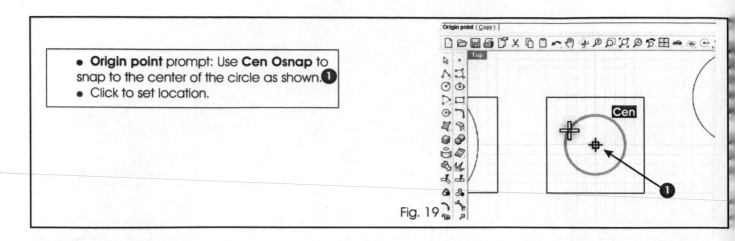

Fig. 19

- **Scale factor or first reference point** prompt: Drag the cursor up to the top of the circle and snap to the upper **quad** point of the circle as shown.
- Click to set location.

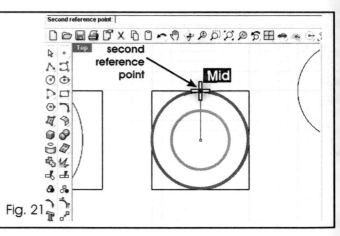

Fig.20

- **Second reference point** prompt: Drag the cursor up to the top of the square and snap to the mid point of the top line of the circle as shown.
- Click to set location.

Fig. 21

- The scaled circle fills the square.

- **Scale 2-D** scaled the circle outward in all directions from the **Origin Point** in the center of the circle.

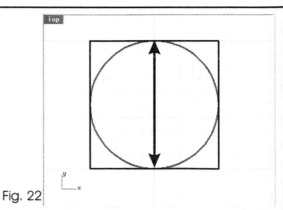

Fig. 22

116

Specifying a Scale Factor

- Zoom in on the circle further over on the right of the screen as shown.

- Click on the **Scale 2-D** command.

Scale 2-D command

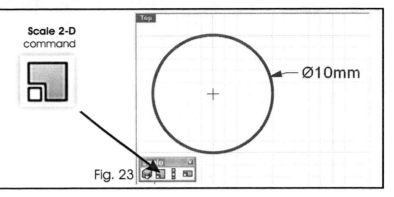

Fig. 23

- **Select objects to scale** prompt: Select the circle and press "enter".

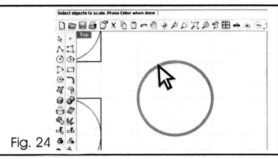

Fig. 24

- **Origin Point** prompt: Snap to the center of the circle and click to set this location.

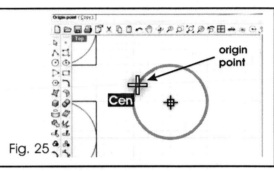

origin point

Fig. 25

- **Scale factor or first reference point** prompt: Type in the number "**1.5**" and press "enter".
  - You have just designated a **Scale Factor.**

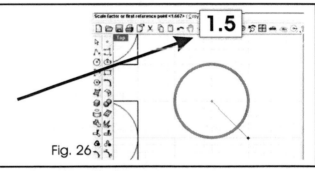

Fig. 26

- After you press **enter,** the command is completed.

- The circle has scaled up to 150% of its original size!

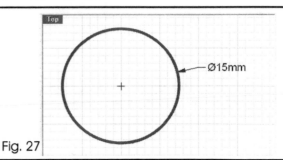

Fig. 27

Quick Rope Twist Necklace Layout with History

• Make 3 layers as shown.

• Make the **construction lines** layer current.

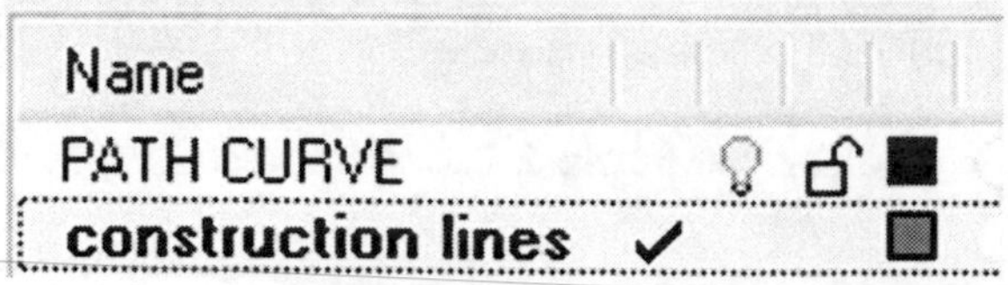

Name			
PATH CURVE	💡	🔓	⬛
construction lines ✓			⬜

Fig. 1

• Using the **Circle: Center, Radius** command, create a circle around **"0"** with a diameter of **129.42mm**.

• Click on the **Zoom Extents** command to zoom out to include a full view of the circle which is very large.

⊕ 🔍 🔍 🔍 🔍 🔄 ⊞

Ø129.4mm

Top

Fig. 2

• **construction lines layer.**

• Click on the **Line: from midpoint** command:
  • **Middle of line** prompt: Snap to the lower **Quad** point of the circle and click to set location.

Line: from Midpoint command

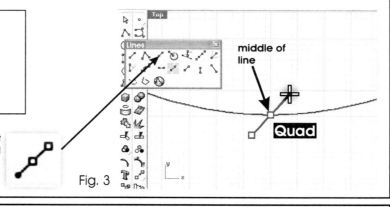

middle of line

Quad

Fig. 3

• **End of line** prompt: Type **"4"** and press "enter". [The finished line will be a total of **8mm long**.]
• **End of line** prompt: type **"<45"** to set an angle of 45-degrees.
• Move the line to the angle shown and click to set location.

Top

8mm

45°

Fig. 4

• Toggle on **History** on the status bar at the bottom of the workspace as shown.

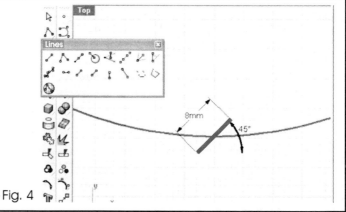

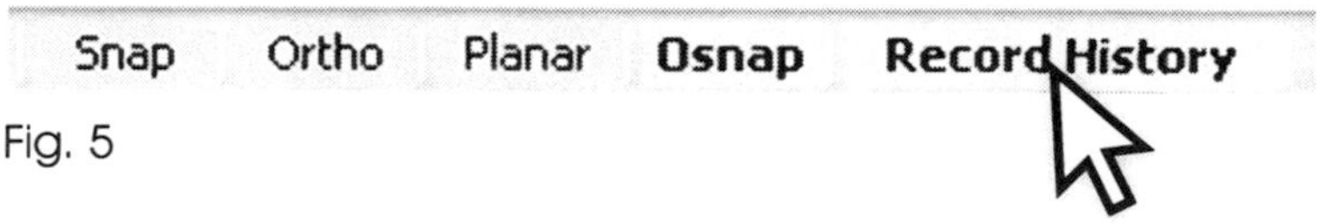

Snap Ortho Planar **Osnap** **Record History**

Fig. 5

- Click on the **Polar Array** command:
  - **Select objects to array** prompt: select the 45-degree angle line just created and press "enter".
  - **Center of polar array** prompt: type "0" and press "enter".
  - **Number of items** prompt: type "60" and press "enter".
  - **Angle to fill or first reference point** prompt: press "enter" to accept the default value of 360.

Polar Array
command

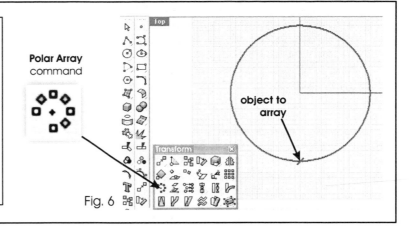

object to array

Fig. 6

- Change the original 45-degree line to the **TECH LINES** layer.

- Make the **TECH LINES** layer current.

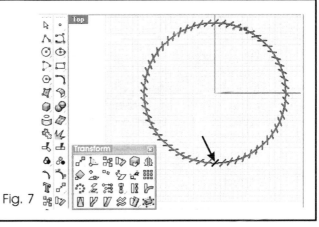

Fig. 7

- Turn on **end osnap**.

- Click on the **Extend Curve, Smooth** command in the **Extend** flyout in the **Curve Tools** toolbar as shown..

accesses the **Extend** toolbar flyout

Extend Curve, Smooth command

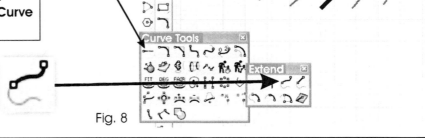

Fig. 8

- **Select curve to extend** prompt: click on the upper end of the diagonal line as shown.

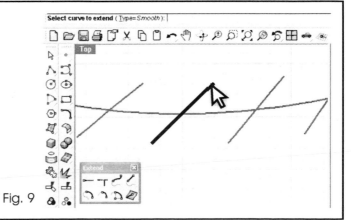

Fig. 9

119

- **End of extension** prompt: move the cursor toward the diagonal line to the right and notice that the selected line to extend "extends" along with the cursor in a very smooth way.

Fig. 10

- Snap to the **end point** of the line next to the original line as shown and click to set the location of this extension.

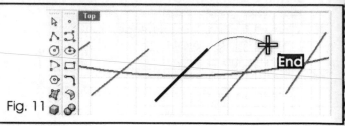

Fig. 11

- **End of extension** prompt: Now click on the other end of the original line and extend it to it's neighbor on the left and clicking to the end point as shown.
- Press "enter" to end the command.

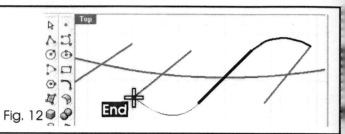

Fig. 12

- After you press "enter". all of the **"children"** will update.

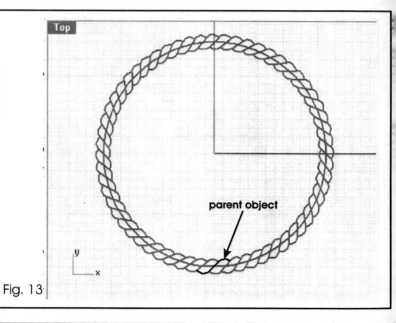

parent object

Fig. 13

- Rebuild the **"Parent"** curve to make it more graceful, staying with the point count of **"7"**.

- The **"Children"** will all update again.

- Notice that, because of the changes in curvature from the rebuilding, the "S" curves all slightly intersect each other.

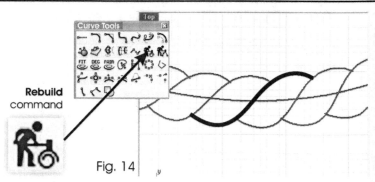

Rebuild command

Fig. 14

- Turn off the **construction lines** laye...

- Turn control points on the **Parent** cu...

- Using **near osnap**, drag the ends of ...
curve so that they touch the curves adjacent
to them as shown.

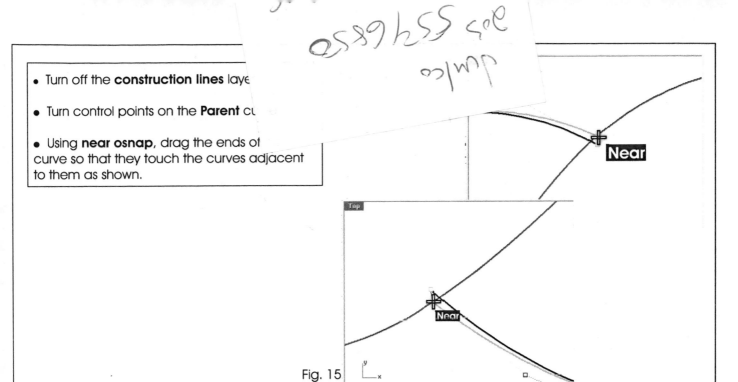

Fig. 15

- The rest of the lines (the **Children**) will
update.

- They will no long intersect each other.

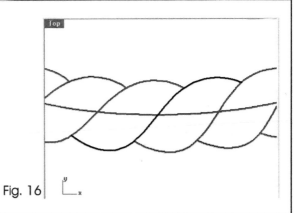

Fig. 16

- Change all "S" curves to the **TECH LINES** layer.

- View the finished necklace layout.

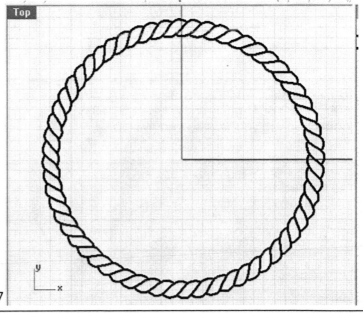

Fig. 17

Arcs

Arc: Center, Start, Angle

- Click on the **Arc: Center, Start, Angle** command in the **Arc** flyout toolbar.
  - **Center of Arc** prompt: left click to set the location of the center of the arc. ❶

Arc: Center, Start, Angle command

accesses the **Arc** toolbar flyout

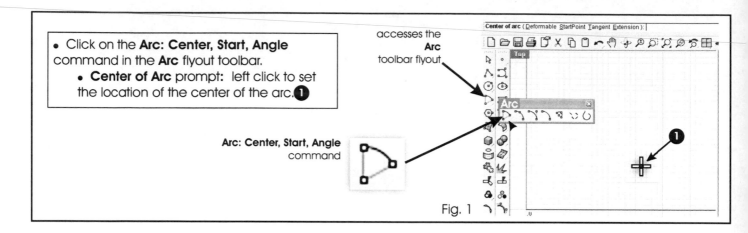

Fig. 1

- **Start of Arc** prompt: left click on the location where you want to start the arc. ❷
- This will actually set the radius of the arc.

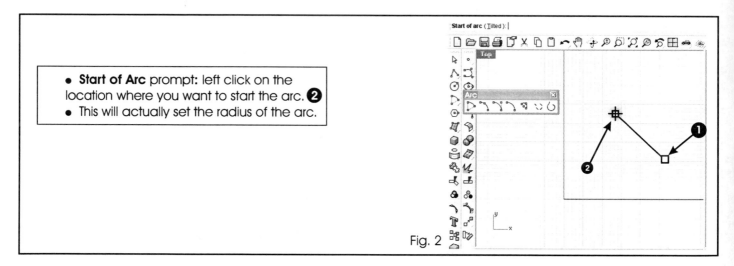

Fig. 2

- **End Point or Angle** prompt: left click at the location where you want to end the arc. ❸

The finished arc

left click

preview lines

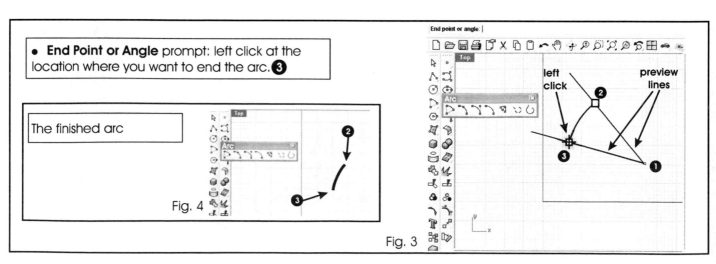

Fig. 4

Fig. 3

Start, End, Point on Arc

- Toggle on **grid snap**.

- Click on the **Arc: Start, End, Point on Arc** command on the **Arc** flyout.
  - **Start of arc** prompt: **left click** on a point on the construction plane. ❶

Arc: Start, End, Point on Arc command

Fig. 5

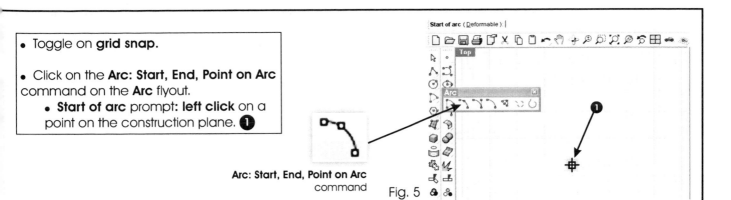

- **End of arc** prompt: left click 20 grid units to the right, using **grid snap** for accuracy. ❷

Fig. 6

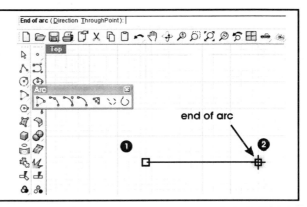

- **Point on arc** prompt: left click on the third and final point of the arc which is it's midpoint as well. ❸

Fig. 7

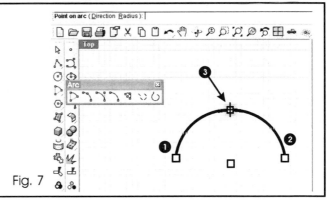

- The completed arc.

Fig. 8

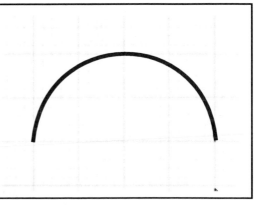

Start, End, Direction at Start

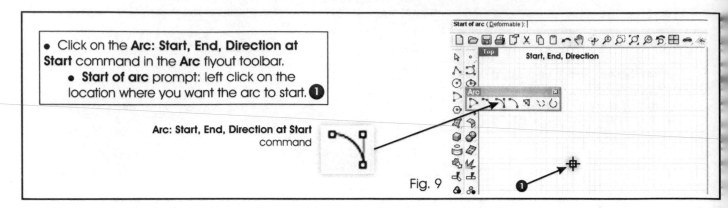

- Click on the **Arc: Start, End, Direction at Start** command in the **Arc** flyout toolbar.
  - **Start of arc** prompt: left click on the location where you want the arc to start. ❶

Arc: Start, End, Direction at Start
command

Fig. 9

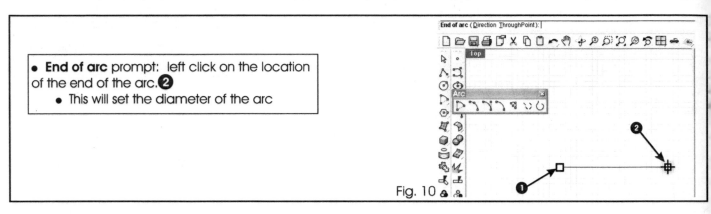

- **End of arc** prompt: left click on the location of the end of the arc. ❷
  - This will set the diameter of the arc

Fig. 10

- **Direction at start** prompt: move the cursor up to set the direction of the arc. Notice the "rubber band" line that follows it.

moving the cursor to
set the direction of the arc

Fig. 11

- **Setting the final direction and radius of the arc.** In this example, **ortho** mode was used to set a perfectly perpendicular direction. This created a 180-degree half circle.

The completed arc

direction at start

Fig. 12

124

Technical Drawing - Bombe Ring
Using Arc commands

- Make layers as shown in the Layers dialog box.

- **TECH LINES** layer current.

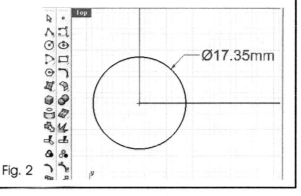

Fig. 1

Name			
TECH LINES	✓		■
construction lnes 1		♀ ♂	■
construction lines 2		♀ ♂	■
dimensions		♀ ♂	■

- Create a circle around 0,0 with a diameter of **17.35mm**.

Fig. 2

Ø17.35mm

- **construction lines 1** layer

- Use the **Line** command to create three small lines from the **3 quad points** of the circle as shown.

- The two horizontal lines are **2mm** long and the one vertical line at the bottom is **1.5mm** long.

Fig. 3

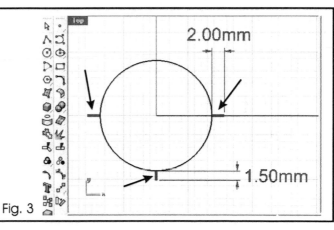

2.00mm

1.50mm

- **TECH LINES** layer

- Use the **Arc: Start, End, Point on Arc** command, to create an arc that snaps to the **end points** of the three small lines as shown.

Arc: Start, Eng, Point on Arc
command

accesses the
Arc toolbar flyout

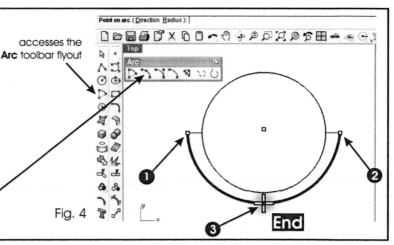

Point on arc (**D**irection **R**adius):

Fig. 4

❶ ❷ ❸ End

125

- Use the **Arc: Start, End, Direction at Start** command, to create the arc shown.
  - Use **end osnap** to set points 1 and 2 to touch ends of the bottom arc as shown.
  - Be sure to use **ORTHO** when setting the final direction as shown.

Arc: Start, End, Direction at Start
command

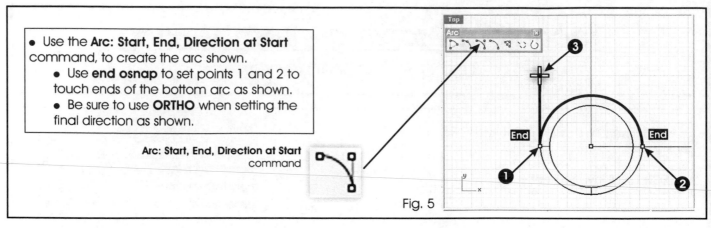

Fig. 5

- **Move** the arc just created straight up **3mm**.
  - Use **ortho.**

Move
command

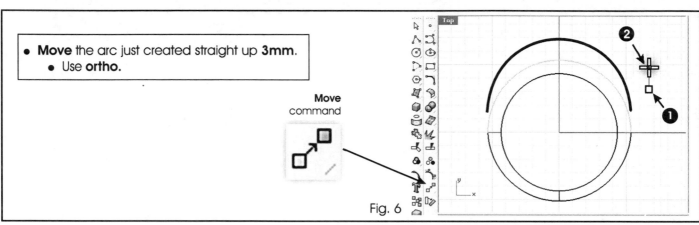

Fig. 6

- Use the **Extend Curve, Smooth** command to extend the ends of the arc just created so that they snap to the ends of the lower arc as shown.
  - Use **End osnap** for accuracy.

Extend Curve, Smooth
command

accesses the
Curve Tools
toolbar flyout

accesses the
Extend
toolbar flyout

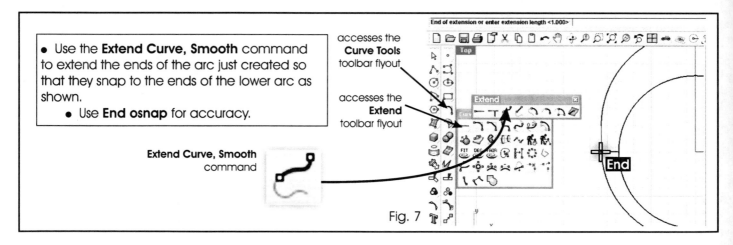

Fig. 7

- When both sides have been extended, **Join** the upper and lower arcs.

- This will result in a closed polyline.

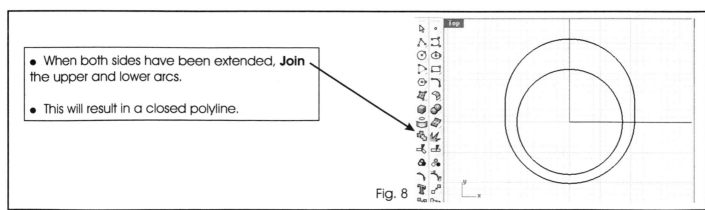

Fig. 8

- Select the closed polycurve and click on the **Adjust Closed Curve Seam** command in the **Curve Tools** toolbar flyout as shown.
    - A point and a white arrow will appear at one side of the closed curve. This is the *curve seam*.
    - The point object indicates the location of the "*curve seam*" - where it starts and ends up.
    - The white arrow indicates the "*direction*" of the curve.

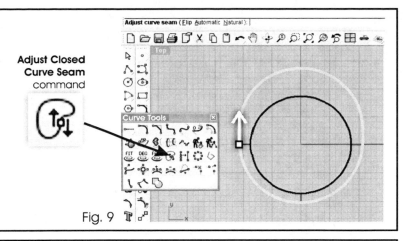

Adjust Closed Curve Seam command

Fig. 9

- Click on the point shown and **draw the cursor to the bottom of the curve until it snaps to the quad point at the bottom.**
    - Click to set this new location for the curve seam.
        - It is necessary to move this seam point to a location that is **symmetrical to both sides of the curve.**
    - Press "enter" to end the command.

- *Now, when you rebuild this curve in the next step, **the arrangement of control points will be symmetrical**. The rebuilt curve will be asymmetrical if you do not do this step first.*

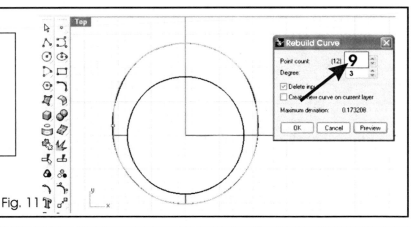

Fig. 10

- **Rebuild** the closed polycurve to the values shown in the **Rebuild Curves** dialog box shown.

- Notice from the dark preview lines that the curve smooths out on the sides after the rebuild.

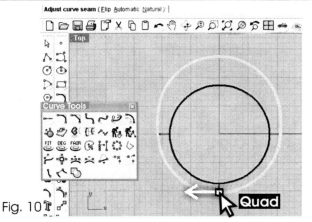

Fig. 11

- If you now turn on the control points for the rebuilt curve you will be able to view the symmetrical arrangement of the control points.

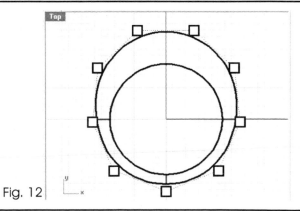

Fig. 12

127

- Switch to the **construction lines 2** layer.

- Use the **Line** command to create the construction lines shown.
  - Create construction lines as shown from the **quad points** straight upward, crossing the center line for the top elevation.
  - Center line for the top elevation is longer on the right side.
  - Note the 45-degree line that extends upward from **"0"** and intersects the center line for the top elevation.
  - Use **ortho.**

Fig. 13

- Create an additional perpendicular line from the intersection of the horizontal and diagonal lines.

Fig. 14

- **TECH LINES** layer.

- Click on the **Ellipse: Diameter** command in the **Ellipse** toolbar flyout.
  - **Start of first axis** prompt: click on the left intersection as shown.❶
  - **End of first axis** prompt: click on the right intersection as shown. ❷
  - **End of second axis** prompt: type **"10"** and press "enter".
  - Draw cursor up and set location.

accesses the **Ellipse** toolbar flyout

end of Second Axis (type "10", press "enter", and left click to set location)

Ellipse: Diameter command

Fig. 15

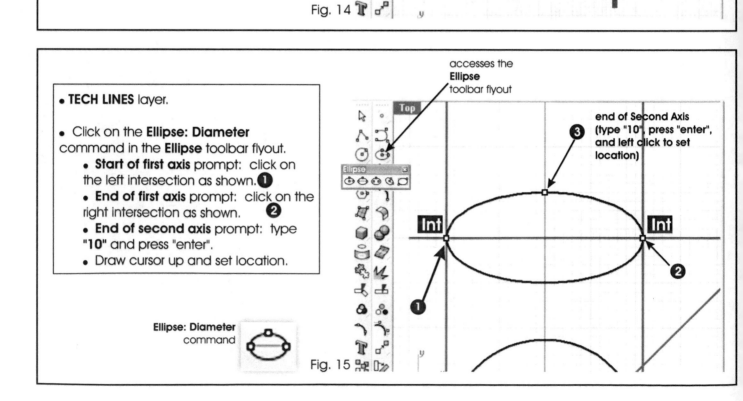

128

- **construction lines** layer.

- From the top and bottom **quad points** of the ellipse just created, create two horizontal lines out to the right that intersect the 45-degree diagonal line as shown.

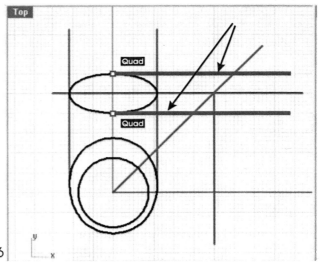

Fig. 16

- From the intersections of the horizontal lines just drawn and the diagonal line, draw two vertical lines as shown.

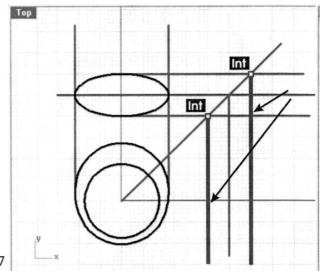

Fig. 17

- Create 4 more horizontal lines from the quad points of the bombe ring front view as shown.

- **quad osnap** and **ortho** are essential here.

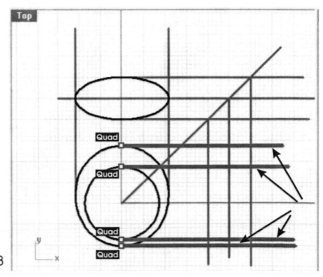

Fig. 18

129

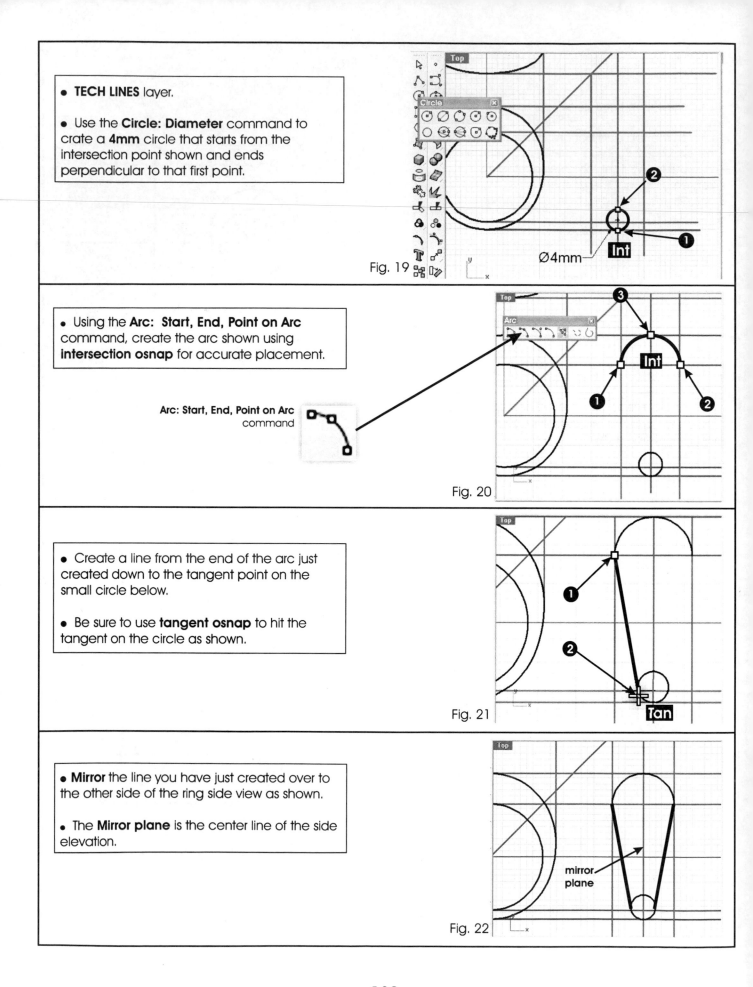

- **TECH LINES** layer.

- Use the **Circle: Diameter** command to crate a **4mm** circle that starts from the intersection point shown and ends perpendicular to that first point.

Fig. 19

Ø4mm

- Using the **Arc: Start, End, Point on Arc** command, create the arc shown using **intersection osnap** for accurate placement.

Arc: Start, End, Point on Arc
command

Fig. 20

- Create a line from the end of the arc just created down to the tangent point on the small circle below.

- Be sure to use **tangent osnap** to hit the tangent on the circle as shown.

Fig. 21

- **Mirror** the line you have just created over to the other side of the ring side view as shown.

- The **Mirror plane** is the center line of the side elevation.

mirror plane

Fig. 22

- **Copy** the side view off to the side as shown.

- **Delete** the two straight lines on the original as shown.

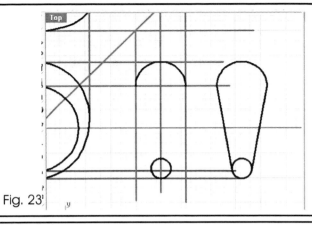

Fig. 23

- Use the **Arc: Start, End, Direction at Start** command to create an arc as shown.
    - Use the **end** and **quad** osnaps for accuracy.

- Make surc to use **ORTHO** when clicking on the third location setting the arc's direction.

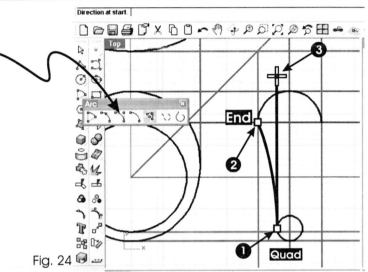

Fig. 24

- **Mirror** the new arc over to the other side of the ring side view.

- **Trim** out both side views.

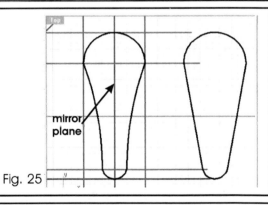

Fig. 25

- In the finished drawing, you can hide lines that you think are not necessary for presentation.

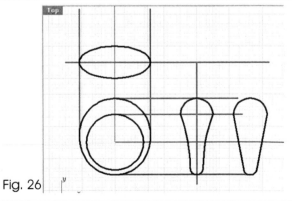

Fig. 26

Point Objects
Points for Reference & the Division of Curves

- Creating **Points** is one of the most useful commands in Rhino.

- **Points** assist you in marking important locations and dividing lines and curves into desired segments.

- The **Point** commands are accessed in the **Point** toolbar flyout.

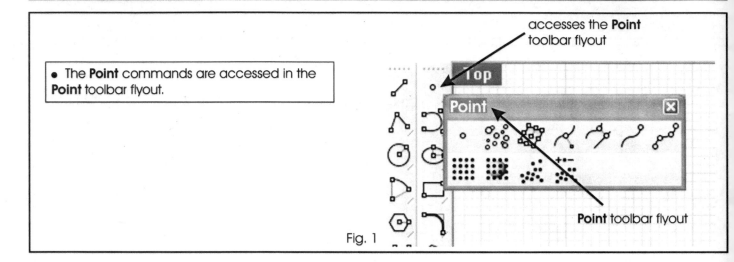

accesses the **Point** toolbar flyout

Point toolbar flyout

Fig. 1

Single Points

- **LEFT CLICK** on the <u>**Single Point**</u> command.
    - This command button is available on the default main toolbar collection as well as in the **Point** toolbar flyout.

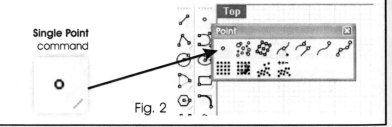

Single Point command

Fig. 2

- **Location of point object** prompt: Click on the desired location.

- A single point will be placed in your chosen location.

- Note: Single or multiple points can be attached to objects with the use of **object snap**.

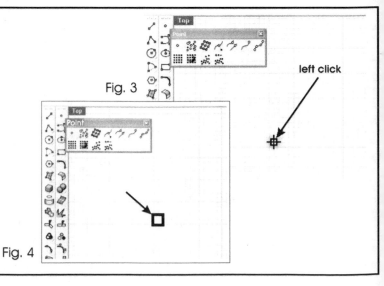

Fig. 3

left click

Fig. 4

Multiple Points

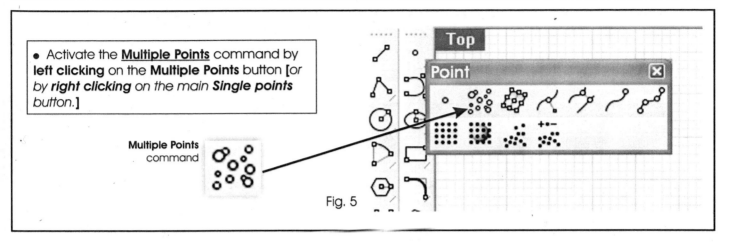

- Activate the **Multiple Points** command by **left clicking** on the **Multiple Points** button [*or by right clicking on the main Single points button.*]

Multiple Points command

Fig. 5

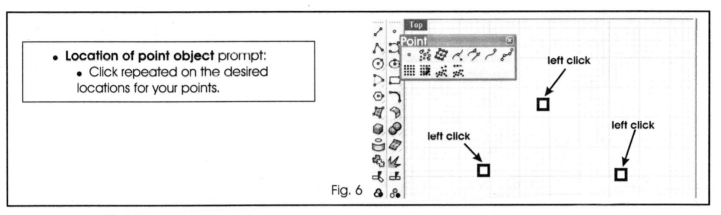

- **Location of point object** prompt:
  - Click repeated on the desired locations for your points.

left click

left click

left click

Fig. 6

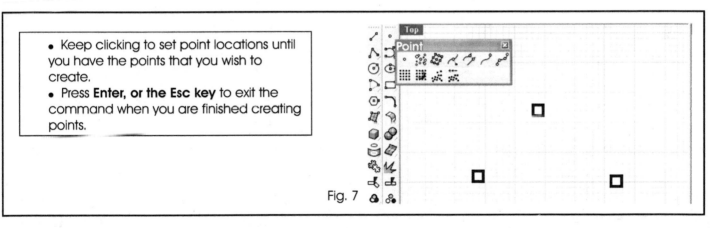

- Keep clicking to set point locations until you have the points that you wish to create.
- Press **Enter, or the Esc key** to exit the command when you are finished creating points.

Fig. 7

Dividing Curves and Lines by Number of Segments

- Create a circle and a straight line.

- Make these objects the same dimensions as shown.

- You do not have to put in dimensions.

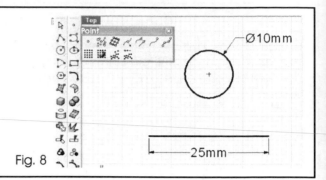

Fig. 8

- **Right click** on the button shown for the **Divide Curve by Number of Segments** command as shown.

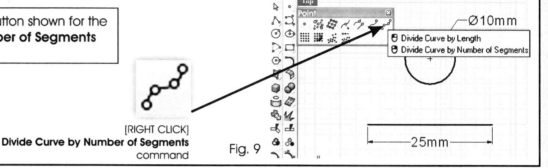

[RIGHT CLICK]
Divide Curve by Number of Segments
command

Fig. 9

- **Select Curves to Divide** prompt: select the circle as shown and press "enter".

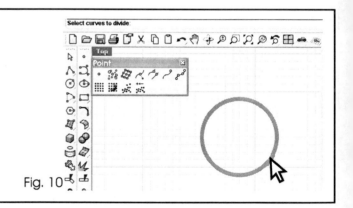

Fig. 10

- **Adjust Curve Seams** prompt:
  - This is a **closed curve** and thus its beginning and end form a **"seam"**. All lines and curves have a beginning and an end, even when they are closed.
  - The point and white arrow represent the seam point. If you want, you can click and drag to move this seam which will effect the distribution of the points that you are creating.

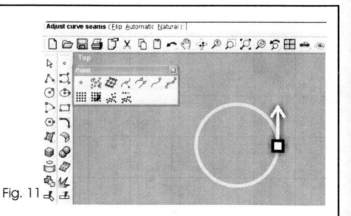

Fig. 11

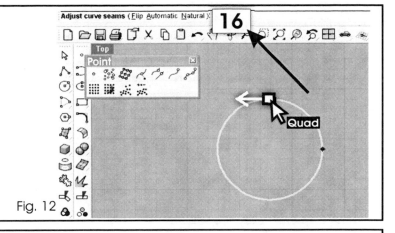

- **Adjust curve seam** prompt: Click on the point shown and guide the curve seam up to the top quad of the circle, using **quad osnap** for accuracy.
  - Click to set this location and press "enter".
- **Number of segments** prompt: Type in the number **"16"** and press "enter".

Fig. 12

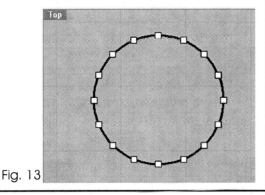

- The circle will be divided up into 16 equal sections by the placement of point objects.

Fig. 13

- Follow this procedure with the line that you created earlier with the circle, dividing it into 60 equal segments as shown.

- You will not be prompted for a curve seam location with the line because it is an **open curve.**

Fig. 14

Dividing Curves and Lines by Length of Segments

- Pan to an unused area of the construction plane and create another circle and another line with the same dimensions as before.

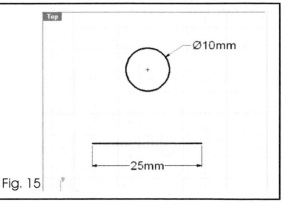

Fig. 15

135

- Select the circle and the line.

- **Left click** on the button shown for the **Divide Curve by Length of Segments** command.

[LEFT CLICK]
Divide Curve by Length of Segments
command

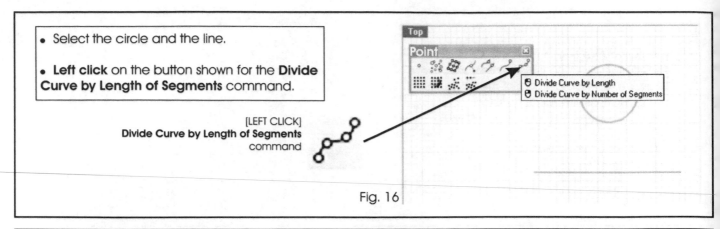

Divide Curve by Length
Divide Curve by Number of Segments

Fig. 16

- **Adjust curve seams** prompt: Press "enter" to accept the default position of the closed curve seam.
  - Notice that this prompt only applies to the circle. This is because the circle is a closed curve. Open curves like the line do not have curve seams.

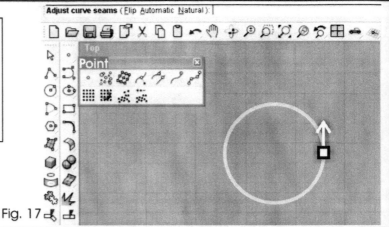

Adjust curve seams (Flip Automatic Natural)

Fig. 17

- **Curve lengths...** prompt: You will be given the information in the **Command Line** of the actual lengths of the selected curves and the length last used.
  - Type "5.45" in the command line and press "enter"

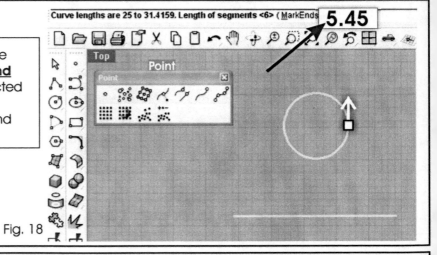

Curve lengths are 25 to 31.4159. Length of segments <6> (MarkEnds

5.45

Fig. 18

- The two selected objects will be divided into segments that are each 5.45mm long.

- Notice that the segments at the end of the curve and circle are not the same length. These are leftover segments that could not be the same length because of overall length constraints of the line and circle.

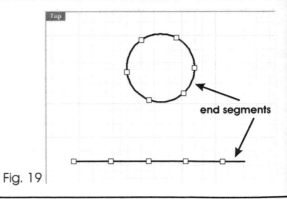

end segments

Fig. 19

Technical Drawing - Necklace Layout

- Create layers as shown.

- Make the **construction lines** layer current.

Fig. 1

- Use the **Circle: Center, Radius** command to create a circle around "**0**" with a diameter of **129.42mm**.

- **Right click** on the **Divide Curve by Number of Segments** command in the **Point** toolbar flyout.
  - **Number of segments** prompt: type "**60**" and press "enter".

- The circle will be divided into 60 segments of equal length by the placement of points.

Divide Curve by Number of Segments command [right click]

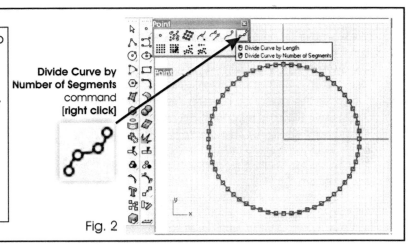

Fig. 2

- Create a vertical line **15mm in length** from the top of the circle - use either **Point Osnap** or **Quad Osnap** to place this line accurately.

- Be sure to use **Ortho**.

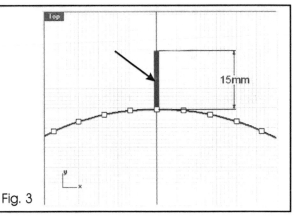

Fig. 3

- Make the **TECH LINES** layer current.

- Using the **Arc: Start, End, Direction at Start** command on the **Arc** toolbar flyout, create an arc as shown.

- When **left clicking** on the final point, make sure you use **ortho**.

Arc: Start, End, Direction at Start command

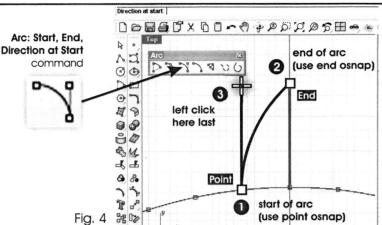

Fig. 4

- Select the arc just created and click on the **Offset Curve** command in the **Curve Tools** toolbar flyout.
  - **Side to offset** prompt: type "**3**" and press "enter".
  - **Side to offset** prompt: draw the cursor to the left of the arc to offset and click to set location.

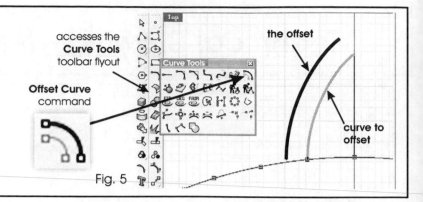

accesses the **Curve Tools** toolbar flyout

Offset Curve command

the offset

curve to offset

Fig. 5

- Click on the **Extend by Arc Keep Radius** command in the **Extend** toolbar flyout:
  - **Select curve to extend** prompt: click on the top end of the offset just created.
  - Draw the cursor upward to extend this curve - it will only extend in an arc that is the same radius as the curve itself. ❶
    - Make sure to extend the curve far enough so that it crosses the Y axis as shown. ❷
  - Click to set location as shown and press "enter".

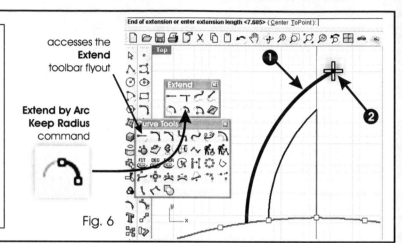

accesses the **Extend** toolbar flyout

Extend by Arc Keep Radius command

Fig. 6

- **Mirror** the two arcs across the Y axis.

- Make sure to use **Ortho** to get an accurate mirror when setting the **mirror plane**.

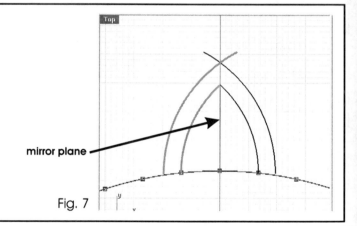

mirror plane

Fig. 7

- Use the **Trim** command to clean up the overlappline lines of the mirrored arcs.

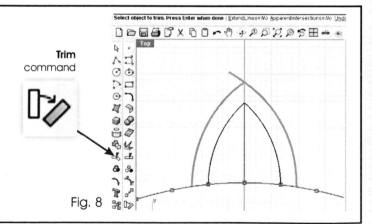

Trim command

Fig. 8

- Click on the **Polar Array** command in the **Transform** toolbar flyout.
  - **Select objects to array** prompt: select the mirrored and joined arcs and press "enter".
  - **Center of polar array** prompt: type "**0**" and press "enter".
  - **Number of items** prompt: type "**30**" and press "enter".
  - **Angle to fill or first reference point** prompt: press "enter" to accept the default of 360.

Polar Array command

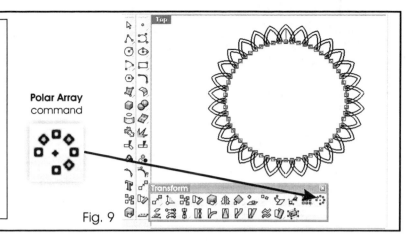

Fig. 9

- The next step is to connect the arcs to each other in a graceful way.

- On the **construction lines layer,** create a line from "**0**" to the point shown.
  - Use **Point osnap.**

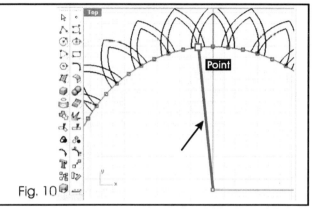

Fig. 10

- Make the **TECH LINES** layer current again.

- Click on the **Blend Curves** command in the **Curve Tools** toolbar flyout.
  - **Select first curve to blend** prompt: click on the end of the arc shown.❶
  - **Select second curve to blend** prompt: click on the end of the other arc shown.❷

- Notice that the **Continuity=Curvature** option is toggled on in the **Command Line.**

Blend Curves command

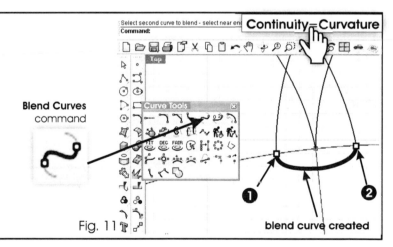

Fig. 11

- Turn on **Near Osnap.**

- Turn on the control points of the blend curve just created.

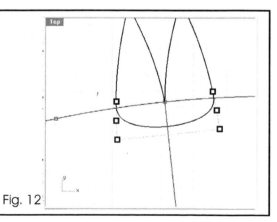

Fig. 12

139

- Select the two center control points of the blend curve and click on the **Move** command.
  - **Point to move from** prompt: snap to the straight line, using **near osnap** and click to set location. ❶
  - **Point to move to** prompt: draw the cursor down the line, using **near osnap** to maintain contact with the line.
  - Click to set location with the blend curve has a graceful shape as shown. ❷

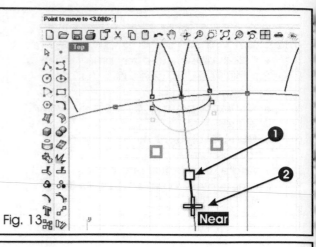

Fig. 13

- **Trim** the loop motif at the top as shown.

Trim command

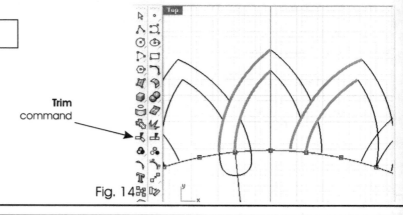

Fig. 14

- Turn off the **construction lines** layer.

- **Delete** all the arrayed curves except the top ones shown.

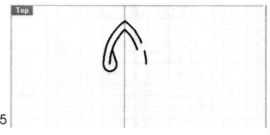

Fig. 15

- **Polar Array** the curves again with the same settings as before:

  - **Center of polar array:** "0".

  - **Number of items:** 30

  - **Angle:** 360

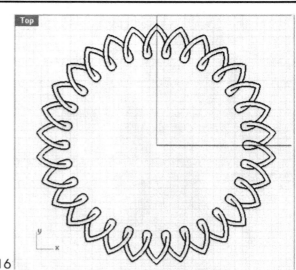

Fig. 16

140

Technical Drawing
Band Ring with Bezel Set Cabochon

- Create the layers shown.

- Make the **STONE TECH LINES** layer current.

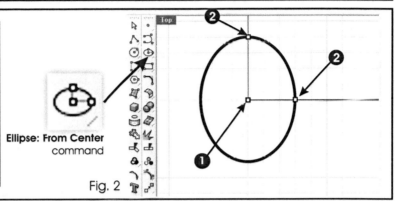

Fig. 1

- Click on the **Ellipse: From Center** command to make a 6 x 8 oval stone.
  - **Ellipse center** prompt: type **"0"** and press "enter". ❶
  - **End of first axis** prompt: type **"3"** and press "enter". Draw cursor to the right and click to set the location. ❷
  - **End of second axis** prompt: type **"4"** and press "enter". Draw cursor up and click to set the location. ❸

Ellipse: From Center
command

Fig. 2

- **tech construction lines** layer.

- Create vertical and horizontal construction lines, starting the lines at the **quad** points of the oval.
  - Make sure to use **ortho** and **Quad Osnap** to place these lines with accuracy.

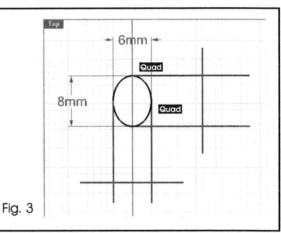

Fig. 3

- Use the **Trim** command to trim off the lines shown.

- Change these two trimmed lines to the **STONE TECH LINES** layer.

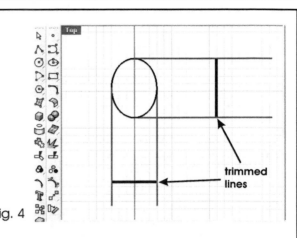

trimmed lines

Fig. 4

- From the **midpoint** of each of these two lines, create smaller lines **2.5mm long**. These lines will be the guides to indicate the height of the cabochons.
- Remember to use **Ortho.**

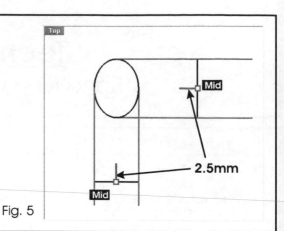

Fig. 5

- Use the **Arc: Start, End, Point on Arc** command to create the arcs shown.
  - Form the arcs by left clicking on the end points of the stone construction lines in the order shown.
- **End Osnap** is essential to place these locations with accuracy.

Arc: Start, End, Point on Arc
command

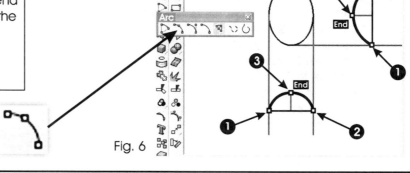

Fig. 6

- Add dimensions as shown.

- Click on the **Rectangle: Corner to Corner** command to frame the stone tech.
  - **First corner of rectangle** prompt: click in the upper left corner as shown. ❶
  - **Other corner or length** prompt: draw the cursor down to the lower right and click to set a rectangle around the technical drawing of the stone as shown. ❷

Rectangle:
Corner to Corner
command

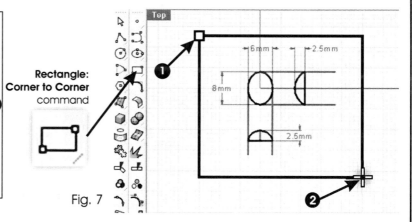

Fig. 7

- Drag the stone tech up out of the way as shown, using **ortho** to ensure that the drag is perpendicular.

- Turn off the **STONE TECH, stone construction lines,** and the **dimensions** layers.

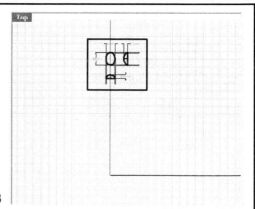

Fig. 8

- **TECH LINES** layer.

- Create a circle around **0** with a diameter of **17.35mm**.

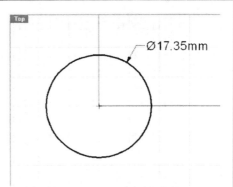

Fig. 9

- Select the circle and click on the **Offset Curve** command in the **Curve Tools** toolbar flyout.
  - **Side to offset** prompt: draw the cursor to the outside of the circle.
  - **Side to offset** prompt: type "**1**" and press "enter".

- The new circle's diameter will be **19.35mm**.

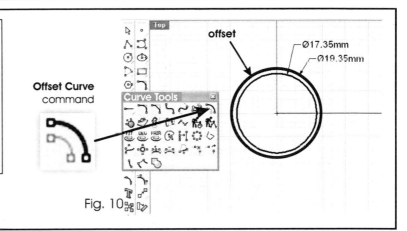

Offset Curve command

Fig. 10

- Offset this offset in turn at a distance of **1mm**.

- The new circle's diameter will be **21.35mm**.

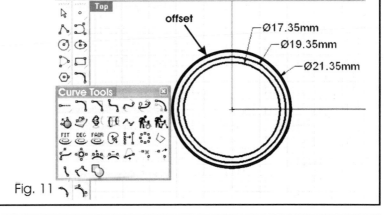

Fig. 11

- **tech construction lines** layer:
  - Use the **Line from Midpoint** command to create a center line for the top elevation of the ring. **❶**
  - Use the **Line** command to draw a perpendicular line up from the quad points of each side of the **outer circle❷**
  - Create a center line upward from **0.❸**

Line command

Line from Midpoint command

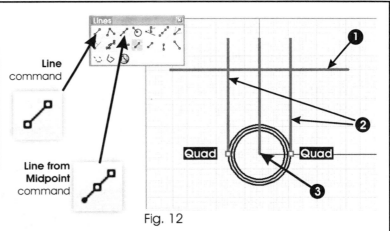

Fig. 12

143

- Turn the **STONE TECH LINES** layer on.

- Select the ellipse of the top view of the stone and click on the **Copy** command:
  - **Point to copy from** prompt: snap to the **center point** of the stone's top view as shown. Click to set location. **1**
  - **Point to copy to** prompt: draw the cursor down and snap to intersection of the top view center line and the center line that extends up from **0**. Click to set location. **2**

- Change the copied stone to the **RING TECH LINES** layer and turn off **STONE TECH LINES** layer.

Copy
command

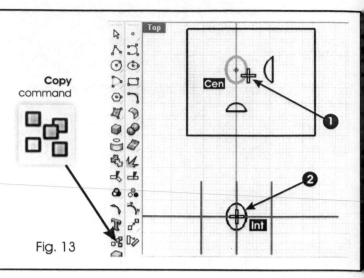

Fig. 13

- Turn on the **TECH LINES** layer and make it current.

- Create a line connecting the upper quad points of the two outer circles on the front projection of the ring as shown.

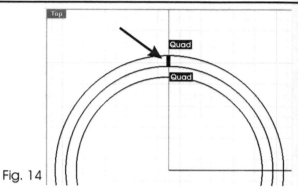

Fig. 14

- Select the line just created and click on the **Polar Array** command in the **Transform** toolbar flyout.
  - **Center of polar array** prompt: type **"0"** and press "enter".
  - **Number of items**: type **"48"** and press "enter".
  - **Angle to fill or first reference point** prompt: press "enter" to accept the default angle of 360.

accesses the **Transform** toolbar flyout

Polar Array command

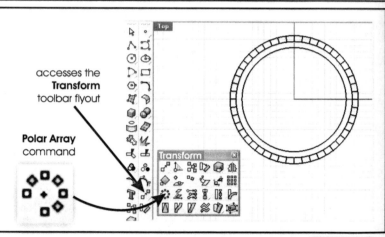

Fig. 15

- **tech construction lines** layer.

- Select the horizontal center line for the top elevation as shown and click on the **Offset Curve** command.
  - **Side to offset** prompt: click on the **BothSides** option in the **Command Line.**
  - **Side to offset** prompt: type **"2"** and press "enter".
  - Click to set the offset.

Offset Curve command

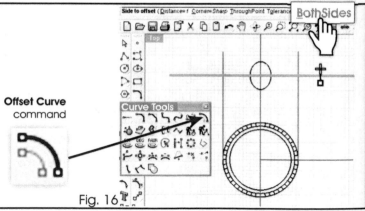

Fig. 16

144

- The line has been offset on both sides for a 4mm wide ring band.

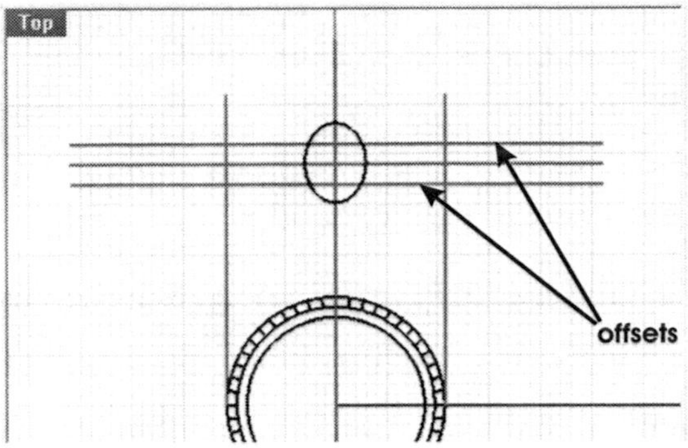

Fig. 17

offsets

- Click on the **Rounded Rectangle** command in the **Rectangle** toolbar flyout.
  - **First corner of rectangle** prompt: click on the **Center** option in the **Command Line** as shown.

Rounded Rectangle command

accesses the **Rectangle** toolbar flyout

First corner of rectangle (3Point Ver

Center

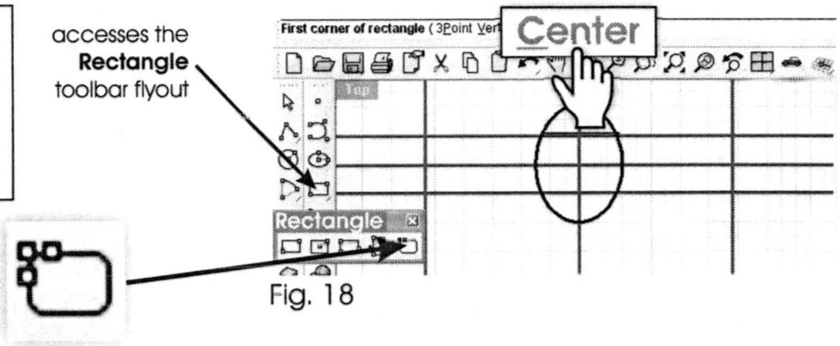

Fig. 18

- **Center of rectangle** prompt: snap to the intersection shown and click to set location.

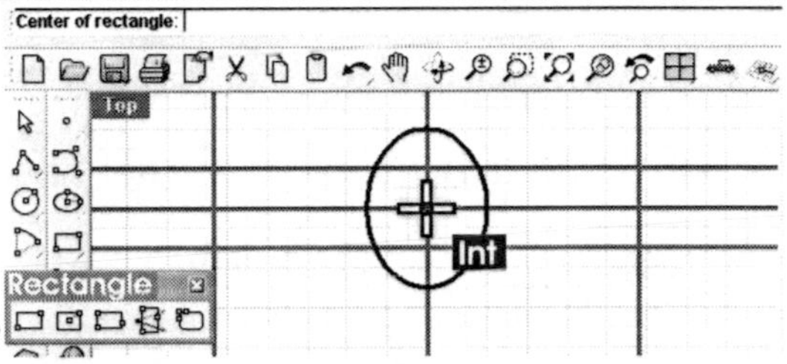

Center of rectangle:

Fig. 19

- **Other corner or length** prompt: draw the cursor down and snap to the intersection on the lower right as shown.
  - Click to set location.

Other corner or length:

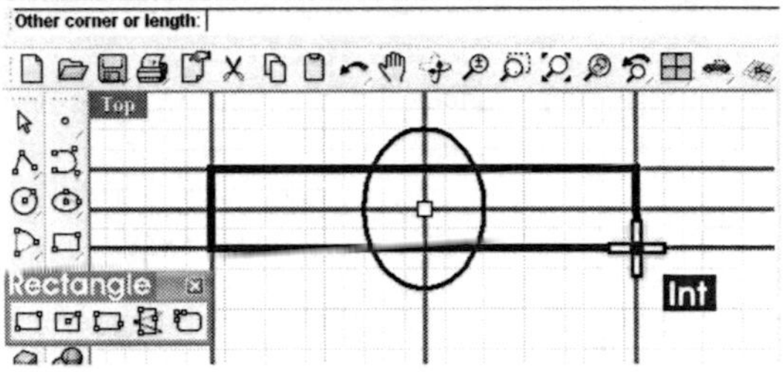

Fig. 20

- **Radius or point for rounded corner to pass through** prompt: draw the cursor to the inside of the rectangle until the end becomes rounded as shown.
  - Click to set location.

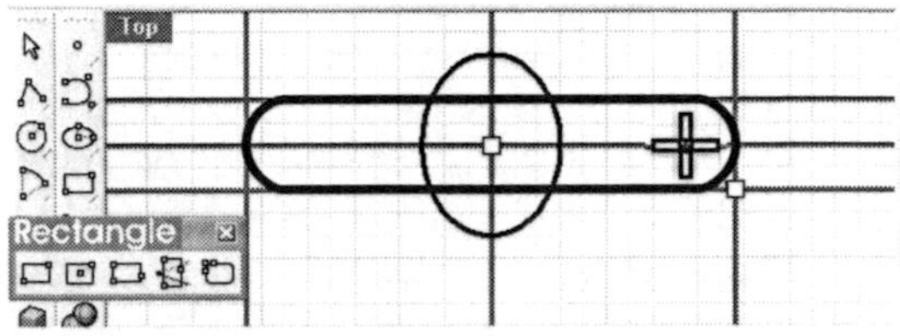

Fig. 21

- The finished ring shank.

- Hide or Delete the two offset construction lines.

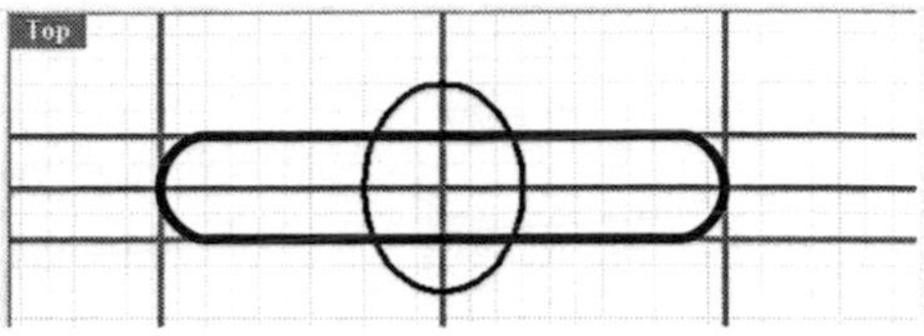

Fig. 22

- **tech construction lines** layer.

- Create two perpendicular lines upward from the **quad** points of the **middle circle** in the front view of the ring band..

- Lines should intersect the top elevation as shown.

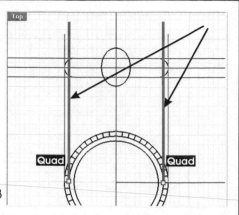

Fig. 23

- **TECH LINES** layer.

- Create two horizontal lines between the intersections of the two new construction lines and the shank as shown.

- These lines represent the dividing line in the middle of the band seen in the front view.

Detail View

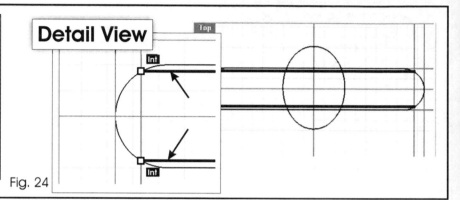

Fig. 24

- Turn off the **tech construction lines** layer.

- Create a new layer named **tech construction lines 2** and make it current.

- Create perpendicular lines from the **inner end points (to the inside of the circle)** of the arrayed lines - **ORTHO** IS ESSENTIAL FOR THIS.

- Make sure that these lines intersect the lines of the top view ring shank as shown.

Detail View

end point

start point

Fig. 25

- Click on the **Object Intersection** command in the **Curve from object** toolbar flyout.
  - **Select objects to Intersect** prompt: select the two parallel lines added to the shank and the perpendicular lines you just created as shown and press "enter".

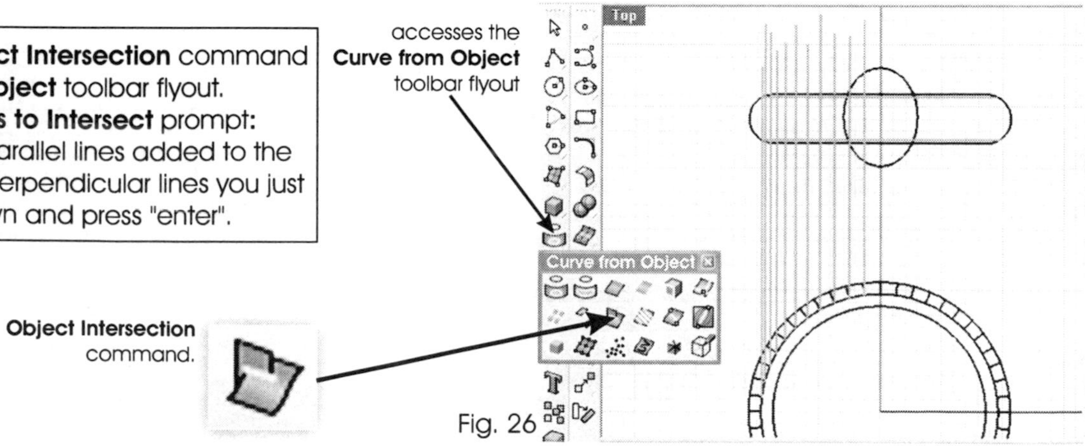

accesses the **Curve from Object** toolbar flyout

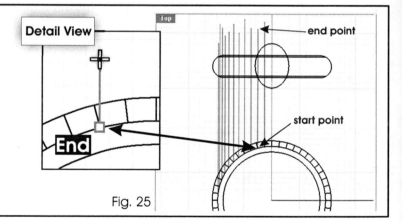

Object Intersection command.

Fig. 26

- At the points where the selected lines intersected, points will appear to mark the intersections.

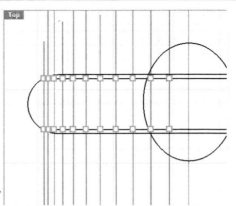

Fig. 27

- **Delete** the lines on the **construction lines 2** layer leaving the points.

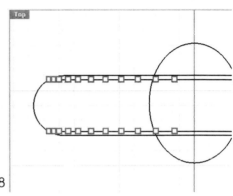

Fig. 28

- Create perpendicular lines from the end points **(to the outside of the circle)** of the arrayed lines this time as shown.

- Make sure that these lines intersect the lines of the top view ring shank as shown.

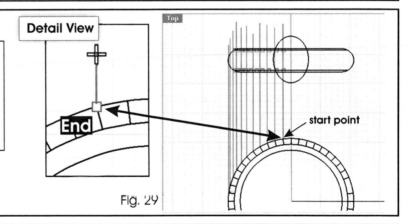

Fig. 29

- **TECH LINES** layer current.

- Turn on **tech construction lines** layer.

- Using the **Arc: Start, End, Point on Arc** command in the **Arc** toolbar, create arcs that start and end on the intersection points as shown.
  - **Int** and **End** osnaps are essential for this step.

Arc: Start, End, Point on Arc
command

Fig. 30

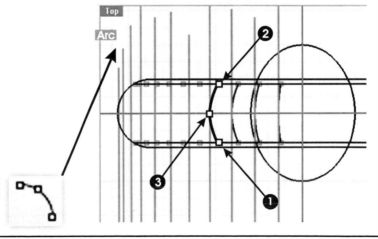

147

- Continue making arcs to the end of the shank, snapping to the points and intersections shown.

- Turn off the **construction lines 2** layer.

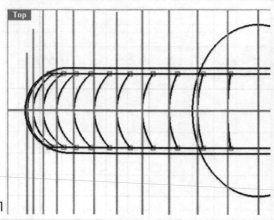

Fig. 31

- **Mirror** the finished arcs over to the other side.

- You can make a line that connects the mid points of both sides of the shank as shown in Fig. 26. This will enable you to use this shank without the stone for a possible matching wedding band.

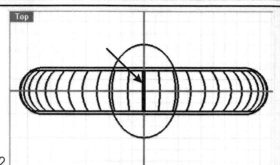

Fig. 32

- Select the top ring band and it's center line as shown and click on the **Rotate** command.
  - **Center of rotation** prompt: click on the **Copy** option in the **Command Line.**
  - **Center of rotation** prompt: type **"0"** and press "enter".
  - **Angle or first reference point** prompt: type **"-90"** and press "enter".
    - *Remember to type a "minus" before the "90" as this is a clockwise rotation.*

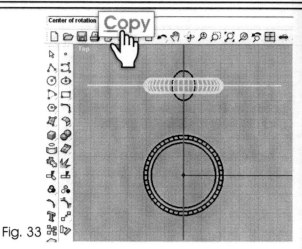

Fig. 33

- A copy of the ring band has been rotated to the side to start the side elevation of this ring.

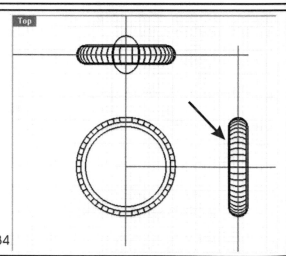

Fig. 34

148

- Use the **Offset curve** command to offset the oval stone outward at a distance of **.3mm**.

- Offset again at a distance of **.3mm** as shown, creating the concentric ovals as shown.

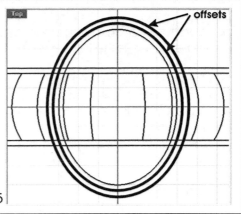

Fig. 35

- Using the outermost circle as a cutting object, **Trim** away unneeded ring shank lines.

- Delete other unwanted lines.

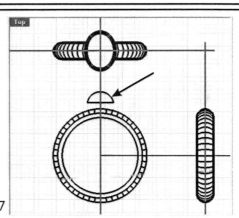

Fig. 36

- Turn on the **STONE TECH LINES** layer.

- Using **ortho, Copy** the front view of the stone from the stone tech to the desired stone height in the front view of the ring as shown.

- Change the copied stone to the **TECH LINES** layer.

- Turn off the **STONE TECH LINES** layer.

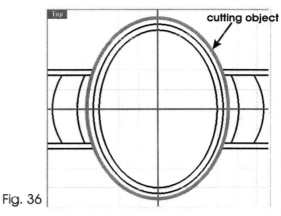

Fig. 37

- **tech construction lines** layer.

- Create a line from **0** at a 45-degree angle and extending out to intersect the two other construction lines shown.

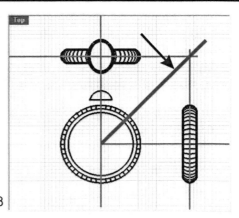

Fig. 38

- Create lines from the quad points of the outer bezel line in the top view. **1**

- Create lines downward from the intersections of these lines with the diagonal line as shown. **2**

- Create a horizontal line from the upper **quad** point of the stone in the front view over to intersect with the center line of the side view as shown. **3**

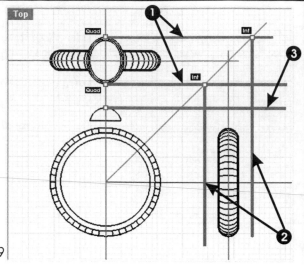

Fig. 39

- Create two perpendicular lines straight down from the **quad** points of the **outer oval** of the top elevation to intersect the front elevation of the ring band as shown. **1**

- **TECH LINES** layer.

- Create a horizontal line across the stone to indicate the height of the stone's bezel. **2**

- *Notice that certain tech construction lines have been hidden for easier viewing.*

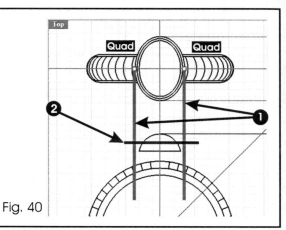

Fig. 40

Trim the **tech construction lines** and **TECH LINES** with each other to achieve the shape shown.

- Change the two lines indicated to the **RING TECH LINES** layer.

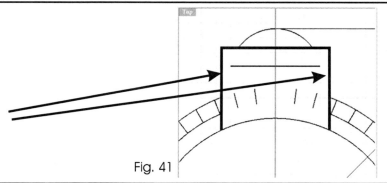

Fig. 41

- **Delete** unwanted lines from the middle of the bezel shape as shown.

- All bezel lines should be changed to the **TECH LINES** layer.

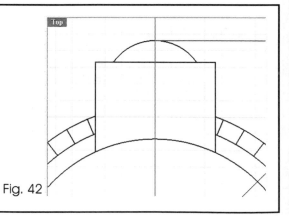

Fig. 42

- **Offset** the top bezel line down **1mm**.

curve to offset ⟶

the 1mm offset ⟶

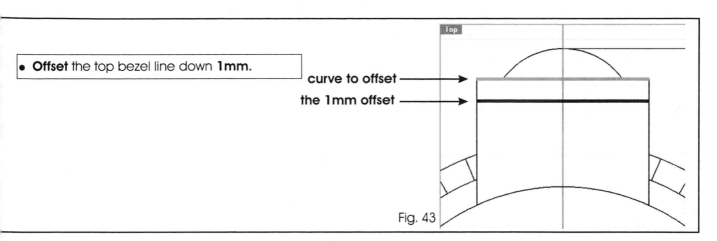

Fig. 43

- **tech construction lines** layer.

- Create two vertical lines down from the **Quad** points of the **middle concentric oval** of the bezel to intersect the bezel of the front elevation as shown.

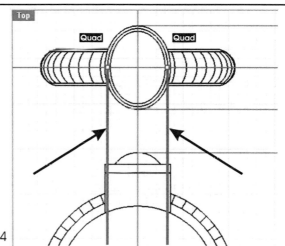

Fig. 44

- **TECH LINES** layer.

- Zoom in to view the bezel and create a diagonal line, snapping to the intersections shown.
    - The angle of the diagonal will represent a slight bevel to the top edge of the bezel.

- **Mirror** this line over to the other side of the bezel.

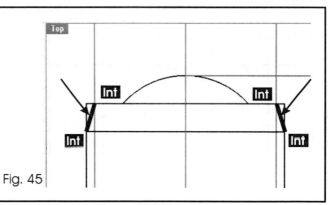

Fig. 45

- Use the diagonal lines to trim away the bezel as shown.

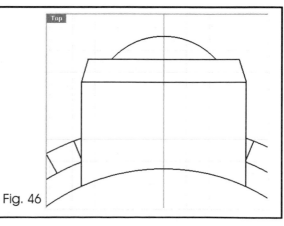

Fig. 46

- **tech construction lines** layer.

- Create the 5 lines shown, horizontal and crossing over and intersecting the ring shank that is the base of the side elevation as shown.

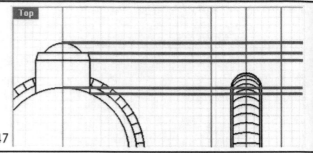

Fig. 47

- Use the **Arc: Start, End, Direction at Start** command to create an arc that defines the bottom curvature of the bezel in the side elevation.
    - **Start of arc** prompt: click on intersection shown.
    - **End of arc** prompt: click on intersection shown.
    - **Point on arc** prompt: draw cursor out as shown and, with **ortho** on, click to set location.

Arc: Start, End, Direction at Start command

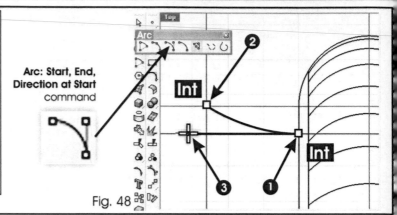

Fig. 48

- **Copy** the small diagonal line from the front bezel elevation to the side bezel elevation as shown.

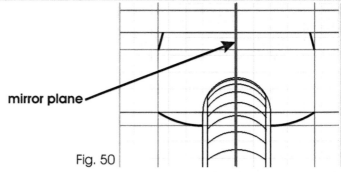

copy

Fig. 49

- **Mirror** the arc and the little diagonal lines across to the other side of the side elevation as shown.

mirror plane

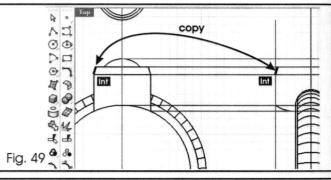

Fig. 50

- **Trim** out the side view of the bezel as shown.

- Switch all lines to the **TECH LINES** layer.

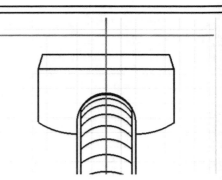

Fig. 51

152

- **STONE TECH LINES** layer.

- **Copy** the side elevation of the stone so that it's quad point rests on the intersection above the side elevation of the ring as shown.

- Select the stone and click on the **Rotate** command.
  - **Center of rotation** prompt: click on the intersection shown.
    - **Angle or first reference point** prompt: type "-90" and press "enter". (remember the "minus")

- The stone will now be oriented in the right direction.

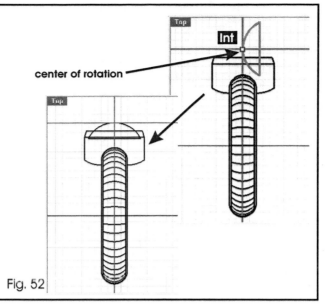

center of rotation

Fig. 52

- **Trim** the stone with the bezel line as shown.

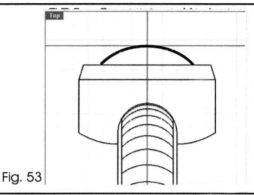

Fig. 53

- Draw a horizontal line from the intersection point of the shank and the bezel in the front view across to intersect the side elevation as shown.

Detail View

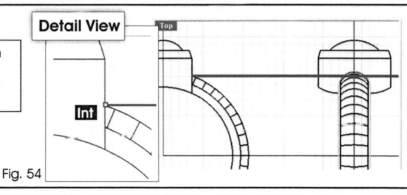

Fig. 54

- **Explode** the outer outline of the ring shank in the side elevation.

- Select the upper arc of the exploded ring shank and click on the **Move** command.
  - **Point to move from** prompt: click on the top of the arc as shown. **1**
  - **Point to move to** prompt: draw the cursor down to the intersection of the horizontal and vertical construction lines shown and click to set location. **2**

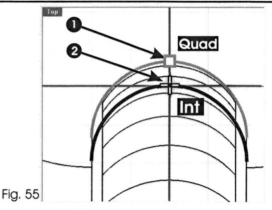

Fig. 55

153

- Use the curve that was just moved as the cutting object that **Trims** the outline of the original shape of the shank.

- Delete the remaining two arcs above.

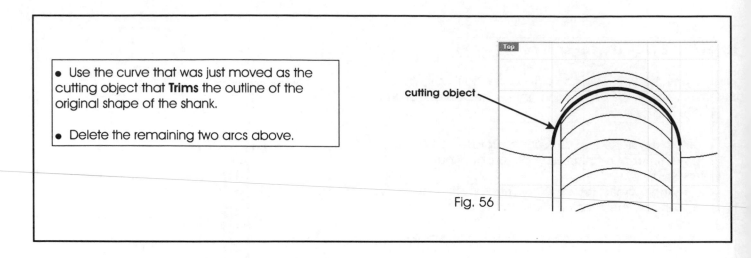

cutting object

Fig. 56

- The finished side elevation showing the reduced shank connecting with the bezel.

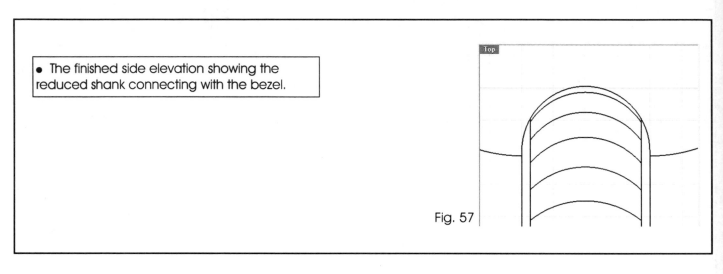

Fig. 57

- Add dimensions to the finished technical drawing.

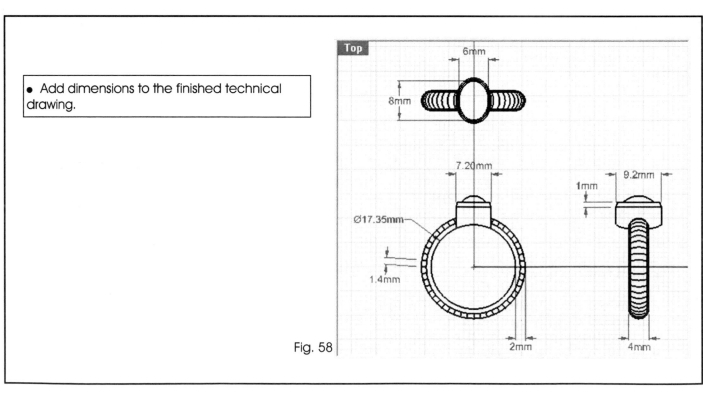

Fig. 58

Bounding Box*

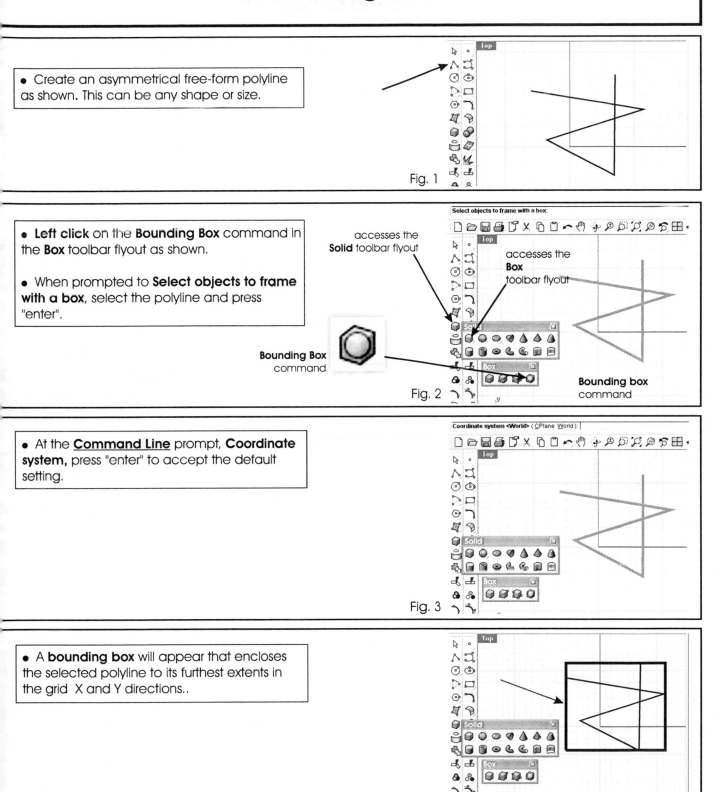

- Create an asymmetrical free-form polyline as shown. This can be any shape or size.

Fig. 1

- **Left click** on the **Bounding Box** command in the **Box** toolbar flyout as shown.

- When prompted to **Select objects to frame with a box**, select the polyline and press "enter".

accesses the **Solid** toolbar flyout

accesses the **Box** toolbar flyout

Bounding Box command

Bounding box command

Fig. 2

- At the <u>**Command Line**</u> prompt, **Coordinate system,** press "enter" to accept the default setting.

Fig. 3

- A **bounding box** will appear that encloses the selected polyline to its furthest extents in the grid X and Y directions..

Fig. 4

*Refer to the Rhino **HELP** menu for additional information on the <u>BoundingBox</u> command.

Watch Dial

- Create the layers shown.

- **TECH LINES** layer current.

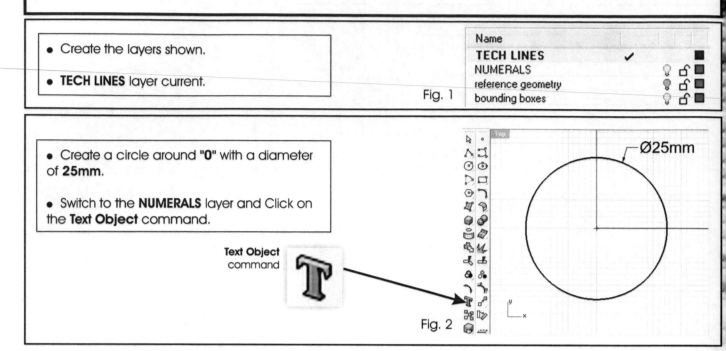

Fig. 1

Name		
TECH LINES	✓	■
NUMERALS		■
reference geometry		■
bounding boxes		■

- Create a circle around **"0"** with a diameter of **25mm**.

- Switch to the **NUMERALS** layer and Click on the **Text Object** command.

Text Object
command

Fig. 2

Ø25mm

- When the **Text Object** dialog box opens, write in the **Text to Create** box, the <u>**numbers 1 through 12**</u> as shown, *making a space between each number.*
- Use the settings shown.
- Click the OK button.

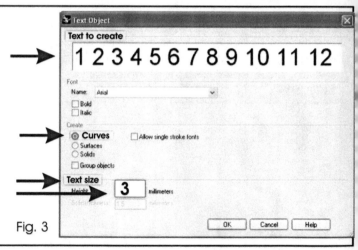

Fig. 3

- **Select insertion point** prompt: the letters will move with the cursor as shown.
- Click to set a location for the letters on the construction plane as shown.

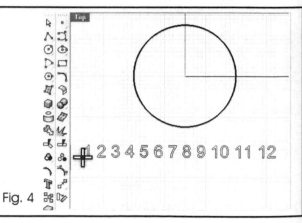

Fig. 4

- **bounding boxes** layer.

- Click on the **Bounding Box** command in the **Box** toolbar.

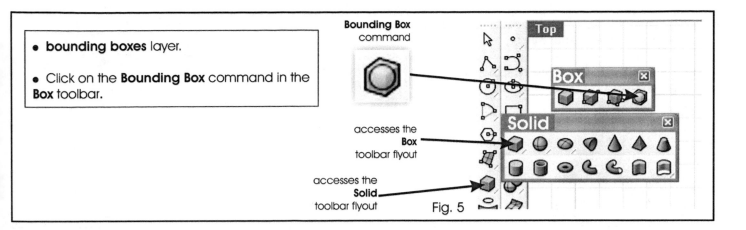

Bounding Box command

accesses the **Box** toolbar flyout

accesses the **Solid** toolbar flyout

Fig. 5

- **Select objects to frame with a box** prompt: select one of the letters and press "enter".
- **Coordinate system** prompt: press "enter" to accept the default **World Coordinate System.**

- A box will surround the selected letter as shown. *This box represents the furthest extant of this object in the X and Y grid directions.*

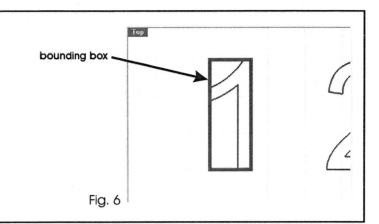

bounding box

Fig. 6

- Two more letters with bounding boxes.

- Note that the extents of the box matches the extents of the letters in the X and Y grid directions.

Fig. 7

- Create bounding boxes for all 12 letters as shown.

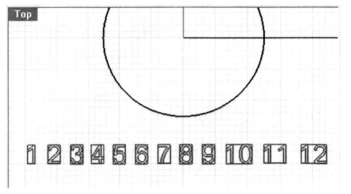

Fig. 8

- **reference geometry layer.**

- Use the **Divide Curve by Number of Segments** command to divide the circle into 12 equal segments.

Divide Curve by Number of Segments
command

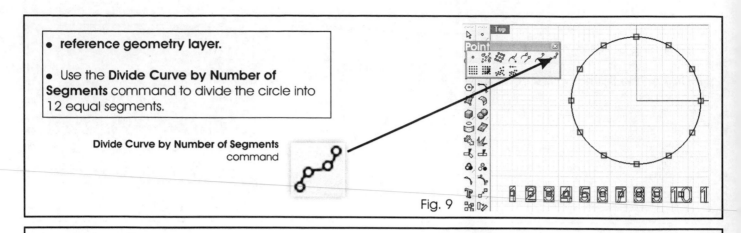

Fig. 9

- **Right-click** on the points button to access the **Multiple Points** command.

- Use **center osnap** to place a point in the center of each bounding box.

Multiple Points
command

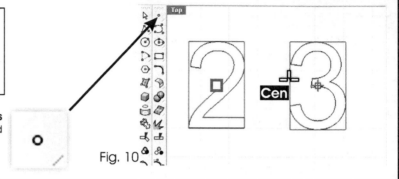

Fig. 10

- Window select the number "1" along with its bounding box and click on the **Move** command.
- **Point to move from** prompt: click on the point in the center of the boundong box. ❶
- **Point to move to** prompt: draw the cursor up to the point on the circle that represents the location of the number "1" on the watch dial.
- Click to set the location of the move. ❷

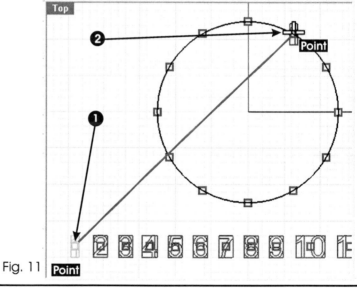

Fig. 11

- Move all numbers and their bounding boxes into position on the dial.

- Turn off the **bounding box** layer.

- **reference geometry** layer current.

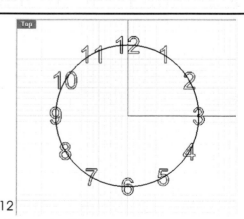

Fig. 12

- Create a **14mm line** straight up from **0** as shown.

- Make sure to use **ortho.**

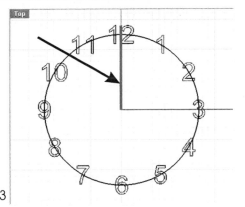

Fig. 13

- **Polar Array** the line around **0**.

- **Number of items: 12**

Polar Array
command

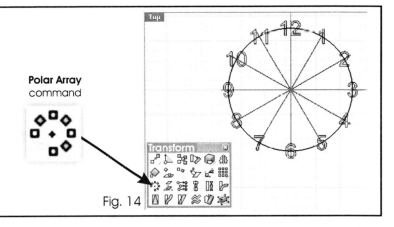

Fig. 14

- Select the **12** numerals and click on the **Move** command.
- **Point to move from** prompt: snap to the outer end of the line as shown. ❶
- **Point to move to** prompt: snap to the intersection of the circle and the line as shown. ❷
- Click to set location.

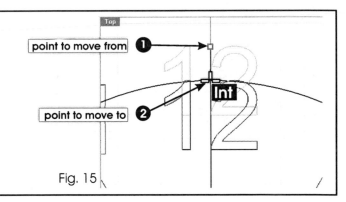

point to move from ❶

point to move to ❷

Fig. 15

- Use the same strategy to move the numeral **1.**

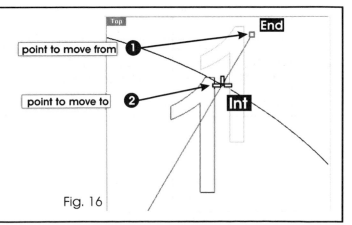

End

point to move from ❶

point to move to ❷

Int

Fig. 16

- Move all numbers, using the same method.

- Notice that the numbers are not evenly aligned to the circle. Some are inside the circle and some are outside.

- It is necessary to create reference geometry in order to accurately place the numerals.
  - The reason for reference geometry is because the letters all have somewhat non-symmetrical shapes but all need to touch the circle for overall symmetry of the watch dial.

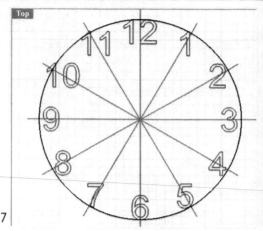

Fig. 17

- Zoom in on the **3** and click on the **Line: Perpendicular to Two Curves** command in the **Lines** toolbar flyout.

Line: Perpendicular to Two Curves
command

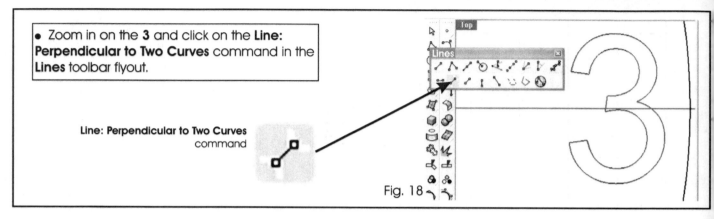

Fig. 18

- **Select first curve near perpendicular point** prompt: click on the lower curvature of the numeral because this curve extends further out in the X direction than the other curvature above it.

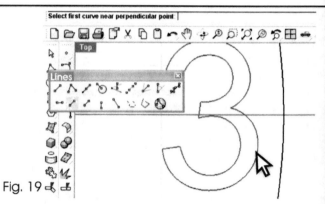

Fig. 19

- **Select second curve near perpendicular point** prompt: click on a location on the circle that is near the first point selected as shown..

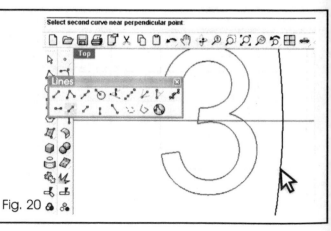

Fig. 20

- A line that is perpendicular to both selected curves has been created.

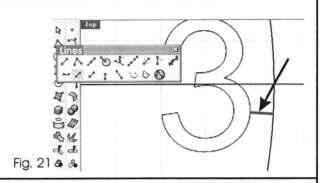

Fig. 21

- Select the horizontal line running through the numeral and click on the **Offset Curve** command.
  - **Side to offset** prompt: click on the **ThroughPoint** option in the **Command Line**.

Offset Curve
command

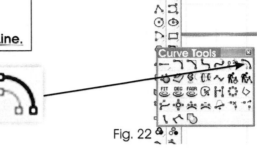

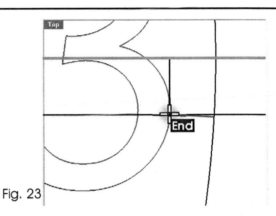

Fig. 22

- **Through point** prompt: draw the cursor down and snap to the end of the little line just created as shown.

- **Lock the original line.**

Fig. 23

- **Move** the numeral from one intersection point to another.

- The numeral will touch the outer circle but will still be properly aligned with the other numerals.

The principle behind this is that the numeral needs to move in the direction of the original line that passes through it. This is the line that originates at "0". Offset makes a line that is parallel to this line. Moving along the new offset line will move the numeral *in the same direction* but will enable snapping to a point of the numeral's curvature that needs to touch the circle.

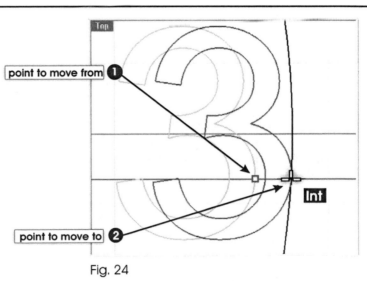

point to move from ①

point to move to ②

Fig. 24

- Zoom in on the bottom of the **6** numeral.

- Select the vertical line and offset as before, locating the offset curve on the lower quad point of the number.
  - Notice that the actual quad point of this numeral is not in the center.

- **Lock** the original vertical line.

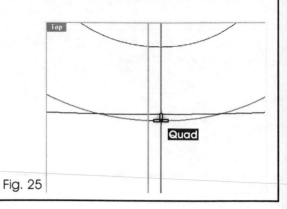

Fig. 25

- As before, use **intersection osnap** to move the numeral so that it touches the circle.

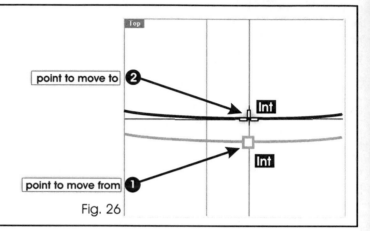

point to move to ❷

point to move from ❶

Fig. 26

- The numeral is now accurately placed inside the circle.

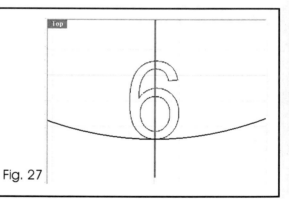

Fig. 27

- Zoom in on the **10** numeral.

- **Offset** the diagonal line to the **intersection** point shown.

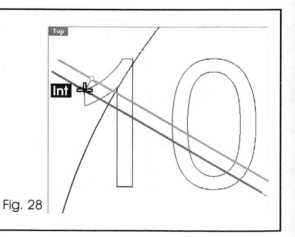

Fig. 28

- **Lock** the original line.

- **Move** the **10** numeral into position, using **intersection osnap** as with the other two examples.

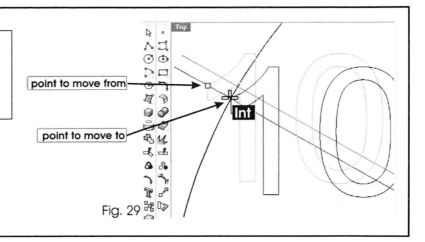

point to move from

point to move to

Int

Fig. 29

- Move all numerals into position.

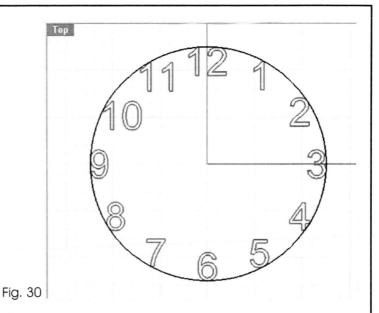

Fig. 30

- **TECH LINES** layer.

- **Offset** the circle at a distance of 1.5mm - or to a distance of your choice.

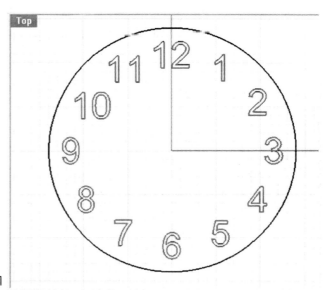

Fig. 31

- Select all numerals and click on the **Hatch** command in the **Dimension** toolbar flyout.

Hatch
command

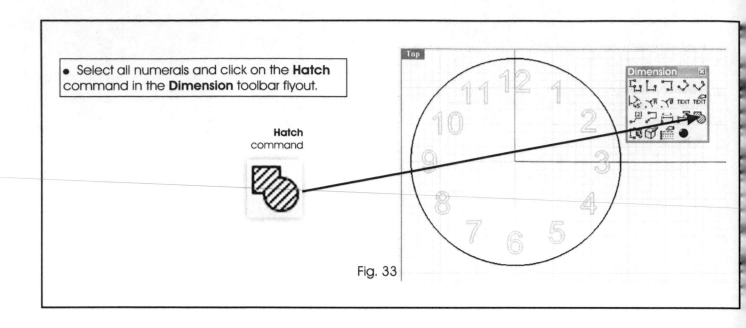

Fig. 33

- The letters will fill with a solid color which is the default setting.
    - The color of the hatch will be the color of the current layer.

- If you select some of the other patters listed, you will see them previewed.

- Click OK to accept the solid color option.

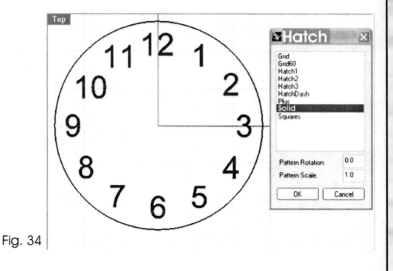

Fig. 34

- As the hatch was added in the **TECH LINES** layer, turn off the **NUMERALS** layer to view the finished watch dial.

- If you leave the **NUMERALS** layer on, the numbers may appear thicker than they actually are because some of the line width of the numerals curves will added to the dimensions of the hatch.

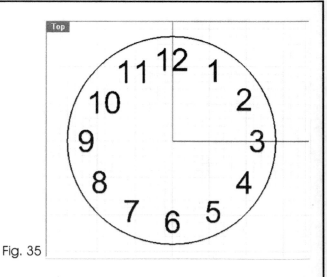

Fig. 35

Creating a Simple Floral Motif

- Create layers as shown.

- **construction lines** layer current.

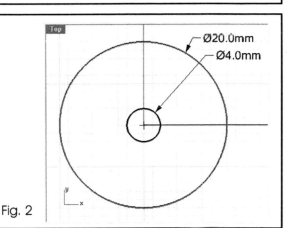

Name
TECH LINES
reference geometry ✓

Fig. 1

- Create the two circles shown around **0**.
  - **Circle diameters: 20mm and 4mm as shown.**

- The larger circle is on the **reference geometry** layer.

- The smaller inside circle is on the **TECH LINES** layer.

Ø20.0mm
Ø4.0mm

Fig. 2

- **reference geometry** layer.

- **Offset** the outer circle inward at an offset distance of **1.5mm** as shown.

- Create a line that connects the top **Quad** points of the inner and outer circles as shown.

the offset
the line
1.5mm

Fig. 3

- **Polar Array** the line around "0".

- **Number of items: 12**

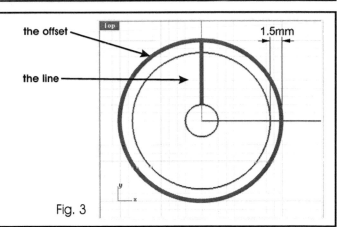

Polar Array
command

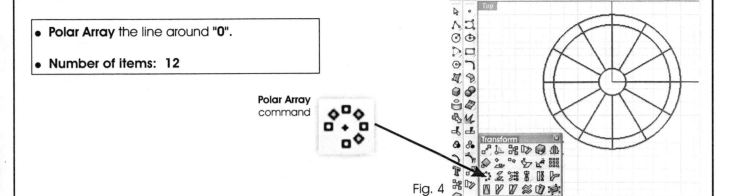

Fig. 4

165

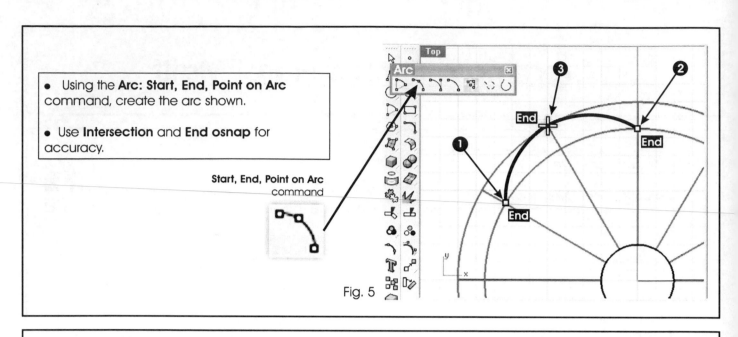

- Using the **Arc: Start, End, Point on Arc** command, create the arc shown.

- Use **Intersection** and **End osnap** for accuracy.

Start, End, Point on Arc command

Fig. 5

- toggle on the **Record History** option on the status bar at the bottom of the workspace.

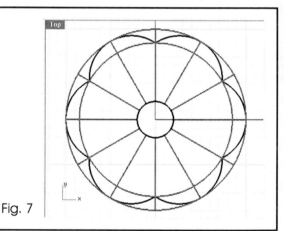

Snap   Ortho   Planar   **Osnap**   **Record History**

Fig. 6

- **Polar Array** the new arc around **0** 6 times as shown.

Fig. 7

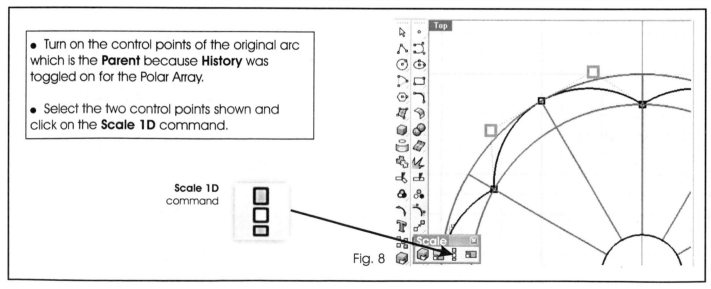

- Turn on the control points of the original arc which is the **Parent** because **History** was toggled on for the Polar Array.

- Select the two control points shown and click on the **Scale 1D** command.

Scale 1D command

Fig. 8

- **Origin point** prompt: snap to the middle point of the arc and click to set the locationt.

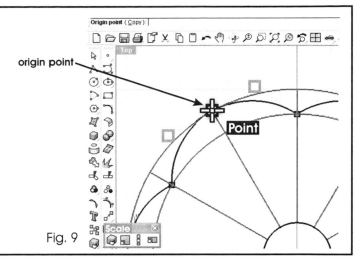

Fig. 9

- **Scale factor or first reference point** prompt: click on one of the selected points as shown.

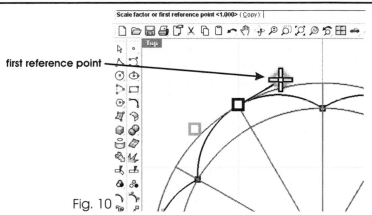

Fig. 10

- **Second reference point** prompt: Draw the cursor outward and note that you are constrained in the direction in which the cursor can move.
- Draw the cursor outward until you like the shape of the preview of the arc.
- Click to set location.

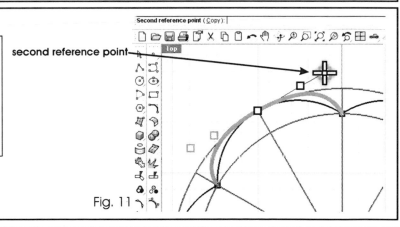

Fig. 11

- Note that after the **Parent** arc is edited, History has updated the rest of the arcs.

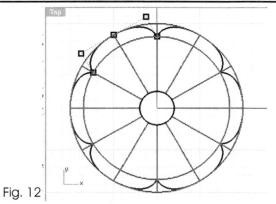

Fig. 12

- Turn off the **reference geometry** layer.

- Create a new line that connects the upper quad of the small inner circle to the end point of the two arcs at the top as shown.

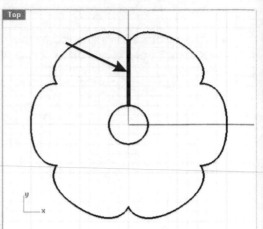

Fig. 13

- **Rebuild** the parent arc to a point count of **7**.

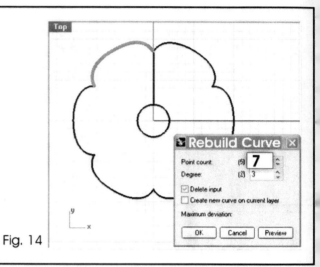

Fig. 14

Rebuild Curve

Point count: (5) **7**
Degree: (3) 3

☑ Delete input
☐ Create new curve on current layer

Maximum deviation:

OK   Cancel   Preview

- **Rebuild** the line to a point count of **4**.

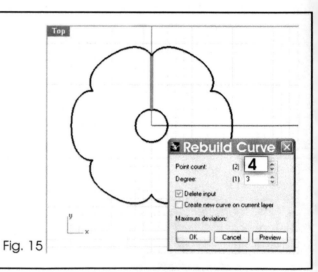

Fig. 15

Rebuild Curve

Point count: (2) **4**
Degree: (1) 3

☑ Delete input
☐ Create new curve on current layer

Maximum deviation:

OK   Cancel   Preview

- toggle on the **Record History** option on the status bar at the bottom of the workspace.

Snap   Ortho   Planar   **Osnap**   **Record History**

Fig. 16

168

- After toggling on the **Record History** option, **Polar Array** the new rebuilt straight line around "0".
  - **Number of items to array: 6**

- Turn control points on both parent objects - the original arc and the original straight line.

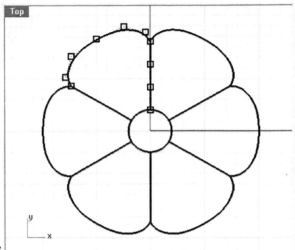

Fig. 17

- As you begin to point edit the objects, the "children" will continue to update.

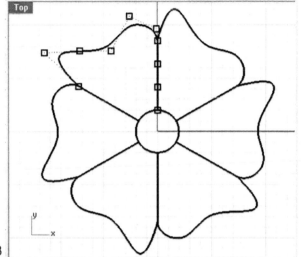

Fig. 18

- See the "children" of the line update when its control points are moved.

- Notice that moving the points on the straight line edited the line to a "degree 3" which results in smooth curves when it is point edited.

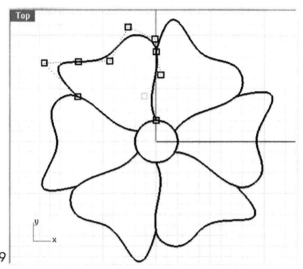

Fig. 19

169

Dimensions
Dimensions and Multiple Dimension Styles

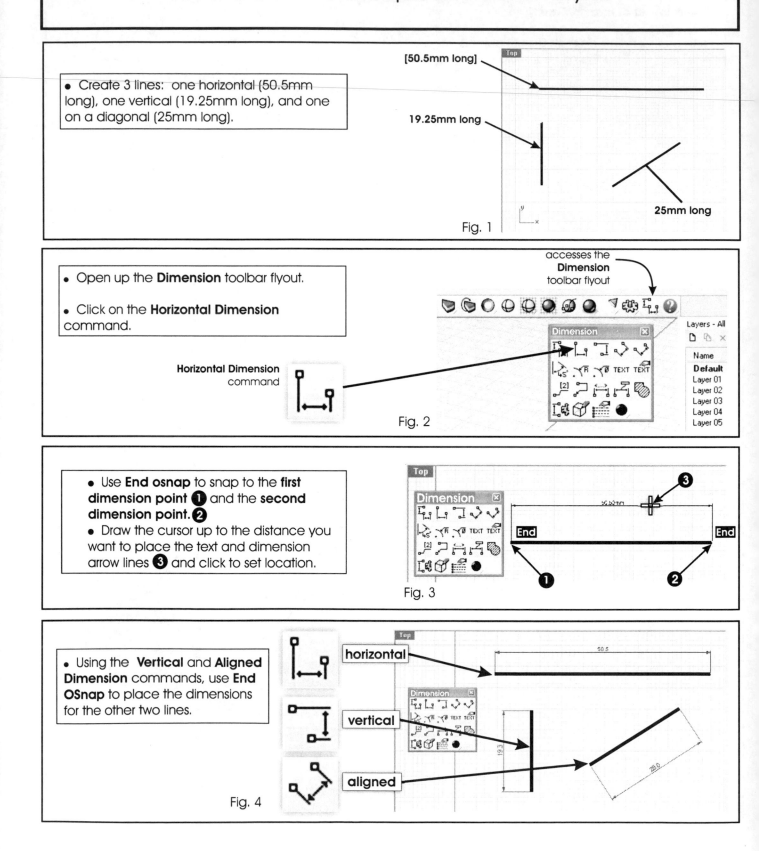

- Create 3 lines: one horizontal (50.5mm long), one vertical (19.25mm long), and one on a diagonal (25mm long).

[50.5mm long]

19.25mm long

25mm long

Fig. 1

- Open up the **Dimension** toolbar flyout.

- Click on the **Horizontal Dimension** command.

Horizontal Dimension command

accesses the **Dimension** toolbar flyout

Dimension

Layers - All

Name
Default
Layer 01
Layer 02
Layer 03
Layer 04
Layer 05

Fig. 2

- Use **End osnap** to snap to the **first dimension point ❶** and the **second dimension point. ❷**
- Draw the cursor up to the distance you want to place the text and dimension arrow lines ❸ and click to set location.

End

End

Fig. 3

- Using the **Vertical** and **Aligned Dimension** commands, use **End OSnap** to place the dimensions for the other two lines.

horizontal

vertical

aligned

Fig. 4

Diameter and Angle Dimensions

- On another part of the construction plane, create a 10mm diameter circle.

- Create a polyline as shown:
  - **Line segment ❶** : **30mm** long
  - **Line segment ❷** : **40mm** long at an angle of **30 degrees** - snapped to the left end point of segment 1.

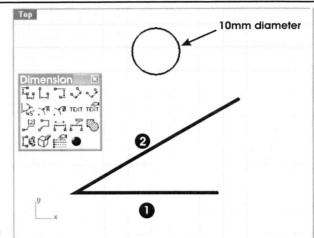

Fig. 5

- Click on the **Diameter Dimension** command.
  - **Select curve for diameter dimension** prompt: select the circle.

Diameter Dimension
command

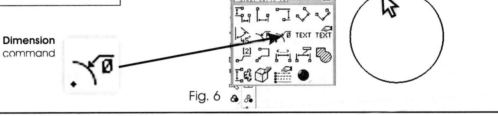

Fig. 6

- **Select dimension location** Prompt: As the cursor is drawn out, the diameter dimension will preview.
  - Click to set a location for the dimension text and leader arrow.

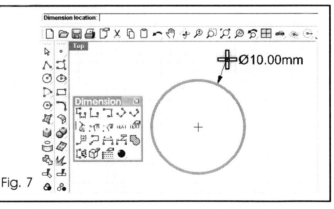

Fig. 7

- You can turn a dimension's **control points** on *[select the dimension and press **F10** as with other objects]* and control point edit to change the location and layout of the dimension text and the leader arrow.

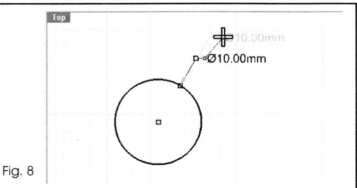

Fig. 8

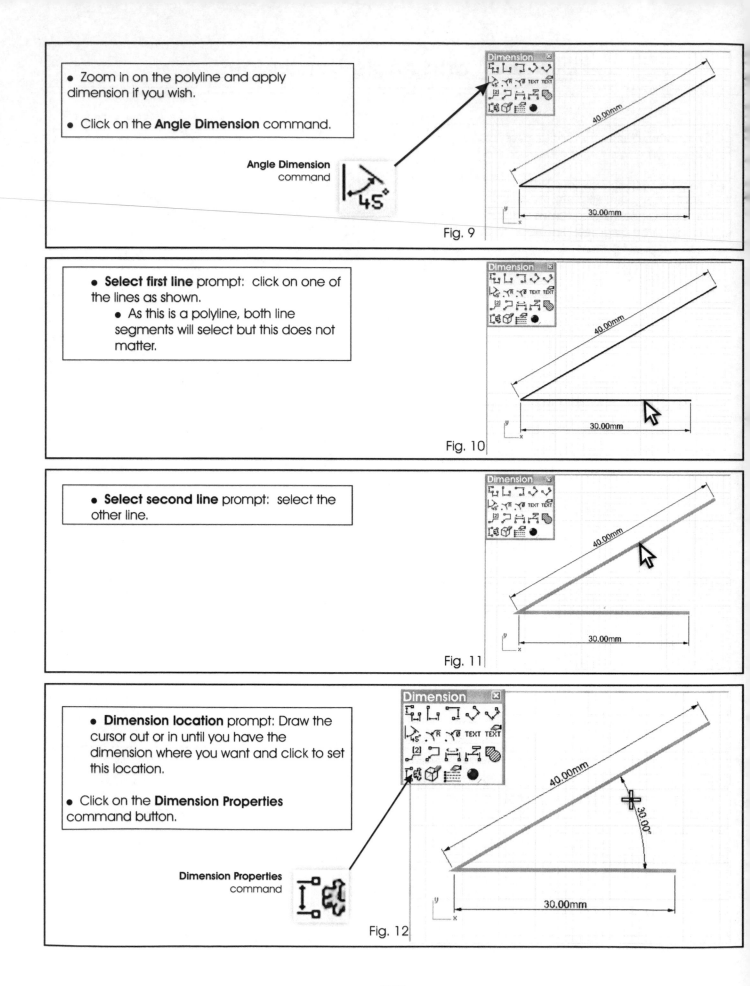

- Zoom in on the polyline and apply dimension if you wish.

- Click on the **Angle Dimension** command.

Angle Dimension
command

Fig. 9

- **Select first line** prompt: click on one of the lines as shown.
  - As this is a polyline, both line segments will select but this does not matter.

Fig. 10

- **Select second line** prompt: select the other line.

Fig. 11

- **Dimension location** prompt: Draw the cursor out or in until you have the dimension where you want and click to set this location.

- Click on the **Dimension Properties** command button.

Dimension Properties
command

Fig. 12

172

Creating Multiple Dimension Styles

- Access the **Dimensions** page and click on the **New** button.

- When the **Dimension Style Name** box appears, name in the new style, "**2mm**". Then left click on the OK button.

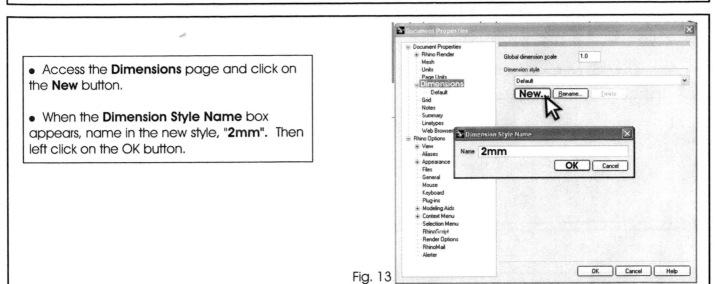

Fig. 13

- The **Dimension Style Name** dialog box will close.

- Notice that the name in the **Dimension Style** box has changed to the newly created style, **2mm**.

- The new dimension style is also now listed in the major drop-down list in the column on the left.

Fig. 14

- Highlight the **2mm** line in the dimensions drop-down and the properties box for that style will become active. Change the settings:

- **Font**
- **Number format**
- **Text Height**
- **Dimension Arrow Length**
- **Text Alignment**

- Click on the OK button to exit the dialog box.

Font Arial Black - **Arial Black**

Fractional

Text height 2.0

Length: 2.0 → Arrow

In dimension line

Fig. 15

173

- Create a new dimension style, **named 3mm.**

- Assign new values as shown.

- Be sure to click on the OK button to exit the dialog box.

Fig. 16

- Select the vertical dimension that you created and press the **F3** keyboard button. The **Properties** dialog box will appear.

Fig. 17

- From the drop-down list at the top of the dialog box, select **Dimension**.

- Notice how the options and configuration of the dialog box changes when you opt for dimension properties.

Fig. 18

- Select the **2mm** style option from the drop-down list at the bottom of the dialog box.

Fig. 19

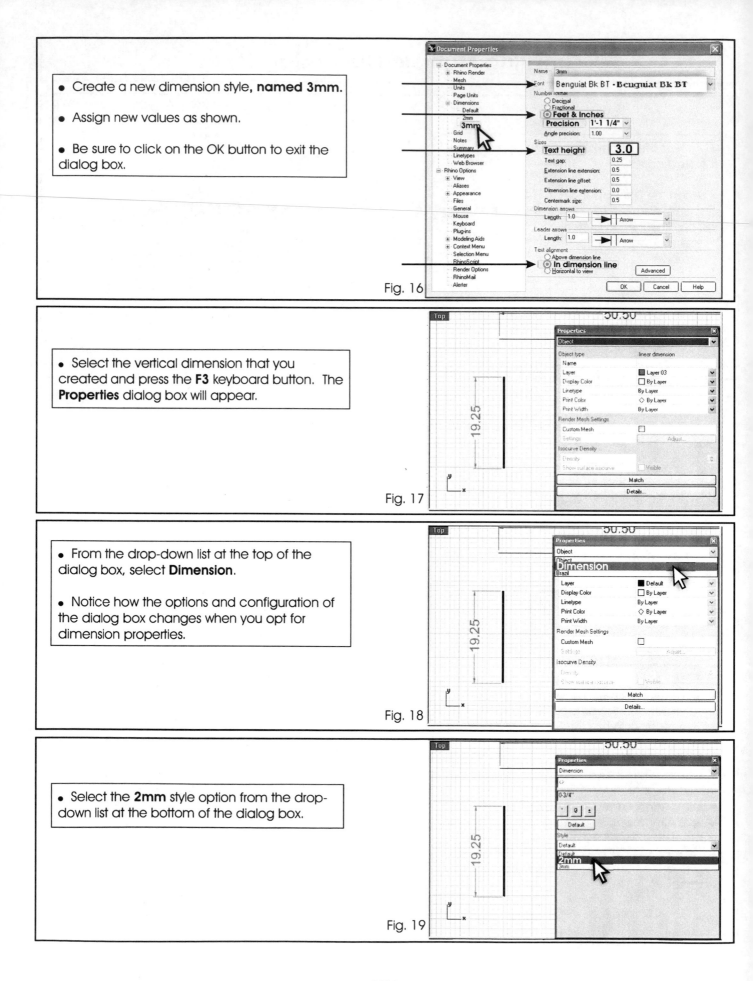

- Notice how as soon as you choose the style, the selected dimension changes to the new style.

- **Keep the Properties dialog box open for the next dimension change.**

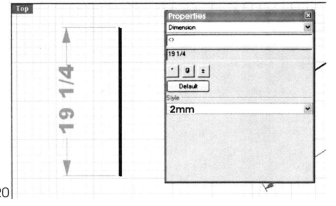

Fig. 20

- Now select the diagonal dimension and, in the **Style** drop-down list, choose the style named **3mm**. Notice the immediate change in the style of the selected dimension.

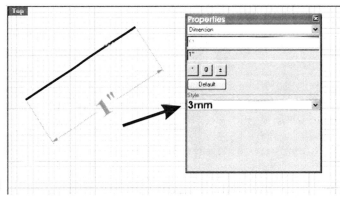

Fig. 21

- Access the **Dimension Properties** page again and adjust the **Text Height** and the **Font** as shown.

- Dimension style **3mm** will be the active dimension that will be adjusted here because that was the last one created.

- Click on the OK button to set the new characteristics of **3mm**.

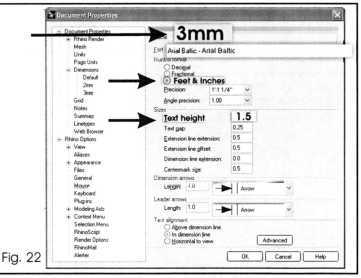

Fig. 22

- The diagonal dimension has taken on the new characteristics assigned to it.

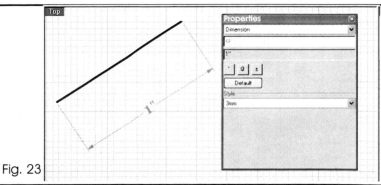

Fig. 23

175

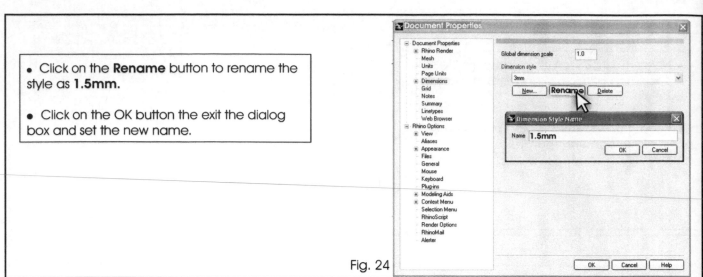

- Click on the **Rename** button to rename the style as **1.5mm**.

- Click on the OK button the exit the dialog box and set the new name.

Fig. 24

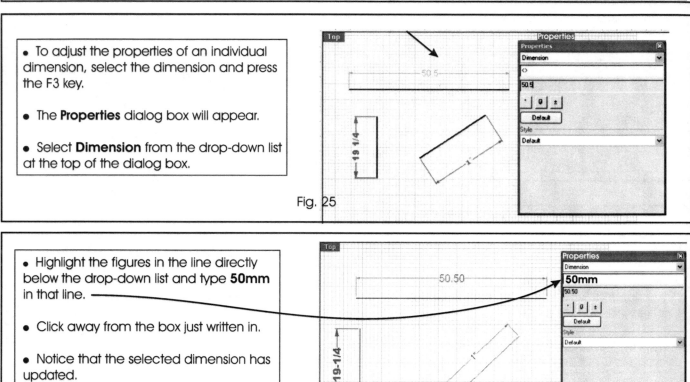

- To adjust the properties of an individual dimension, select the dimension and press the F3 key.

- The **Properties** dialog box will appear.

- Select **Dimension** from the drop-down list at the top of the dialog box.

Fig. 25

- Highlight the figures in the line directly below the drop-down list and type **50mm** in that line. ———

- Click away from the box just written in.

- Notice that the selected dimension has updated.

Fig. 26

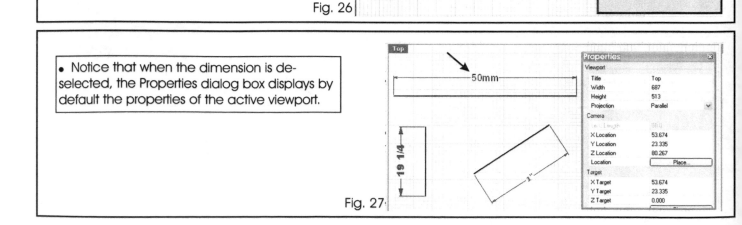

- Notice that when the dimension is de-selected, the Properties dialog box displays by default the properties of the active viewport.

Fig. 27

176

- In this example, a horizontal dimension has been applied to a 2mm line.

- Notice how the small dimension size has not allowed much room for the placement of the dimension text.

Fig. 28

- **Double-clicking on the dimension text** will open a little text editing box.

- Two < > symbols shown represent the text in its present form

Fig. 29

- Select the symbols and write your desired text as shown.

- Click away from the box to close it.

- The text will update.

Fig. 30

- Select the Dimension and press **F10** to turn on control points.

- Select the middle of the three points that are aligned across the text.

- Drag the selected point up (or to the side) to move it clear of the dimension lines.

Fig. 31

- The layout of the dimension has been edited with a more successful placement.

Fig. 32

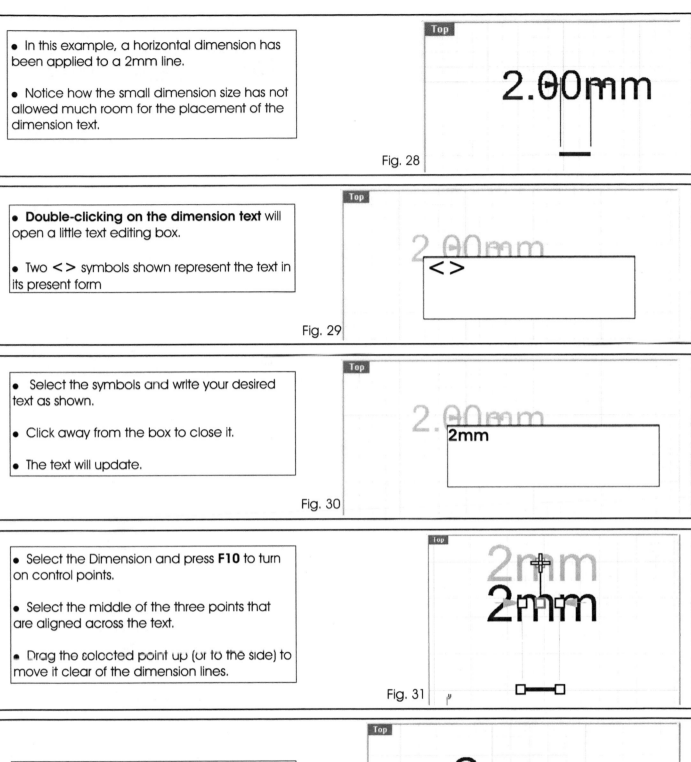

Print Width & Linetypes for 2D Drawings

• Open the Rhino file **PEARL RING.3dm**.

• **If you do not have this file saved from the previous tutorial, you can open another file that features linework.**

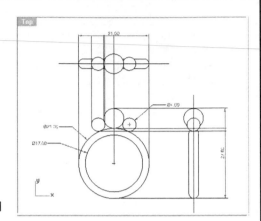

Fig. 1

• **Right click** on the line shown in the **Layers** dialog box.

• A context box will drop down, showing the categories that are presently showing in the **Layers** dialog box.

• If any of the listed items are not checked, click on them to check them as they need to be visible for this exercise.

Name	
TECH LINES	✔ Name
construction lines	✔ Current
dimensions	✔ On
Layer 03	✔ Lock
Layer 04	✔ Color
Layer 05	✔ Material
	✔ Material Library
	✔ Linetype
	✔ Print Color
	✔ Print Width

Fig. 2

• Pull out the borders of the **Layers** dialog box so that all columns are in view.

• Left click on the **Print Width** column on the **TECH LINES** layer line.

• The text in this column reads **default** but this will be changed.

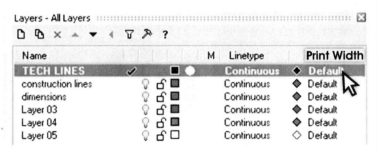

Fig. 3

178

- The **Select Print Width** dialog box will appear.

- Click on the desired print width. **In this example, the selected print width is .60mm.**

- Click on the OK button.

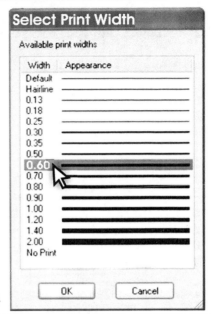

Fig. 4

- A quick check of the drawing shows no change in the appearance of the lines in the **TECH LINES** layer <u>but the lines will print to the assigned line width.</u>

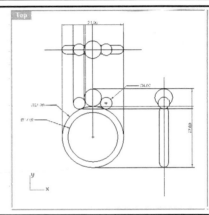

Fig. 5

- You can access the **Print** command to preview the Line width of the **TECH LINES** layer. The quickest way to do this is to press **ctrl+P** on your keyboard. You can also use the drop-down from **File** in the Menu Bar at the top of the screen.

- Notice that the black lines of the **TECH LINES** layer are thicker than the red lines on the **construction lines** layer.

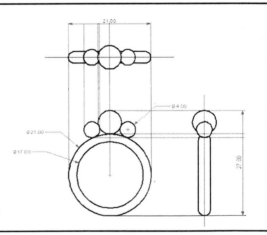

Fig. 6

- Left click in the **Linetype** column on the **construction lines** line.

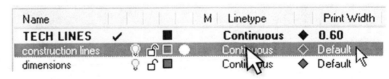

Fig. 7

Name					M	Linetype		Print Width
TECH LINES	✓		■			**Continuous**	♦	**0.60**
construction lines				●		Continuous	◇	Default
dimensions			■			Continuous	♦	Default

179

- The **Select Linetype** dialog box will appear.

- Highlight the **Dashed** option.

- Click on the OK button.

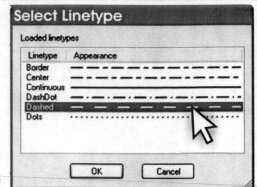

Fig. 8

- After clicking OK, if you do not see an updated linetype, type **"LinetypeDisplay"** in the **Command Line** and press "enter".

- Click on the **DisplayLinetypes=No** link to toggle on **DisplayLinetypes=Yes** and press "enter".

- Reverse this process to toggle Linetypes off.

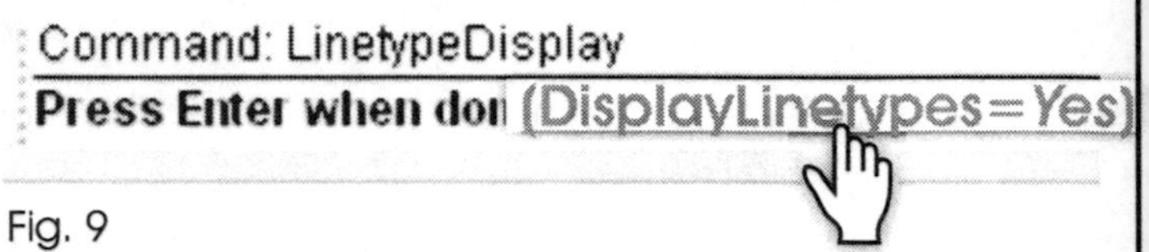

Command: LinetypeDisplay
Press Enter when do (DisplayLinetypes=Yes)

Fig. 9

- You will now see the new linetype for the **construction lines** layer.

- It is necessary to **create a new Linetype** that will fit better with drawings of smaller objects.

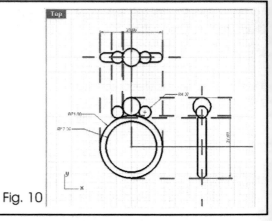

Fig. 10

- Click on the **Options** button to access the **Rhino Options** dialog box.

- Highlight the **Linetypes** category to access the **Linetypes** page..

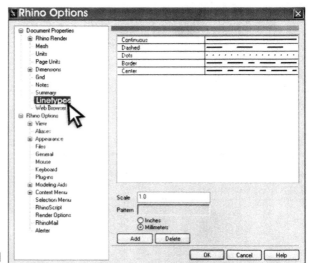

Fig. 11

180

- Click on the **Add** button.

- A new line appears in the list of Linetypes.

- Make sure that the millimeters option is selected.

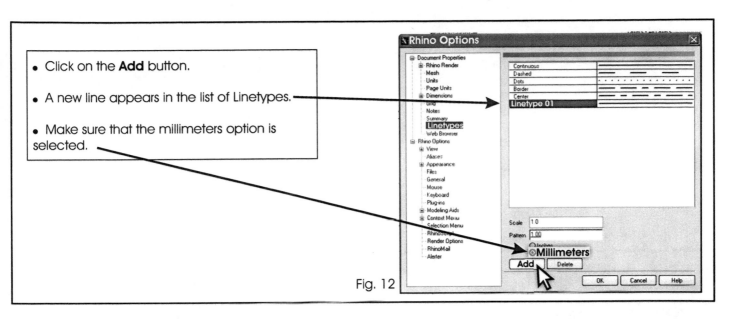

Fig. 12

- In the **Pattern** box, type "**1,1**".
  - **First number will be underlined:** sets the length of the dash.
  - **The number without an underline:** represents the length of the space between dashes.

- The new linetype will be previewed on the line entitled "Linetype 01" as shown.

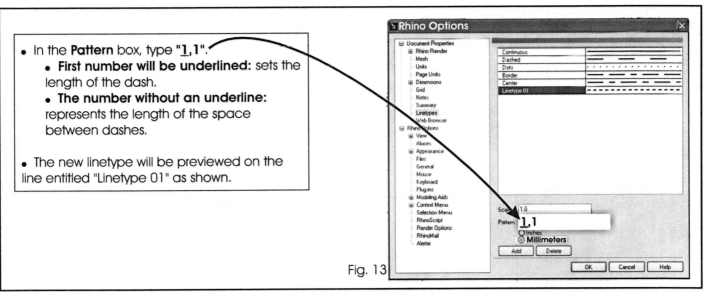

Fig. 13

- Click in the name box and rename the Linetype, **"Dashes - 1mm-1mm"**.

- This will give you a linetype with 1mm dashes separated by 1mm spaces.

- Click on the OK button.

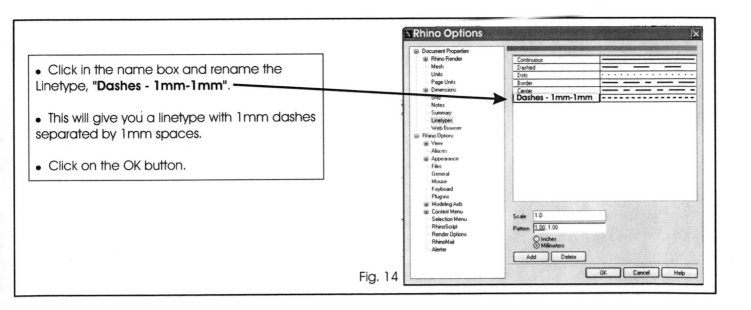

Fig. 14

- Click in the **Linetypes** column in the **construction lines** line once again.

- Notice that the new linetype now appears in the **Select Linetype** dialog box.

- Highlight the new Linetype, **Dashes 1mm-1mm** and click OK.

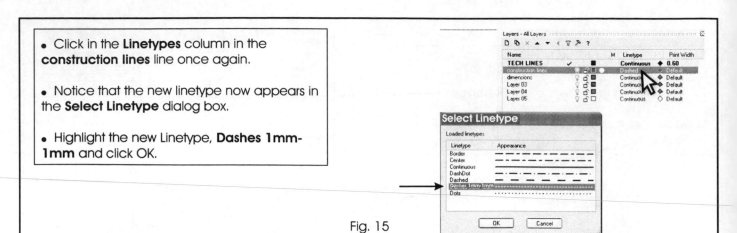

Fig. 15

- Notice that the dashed line is in better proportion to the scale of the drawing.

- Click on the **(DisplayLinetypes=NO)** option and press "enter".

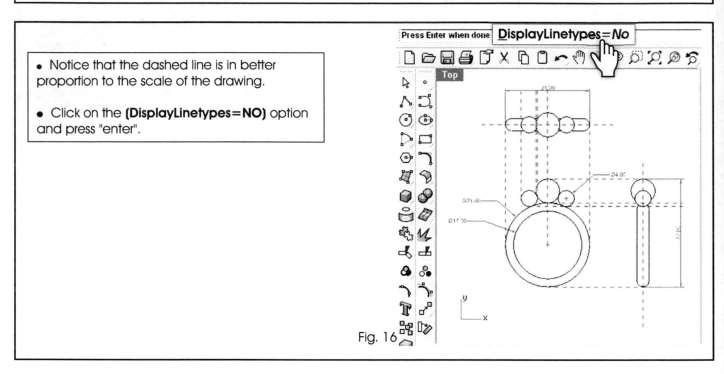

Fig. 16

- The Linetypes will not show.

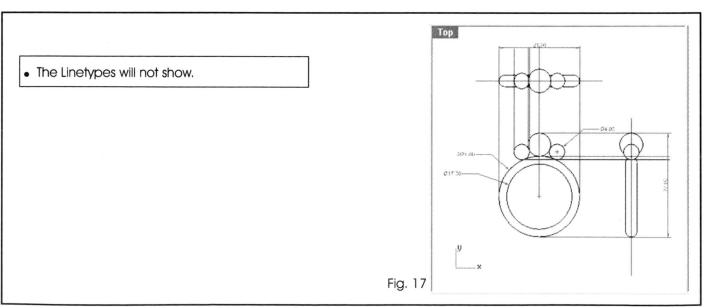

Fig. 17

Simple Printing of 2D Drawings

- Go to the File<print command from the **File** drop-down menu in the menu bar at the top of the Rhino screento get the **Print** dialog box.

Fig. 1

- Use the settings shown on the right for a basic printing in which the printed images will be to exact scale and centered on the page.

experiment with the scale drop-down list to scale the printed image up or down.

check this box to center the image on the printed page.

*Refer to the Rhino HELP menu for additional information on this command.
Keyword: Print

Fig. 2

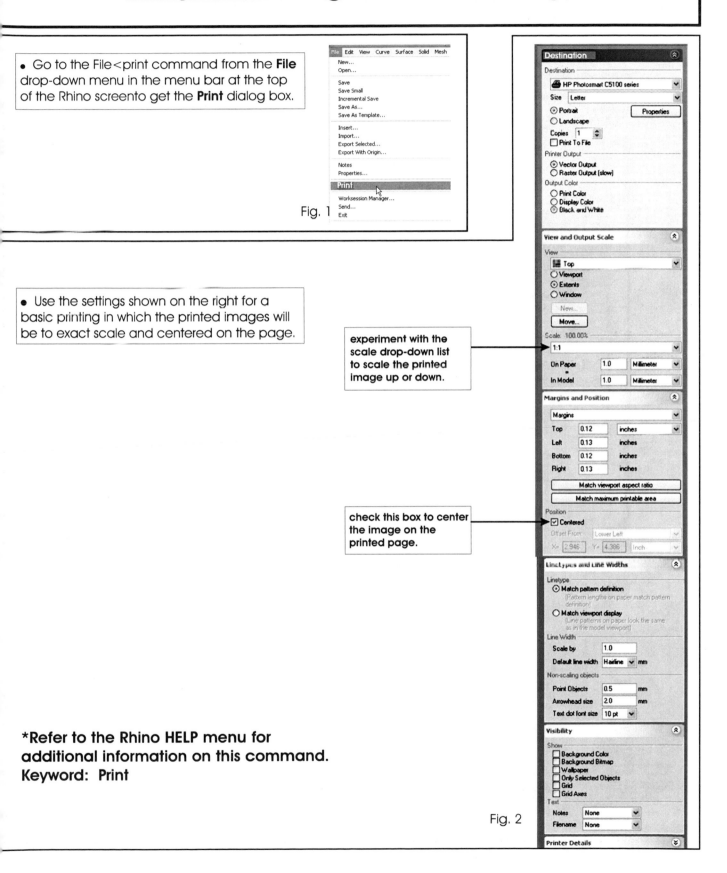

- The screen as it looks with the **Print Setup** dialog box which includes a print preview.

- After creating the settings, click the OK button to initiate the print.

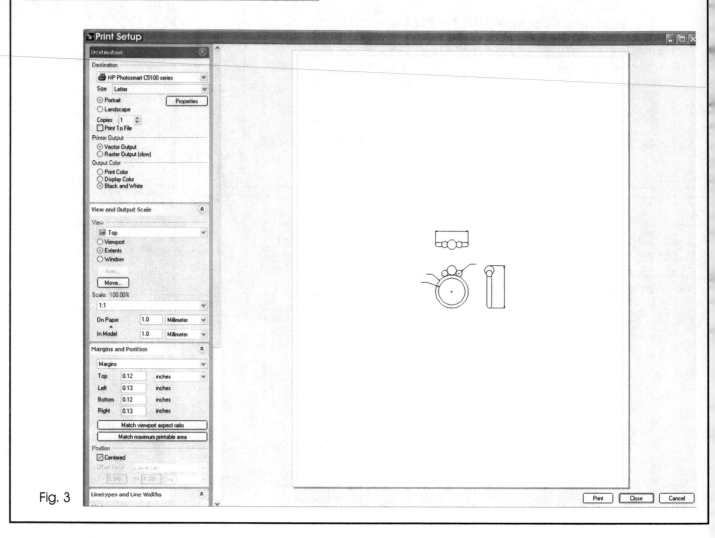

Fig. 3

184

Working in Different Viewports

A simple first experience with different viewports, construction planes and working in 3d space.

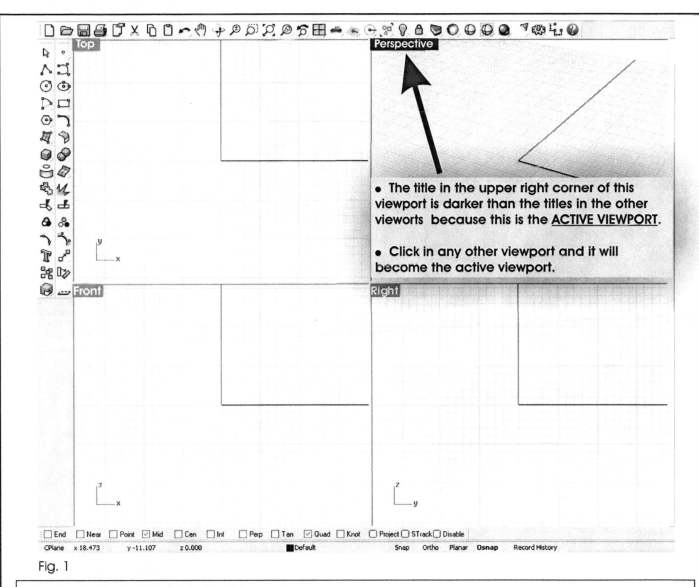

Top   Perspective

- The title in the upper right corner of this viewport is darker than the titles in the other vieworts because this is the <u>ACTIVE VIEWPORT</u>.

- Click in any other viewport and it will become the active viewport.

Front   Right

☐ End ☐ Near ☐ Point ☑ Mid ☐ Cen ☐ Int   ☐ Perp ☐ Tan ☑ Quad ☐ Knot ☐ Project ☐ STrack☐ Disable

CPlane   x 18.473   y -11.107   z 0.000   ■Default   Snap   Ortho   Planar   **Osnap**   Record History

Fig. 1

- the four default viewports in the Rhino workspace.

- Each viewport represents a different view of your work area and the object that you create.

- In addition to the different views, these viewports represent 3 separate construction planes - the TOP, FRONT, and RIGHT construction planes.

- The default perspective viewport uses the TOP construction plane, also known as "World TOP".

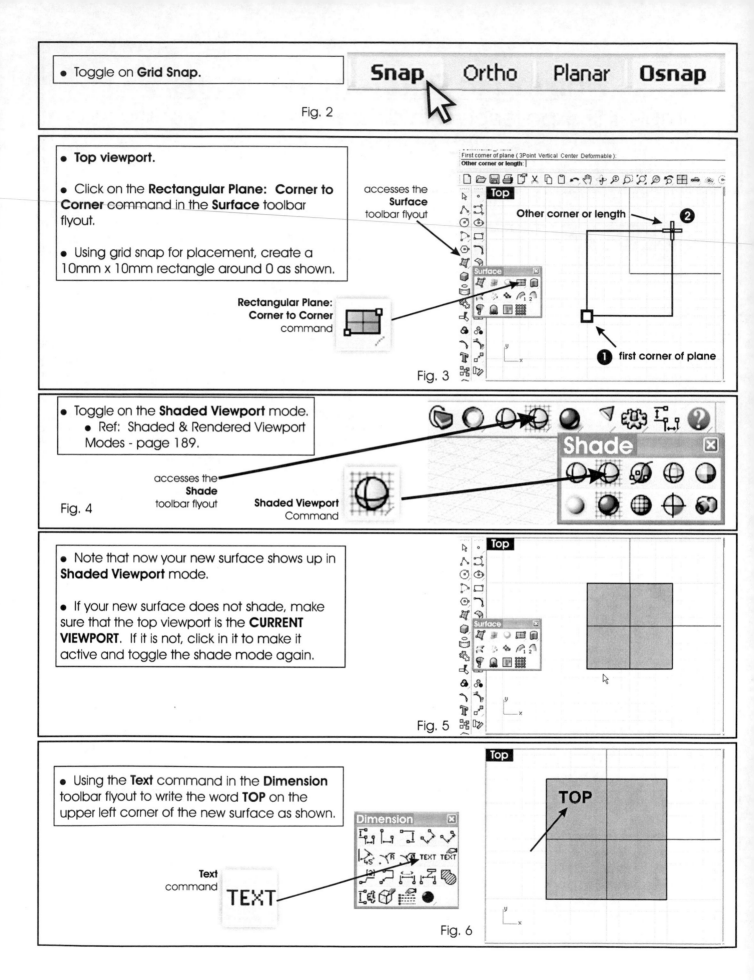

- Toggle on **Grid Snap**.

Snap   Ortho   Planar   Osnap

Fig. 2

- **Top viewport.**

- Click on the **Rectangular Plane: Corner to Corner** command in the **Surface** toolbar flyout.

- Using grid snap for placement, create a 10mm x 10mm rectangle around 0 as shown.

accesses the **Surface** toolbar flyout

Rectangular Plane: Corner to Corner command

First corner of plane (3Point Vertical Center Deformable):
Other corner or length:

Top

Other corner or length → ②

① first corner of plane

Fig. 3

- Toggle on the **Shaded Viewport** mode.
  - Ref: Shaded & Rendered Viewport Modes - page 189.

accesses the **Shade** toolbar flyout

Shaded Viewport Command

Shade

Fig. 4

- Note that now your new surface shows up in **Shaded Viewport** mode.

- If your new surface does not shade, make sure that the top viewport is the **CURRENT VIEWPORT**. If it is not, click in it to make it active and toggle the shade mode again.

Top

Surface

Fig. 5

- Using the **Text** command in the **Dimension** toolbar flyout to write the word **TOP** on the upper left corner of the new surface as shown.

Text command

TEXT

Dimension

TEXT TEXT

Top

TOP

Fig. 6

- Repeat the process in both the **Front viewport** and the **Right viewport** in turn.

- Note that you can not see the other surfaces because, as you are viewing them from the top or side, they are just look like straight lines.

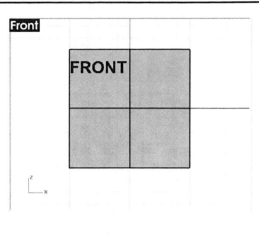

Fig. 7

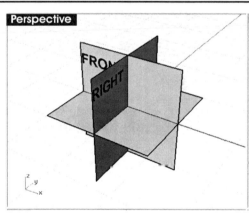

Fig. 8

- Now switch to the **Perspective viewport** and you will see what you have created by working in three different views and construction planes.

- Rotate the view to see the different labels that you have created for the three surfaces.

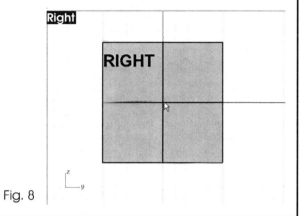

Fig. 9

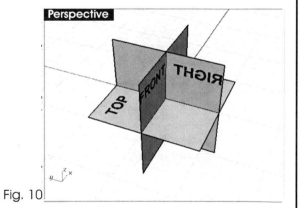

Fig. 10

Navigating in 3D Space
Panning, Zooming and Rotating Your View

- Panning your view in the Perspective Viewport is slightly different than in the "parallel" view orientations of the top, front, right, and left viewports.

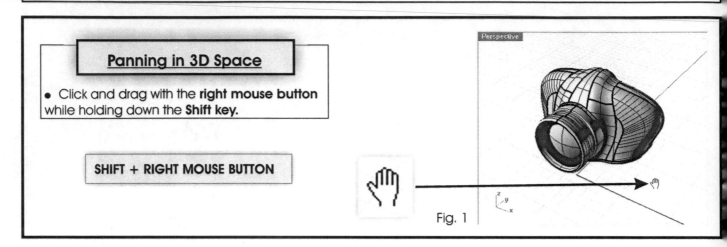

Panning in 3D Space

- Click and drag with the **right mouse button** while holding down the **Shift key.**

SHIFT + RIGHT MOUSE BUTTON

Fig. 1

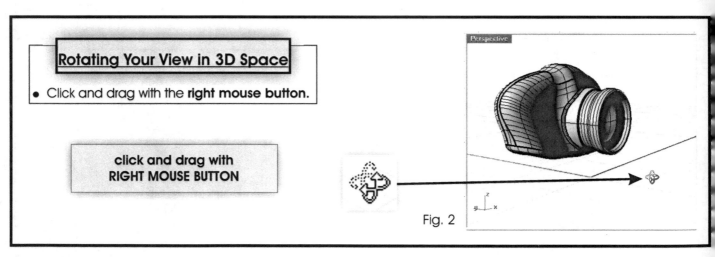

Rotating Your View in 3D Space

- Click and drag with the **right mouse button.**

click and drag with RIGHT MOUSE BUTTON

Fig. 2

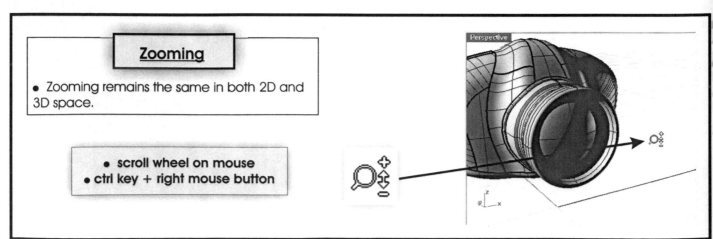

Zooming

- Zooming remains the same in both 2D and 3D space.

- scroll wheel on mouse
- ctrl key + right mouse button

Shaded & Rendered Viewport Modes
For Visibility While Modeling

- **Front viewport.**

- Click on the **Torus** command in the **Solid** toolbar flyout.
  - **Center of torus** prompt: type **"0"** and press "enter".

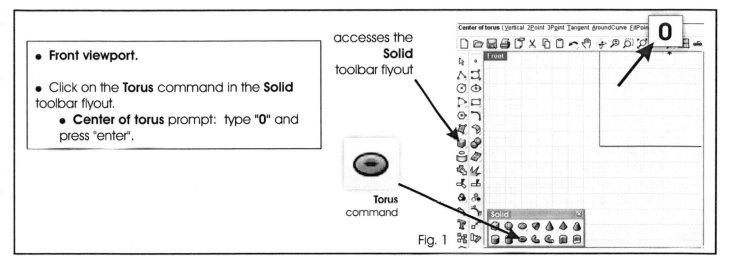

accesses the **Solid** toolbar flyout

Torus command

Fig. 1

- **Radius** prompt: type **"20"** and press "enter"

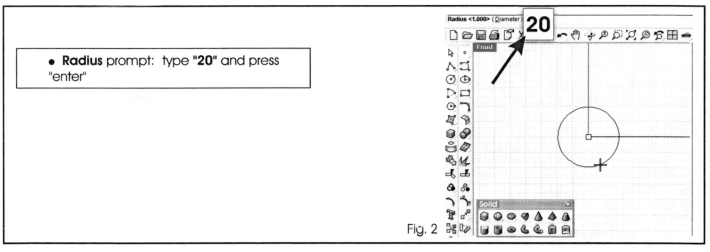

Fig. 2

- **Second radius** prompt: type **"10"** and press "enter".

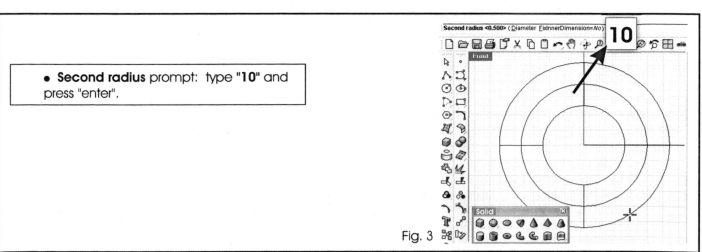

Fig. 3

- **Top perspective** viewport.

- This illustration shows the newly created torus object in perspective view.

- It is shown in **Wireframe mode** which is the basic display mode in Rhino.

- The thin lines that run across the surface in two different directions are the isocurves. The isocurves indicate the shape and geometry of surfaces.

- The thicker lines indicate the location of the surface edges and seams.

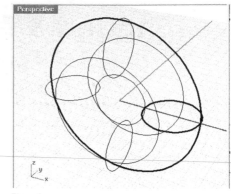

Fig. 4

- Open the **Shade** toolbar flyout as shown.

accesses the
Shade toolbar flyout

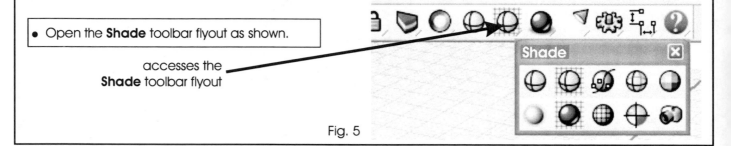

Fig. 5

- Click on the **Shade** command button.

- By default, in the current viewport, the grid will turn off and the surface of the torus will take on a solid, shaded appearance as shown.

- Note that you can toggle different options on and off in the **Command Line.**

Shade
command

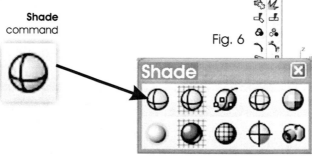

Fig. 6

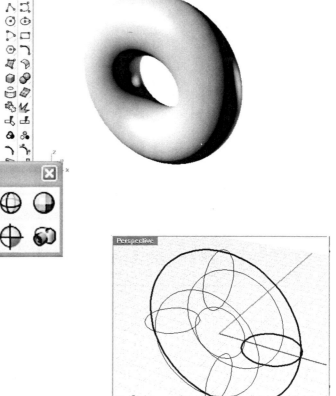

- Click somewhere in the viewport to return to the previous viewport mode which, in this case, is wireframe mode.

- This **Shade** command is good for quickly checking out how your model looks in a mode different from the one in which you are working.

Fig. 7

- In order to keep your images shaded while you work on them, click on the **Shaded Viewport** command as shown.

- By default, in the current viewport, your piece will be shaded and also show surface geometry as shown. The grid will also show.

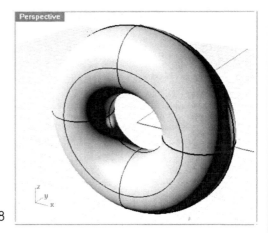

Perspective

Fig. 8

Shaded Viewport
mode

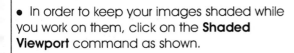

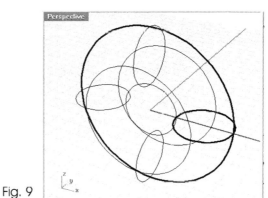

- **Right click** on this same button to get back to **wireframe mode**.

Perspective

Fig. 9

- Click on the **X-Ray Viewport** button.

- The objects in the current viewport will appear transparent with the geometry on the far side showing with equal value as the geometry on the near side.

Perspective

Fig. 10

X-Ray Viewport
command

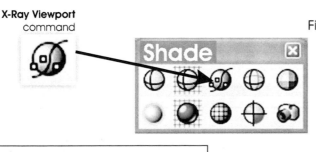

- **Right click** on the **Shaded Viewport** button to return to **Wireframe mode** in the current viewport.

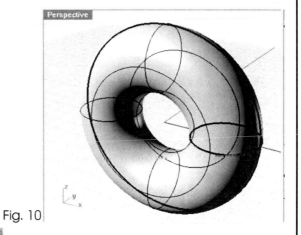

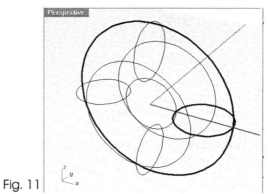

Perspective

Fig. 11

- Click on the **Ghosted Viewport** button.

- The object in the current viewport takes on the look of a transparent object in which the lines on the far side of the piece look paler than those on the near side.

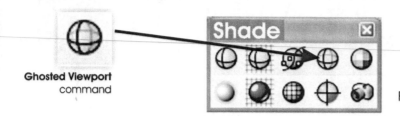

Ghosted Viewport
command

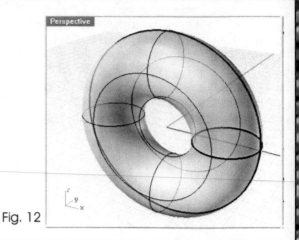

Fig. 12

- Click on the **Rendered Viewport** button.

- The object will take on a shaded aspect and all surface geometry will be hidden. By default, the shaded color will be the color of the object's assigned layer.

Rendered Viewport
command

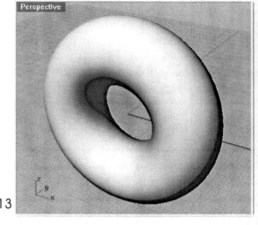

Fig. 13

- *Note: To change the properties of these viewport modes, refer the chapter in this book, Settings for Rhino Options.*

- Click on the **Toggle Flat Shade Mode** button.

- Any display mode that uses shading will not be smoothed but will show the individual render mesh faces.

- *For beginners, it is advised to leave this mode toggled off.*

Fig. 14

- If you click on the **Toggle Shade Selected Mode** button, every object you select will be shaded until it is de-selected.

- *For beginners, it is advised to leave this mode toggled off to avoid confusion.*

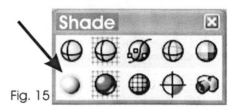

Fig. 15

- Either right click or left click on the button shown to get eigher Render Mesh Settings of Advanced Display settings.

- Refer to the chapers, **_Settings for Rhino Options_** and **_Render Mesh Options_** for more information.

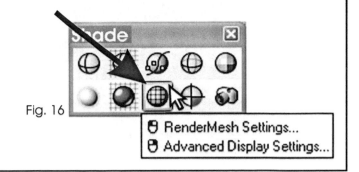

Fig. 16

- Left clicking on the button shown will enable you to set **separate** display options for selected objects.

- These assigned display options will remain the same, even when the current viewport display options are changed.

- Right click to disable this custom display arrangement.

- **_For beginners, it is advised to use this command with caution to avoid confusion._**

Fig. 17

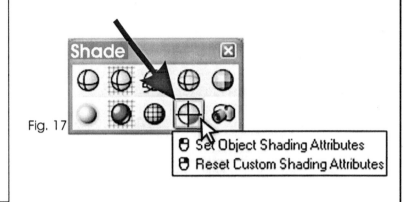

- Either left click or right click on the button shown to create a bitmap image of the current viewport, either to the clipboard (to be pasted into another file or email) or to a bitmap file in a location of your choosing.

Fig. 18

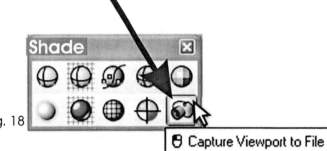

Render Mesh Options

- **Perspective viewport.**

- Click on the **Rectangular Plane: Corner to Corner** command in the **Surface** toolbar flyout.
    - **First corner of plane** prompt: click where you want the lower left corner to be.
    - **Other corner or length,** type **"30"** and press "enter".
        - This determines the plane's dimension along the X axis.
    - **Width,** type **"20"** and press "enter".
        - This determines the plane's dimension along the Y axis.

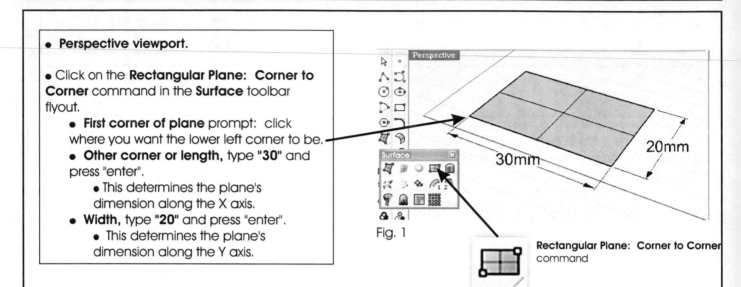

Fig. 1

Rectangular Plane: Corner to Corner
command

- **Rebuild** the surface so that it will have **16 control points in both U and V directions** as shown.

- Turn on control points.

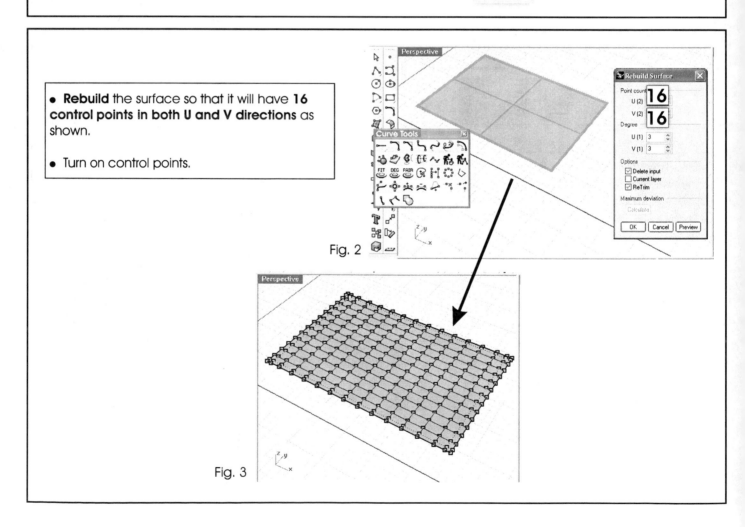

Fig. 2

Fig. 3

194

- Select a number of control points somewhere in the middle of the surface as shown.

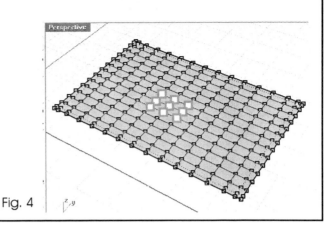

Fig. 4

- Hold down the Ctrl key and drag the selected control points upward as shown.

- Notice that, although the wireframe lines show the new shape given to the surface, the rendering mesh has not updated sufficiently and thus looks angular as shown.

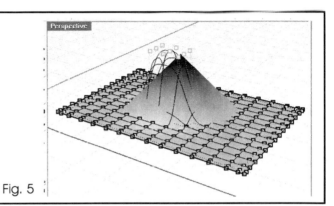

Fig. 5

- To clear and reset the render mesh, you can type the command **"ClearAllMeshes"** in the command line.

- Another way to do this is to access the command button for this purpose, access the **Utilities** toolbar flyout and click on the **Clear All Meshes** button as shown.

Fig. 6

Comman **ClearAllMeshes**

- **ClearAllMeshes** is a useful command when closing large files as the size of the file is dramatically reduced. which is a strong consideration when sending or storing your work.

Fig. 7

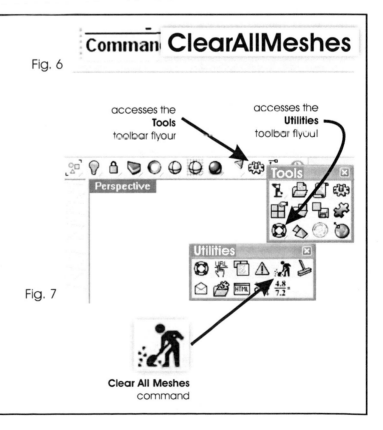

accesses the **Tools** toolbar flyour

accesses the **Utilities** toolbar flyoul

Clear All Meshes command

- Click on the **Shaded Viewport** command and note how the render mesh has updated.

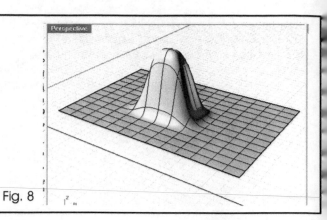

Fig. 8

- If Clear All Meshes does not work, you can try the adjust the mesh settings to **Smooth and Slower** or to **Custom** as shown in the **Rhino Options** dialog box.

- **Custom** is a more advanced category that deals with specific mesh values and characteristics. It is suggested that you avoid this option if you are just starting to learn Rhino or are unfamiliar with the concepts and techniques of mesh settings.

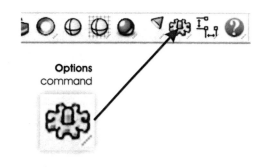

Options
command

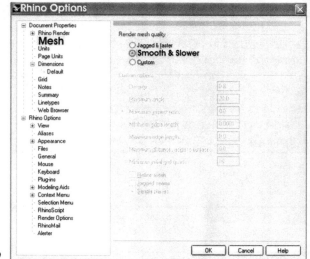

Fig. 9

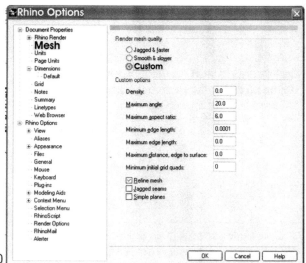

Fig. 10

Viewport Navigation
Using the SetView Command to set a Perspective view

- **Front viewport.**

- Click on the **Torus** command in the **Solid** toolbar flyout.
  - **Center of torus** prompt: type "**0**" and press "enter".
  - **Radius** prompt: type "**4**" and press "enter".
  - **Second Radius** prompt: type "**2**" and press "enter".

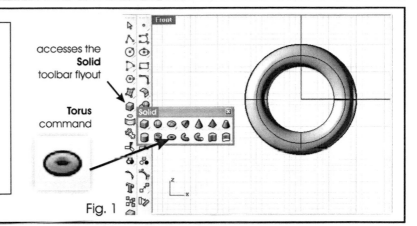

accesses the
Solid
toolbar flyout

Torus
command

Fig. 1

- Access the **Set View** toolbar flyout as shown.

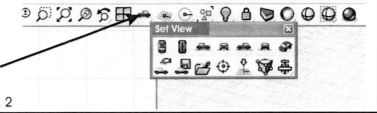

accesses the
Set View
toolbar flyout

Fig. 2

- Click the **Top View** command button ❶ and then the **Perspective View** command button. ❷

- Notice that because it was created in the **Front Viewport**, the torus object has been constructed so that it sits vertically on the **top construction plan** which is the default construction plane for the **Perspective Viewport.**

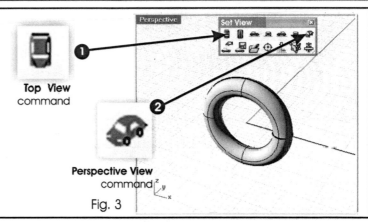

Top View
command

Perspective View
command

Fig. 3

- Click the **Front View** button as shown.

- Notice that you have now switched back to the **Front Viewport.**

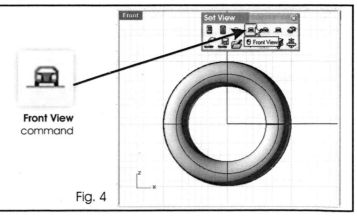

Front View
command

Fig. 4

- Now click on the **Perspective View** button.

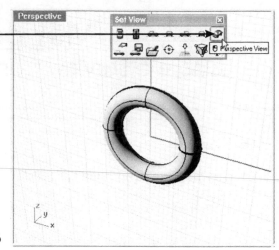

- See the viewport change to a **Perspective Viewport**.

- Notice, however, that the _**construction plane is still the front construction plane.**_

- This is a good way to see the viewport in perspective even though one needs to work with the **front construction plane** active.

Fig. 5

- Getting back to the default **Perspective Viewport** that features the **Top construction plane**, involves a couple of steps more.

- **Step 1:** Click on the **Top View** button as shown. See that the torus is now viewed from the top.

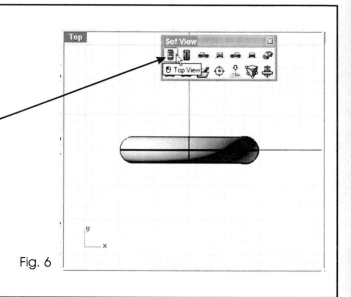

Fig. 6

- **Step 2:** Now click on the **Perspective View** button and the **Perspective Viewport** is restored with the **top construction plane**.

- You are now looking at the torus in _World Top Perspective_.

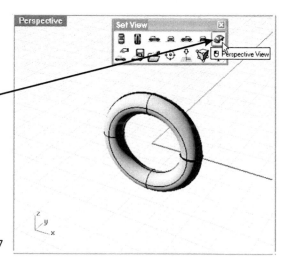

Fig. 7

Creating a "Perspective View - TOP" Button Command

- This exercise will now show you how to adjust the settings on the **Perspective View** command button in order to streamline getting back to the default Top perspective view.

- Open the **Set View** toolbar flyout.

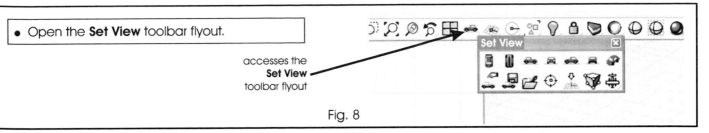

accesses the
Set View
toolbar flyout

Fig. 8

- Hover the cursor over the **Perspective View** button and notice the tooltip.

- Notice that there is no command for the **right mouse button.**

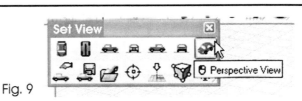

Fig. 9

- **RIGHT CLICK** on the **Perspective View** button **WHILE HOLDING DOWN THE SHIFT KEY.** Notice that the tooltip changes when the shift key is held down.
    - The word **"Edit"** refers to the option of editing the toolbar button.

- The **Edit Toolbar Button** dialog box will open.

- Notice the "**Perspective View**" tooltip in the left tooltip text box.

- Notice the command script in the **Left Mouse Button Command** text box.

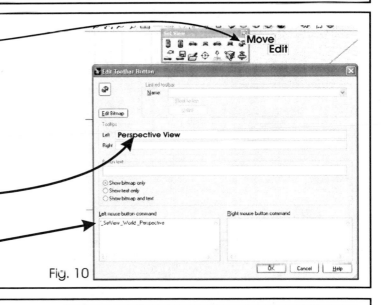

Fig. 10

- In the **Right Mouse Button Command** text box, write the following script: _note that after each word there is a space - indicated here by the arrows._

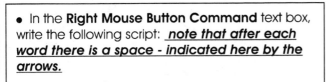

space   space space

- The script: **!_SetView _World _Top _Perspective**

- Add a tooltip in the **Right** box as shown.

- Click OK.

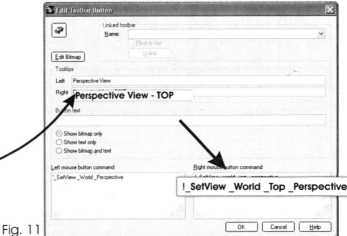

Fig. 11

- New when you hover the cursor over the button, note the newly created tooltip for the **right mouse button**.

Fig. 12

Testing the New Button Command

- To test the new button command, click on the **Front View** command as shown.

- Your viewport will be changed to the **Front** view.

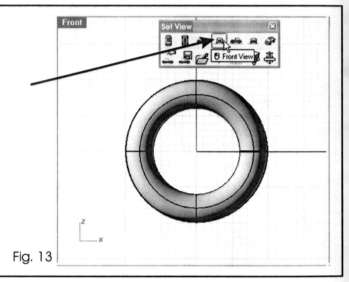

Fig. 13

- **RIGHT CLICK** on the newly created **Perspective View-TOP** command as shown.

- You are now switched to a **Perspective Viewport** that features the **top construction plane**.

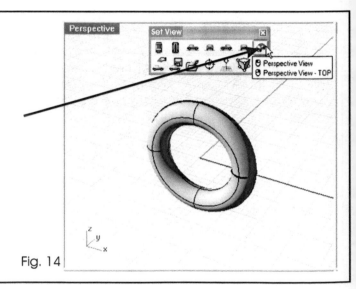

Fig. 14

200

Control Point Editing
Torus - Sculpting with Control Points

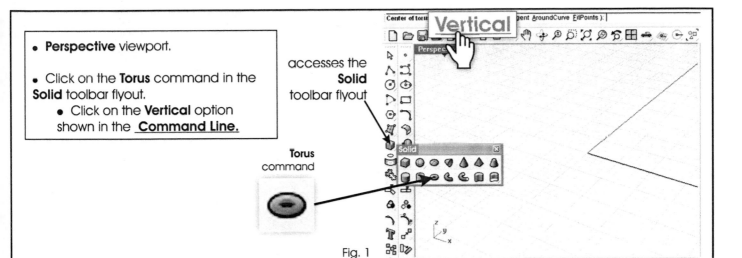

- **Perspective** viewport.

- Click on the **Torus** command in the **Solid** toolbar flyout.
  - Click on the **Vertical** option shown in the **Command Line.**

accesses the **Solid** toolbar flyout

Torus command

Fig. 1

- **Center of Torus** prompt: type **"0"** and "enter".
- **Diameter** prompt: type **"19"** and press "enter".
  - Make sure to click on diameter option in the **Command line!)**
- Click to set location using **ORTHO**.
- **Second Radius** prompt: type **"1.5"** and press "enter".

- Toggle on **Shade** mode for better visibility.

- The resulting object is a **Torus,** made up of a single closed surface. Because this is a single surface, it is possible to turn on and edit it's control points.

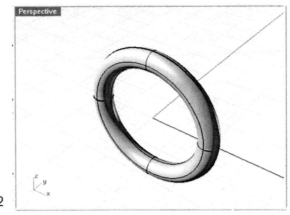

Fig. 2

- Select the Torus and press the **F10** key on your keyboard to turn on it's control points.

- Notice the squared up look to the control point configuration.

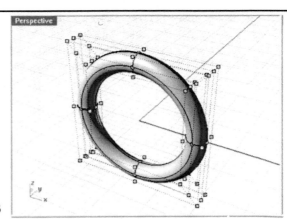

Fig. 3

- Window select the two groups of control points in the upper corners of the torus as shown.

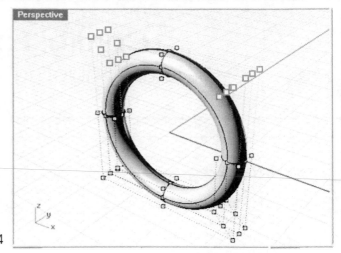

Fig. 4

- Drag the points straight back a short distance.

- Notice the sharpness of the bends in the shape. Notice the kink on the left side where the surface seam is located.

- In order to get a more even and graceful bending, it is necessary to **Rebuild** this surface.

- Press **Undo** to get back to the original shape of the torus.

- Press the **Esc** key a couple of times to turn off control points.

Fig. 5

- Click on the **Analyze Direction** button and select the Torus shape when prompted in the **Command Line.**

- Note that, in addition to a series of white arrows that appear all over the surface of the Torus, the cursor itself turns into a small icon with two arrows, indicating the **U Direction (red arrow)** and the **V Direction (green arrow)** of the surface.

- All surfaces have these two directions.

Analyze Direction
command

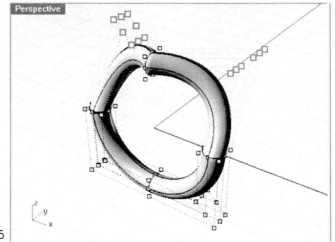

Green arrow indicates the "V" direction

Red arrow indicates the "U" direction

Fig. 6

- Select the torus and click on the **Rebuild Surface** button on the **Surface Tools** toolbar flyout.
  - The **Rebuild Surface** dialog box will appear.
    - The numbers in parentheses to the left that can not be changed show the existing point count of the torus in both the U and the V directions.
  - Enter the values shown in the white boxes to the right.
  - Click OK to exit the dialog box.

Rebuild Surface command

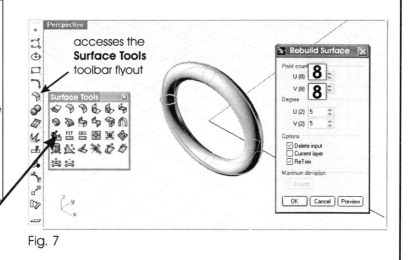

Fig. 7

- Notice that the torus has more isocurves (lines on the surface) now in both the U and the V direction.

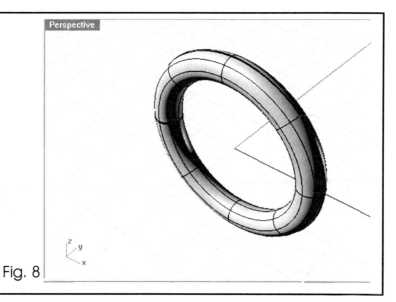

Fig. 8

- Select the torus and press the **F10** key to turn on the control points.

- Notice how the distribution of the control points has changed.

- Moving control points now will result in more even and graceful control point editing.

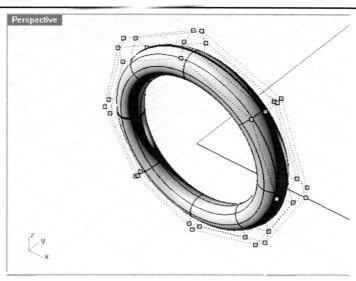

Fig. 9

- **Front Viewport.**

- Window select the two control points at the top of the torus as shown.

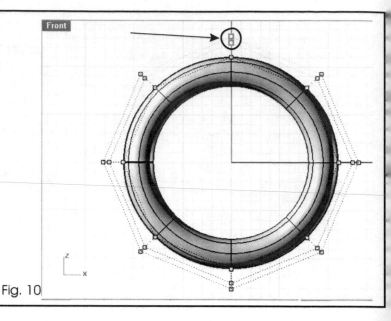

Fig. 10

- Zoom in on the selected points and turn the view slightly and you will see that you have actually selected three control points.

- In the **Front** view, the bottom two points are directly in line with each other and look like only two points.

- Window selection insures that all three points will be selected.

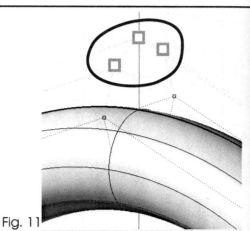

Fig. 11

- Click on the **Front View** button on the **Set View** toolbar flyout to get back to the **Front View.**

accesses the **Set View** toolbar flyout

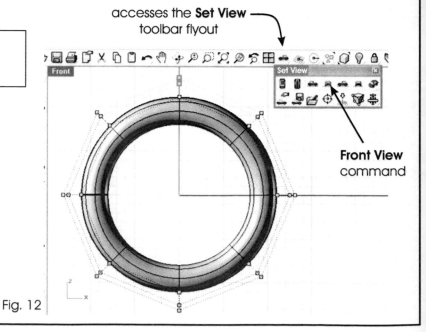

Front View command

Fig. 12

- Drag the selected control points so that the surface assumes the approximate shape shown.

- Use **ortho mode** to ensure that you are dragging straight up.

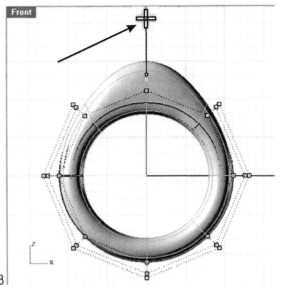

Fig. 13

- Carefully window select the two sets of three control points on either side of the previously selected and moved control points.

- Use the Shift key when making these 2 window selections.

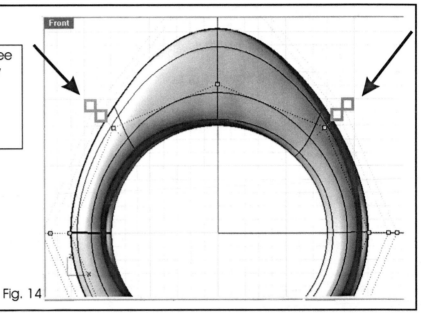

Fig. 14

- Drag the selected points so that they line up slightly below the previously moved points. Try to achieve the approximate shape of the surface shown.

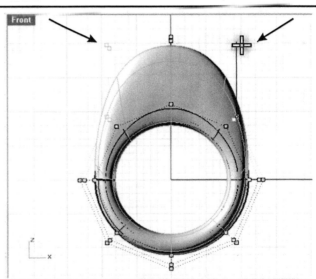

Fig. 15

- Window select all three sets of points shown.

- Drag these points down together so that the shape of the surface looks as shown.

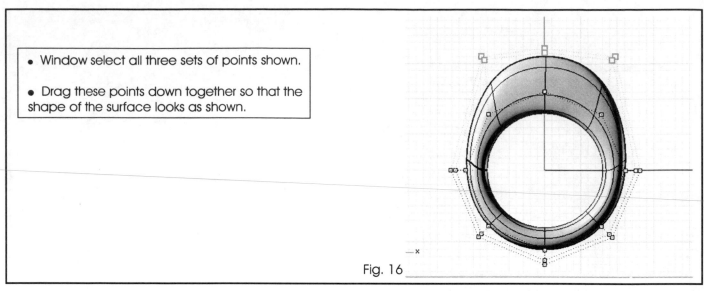

Fig. 16

- **Right Viewport.**

- Zoom in on the top of the torus.

- Window select the two groups of points shown.

- Use **Scale 1-D** to widen the upper part of the torus as shown.

Scale 1-D command

accesses the **Scale** toolbar flyout

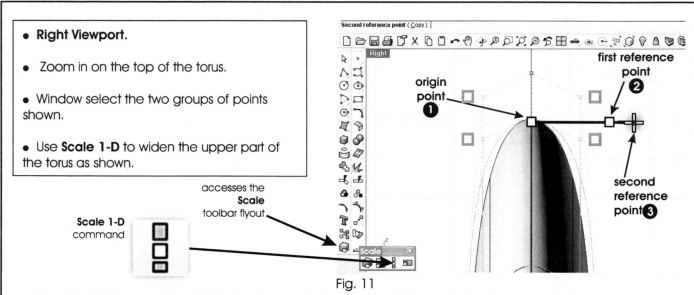

Second reference point (Copy):

origin point ❶

first reference point ❷

second reference point ❸

Fig. 11

- The top of the torus has been widened.

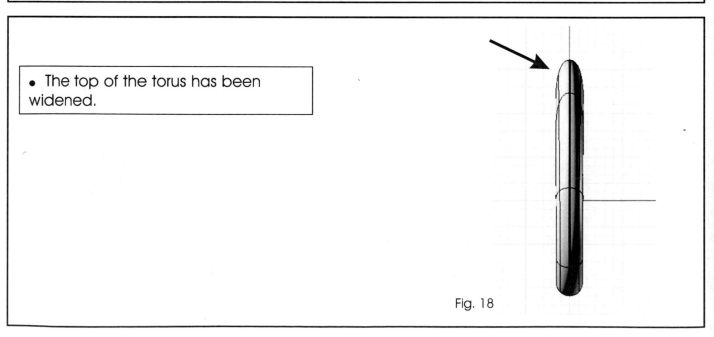

Fig. 18

- **Perspective TOP Viewport.**

- Window select the top three control points and drag them back along the Y Axis.

- Use **Ortho** for symmetry.

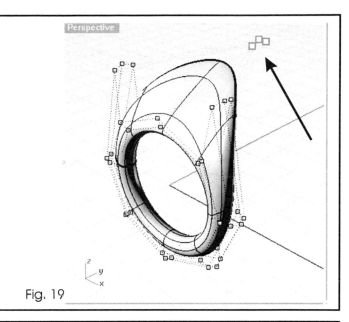

Fig. 19

- Carefully window select the groups of 3 points on either side of the points just moved.

- Either drag or use the **Move** command to move these points in direction shown.

- Use **Ortho** mode if you want the resulting shape to be symmetrical.

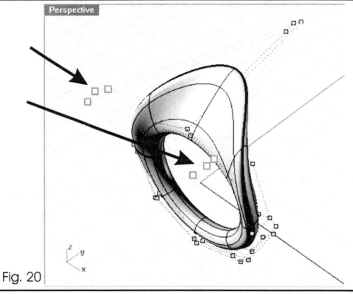

Fig. 20

- Keeping these points selected, use the **Move** command, this time selecting the **Vertical** option offered in the **Command Line** to move these points vertically up from the construction plane.

- Use this **Vertical** option again to move other points, if desired.

- Continue to manipulate control points if desired to achieve more variations on the shape of this closed surface.

- **Note:** You can also **Drag vertically** if you keep the **Ctrl button depressed.**

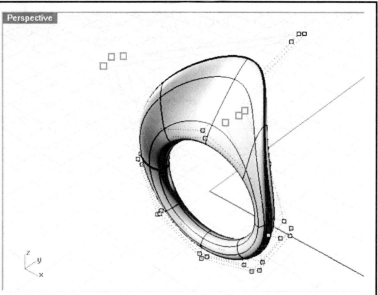

Fig. 21

Loft Command
Simple Sculpted Rings

- Create layers as shown.

- **Construction lines** layer current.

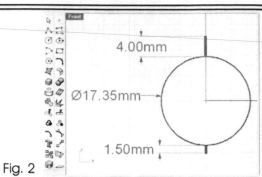

Name			
RING		💡 🔓 ■	
construction lines ✓		■	

Fig. 1

- **Front Viewport.**

- Create a **Circle** around 0 with a diameter of **17.35mm**.

- Create two perpendicular lines from the top and the bottom quad points as shown.
  - **top line:** 4mm.
  - **bottom line:** 1.5mm.

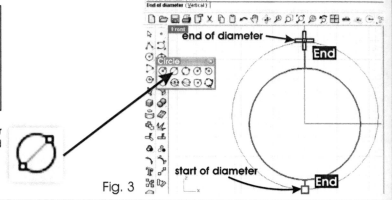

4.00mm

Ø17.35mm

1.50mm

Fig. 2

- Use the **Circle: Diameter** command to create a circle with a diameter that starts and ends at the end points of the two lines created in Fig. 2.

- **End osnap** is essential for this step.

Circle: Diameter command

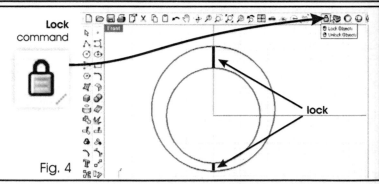

Start of diameter (Vertical)
End of diameter (Vertical)

end of diameter
End

start of diameter
End

Fig. 3

- Use the **Lock** command to lock the two straight lines as shown.

- You will not need them again and you want to avoid selecting them in subsequent steps of this exercise.

- You can also choose to **Hide** them.

Lock command

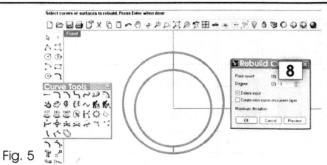

lock

Fig. 4

- **Rebuild** the two circles as shown.

- **Point count: 8**.

Select curves or surfaces to rebuild. Press Enter when done

Curve Tools

Rebuild C   8
Point count
Degree
Delete input
Create new curve on current layer
Maximum deviation
OK   Cancel   Preview

Fig. 5

- Turn control points on for the **outer circle** and move on to create a similar shape to the one shown.

- Then, turn control points on for the inner circle and select the upper left point as shown so that the upper left control points of both inner and outer curves are now selected.

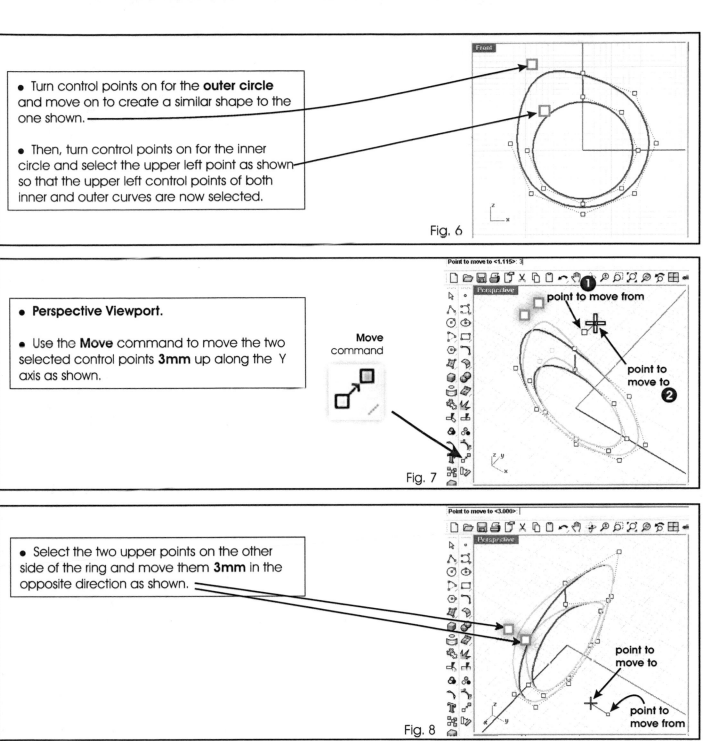

Fig. 6

- **Perspective Viewport.**

- Use the **Move** command to move the two selected control points **3mm** up along the Y axis as shown.

Move command

Fig. 7

- Select the two upper points on the other side of the ring and move them **3mm** in the opposite direction as shown.

Fig. 8

- Rotate your view to see the graceful "S" curve that the top of the ring has assumed as a result of moving control points in opposing directions.

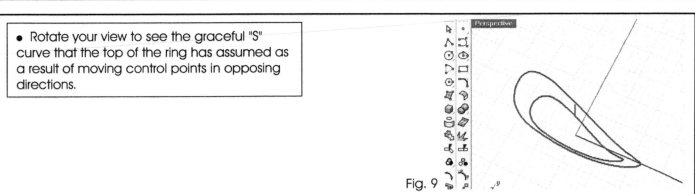

Fig. 9

209

- **Rebuild** both curves as shown.
  - **Point count: 9**

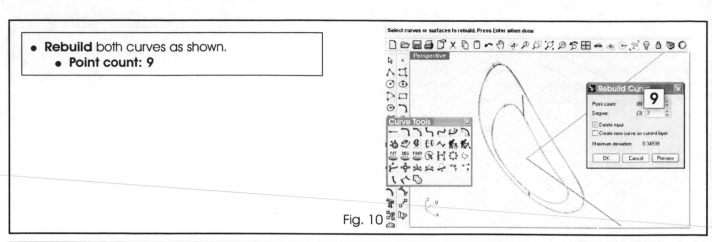

Fig. 10

- **Copy** both curves 3mm up along the Y axis.

- Then, copy downward along the Y axis the same distance.

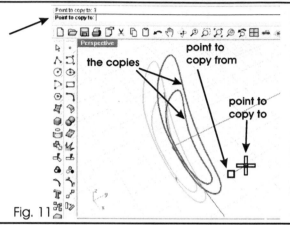

the copies

point to copy from

point to copy to

Fig. 11

- **Hide** the original curves.

- The two copies are now placed at equal 3mm distances on either side of the X axis as shown.

- Switch to the **RING** layer.

Fig. 12

- Click on the **Loft** command in the **Surface** toolbar flyout.
  - **Select curves to loft** prompt: select all of the curves in the order shown and press "enter".

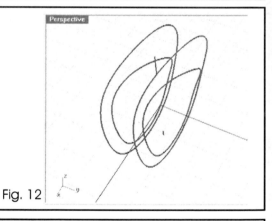

accesses the **Surface** toolbar flyout

Loft command

Fig. 13

210

- **Adjust curve seams** prompt: click and drag seam points to line up with each other at the lower **Quad** points of the bottoms of the curves as shown.
- Press "enter" when finished adjusting all 4 seams.

Note: if a finished loft does not appear at the end of this command, repeat the loft command, omitting this step.

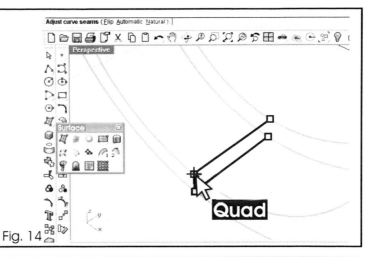

Fig. 14

- When the **Loft Options** dialog box appears, set values and options as shown.
  - Click to engage the **closed loft** option.
  - When finished selecting options, click OK.

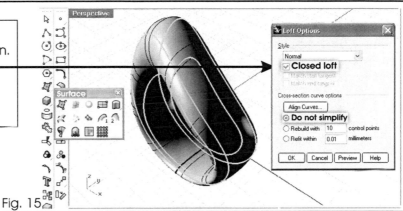

Fig. 15

- The finished loft.

- A graceful intuitive shape has been created from the loft curves.

- Because the loft curves did not have any kinks in them, this is a single closed surface so control points can be turned on for sculpting

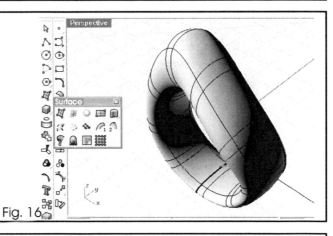

Fig. 16

- **Drag** the ring shape you have just created back so that the original loft curves are standing clear as shown.

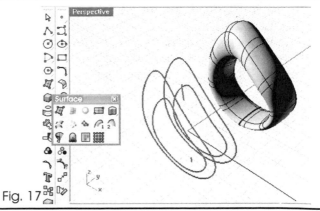

Fig. 17

- **Loft** the curves again, this time using the **rebuild** setting shown in the **Loft Options** dialog box.
    - Accept the default number of 10 control points.

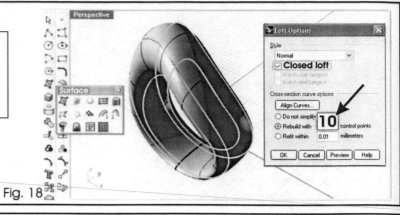

Fig. 18

- Compare the two ring shapes created so far.

- The new shape with the rebuilt surface pulls away from the original loft curves and has a slightly more graceful shape.

- Also, notice the regularity of the surface isocurves in contrast to the first shape.

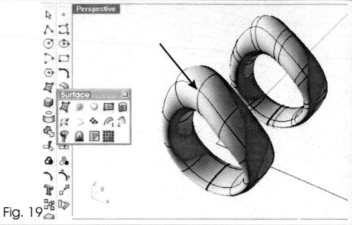

Fig. 19

- Drag both ring shapes up and away from the original loft curves as shown.

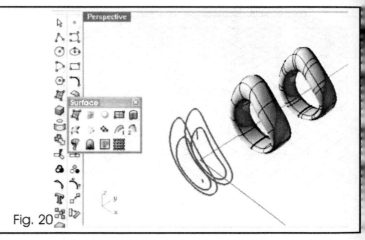

Fig. 20

- **Loft** the curves again and change the settings in the **Loft Options** dialog box by *not checking the closed loft option*.

- This will be an **open loft** as shown in the loft preview.

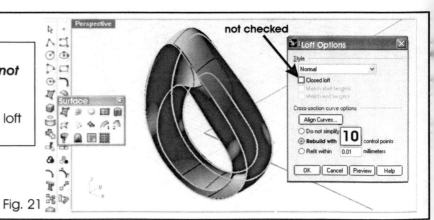

Fig. 21

- The finished open loft.

- Because the rebuild setting was enabled for this loft, notice that the edges of the loft surface are not exactly along the original loft curves.

- Turn off the **construction lines** layer.

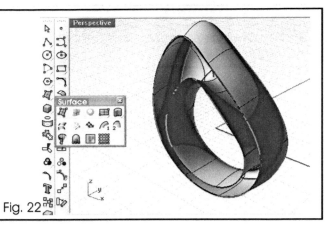

Fig. 22

- Click on the **Loft** command and, when prompted to **Select curves to loft**, select the two surfaces edges as shown.

- Click OK.

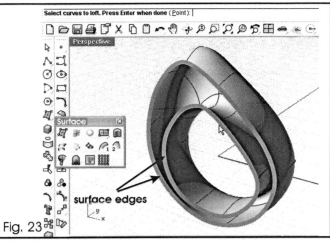

surface edges

Fig. 23

- Select the **Tight** option in the drop-down list at the top of the **Loft Options** dialog box as shown.

- This is to ensure that the selected lines will be followed accurately in the loft. This is essential to achieve a completely closed polysurface in the next step.

- Click OK.

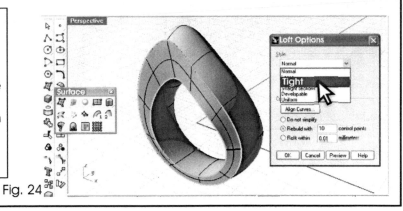

Fig. 24

- The resulting surface is a straight section because only two loft lines were selected.

- **Join** the two surfaces together as shown.

- Note that, because there is one straight section, *that this is a closed polysurface, not a closed surface* like the previous two ring shapes created.

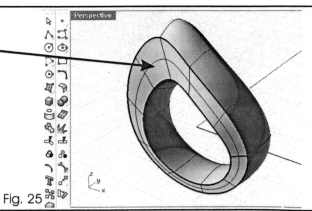

Fig. 25

- Drag all of the rings back and clear of the original loft curves.

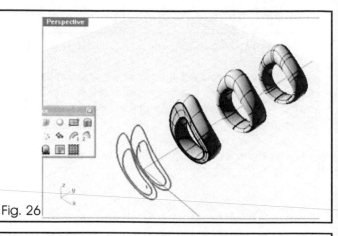

Fig. 26

- Call up the **Loft** command and select the **Straight sections** option in the drop-down list as shown.

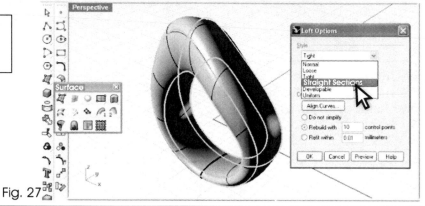

Fig. 27

- Enable the **Closed loft** option.

- Notice from the preview image how different this ring shape is from the others.

- Click OK.

- **Join** all the surfaces together.

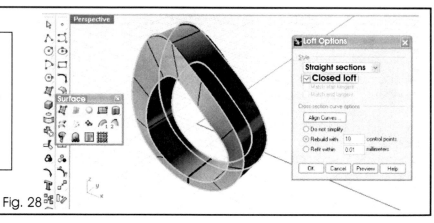

Fig. 28

- Compare all the rings.

- Select all 4 rings and try to turn on control points by pressing the **F10** key on your keyboard.

- Notice that control points can only turned on with two of the rings. These are single surfaces.

- This is because the other two shapes are both polysurfaces and you can not turn control points on with polysurfaces.

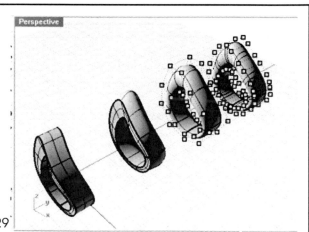

Fig. 29

- Click on the **Record History** button in the status bar at the bottom of the Rhino screen to toggle on the **History** function for the following **Loft** command.

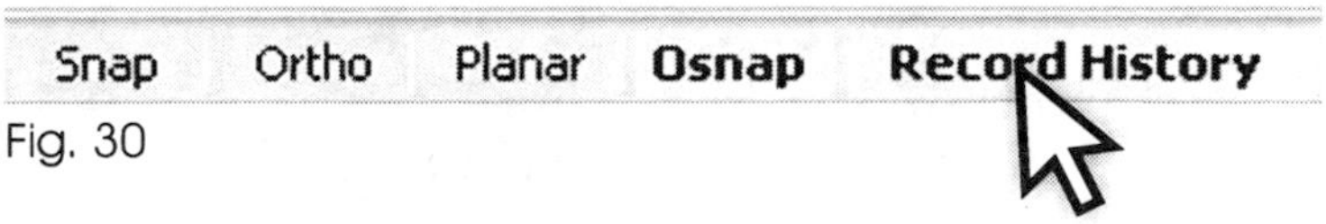

Snap   Ortho   Planar   **Osnap**   **Record History**

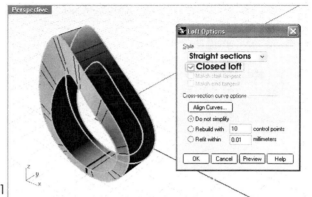
Fig. 30

- Select the 4 curves and click on the **Loft** command.
  - Use settings shown in the **Loft Options** dialog box.

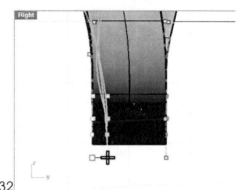
Fig. 31

- Select all 4 curves and turn on their control points.

- Select and drag some of the control points as shown.
  - In this example, in the **Right viewport** some points at the bottom of the ring are being dragged to the right as shown.

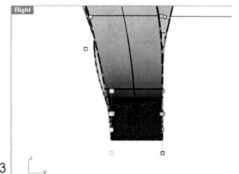
Fig. 32

- The shape of the ring has updated to the new shape of the **Parent** curves because **History** was enabled.

Fig. 33

- More control point editing of the parent curves has refined the shape of the bottom of the ring.

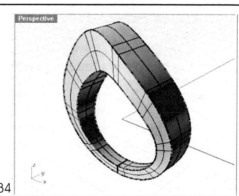
Fig. 34

Revolve Command - Ring Band
Creating a ring and using History to make variations

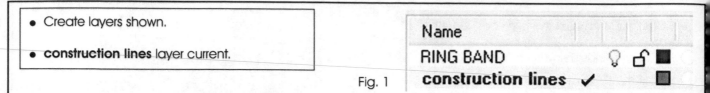

- Create layers shown.

- **construction lines** layer current.

Fig. 1

Name			
RING BAND	💡	🔓	⬛
construction lines ✓			⬜

- **Front Viewport.**

- Create a circle around **0** with a diameter of **17.35**.

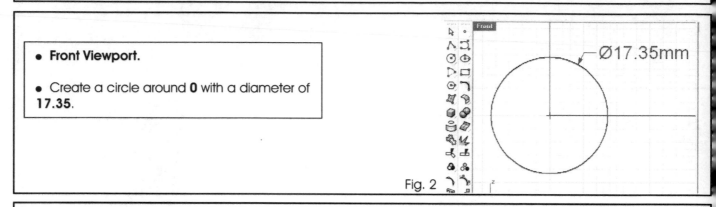

Ø17.35mm

Fig. 2

- **LEFT CLICK** on the **Point** command.

- Place a point object on the to quad point of the circle.

- This will serve as reference geometry for the following steps.

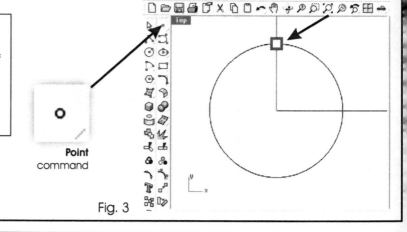

Point command

Fig. 3

- **Right viewport.** Circle is seen from the side.

- **LEFT CLICK** on the **Arc: Center, Start, Angle** command.
  - **Center of arc** prompt, snap to the point at the top of the circle and click to set the location. ❶

Arc: Center, Start, Angle command

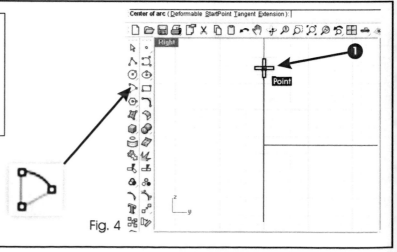

Fig. 4

216

- **Start of arc** prompt: type "**5**" and press "enter".
  - The radius of the arc will be constrained to 5mm.
- Draw the cursor to the left, using **ortho.**
- Click to set location. **2**

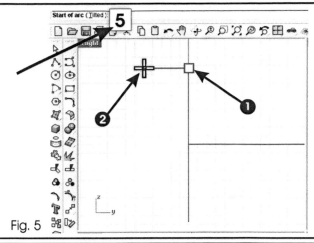

Fig. 5

- **End point or angle** prompt: draw the cursor clockwise around to the other side and, using **ortho,** click to set location. **3**

- A 180-degree arc has been created.

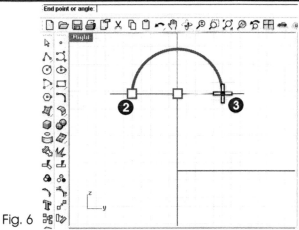

Fig. 6

- Create a perpendicular line 2mm long straight up from the point as shown.

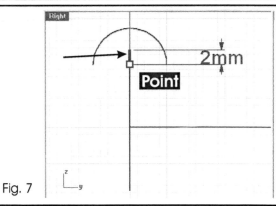

Fig. 7

- Turn on the arc's control points.

- Select the top three control points as shown.

- Drag all three control points down, snapping the center control point on the top of the little line created din Fig. 7.

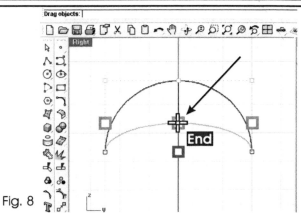

Fig. 8

- Click on the **Record History** button at the bottom of the workspace.

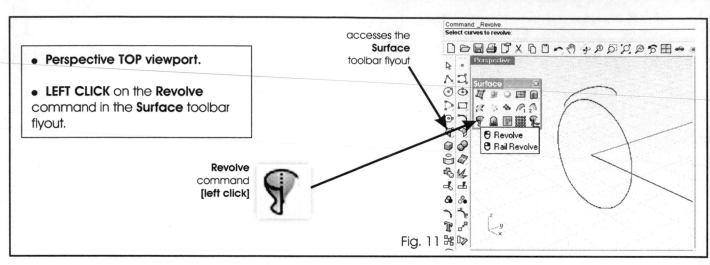

Fig. 10

- **Perspective TOP viewport.**

- **LEFT CLICK** on the **Revolve** command in the **Surface** toolbar flyout.

Revolve
command
[left click]

accesses the
Surface
toolbar flyout

Fig. 11

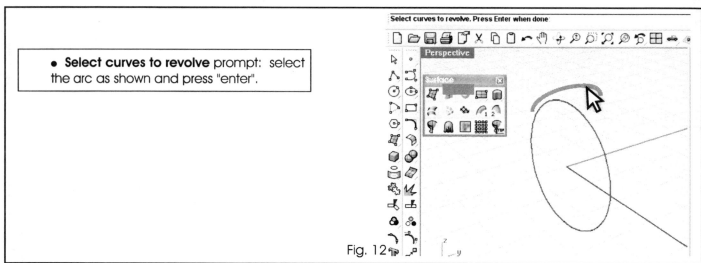

- **Select curves to revolve** prompt: select the arc as shown and press "enter".

Fig. 12

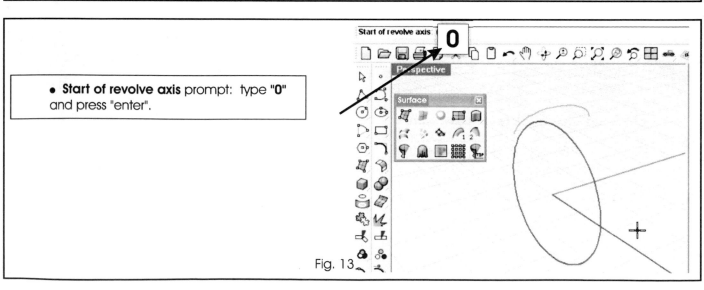

- **Start of revolve axis** prompt: type **"0"** and press "enter".

Fig. 13

- **End of revolve axis** prompt: engage **ortho** and draw the cursor along the **Y** axis as shown.
- Left click anywhere on this line to set the location of the end of the revolve axis. **2**
- **Start angle** prompt: accept the default value of **"0"** by pressing "enter".
- **Revolution Angle** prompt: accept the default value of 360-degrees by pressing "enter".

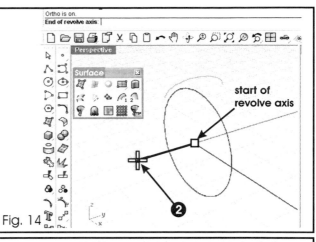

start of revolve axis

Fig. 14

- View the finished surface in **Shade mode.**

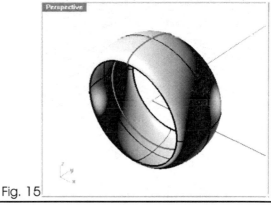

Fig. 15

- **Right perspective viewport.**

- Carefully select the arc that was used to revolve the new surface.

- Turn on the arc's control points.

- *NOTE: do not turn on the control points for the surface, just the control points for the arc as shown.*

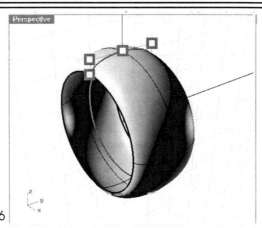

Fig. 16

- Select the center control point and, with ortho engaged, drag this point upward a short distance as shown.

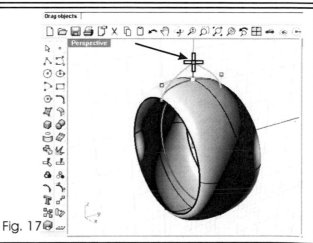

Fig. 17

- The ring band will immediately update to take on the new shape defined by it's parent curve.
  - Parent: the arc
  - Child: the revolved ring surface

- This is an example of the **History** function at work with the **Revolve** command.

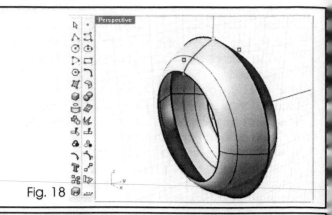

Fig. 18

- **Copy** the ring band over to the side.

- **Rebuild** the original arc with 5 control points which will change its shape, even though the number of control points remains the same.

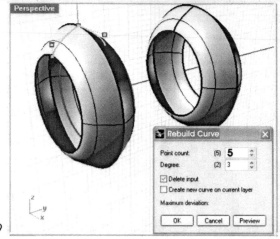

Fig. 19

- Rebuilding the arc **(the parent)** has smoothed out its shape and this is also reflected in the updated shape of the ring band surface **(the child)**.

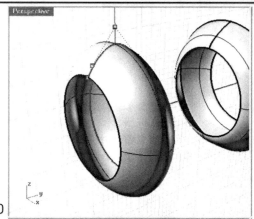

Fig. 20

- If you continue to edit this curve, the surface will continue to update.

- You can rebuild to increase or decrease the number of control points as well and the surface will update.

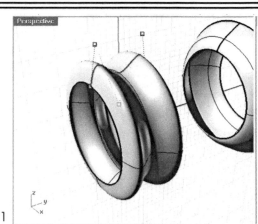

Fig. 21

220

- **Hide** the copy of the ring band that you made earlier.

- Turn on control points for the remaining surface as shown.

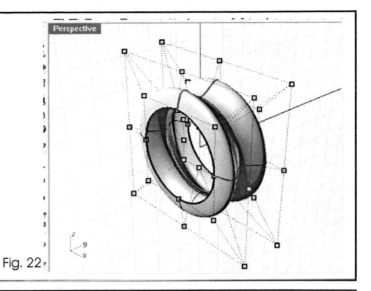

Fig. 22

- Window select the top two control points as shown.

- Drag them upward and click to set a new location.

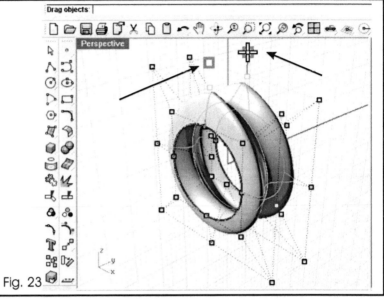

Fig. 23

- The **History Warning** dialog box will appear.

- **History** will be broken if you edit the surface because it is the "child" of the "parent" piece which is the curve that was revolved to create it.

You can copy this band **with history toggled on** and it will **update when the parent band updates.**

- But any copy you make **without history toggled on** will **not** be bound by History to the parent **ring**.

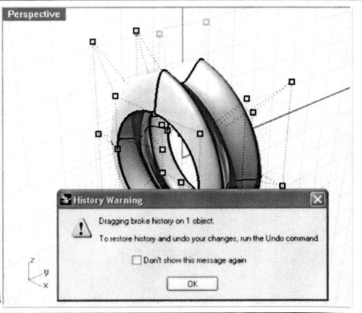

Fig. 24

Rail Revolve & Sweep 1Rail Commands
Cabochon Stone in a Bezel

- Open Rhino and save this file as **6x8 cabochon in bezel.3dm.**

- Create layers as shown.

- Make the **stone construction lines** layer current.

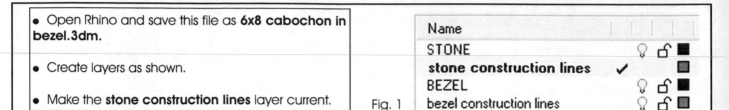

Fig. 1

Name			
STONE	💡	🔓	⬛
stone construction lines	✓		⬛
BEZEL	💡	🔓	⬛
bezel construction lines	💡	🔓	⬛

- Create an **Ellipse** measuring **8mm x 10mm** around "**0**".

Ellipse command

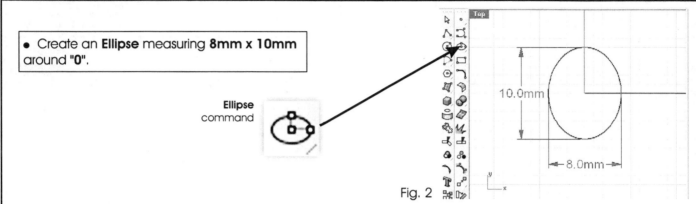

Fig. 2

Create a vertical line from "**0**" with a length of **4mm**.

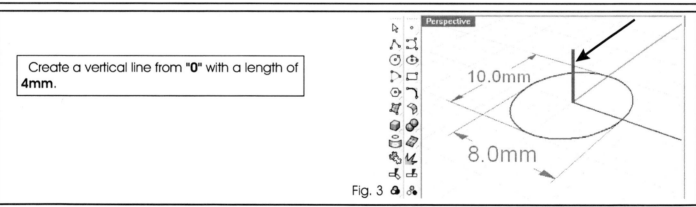

Fig. 3

- Create an arc using the **Arc: Start, End, Point on Arc** command to create the arc shown.

- Use **Quad** and **End** snap for accurate placement.

Arc: Start, End, Point on Arc command

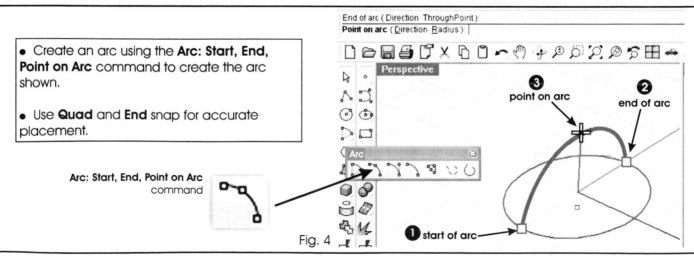

Fig. 4

- **Trim** off one end of the arc as shown.

- Switch to the **STONE** layer.

- Select the arc and **right-click** on the **Rail Revolve** command in the **Surface** toolbar flyout.
  - **Select rail curve** prompt: select the ellipse. **❶**
  - **Start of RailRevolve axis** prompt: type "0" and press "enter". **❷**
  - **End of RailRevolve axis** prompt: snap to the upper end point of the vertical line as shown. **❸**

Rail Revolve
command
[right click]

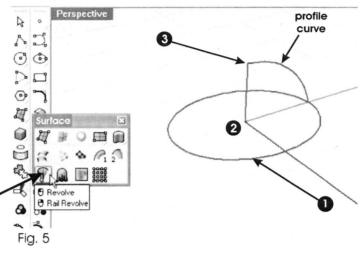

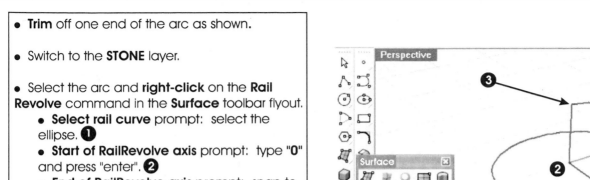

profile curve

Fig. 5

- The finished revolve will create the top surface of the cabochon.

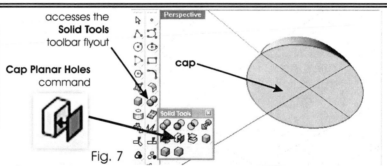

Fig. 6

- Select the new revolved surface and click on the **Cap Planar Holes** command in the **Solid Tools** toolbar flyout.
  - A flat surface will form to close the open planar hole at the bottom of the surface.
  - This is called a "cap".

accesses the **Solid Tools** toolbar flyout

Cap Planar Holes command

cap

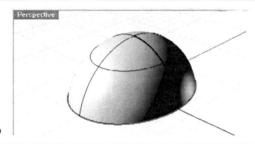

Fig. 7

- **Front Viewport.**

- **bezel construction lines** layer.

- Click on the **Rectangle: Corner to Corner** command.
  - **First corner of rectangle** prompt: click on the quad point of the circle as shown. **❶**
  - **Other corner or length:** type "-.7" and press "enter". *The "minus" sign must be included because this dimension will extend to the left of the first corner. This is in the negative (or "minus") grid direction.*
  - **Width:** type "2" and press "enter".

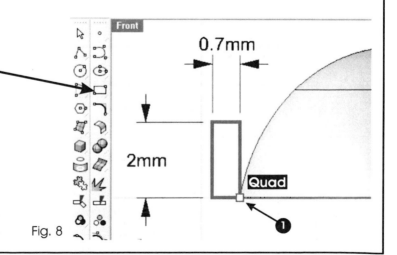

0.7mm

2mm

Quad

Fig. 8

- Click on the **Rectangle** command again.
  - **Start of rectangle** prompt: use **end osnap** to click on the lower left corner of the first rectangle. **①**
  - **Other corner or length** prompt: type "**1.5**" and press "enter".
  - **Width** prompt: type "**-.7**". *The "minus" is because the rectangle's width will extend downward which is a negative, or "minus" grid direction.*

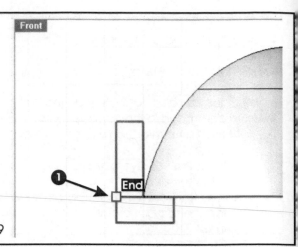

Fig. 9

- Select both rectangles and click on the **Curve boolean** command in the **Curve Tools** toolbar flyout.
  - **Click inside regions to keep** prompt: click on the **DeleteInput=*None*** link as shown.
    - **DeleteInput** prompt: click on the **All** option as shown.

DeleteInput <All> (None Use

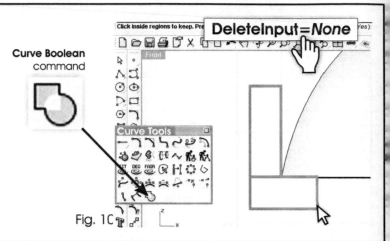

Curve Boolean command

DeleteInput=*None*

Fig. 10

- **Click inside regions to keep** prompt: click with the cursor inside first one rectangle, than the other.
- When you click inside a rectangle, a thin black line will outline it's perimeter.
- When you have clicked inside both rectangles, press "enter".

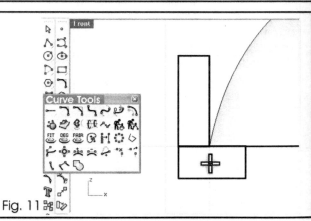

Fig. 11

- The two rectangles are now trimmed and joined into one closed polyline.

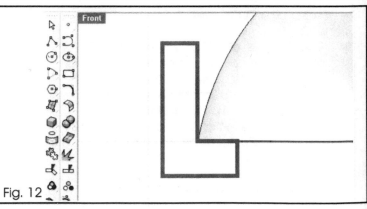

Fig. 12

- Click on the **Chamfer Curves** command in the **Surface Tools** toolbar flyout.
    - Toggle on the **Distances=1,1** link in the **Command Line.**
    - **First chamfer distance** prompt: type "**.3**" and press "enter".
    - **Second chamfer distance** prompt: type "**1**" and press "enter".

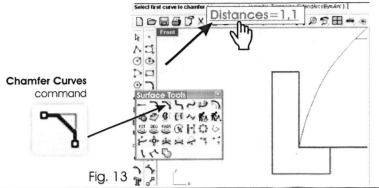

Chamfer Curves
command

Fig. 13

- **First curve to chamfer:** click on the short line segment at the top of the polyline as shown. **①**
- **Second curve to chamfer:** click on the longer line segment on the left side of the polyline as shown. **②**

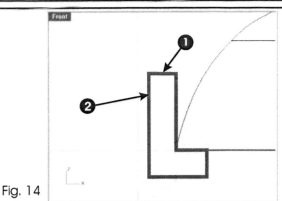

Fig. 14

- The two lines selected to chamfer have been trimmed to the specified lengths and a diagonal line has been added to bridge the gap created by the chamfer.

- **Join** the diagonal line to the polyline to create a closed polyline.

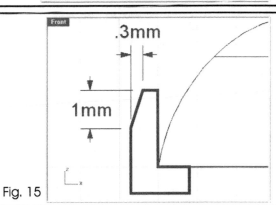

.3mm

1mm

Fig. 15

- **Perspective TOP** viewport.

- **BEZEL** layer.

- Use the **Sweep 1 Rail** command to create a bezel.

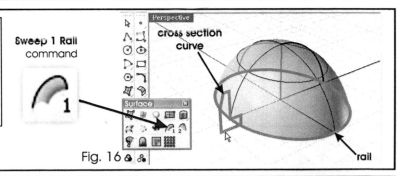

Sweep 1 Rail
command

cross section curve

rail

Fig. 16

- The finished stone and bezel.

Fig. 17

225

Rail Revolve Command - Puffed Heart
Rail Revolve and Point Editing

- Create layers as shown.

- **reference geometry** layer current.

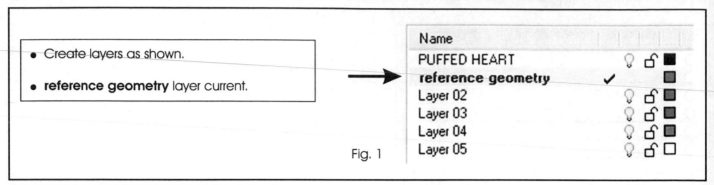

Fig. 1

- **Top Viewport.**

- Use the **Circle: Diameter** command to create a circle **10mm** in diameter.

- Diameter starts at "0" ❶ and extends **10mm** straight along the X axis. ❷

- Use **ORTHO** for accuracy.

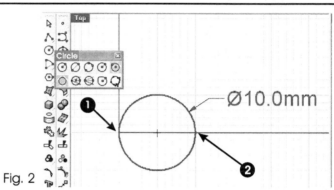

Fig. 2

- **Mirror** the circle horizontally as shown.

- Create a **Line** that connects the two outer **quad** points of the two circles as shown.

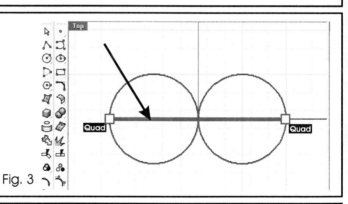

Fig. 3

- **Trim** off the lower half of both circles, using the line as the cutting object.

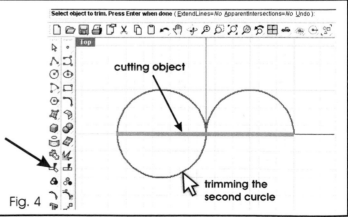

Fig. 4

- When the trim is completed, you can delete the line used as the cutting object.

- Use the **Point** command to place a single point **15mm** below "**0**" as shown.

- The quickest way to do this is to toggle on **grid snap** and snap to this location to set the point.

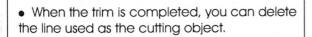
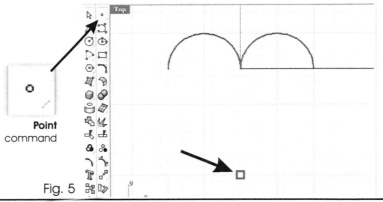

Point
command

Fig. 5

- Use the **Extend by Arc to Point** command to extend the end of both of the arcs as shown to the point below.

- Use **point osnap** to set this location with accuracy.

Extend by Arc to Point
command

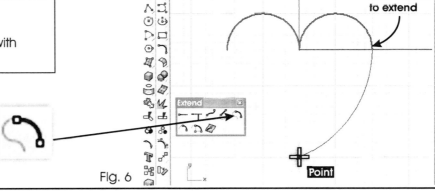

select curve to extend

Point

Fig. 6

- Both arcs have been extended down to the point below.

Fig. 7

- Click on the **Fillet Curves** command in the **Curve Tools** toolbar flyout.
  - Type **.5** to set the Fillet Radius.
  - Note the fillet options in the **Command Line.**
  - **Select first curve to fillet** prompt: click on one side of the angle of the two curves as shown.
  - **Select second curve to fillet** prompt: click on the curve on the other curve as shown.

- The finished fillet will round off the sharp angle at the top of the heart.

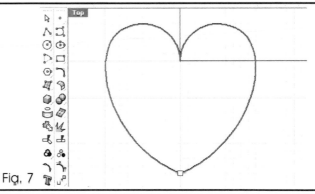
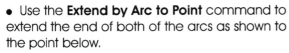
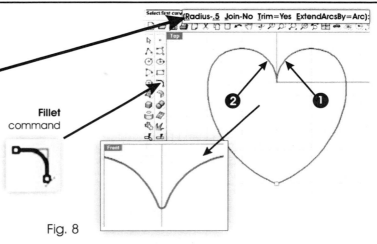

Fillet
command

(Radius-.5 Join-No Trim=Yes ExtendArcsBy=Arc):

Fig. 8

- Click on the **Fillet Curves** command in the **Curve Tools** toolbar flyout.
  - **Select first curve to fillet** prompt: type "4" and press "enter".
  - At the **Command Line** prompts, select the two curves at the point at the bottom of the heart to create a fillet with a radius of **4mm**.

- **Join** all segments.

- You can **Hide** or delete the point at the bottom.

Fillet Curves command

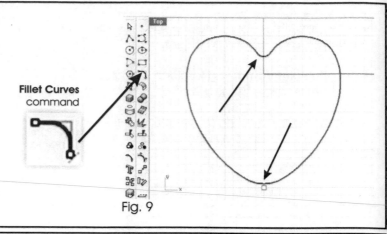

Fig. 9

- Select the heart and click on the **Adjust Closed Curve Seam** command in the **Curve Tools** toolbar flyout.
  - **Adjust curve seam** prompt: click and drag the curve seam so that it snaps to the lower **quad** point of the heart as shown, assuring control point symmetry for the rebuilding in the next step.
    - **quad osnap** is essential here for accuracy.

Adjust Closed Curve Seam command

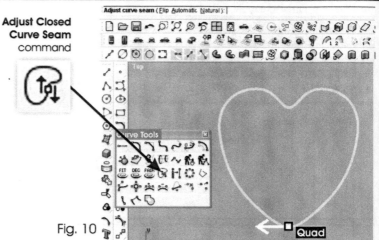

Fig. 10

- **Rebuild** the polyline with 20 control points as shown.

- Fig. 11 shows the distribution of control points before rebuilding.

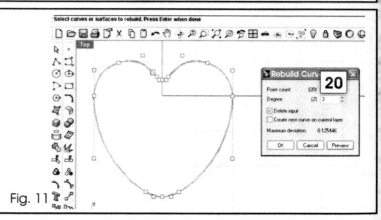

Fig. 11

- The rebuilt curve.

- *Notice the symmetrical placement of points because you adjusted the curve seam to a middle point that ensured symmetry.*

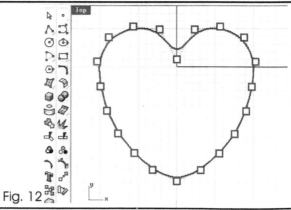

Fig. 12

- Create a **Line** that connects the **quad** points of the top and bottom fillets as shown.

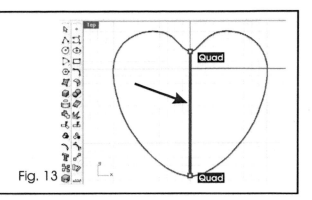

Fig. 13

- **Perspective TOP viewport.**

- Select the line you just created and **Right click** on the **Divide Curve by Number of Segments** command in the **Point** toolbar flyout.
    - **Number of segments** prompt: type "5" and press "enter".

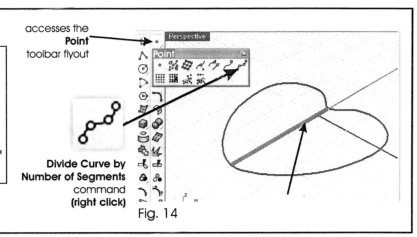

accesses the **Point** toolbar flyout

Divide Curve by Number of Segments command (right click)

Fig. 14

- Your line will be divided into 5 equal segments with points as the dividers.

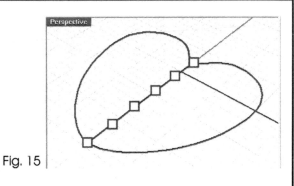

Fig. 15

- Click on the **Line** command and toggle on the **Vertical** option in the **Command Line.**
    - Create a vertical **4mm** line straight up from the third point down from the top of the heart as shown.

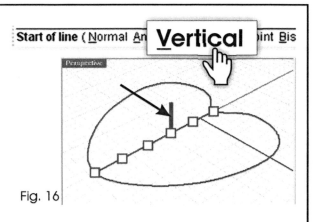

Fig. 16

229

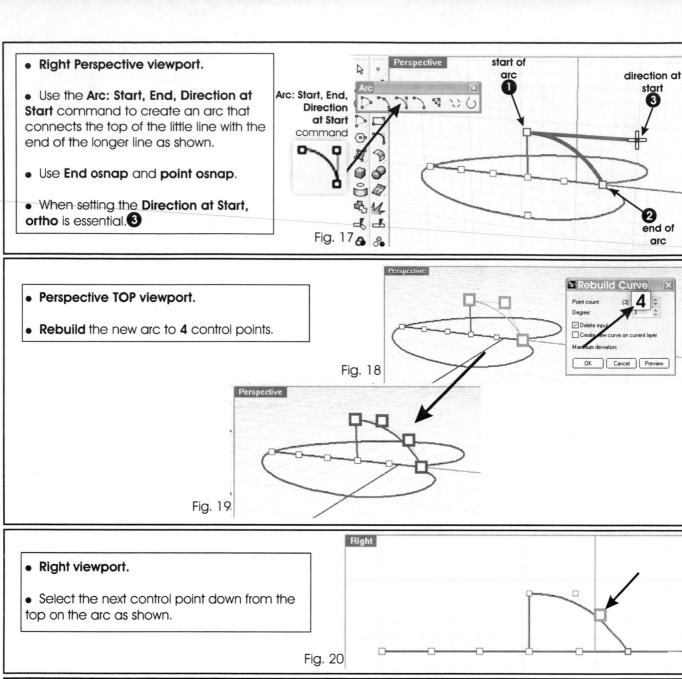

- **Right Perspective viewport.**

- Use the **Arc: Start, End, Direction at Start** command to create an arc that connects the top of the little line with the end of the longer line as shown.

- Use **End osnap** and **point osnap**.

- When setting the **Direction at Start**, **ortho** is essential.❸

Arc: Start, End, Direction at Start command

start of arc ❶

direction at start ❸

❷ end of arc

Fig. 17

- **Perspective TOP viewport.**

- **Rebuild** the new arc to **4** control points.

Fig. 18

Rebuild Curve

Point count: (3) **4**
Degree: 3
☑ Delete input
☐ Create new curve on current layer
Maximum deviation:

OK   Cancel   Preview

Fig. 19

- **Right viewport.**

- Select the next control point down from the top on the arc as shown.

Fig. 20

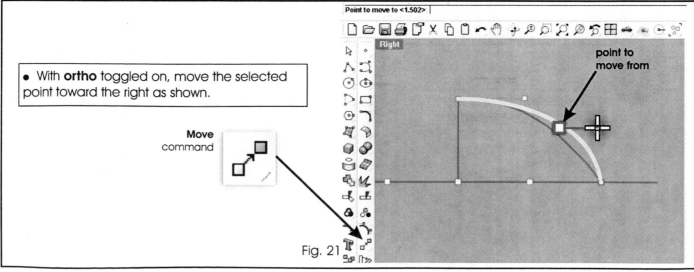

- With **ortho** toggled on, move the selected point toward the right as shown.

Move command

Point to move to <1.502>

point to move from

Fig. 21

- Tap the **Tab** key on your keyboard.

- When you do this, notice the rubber band line becomes white in color, signifying a constraint. The direction of the move is now constrained to the right as shown.

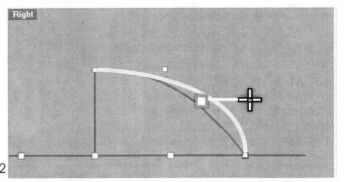

Fig. 22

- Snap to the last point on the arc. An additional perpendicular constraint line will appear.

- The selected point that you are moving will be re-located to a position exactly above and perpendicular to the point you are snapping to.

- You can **Hide** the center line and points.

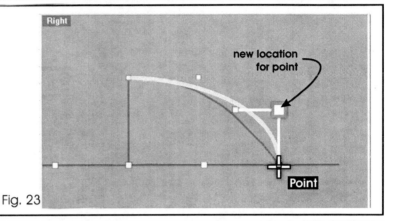

new location for point

Point

Fig. 23

- **Perspective TOP viewport.**

- **PUFFED HEART** layer.

- **RIGHT CLICK** on the **Revolve** button to access the **Rail Revolve** command.

- When prompted, select the **Profile Curve**, **Rail Curve**, and **Start of Revolve Axis**, and **End of Revolve Axis** in turn.

Rail Revolve
command
[right click]

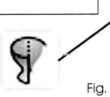

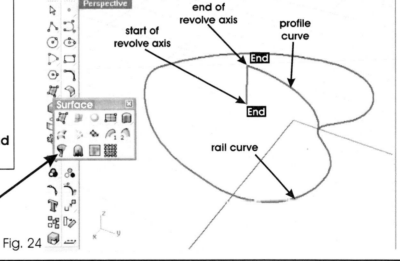

end of revolve axis

start of revolve axis

profile curve

End

End

rail curve

Fig. 24

- **Rail Revolve** has produced a heart-shaped surface.

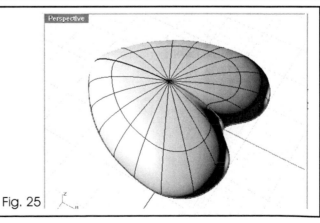

Fig. 25

- Turn off the **reference geometry** layer.

- Turn on the surface's control points.

- Notice that the first two rows of control points in from the edge of the surface are **perpendicular to each other**. This is because of the control point editing that you did to the arc which is the profile curve.

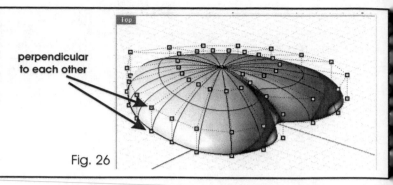

perpendicular to each other

Fig. 26

- **Top viewport.**

- Window select the two points shown. Note that, because the outer two rows of control points are perpendicular to each other, *they look like one point from the top.*

- You are looking at two selected control points in this example!

- Click on the **Select V** command in the **Select Points** toolbar flyout.

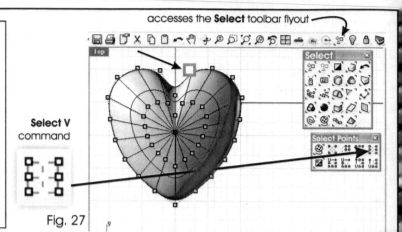

accesses the **Select** toolbar flyout

Select V command

Fig. 27

- All of the control points in the surface's **V** direction become selected.

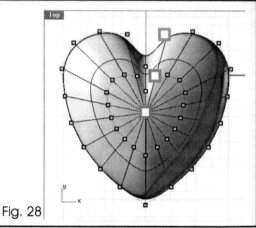

Fig. 28

- Click on the **Rotate** command.
  - **Center of rotation** prompt: snap to the control point in the center of the heart as shown. Use **point osnap** to hit this location with accuracy.

Rotate command

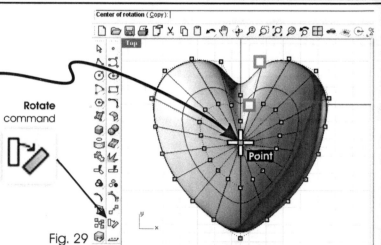

Point

Fig. 29

- **Angle or first reference point** prompt: click on the outermost point as shown.

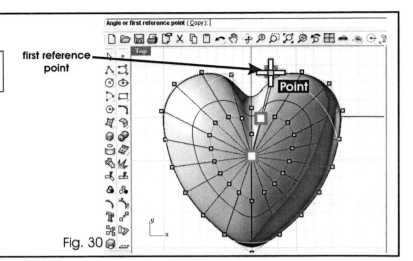

Fig. 30

- **Second reference point** prompt: draw the cursor toward the left until the **yellow wireframe preview** shows a shape that you like.
- Click to set the new shape.

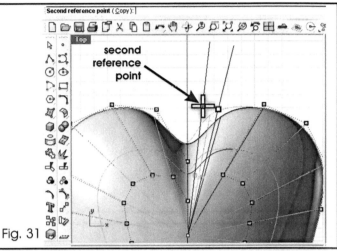

Fig. 31

- **reference geometry** layer.

- Use the **Point** command to place a point on the outermost control point as shown.

- Actually there are two points in this location, one under the other but this does not matter in this instance.

Point command

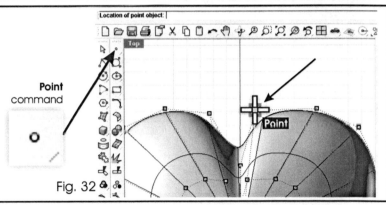

Fig. 32

- Turn off the control points and you can see the point object that you just created.

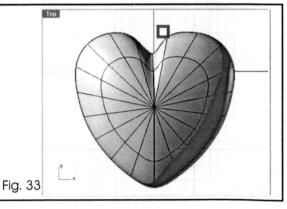

Fig. 33

233

- **Mirror** the point across the Y axis as shown.

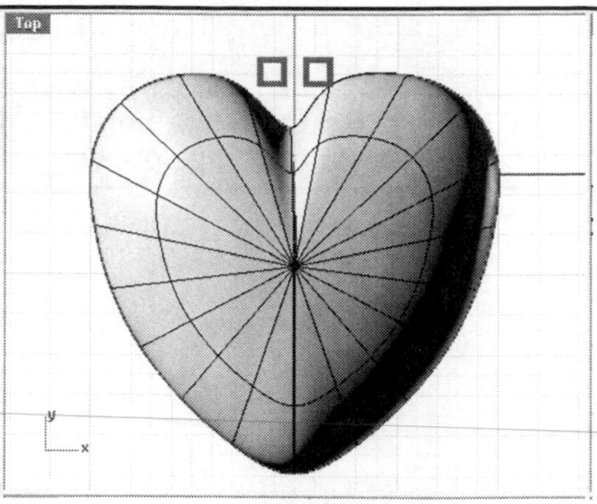

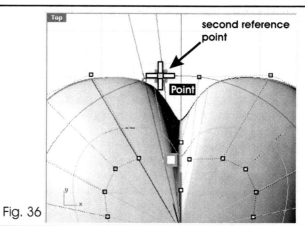

Fig. 34

- Select the row of control points on the other side of the heart with the same steps as you did before on the right side of the surface.

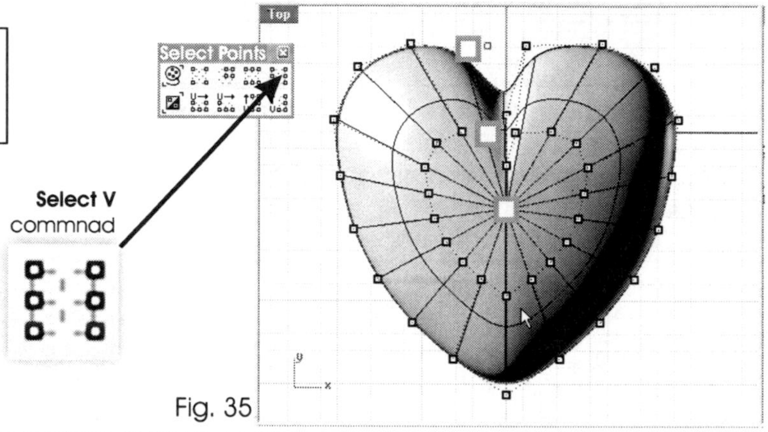

Select V commnad

Fig. 35

- **Rotate** this row of points as before but in the other direction..

- When prompted for the **Second reference point,** this time, snap to the point that you just mirrored over from the other side across the Y axis.

second reference point

Fig. 36

- The heart is now symmetrical again but you might want to do some more editing to refine the shape.

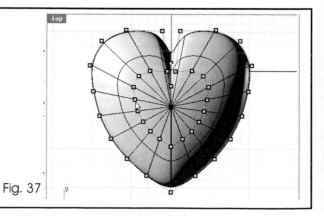

Fig. 37

234

• You can move the two sets of points upward as shown to achieve a rounder shape at the two top lobes of the neart.

• *Make sure to window select these points. They look like single points but they are actually sets of 2 points, one behind the other. The selected points shown look like 2 points but actually 4 points are selected.*

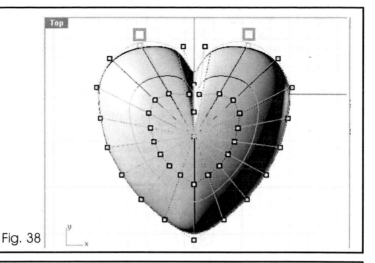

Fig. 38

• The heart might now benefit from spreading the **darkened** points outward, using **Scale 1D** so that they travel outward symmetrically from the designated **origin point.**

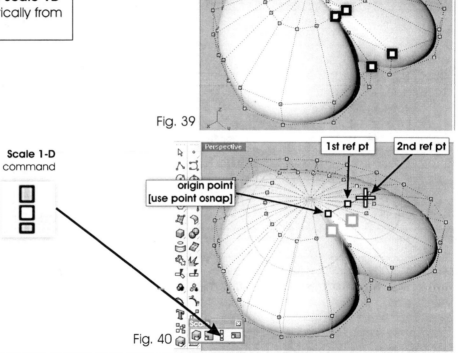

Fig. 39

Scale 1-D
command

1st ref pt   2nd ref pt

origin point
[use point osnap]

Fig. 40

• After using the **Scale 1D** command on both sets of points suggested, the cleft of the heart is more gradual.

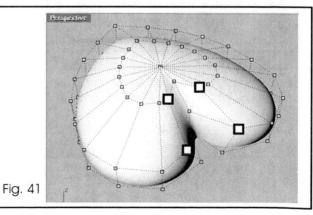

Fig. 41

- **Move** the center point shown **up toward the top of the heart** as shown to reduce the length of the cleft.

- _**Note: remember that you can drag vertically if you hold down the Ctrl key.**_

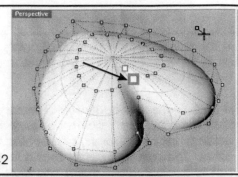

Fig. 42

- Select one point in the row directly perpendicular to the edge of the surface.

- Then click on the **Select U** command to select the rest of the points in that row.

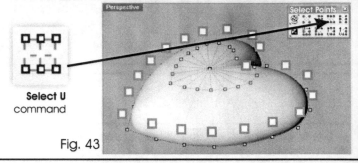

Select U command

Fig. 43

- Use **Scale 1D** again to scale back the selected row of points so that they withdraw a bit from the bottom of the heart.

- The aim here is to make the slope of the surface a little more gradual at the bottom of the heart.

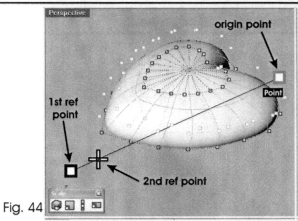

origin point

1st ref point

Point

2nd ref point

Fig. 44

- To minimize the small ridge that forms between the center and bottom tip of the heart, select and move the two points shown upward toward the top of the heart..

- Move them upward about 1mm.

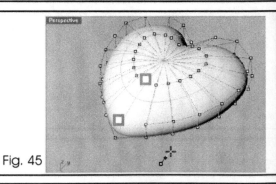

Fig. 45

- Move and Scale are very powerful ways to control point edit the surface of a heart.

- Keep point editing to get the shape that you want.

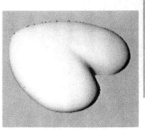

Fig. 46

Sweep 1 Rail Command
Simple Ring band

- Create layers as shown.

- **construction lines** layer current.

Fig. 1

Name			
RING		♀ 🔓 ⬛
construction lines	✓	. - . ⬛

- **Front viewport.**

- Create a **Circle** around 0 with a diameter of 17.35mm.

Ø17.35mm

Fig. 2

- **Right viewport.**

- **Left click** on the **Ellipse: Diameter** command in the **Ellipse** toolbar flyout.

accesses the **Ellipse** toolbar flyout

Ellipse: Diameter command

notice how right view of circle looks like a straight line

Fig. 3

- **Start of first axis** prompt: click on the top of the circle, using **quad osnap** for proper placement on top of the circle.
- **End of first axis** prompt: type "**3**" and press "enter".
- Click to set location using **ortho**.

End of first axis **3**

Start of first axis (Vertical):

Quad

Fig. 4

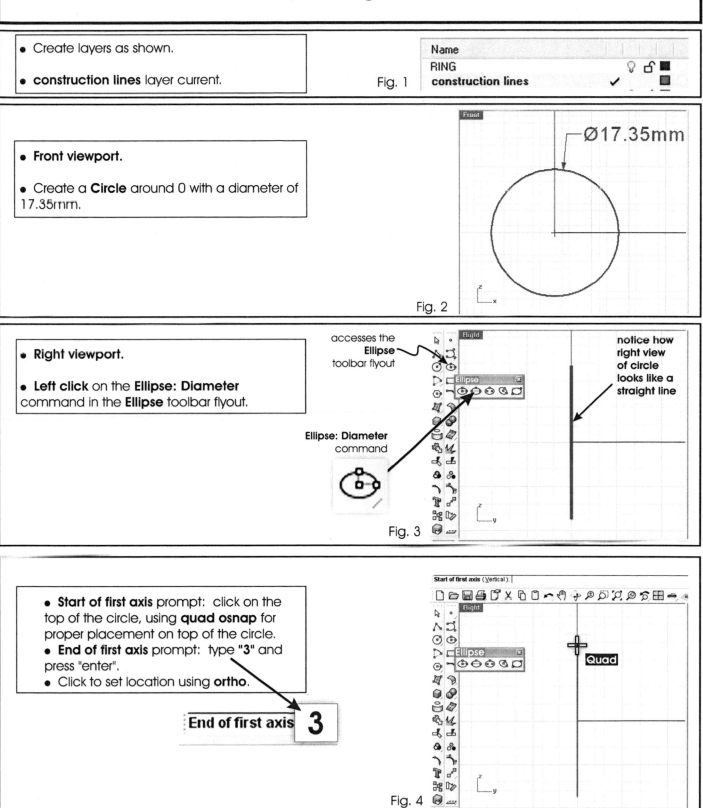

237

- When prompted for the **End of second axis,** type **"10"** and press "enter".

End of second axis: **10**

Fig. 5

- **Left click** to set the end of the second axis as shown.

Fig. 6

- Using the same technique, create an ellipse at the bottom of the circle as shown.

- Remember to use **quad osnap** to place the location at the bottom of the circle.

- **End of first axis:** type **"2"**

- **End of second axis:** type **"4"**

Fig. 7

- **Perspective TOP viewport.**

- **RING** layer current.

Fig. 8

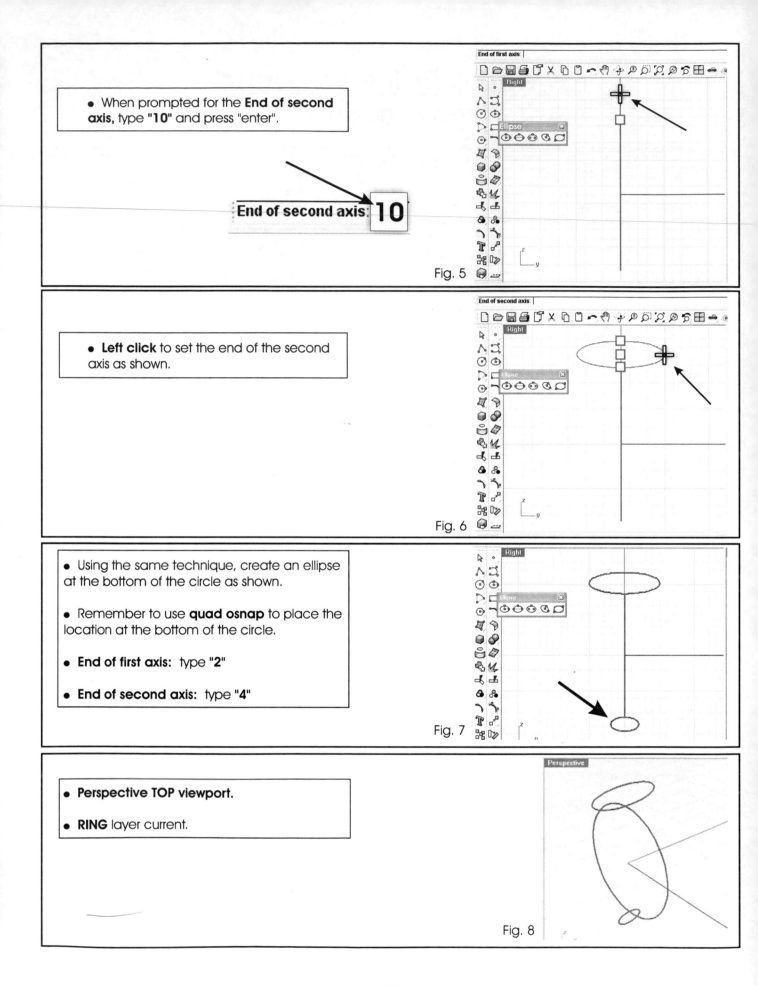

- **Left click** on the **Sweep 1 Rail** command in the **Surface** toolbar flyout.
  - **Select rail** prompt: select the circle.
  - **Select cross section curve** prompt: select the two ellipses and press "enter".

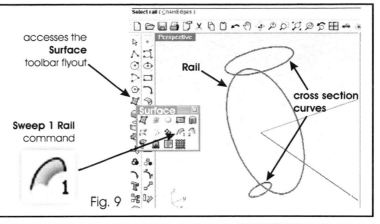

accesses the **Surface** toolbar flyout

Sweep 1 Rail command

Rail

cross section curves

Fig. 9

- Since the ellipses are closed curves, you will be prompted to **Adjust curve seams.**
  - Notice the curve is shown as a line between two points, one on each of the closed curves.
  - The two white arrows indicate the direction of the curves.

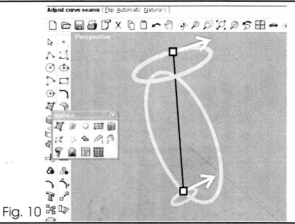

Fig. 10

- Click on the top curve seam point and drag it around until you snap to the quad point shown.
- **Left click** to set this new location for this end of the curve seam.
- Press "enter".

- *Note: The two white arrows are no longer pointing in the same direction. You can use the Flip option in the <u>Command Line</u> to remedy this but leave that alone for this exercise.*

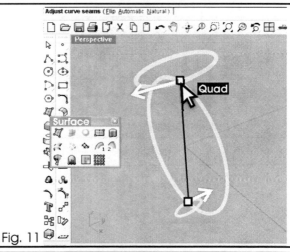

Quad

Fig. 11

- If you look at Fig. 11, you will notice that the white arrows on each end of the seam are pointing in different directions - one is pointing forward and the other is pointing backward.
  - For this reason, the preview of the ring has a twisted surface.
- Click on the **Align Shapes** button in the **Sweep 1 Rail options** dialog box.

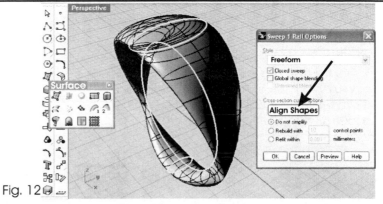

Fig. 12

- **Click on end of shapes to reverse**
  prompt: click on one of the points of the
  seam as shown.

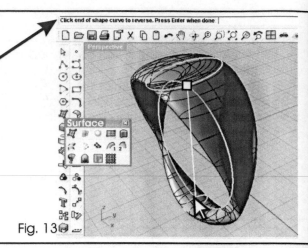

Fig. 13

- Notice how the preview of the ring is no
  longer twisted.
- Press "enter".

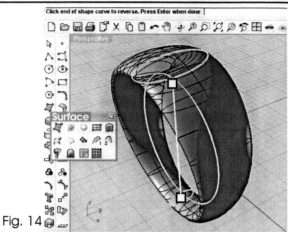

Fig. 14

- **Closed Sweep** option is toggled on as
  shown.
- Click on the OK button to exit the dialog
  box and end the command.

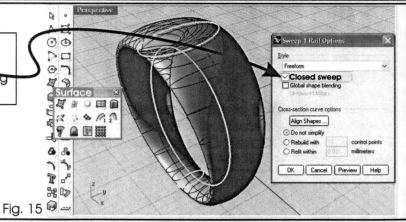

Fig. 15

- The finished ring is shaped by the two **profile
  curve**s that have swept a surface between
  them following the direction of the circle which
  is the **rail curve**.

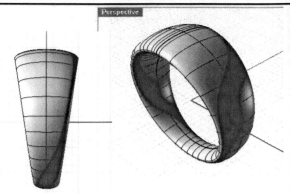

Fig. 16

Sweep 2 Rails Command
Wavy Ring Band

- Create layers as shown.

- **reference geometry** layer current.

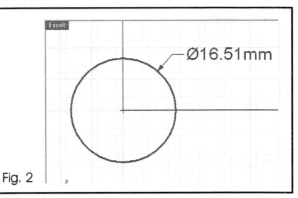

Fig. 1

Name			
RING 1	💡	🔓	◼
RING 2	💡	🔓	◼
reference geometry	✓		◼

- **Front viewport.**

- Create a circle around "**0**" with a diameter of **16.51mm**.

Ø16.51mm

Fig. 2

- **Perspective TOP viewport.**

- **Rebuild** the circle to 12 control points.

- Select every other control point, starting with the top one as shown.

Rebuild command

Fig. 3

- Click on the **Move** command.
  - **Ortho** mode toggled on.
  - **Point to move from** prompt: click on the construction plane.
  - **Point to move to** prompt: type "**6**" and press "enter". Distance will be constrained.
  - **Point to move to** prompt: draw the cursor upwards along the Y axis and click to set location.

- The circle will now resemble the highlighted wavy curve shown as a preview during the move.

Move command

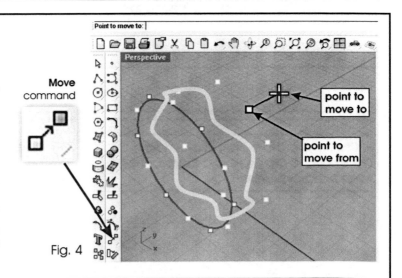

point to move to

point to move from

Fig. 4

- Select the wavy curve and type **"mv"**, activating the **Mirror** command using one of the custom aliases described in the **Rhino Options: Keyboard Aliases** chapter of this book - **page 421**.
  - *You must pre-select for this to work.*
  - Press "enter" to end the command.

- The wavy curve will be **mirrored vertically** to the other side of the X axis as shown.

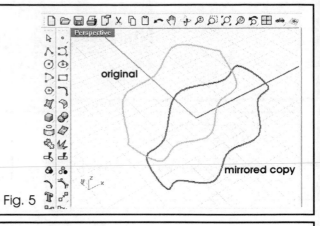

Fig. 5

- Create a **Line** as shown between the two quad points of the two curves at the top of the ring band reference geometry.

Line command

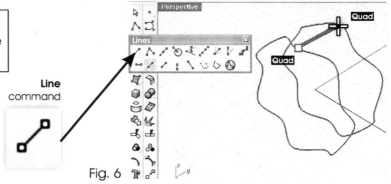

Fig. 6

- Click on the **Line** command again..
  - Click on the **Vertical** option in the **Command Line.**

Fig. 7

- **Start of line** prompt: use **mid osnap** to click on the mid point of the line just created.
- **End of line** prompt: type **"3.25"** and press "enter", constraining the line to that length.
- **End of line** prompt: draw the cursor upward and click to set location.

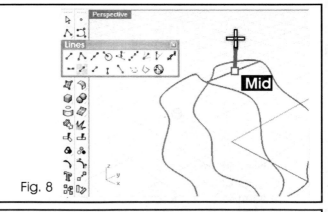

Fig. 8

- Use the **Arc: Start, End, Point on Arc** command to create an arc that touches all three end points shown.

Arc: Start, End, Point on Arc command

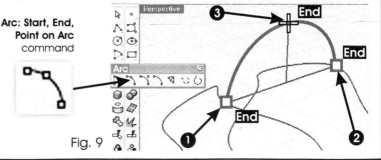

Fig. 9

242

- **RING 1** layer.

  - Click on the **Sweep 2 Rails** command in the **Surface** toolbar flyout.

Sweep 2 Rails
command

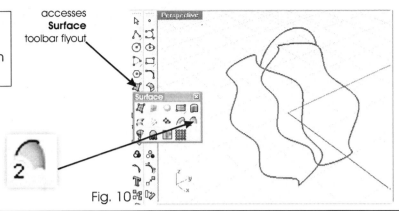

Fig. 10

- **Select first rail** prompt: Select one of the wavy curves.
- **Select second rail** prompt: select the other wavy curve.
- **Select cross section curves** prompt: select the arc.
- Press "enter".

cross section curve

the two rails

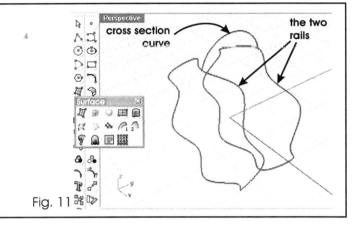

Fig. 11

- When he **Sweep 2 Rails Options** dialog box will appears. make sure that the settings are as shown.
  - A preview of the new surface will be visible. Press the **Preview** button if you do not see a preview.
  - Click OK.

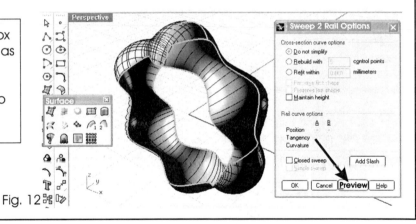

Fig. 12

- A surface has been created that has its edges defined by the two rails that have constrained its shape as shown.

- The arc has defined its modulation.

- Notice how the surface undulates in its modulation, depending on the proximity of the two rails to each other as they proceed around the ring band.

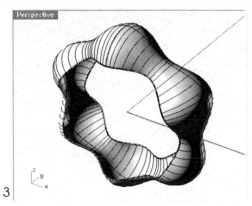

Fig. 13

- Turn off the **RING 1** layer.

- **RING 2** layer current.

- Perform the **Sweep 2 Rails** command as before.
    - This time when the **Sweep 2 Rails Options** dialog box appears, put a check in the box to enable the **Maintain Height** option.
        - Click OK.

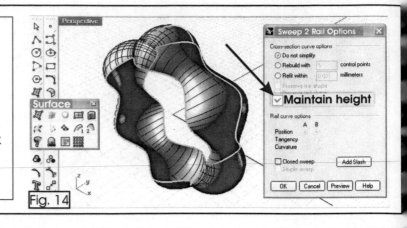

Fig. 14

- There is now no modulation in the height of the band as the **Maintain Height** option has constrained it to the height of the arc which is the cross-section curve.

- Turn off the **RING 2** layer.

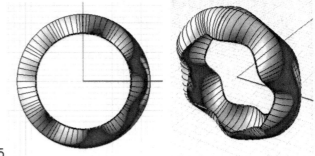

Fig. 15

- Turn on the **RING 1** layer.

- Navigate to the underside of the ring top.

- The next step is to sweep a surface on the inside of the ring band.

- **reference geometry** layer current.

- Create a **Line** that snaps to the end points of the arc at the top of the ring as shown.

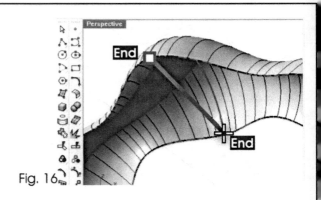

Fig. 16

- Click on the **Sweep 2 Rails** command.
    - **Select first rail** prompt: click on one of the surface edges of the ring surface.
    - When the **Selection Menu** appears, click on the **"Surface Edge"** option.

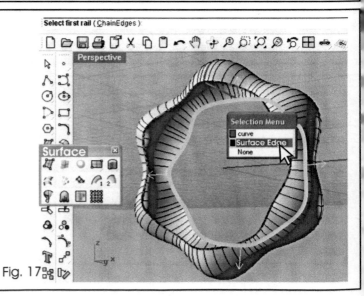

Fig. 17

- **Select second rail** prompt: select the other surface edge, selecting the **"Surface Edge"** option as before.

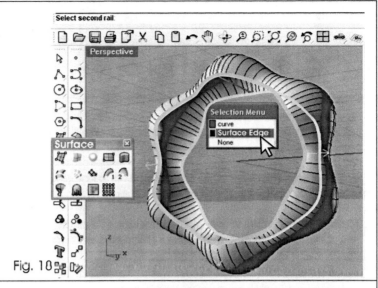

Fig. 18

- **Select cross section curves** prompt: select the line on the underside of the band as shown.
- Press "enter"

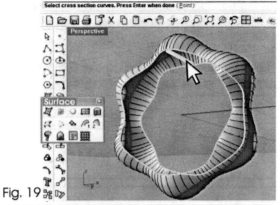

Fig. 19

- Use the settings shown.

- Click OK.

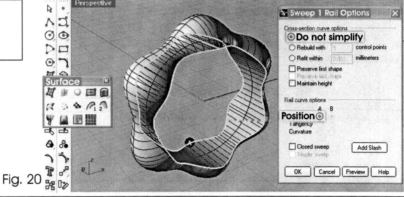

Fig. 20

- **Join** the inner and outer surfaces together.

- The finished ring is a closed polysurface.

- Check for naked edges.
  - Ref: Naked Edges chapter - page 246.

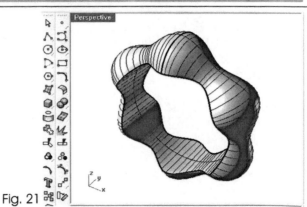

Fig. 21

245

Naked Edges
The need for closed surfaces and polysurfaces.

- If you are modeling for design visualization and the aim is just to create images for illustration purposes, than the issue of whether or not the surfaces are or are not joined together may not be important. But certain commands, such as the booleans, will not always work with open polysurfaces.

- But if you are modeling with the purpose of sending your file for prototyping, then you need to make sure that you do not have any open surfaces or polysurfaces. Models need to be "watertight".

- **Naked Edges** refers to the edges of surfaces that are not joined to other surface edges.
  - Checking for open surfaces or polysurfaces involves *Checking for Naked Edges.*

- This exercise will use the file of the **Wavy Ring Band** that was created with the **2 Rail Sweep** command.

- Select the ring and click on the **Show Edges** command in the **Analyze** toolbar flyout.

Show Edges
command

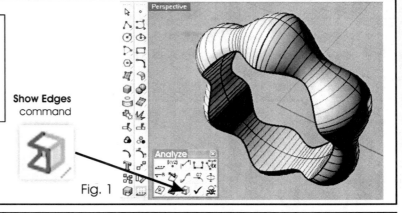

Fig. 1

- the **Edge Analysis** dialog box will appear.

- All seams on the polysurface will light up with a bright pink color.

- The ends of edges will be indicated by point pbjects.

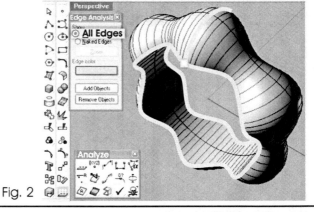

Fig. 2

- Click on the **Naked Edges** option and no seams will select as this is a closed polysurface.

- All edges are joined to other edges.

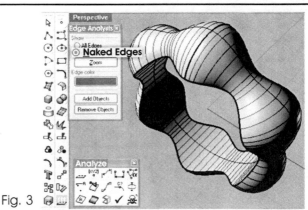

Fig. 3

- In this example, a polysurface was tested for Naked Edges.

- The History line informs you both of the total number of edges in the model and the number of Naked Edges if they exist.

- In this example, there are 2 Naked Edges.

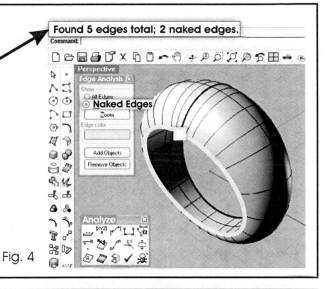

Fig. 4

- A closer look at the inside surface at the top of the ring reveals that the two surfaces are not meeting at their respective edges.

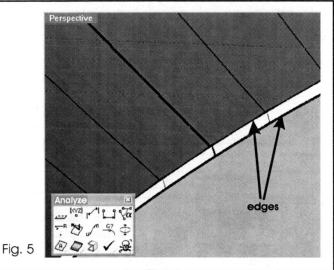

Fig. 5

- Hide or turn off the ring layer and inspect all curve intersections.

- In this example, the reason for the naked edges becomes apparent. *One of the lines was not properly snapped to the curve it was supposed to touch.*

- To remedy this problem, you can re-draw the line and sweep the inside of the ring once again.

- Or, you can turn on the line's control points and edit the line so that the control point at the end shown snaps to the end of the arc.

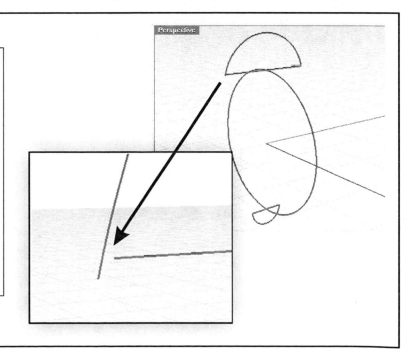

Fig. 6

Surface from Network of Curves Command
Bombe Ring - Basic Shapes

- Save a file off as **bombe ring shape.3dm.**

- Create Layers as shown.

- Make the **construction lines** layer current.

Fig. 1

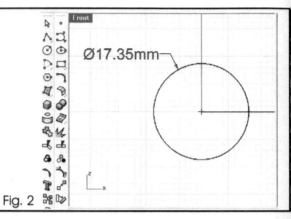

Name			
RING BODY		💡 🔓 ⬛
construction lines	✓	🔓 ⬛
2D curves		💡 🔓 ⬛

- **Front Viewport.**

- Create a circle around **0** with a diameter of **17.35mm.**

- *Remember to make sure you check in the* <u>*Command Line*</u> *to make sure that you are specifying the diameter, not the radius!*

➤ **Diameter <17.350>** (**R**adius):

Fig. 2

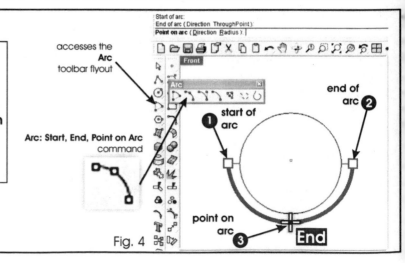

Ø17.35mm

- Create three small lines at the circle's three quad points as shown.

- Use your **QUAD osnap** for accuracy.

- Use **ORTHO.**

- You can **toggle off the grid** by pressing the **F7** key. Press it again to toggle the grid back on.

Fig. 3

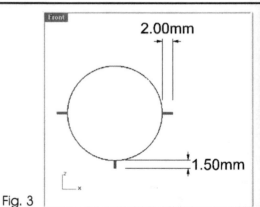

2.00mm

1.50mm

- Using the **Arc: Start, End, Point on Arc** command, create an arc touching the ends of all three lines as shown.
- Follow <u>**Command Line**</u> prompts for placing the **Start of arc❶**, **end of arc❷**, and **Point on arc.❸**

- Use **end osnap.**

accesses the Arc toolbar flyout

Arc: Start, End, Point on Arc command

Start of arc:
End of arc (Direction ThroughPoint):
Point on arc (Direction Radius):

start of arc ❶
end of arc ❷
point on arc ❸
End

Fig. 4

- Using the **Arc: Start, End, Direction at Start** command, draw an arc over the top of the circle as shown.
- Follow prompts for **Start of arc❶**, **End of arc,❷** and **Direction at start.❸**

- Use **ORTHO** when setting the last point.

Arc: Start, End, Direction at Start command

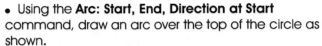

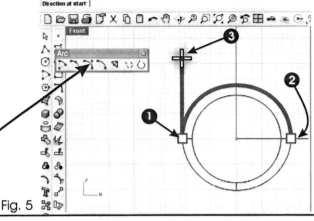

Fig. 5

- Use the **Move** command to move the arc up **3mm**.

- Follow the prompts in the **Command Line** for the proper sequence of steps.

- For the **Point to move to,** type "3", toggle on **ORTHO**, and click on the **point to move to** as shown.

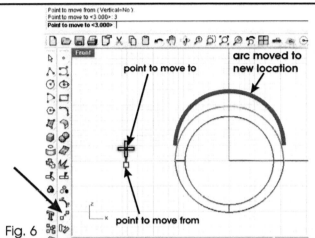

point to move to

arc moved to new location

point to move from

Fig. 6

- Using the **Extend Curve, Smooth** command, extend the ends of the arc just created so that they snap to the endpoints of the lower arc.
  - **Start of extension** prompt: click on the end of the upper arc. ❶
  - **End of extension** prompt: snap to the end point of the lower arc and click to set location.❷
  - Extend the arc on the other side of the ring as well.

accesses the **Extend** toolbar flyout

Extend Curve, Smooth command

End

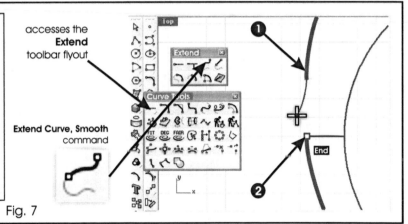

Fig. 7

- When top arc has been extended on both sides, press "enter" to end the command.

- **Join** the top and bottom arcs to get a closed polyline.

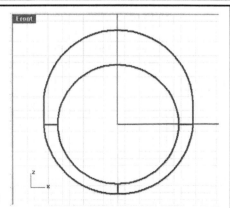

Fig. 8

249

- Before rebuilding the outer polyline, you need to make sure that the "closed curve seam" or "curve seam" of this polycurve is centered.

- Select the polycurve and click on the **Adjust Closed Curve Seam** command.
  - The location of the curve seam will be indicated by a point and a white arrow.

Adjust Closed
Curve Seam
command

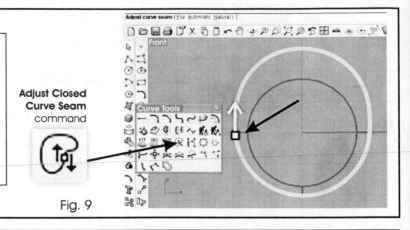

Fig. 9

- Click on the curve seam's single control point and drag the seam indicator down to the lower quad point as shown.

- Snap to the lower **quad** point of the circle as shown and click to set the new location for the curve seam.

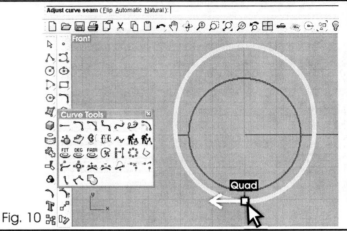

Fig. 10

- **Rebuild** this curve for a smoother shape.
  - **Point count: 25**

- Turn on the control points. Notice the symmetry.

- Turn off the control points.

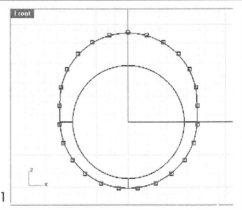

Fig. 11

- **Perspective TOP Viewport.**

- Use the **Line: from Midpoint** command to create two lines from the upper and lower quad points of the inner circle as shown.
  - **Ortho** is essential for this step.
  - **Upper line: 10mm long** [type "5" and press "enter"].
  - **Lower line: 4mm long** [type "2" and press "enter"].

- Use **Quad osnap.**

Line:
from Midpoint
command

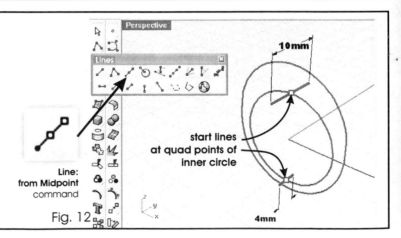

Fig. 12

- Make the **2D Curves** layer current.

- Using the **Line** command, create the line shown with both start and end points on the endpoints of the two lines just created in Fig. 12.
  - Make sure to use **End Osnap** for accurate placement of both start and end of the line.

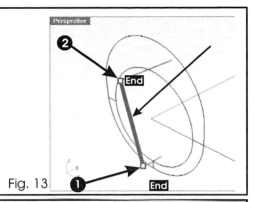

Fig. 13

- Click on the **Extend** command to extend each end of the line by **1mm**.
  - **Select boundary objects or enter extension length** prompt: type "**1**" and press "enter".
  - **Select curve to extend** prompt: Click on each end of the line in turn and you will notice that each time you click, an extra 1mm length grows onto the end of the line where you click.
  - Press "enter" or "esc" to exit the command.

Extend command

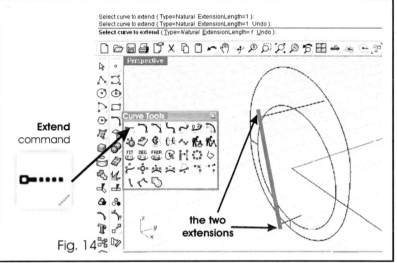

the two extensions

Fig. 14

- Click on the **Curve from 2 Views** command in the **Curve Tools** toolbar.
  - **Select first curve** prompt: select the inner circle. ❶
  - **Select second curve** prompt: select the straight line created in Fig. 12. ❷
  - A third curve will immediately appear which is a combination of the two selected curves. ❸

Curve from 2 Views command

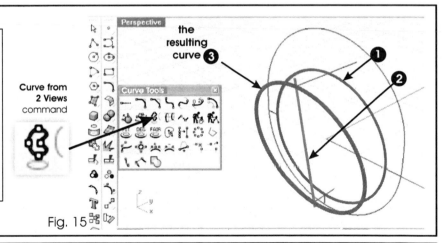

the resulting curve ❸

Fig. 15

- Turn off the **2D curves** layer.

- **Mirror** the curve made in the previous step over to the other side of the ring.

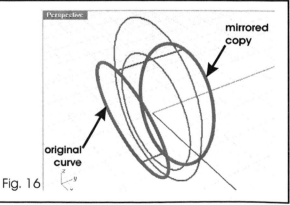

mirrored copy

original curve

Fig. 16

251

- Using the **Arc: Start, End, Point on Arc** command, create arcs at the top and bottom of the ring.

- Use **End** and **quad** osnaps for accurate placement.

Arc: Start, End, Point on Arc
command

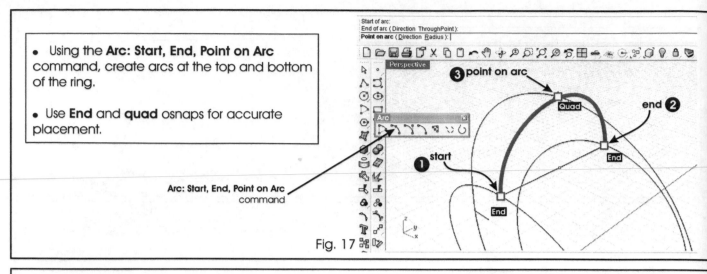

Fig. 17

- **Hide** all inner construction lines - the straight lines and the original inner circle.

- Leave only the 5 curves shown here.

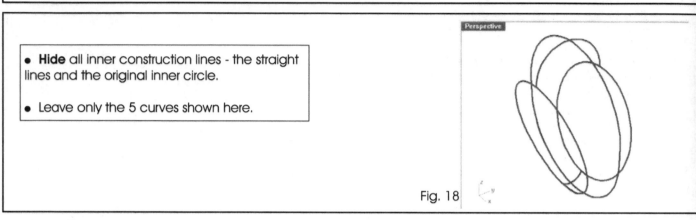

Fig. 18

- **Front viewport.**

- Select the inner and outer closed curves and click on the **Cutting Plane** command in the **Plane** toolbar.

Cutting Plane
command

accesses the
Surface
toolbar flyout

accesses the
Plane
toolbar flyout

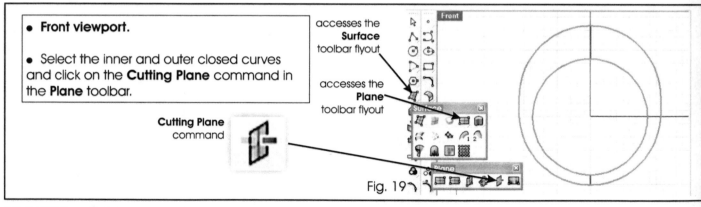

Fig. 19

- **Start of cut plane** prompt: type "0" and press "enter". ❶
- **End of cut plane:** draw the cursor to the side, using **ortho,** and click somewhere on this line to indicate the direction of the cutting plane. ❷

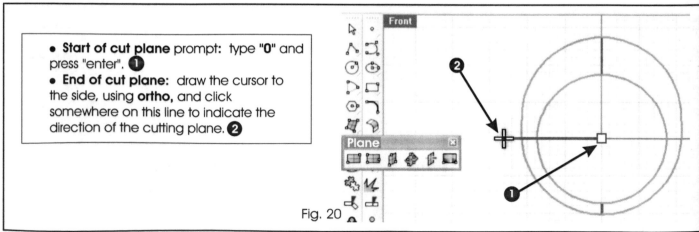

Fig. 20

- A **cutting plane** surface will be created that forms itself so that it cuts through the designated objects.

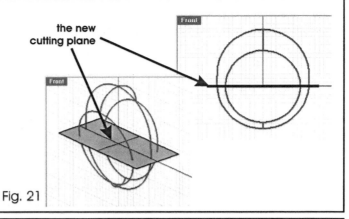

the new cutting plane

Fig. 21

- Click on the **Object Intersection** command in the **Curve from Object** toolbar flyout.

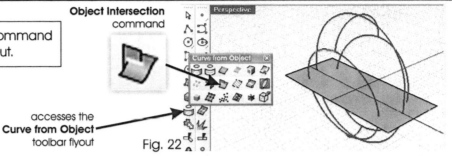

Object Intersection command

accesses the **Curve from Object** toolbar flyout

Fig. 22

- **Select objects to intersect** prompt: select the new **cutting plane surface** and **all the curves that intersect it** - the three closed curves shown.
  - Press "enter".

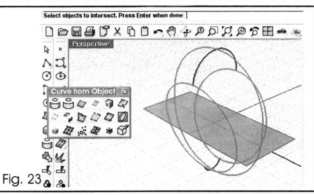

Select objects to intersect. Press Enter when done

Fig. 23

- At the points where the curves intersect the cutting plane surface, point objects will be created.

- This illustration is viewed in **Ghosted viewport mode**.

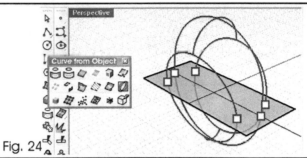

Fig. 24

- Use the **Arc: Start, End, Point on Arc** command to connect the three points on one side of the ring's construction lines as shown.

- **Mirror** this arc over to the other side of the ring.

- You can delete the cutting plane and the points or move them to a new layer.

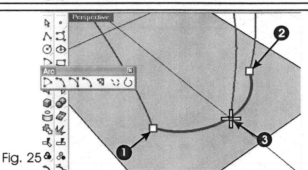

Fig. 25

- A **network of curves** has been created.

- This curve network consists of:
  - **3 closed curves**
  - **4 open curves (the arcs)**

- Any straight lines and the original inner ring circle must be locked or hidden now.

Fig. 26

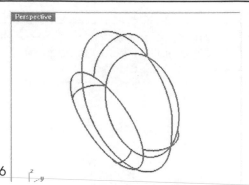

- **RING BODY** layer.

- Select all 7 curves.

- Click on the **Surface from Network of Curves** command in the **Surface** toolbar flyout.

Surface from Network of Curves command

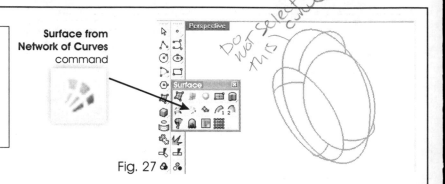

Fig. 27

- The **Surface from Curve Network** dialog box will appear.
- Accept the default values shown in the dialog box.
- Click OK.

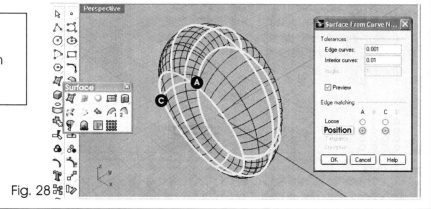

Fig. 28

- Turn off the **construction lines** layer and turn on **Shaded Viewport** mode to view the finished surface.

Fig. 29

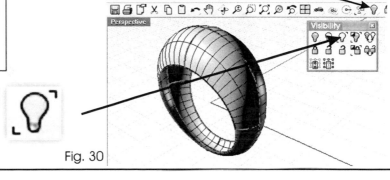

accesses the **Visibility** toolbar flyout

- Turn on the **construction lines** layer again.

- Click on the **Show Selected Objects** command in the **Visibility** toolbar flyout.

Show Selected Objects command

Fig. 30

- All of the previously **Hidden** lines and curves will appear.

- The ring and the network lines will temporarily not be visible.

- Select the longer single line segment on the top of the ring as shown.

- Press "enter".

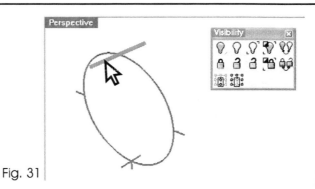

Fig. 31

- The ring and network lines will reappear.

- Navigate so that you can inside the top of the ring surface and you will see that the selected line in the previous step is now showing - it has been "un-hidden".

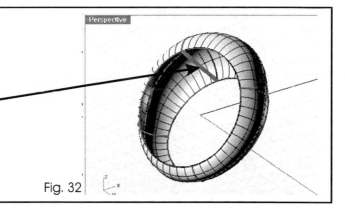

Fig. 32

- Click on the **Sweep 2 Rails** command in the **Surface** toolbar flyout.
    - **First rail** prompt: click on one of the surface edges and select the **surface edge** option from the little drop-down **Selection Menu** as shown. ❶
    - **Second rail** prompt: follow the same procedure as with the first rail, selecting the **surface edge** as before. ❷
    - **Cross section curve** prompt: Select the straight line in the top of the ring that was "un-hidden" previously. ❸

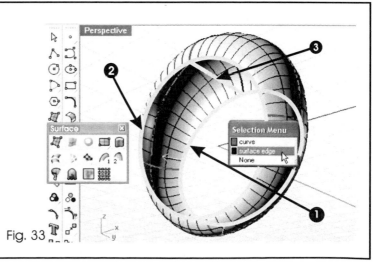

Fig. 33

- Accept the settings in the **Sweep 2 Rails Options** dialog box as before.

- Click OK.

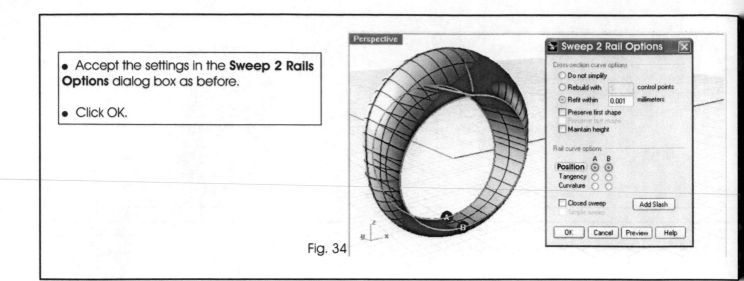

Fig. 34

- **Join** the inner and outer surfaces together.

- Check for Naked Edges.
  - Ref: Naked Edges chapter - page 246.

- Switch to **Render Mode** and toggle off the grid to view your finished basic bombe shape.

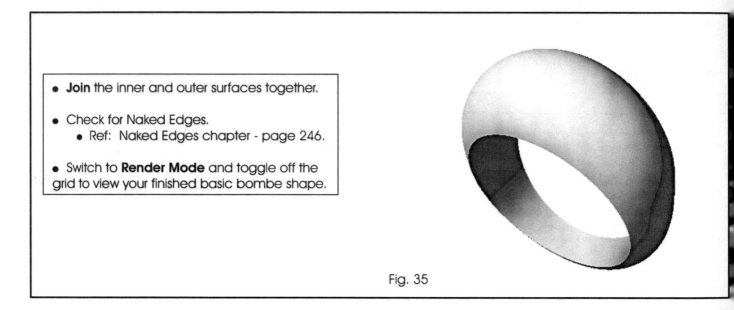

Fig. 35

- Drag the finished ring shape aside.

- **Do not drag the construction lines along with the ring shape.**

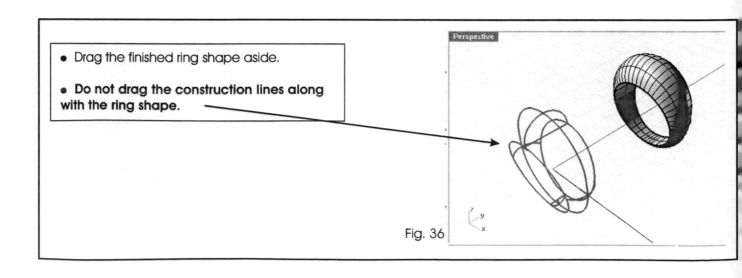

Fig. 36

Basic Bombe ring shape - Version 2

- Name a new layer **RING BODY 2.**

- Make the **2D curves** layer current.

- Turn off the **RING BODY** layer.

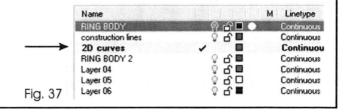

Fig. 37

- **Hide** all curves except for the ones shown.

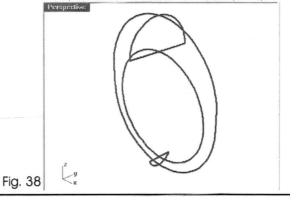

Fig. 38

- **Right Viewport.**

- Click on the **Arc: Start, End, Direction at Start** command to create the arc shown.
  - **Start of arc** prompt: snap/click on the end pont of the lower line as shown.❶
  - **End of arc** prompt: snap/click on the end point of the upper line as shown.❷
  - **Direction at start** prompt: Draw the cursor straight up, using **ortho**, and click to set direction. ❸

Arc: Start, End, Direction at Start command

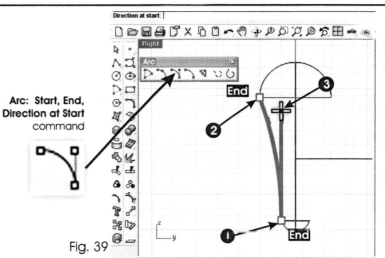

Fig. 39

- A new curve has been created in order to form a different bombe shape.

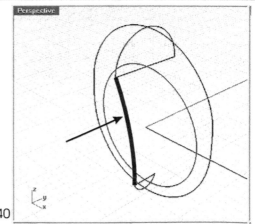

Fig. 40

257

- As before, use the **Extend** command to extend both ends of the new line by **1mm** each.

- **construction lines** layer.

- Select the two curves shown and click on the **Curve from 2 Views** command in the **Curve Tools** toolbar.

Curve from 2 Views command

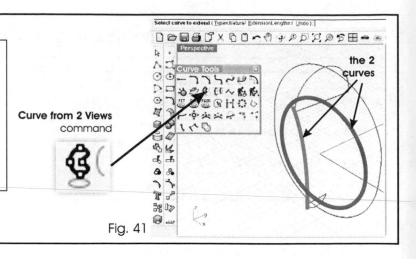

the 2 curves

Fig. 41

- A third curve will immediately appear which is a combination of the two selected curves.

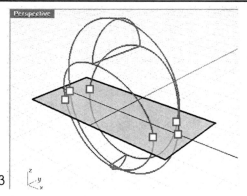

the new curve

Fig. 42

- Create a **cutting plane** as before.

- Use the **Object Intersection** command to create the points shown, as before.

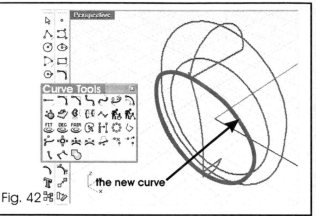

Fig. 43

- Use the **Arc: Start, End, Point on Arc** command to connect the points on one side of the ring as before.

- **Mirror** this arc over to the other side of the ring as before.

- You can delete the cutting plane and the points or move them to a new layer.

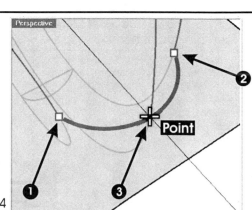

Point

Fig. 44

- The new network of 7 curves.

- Made sure all other lines are hidden so that they do not get selected by mistake in the upcoming **Surface from Network of Curves** command.

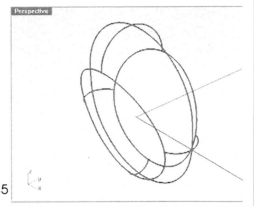

Fig. 45

- **RING BODY 2** layer.

- **Surface from Network of Curves** command.

- Accept the default settings as before and click OK.

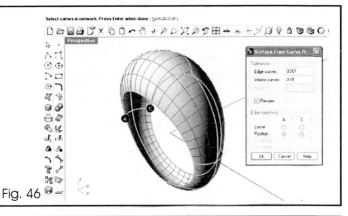

Fig. 46

- A new ring surface has been created.

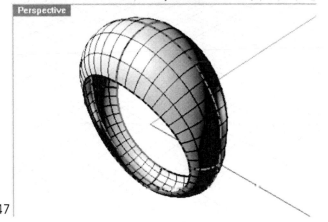

Fig. 47

- Click on the **Show Selected Objects** as before.

- Select the top line to "unhide" as before and press "enter".

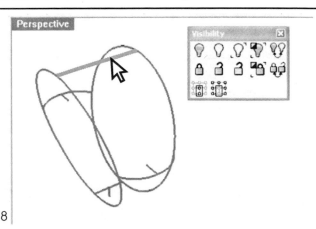

Fig. 48

- Use the **Sweep 2 Rails** command once again to create the inner surface of the ring.

- Notice the **Refit** option in the **Sweep 2 Rails Options** dialog box. This will ensure a very precise fit of the resulting surface to the network curves.

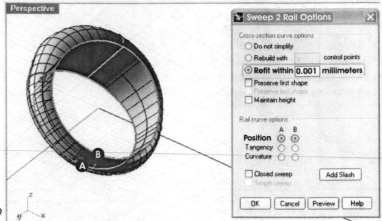

Fig. 49

- **Join** the two surfaced to achieve a closed polysurface.

- Test for naked edges.

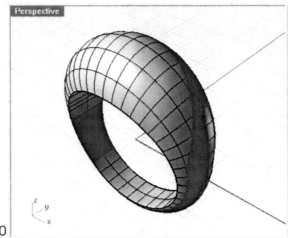

Fig. 50

- **Right Viewport.**

- Turn on the **RING BODY** layer and notice how these two versions look different from each other.

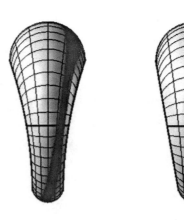

Fig. 51

Bombe Ring - Hollowing Out
Creating a cutting tool and using the Boolean Difference command

- Open the Rhino file called **bombe ring shape.3dm.**

- Save the file as **BOMBE RING hollowed out.3dm**

- **Explode** the ring and **Hide** the inner surface.

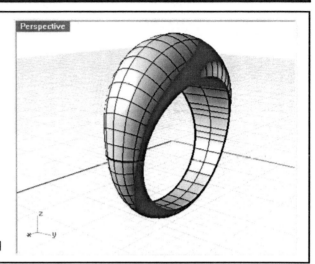

Fig. 1

- **Perspective TOP viewport.**

- Notice the seam the runs over the side of the bombe surface - the seam may be on the top of the ring in your file.

- It is necessary to have this seam at the bottom of the ring shape because otherwise it may get in the way of hollowing out the ring.

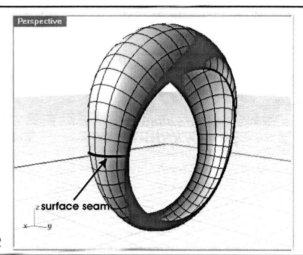

surface seam

Fig. 2

- Click on the **Adjust Surface Seam** command in the **Surface Tools** toolbar flyout.
  - **Select closed surface for seam adjustment** prompt: select the surface.
  - The surface seam will immediately be released to move with the cursor.

Adjust Closed Surface Seam
command

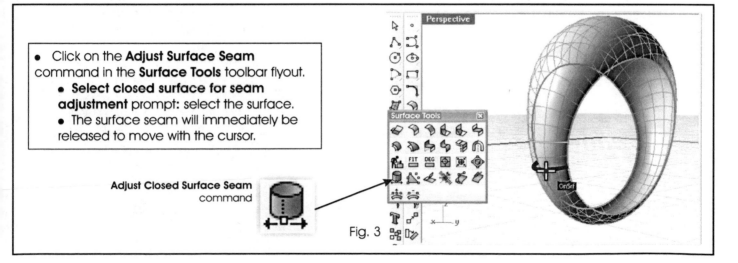

Fig. 3

- **Adjust surface seam** prompt: Drag the cursor down to the middle of the bottom of the ring shape and use **quad osnap** to snap to the exact center as shown.
- Click to set this new location for the closed surface seam.

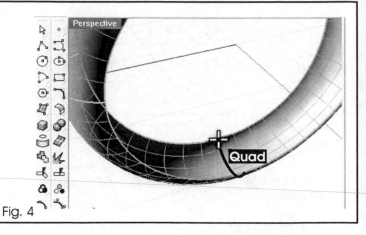

Fig. 4

- The seam has now been moved to the bottom of the ring surface.

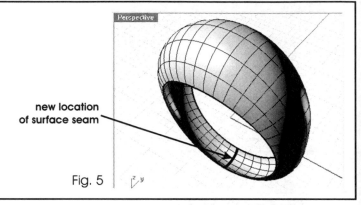

new location
of surface seam

Fig. 5

- **CUTTER** layer.

- Select the ring surface and click on the **Offset Surface** command in the **Surface Tools** toolbar flyout.
    - The surface will immediately display a series of white arrows. These arrows indicate the direction of the offset.
        - These arrows must be pointed inward so that the offset will end up on the inside of the ring surface.

Offset Surface
command

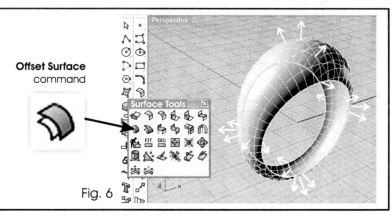

Fig. 6

- Click on the **FlipAll** option in the **Command Line.**
- The direction of the white arrows will be reversed.
    - The illustration shows the correct inward pointing direction of the arrows for this offset.
- Type "**.8**" and press "enter" to set the **Offset distance.**
- Press "enter".

Offset distance <0.800> **FlipAll** (Loose Tolerance=0.001 BothSides):

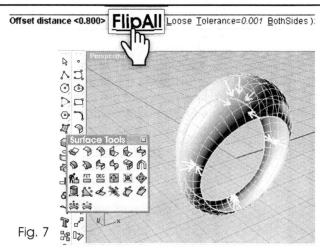

Fig. 7

262

- The offset has been created on the inside of the ring's outer surface as shown.

- This is the surface of the CUTTER that will eventually hollow out the ring.

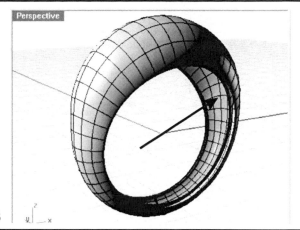

Fig. 8

- If you **Unhide** the inner surface of the ring, you will see that the new offset, which will be the cutter, barely sticks out from the inside of the ring.

- At the top of the ring, the offset does not stick out at all.

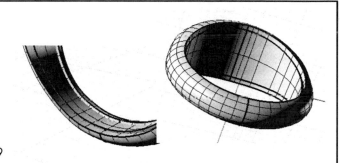

Fig. 9

- It is now necessary to extend the edges of the cutter so that they extend past the inner surface of the ring. Otherwise, the cutter will not get the clearance it needs to hollow out the ring.

- Turn off the **RING BODY** layer.

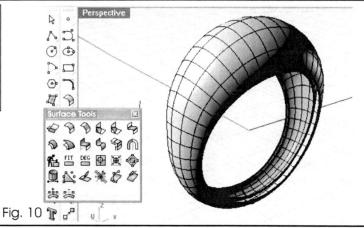

Fig. 10

- Click on the the **Extend Untrimmed Surface** command in the **Surface Tools** toolbar flyout.
    - **Select edge of surface to extend prompt:** click on one of the edges as shown.
    - **Extension factor** prompt: type ".5" and press "enter".

Extend Untrimmed Surface
command

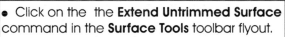

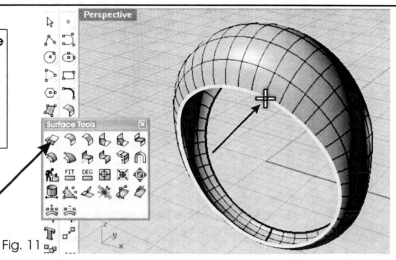

Fig. 11

- The selected edge will be extended by .5mm.

- Repeat this process with the other edge.

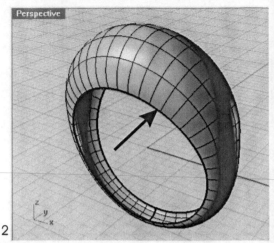

Fig. 12

- **Rebuild** the cutter with the values shown.

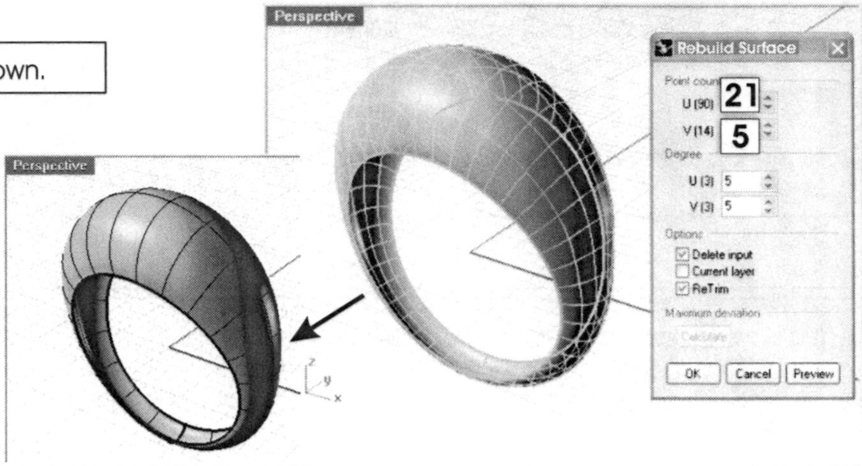

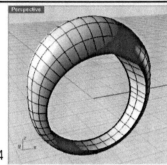

Point count
U (90) **21**
V (14) **5**

Degree
U (3) 5
V (3) 5

Options
☑ Delete input
☐ Current layer
☑ ReTrim

Maximum deviation
Calculate

OK   Cancel   Preview

Fig. 13

- Turn on the **RING BODY** layer and **Unhide** the inner surface of the ring.

- **Join** both together to create a closed polysurface.

Fig. 14

- It is possible that these two surfaces may not join. This will be because, when the closed curve seam was moved, the geometry changed slightly, making it necessary to create a new inner surface.

- Delete the inner surface and click on the **Sweep 2 Rails** command.

- Select one of the surface edges as the first rail. *Notice that only part of the edge selects. The edge is broken and needs to be fixed.*

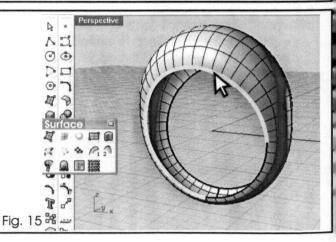

Surface

Fig. 15

- **Select edge to merge**
  prompt: select one of the edges as shown.
    - The edge will repair itself as shown.
  - Repeat this process with the other edge.

Merge Edge command (right click)

accesses the **Edge Tools** toolbar lfyout

accesses the **Analyze** toolbar flyout

Fig. 16

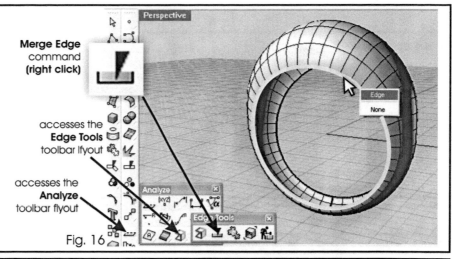

- Create an inner surface, using the **Sweep 2 Rails** command.

- **Join** the inner and outer surfaces.

- Check for Naked Edges.

rails

cross section curve

Fig. 17

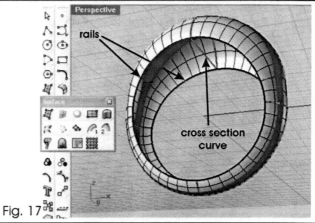

- **Front viewport.**

- **Ghosted viewport mode.**

- Turn on the **cutter** layer and turn on the cutter's control points.

- Window select the bottom three rows of control points as shown.

Fig. 18

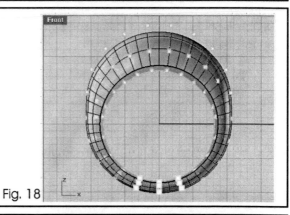

- **Move** or **Drag** the selected control points upward so that part of the cutter lifts off the bottom of the ring as shown.
    - The preview lines will show you the new shape of the cutter as it lifts out of the ring band as shown.

- Click to set a new location for the control points.

Fig. 19

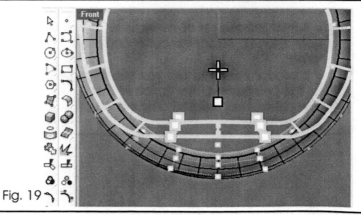

265

- **Perspective TOP viewport.**

- Turn off control points.

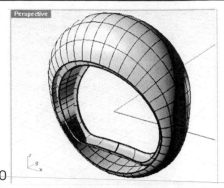

Fig. 20

- Turn off or hide the RING BODY and click on the **Analyze Direction** command.
  - **Select objects for direction display** prompt: select the cutter.
    - The white arrows that appear on its surface **must point outward** for the Boolean Difference in the next step to work properly.
  - Click on the surface or click on the **Flip** option in the **Command Line** to change the direction of the arrows.

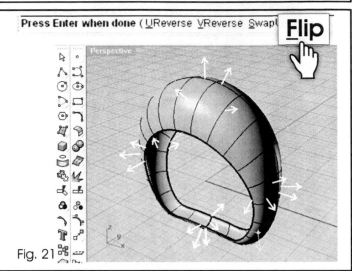

Fig. 21

- Click on the **Boolean Difference** command in the **Solid Tools** toolbar flyout.
  - **Select first set of surfaces or polysurfaces** prompt: select the ring body and press "enter".

Boolean Difference command

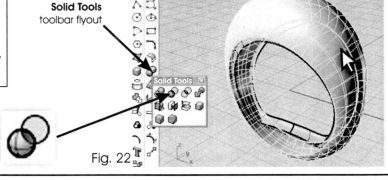

Fig. 22

- **Select second set of surfaces or polysurfaces**: select the cutter and press "enter".
  - It is recommended that you also toggle on the **DeleteInput=No** option so that your cutter is not deleted after this step.
  - Press "enter".

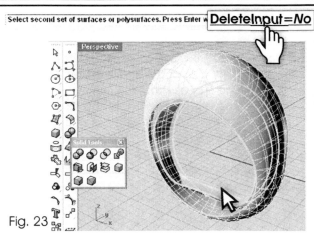

Fig. 23

266

- The cutter has hollowed out the ring.

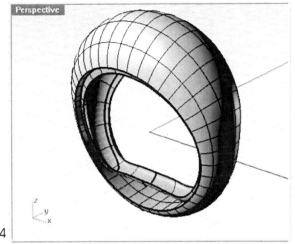

Fig. 24

- Turn off the **cutter** layer and view the finished ring.

- View the finished ring in **Rendered Viewport** mode with the grid turned off (press F7 to toggle the grid off and on).

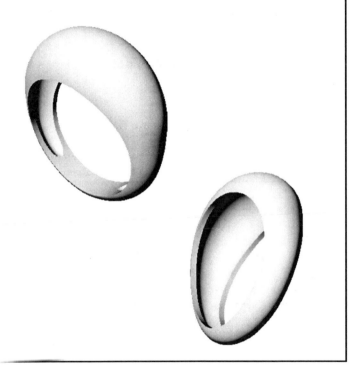

Fig. 25

BOMBE RING - Blended Bezel at Top
Blend Surface command

- **Import** the file **BOMBE RING - Hollowed Out.3dm** from the previous chapter.

- Save this file as **bombe ring with stone.3dm**.

- Turn off both the **RING BODY** and the **RING BODY 2** layers.

Import/Merge command [right-click]

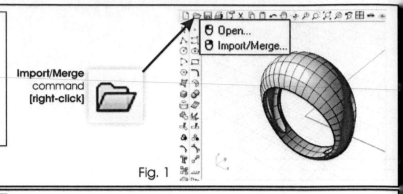

Fig. 1

- **Top viewport.**

- Create two new layers called **cabochon** and **cabochon curves**.

- **cabochon curves** layer current.

- Create an **Ellipse** measuring **6mm x 8mm** around "**0**".

Ellipse command

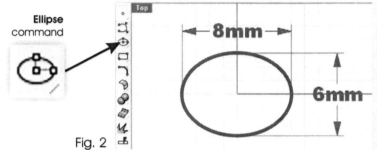

Fig. 2

- **Perspective TOP viewport.**

- Create a vertical line from "**0**" with a length of **3mm**.
    - *Remember that when you are in the **Line** command, if you click on the **Vertical** option in the **Command Line** and you can create this line in the Perspective top viewport as shown.*

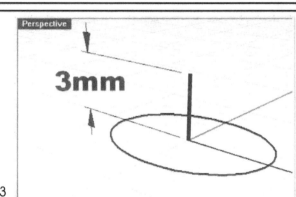

Fig. 3

- Create an arc using the **Arc: Start, End, Point on Arc** command in the **Arc** toolbar flyout.
    - **Start of arc** prompt: **①**
    - **End of arc** prompt: **②**
    - **Point on arc** prompt: **③**
- Use **Quad** and **End** snap for accurate placement.

Arc: Start, End, Point on Arc command

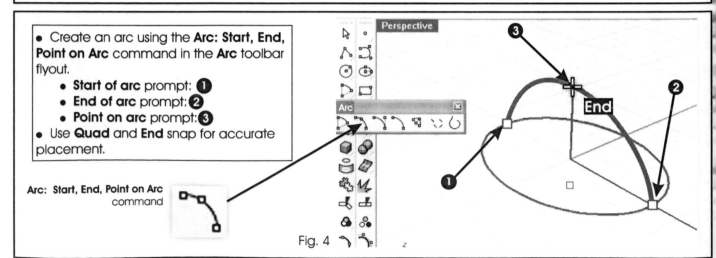

Fig. 4

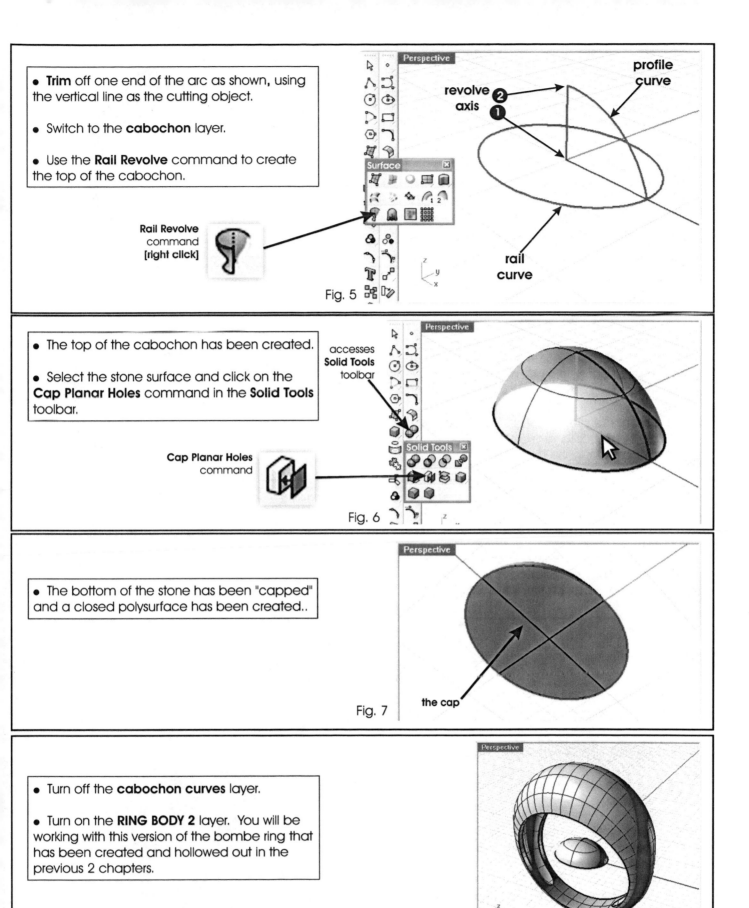

- **Trim** off one end of the arc as shown, using the vertical line as the cutting object.

- Switch to the **cabochon** layer.

- Use the **Rail Revolve** command to create the top of the cabochon.

Rail Revolve
command
[right click]

Fig. 5

profile curve

revolve axis ② ①

rail curve

- The top of the cabochon has been created.

- Select the stone surface and click on the **Cap Planar Holes** command in the **Solid Tools** toolbar.

accesses **Solid Tools** toolbar

Cap Planar Holes command

Fig. 6

- The bottom of the stone has been "capped" and a closed polysurface has been created..

Fig. 7

the cap

- Turn off the **cabochon curves** layer.

- Turn on the **RING BODY 2** layer. You will be working with this version of the bombe ring that has been created and hollowed out in the previous 2 chapters.

Fig. 8

269

- **Front Viewport.**

- **Move** the stone upward to a distance of **13.5mm** so that it rests on top of the ring as shown.

- Use **ortho.**

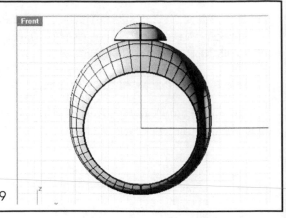

Fig. 9

- Create a new layer called **cutter 2** and make it current.

- Select the ring and click on the **Cutting Plane** command in the **Plane** toolbar flyout.
  - **Start of cut plane** prompt: click on the construction plane on a point to the left of the ring as shown. ❶
  - **End of cut plane** prompt: using **ortho**, draw the cursor to the right and click anywhere along this direction. ❷

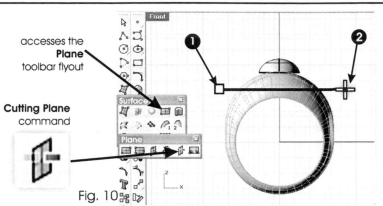

accesses the **Plane** toolbar flyout

Cutting Plane command

Fig. 10

- The finished cutting plane.

- If you change the view, you can see how the cutting plane has adjusted its width to make sure that it completely intersects the ring.

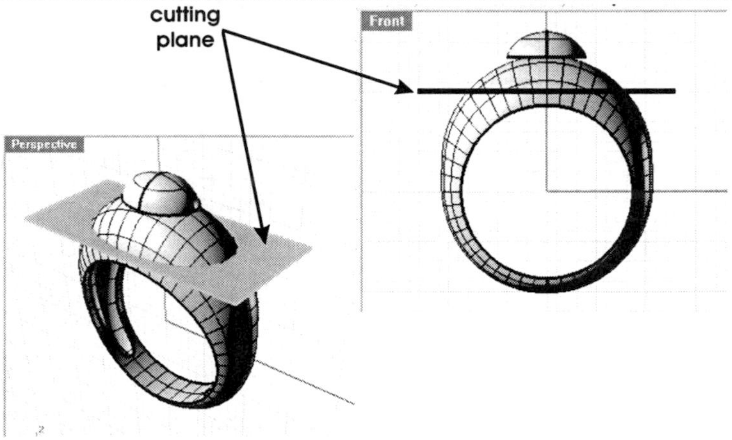

cutting plane

Fig. 11

- **Perspective TOP viewport.**

- You can turn off the **cabochon** layer for better visibility.

- Click on the **Trim** command.
  - **Select cutting objects** prompt: select the cutting plane and press "enter". ❶
  - **Select object to trim** prompt: select the top of the ring that sticks up out of the cutting plane. ❷

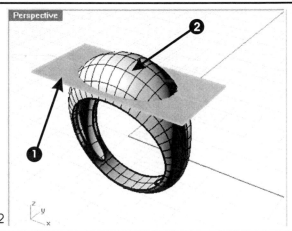

Fig. 12

270

- **Object to trim:** select the top of the ring.
    - You will have to trim the inner wall of the ring as well after you have selected the outer.

- Illustration shows the completed trim.

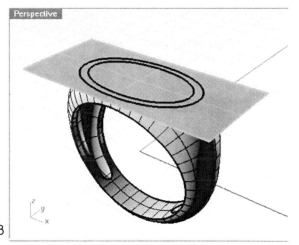

Fig. 13

- Turn off the **cutter 2** layer.

- Notice that the ring is now open at the top. It is an open polysurface because the top has been trimmed off.

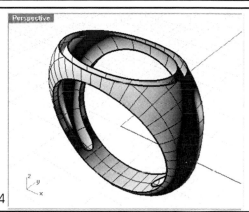

Fig. 14

- Turn on the **cabochon** layer.

- Turn off the **RING BODY 2** layer.

- Toggle on **Ghosted Mode**

- Create a new layer called **extrusions** and make it current.

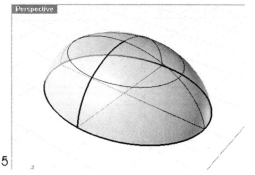

Fig. 15

- Click on the **Offset Curve** command to create an offset curve on the inside of the cabochon.
    - **Select curve to offset:** select the outside edge of the cabochon. This surface edge will be selected as the curve to offset. **①**
    - **Side to offset:** type ".5mm" and press "enter".
    - **Side to offset:** draw the cursor to the inside of the stone and click to set the offset location. **②**

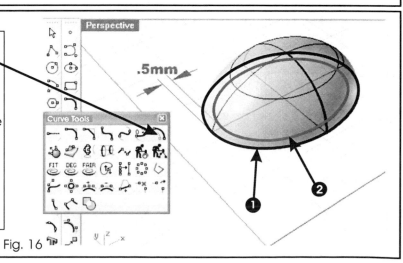

Fig. 16

271

- **Offset** the curve just created to the outside.
  - **Offset distance: 1.2mm**

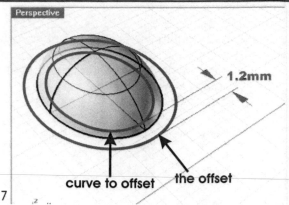

1.2mm

curve to offset   the offset

Fig. 17

- Turn off the **cabochon** layer.

- Select the two concentric ellipses and click on the **Extrude Straight** command in the **Surface** toolbar flyout.

Extrude Straight
command

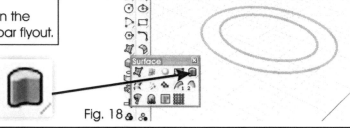

Fig. 18

- **Extrusion distance** prompt: type **"1"** in the and press "enter".

- Two little surfaces will be extruded upward from the two selected ellipses as shown.

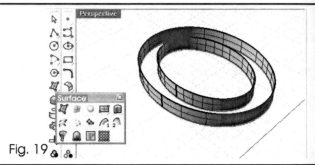

Fig. 19

- **Front Viewport.**

- turn the **cabochon** layer back on.

- **Move** the two extruded surfaces and their curves upward to a distance of **1.5mm**.

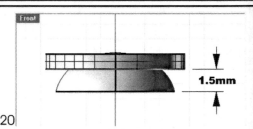

1.5mm

Fig. 20

- **Perspective TOP viewport.**

- Turn off the **cabochon** layer.

- Turn on the **RING BODY 2** layer.

- View the project so far.

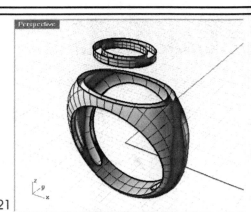

Fig. 21

272

- Click on the **Blend Surface** command in the **Surface Tools** toolbar flyout.
  - **Select segment for first edge** prompt: select the lower edge of the inner little extrusion as shown and press "enter".

Blend Surface command

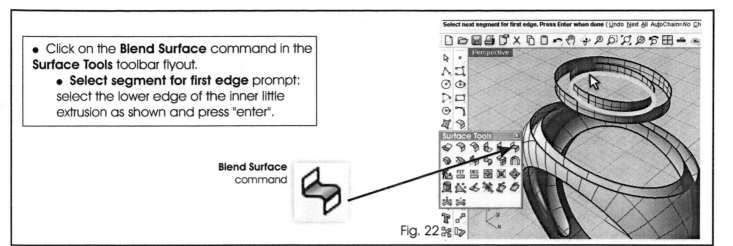

Fig. 22

- **Select segment for second edge** prompt: select the surface edge of the inside of the ring as shown.
- The **surface seam** will immediately appear and you will be prompted to **Adjust closed curve seam.**
  - It is advised to drag the two points of this seam to a symmetrical position so that the resulting blend surface is symmetrical and not wrinkled.

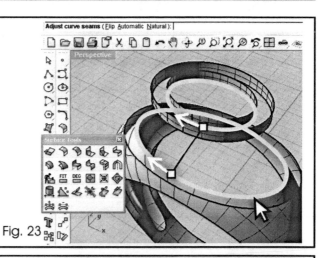

Fig. 23

- **Drag** the ends of the curve seam around to one the quad points of the surface edges as shown.
- Click to set the new seam locations.

Fig. 24

- Dragging the second point of the curve seam into place.
- Press "enter".

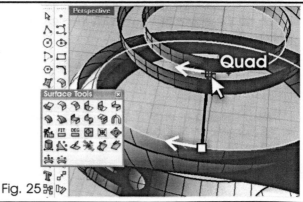

Fig. 25

- A preview line of the modulation of the blend surface will appear along with the **Adjust End Bulge** dialog box.
  - This preview can be point edited by dragging the points or by use of the sliders in the dialog box.
  - For this exercise, accept the default blend shape by clicking the OK button.

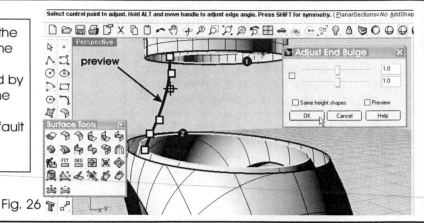

Fig. 26

- A surface will appear that smoothly blends the inner ring surface with the little inner extrusion at the top.

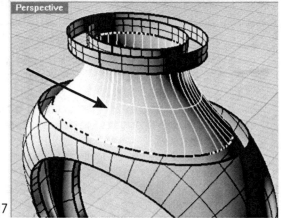

Fig. 27

- Use the same technique to create a blend between the two outer surfaces as shown.

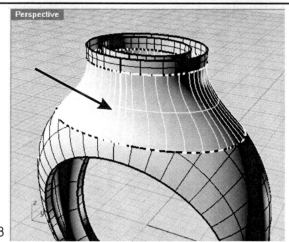

Fig. 28

- Turn off the **extrusions** layer with the two little utility surfaces..

- **Join** the two new blend surfaces to the rest of the ring as shown.

- Select the ring and click on the **Cap Planar Holes** command in the **Sold Tools** toolbar flyout.

Cap Planar Holes command

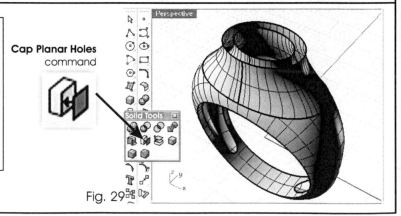

Fig. 29

- A new surface will appear at the top, **"capping"** the polysurface so that it is now a *closed polysurface.*

the cap

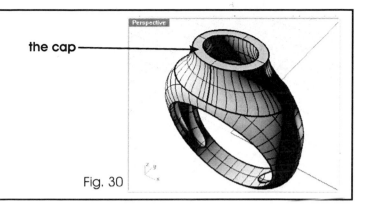

Fig. 30

- Click on the **New Layer** button at the top of the **Layers** box as shown.

- Make this new layer current. No need to give this layer a name. It is of very temporary use.

New Layer
command

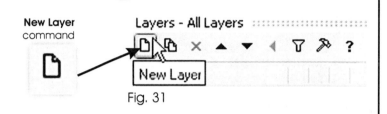

Fig. 31

- Click on the **Pipe** command in the **Solid** toolbar flyout.

Pipe
command

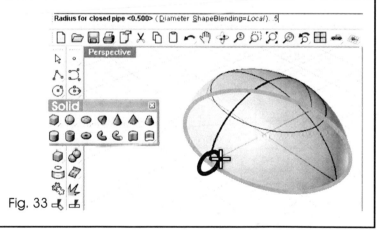

Fig. 32

- **Select curve to create pipe around** prompt: select the bottom edge of the stone.
    - A little radius preview circle will appear and you will be prompted to specify the **Radius for closed pipe.**
        - Type ".5" and press "enter".
- **Point for next radius** prompt press "enter".

Fig. 33

- A tube-like "pipe" will form itself perfectly around the designated lower edge of the stone as shown.

- This is a single closed surface.

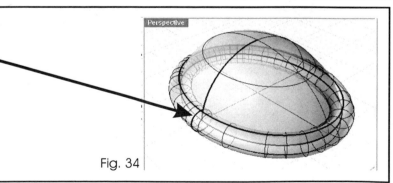

Fig. 34

- Turn off the **cabochon** layer and turn on the the **RING BODY 2** layer once again.

- The newly created "pipe" will be seen mostly buried withing the upper walls of the ring as shown.

- Click on the **Boolean Union** command.

pipe is
just visible

Boolean Union
command   Fig. 35

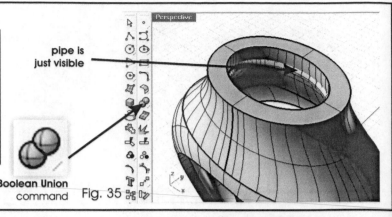

- **Select surfaces or polysurfaces to union** prompt: select both ring and pipe. and press "enter".

Select surfaces or polysurfaces to union. Press Enter when done:

Fig. 36

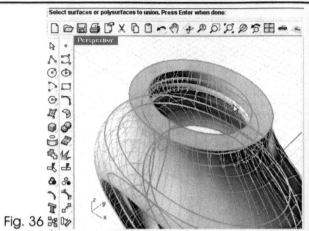

- The ring and the pipe are now one closed polysurface.

- Notice the new seams at the top and bottom of where the pipe sticks out of the inner wall of the ring top.

- Create a new layer and call it **stone seat cutter** and make it current.

Fig. 37

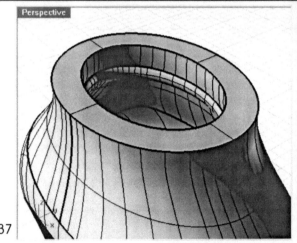

- Turn off the **RING BODY 2** layer and turn on the **cabochon** layer.

- Click on the **Extrude closed planar curve** command in the **Solid** toolbar flyout.
  - **Select curves to extrude** prompt: select the lower seam of the stone and press "enter".

Extrude Closed Planar Curve
command

Fig. 38

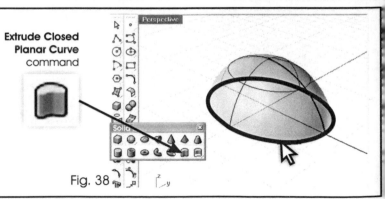

- After you press "enter" a polysurface will immediately start to grow out of the selected curve.
- Draw the cursor upward so that the extrusion created is higher than the stone. You can do this by eye.
- Click to set the height of the extrusion.

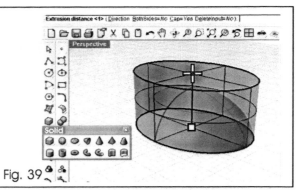

Fig. 39

- The extrusion is capped by default. This means that it is a **closed polysurface.**

- The reason for this is that this is a solid extrusion that is part of the group of solid commands.

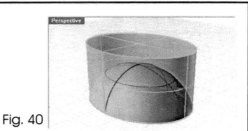

Fig. 40

- Turn on the **RING BODY 2** layer and turn off the **cabochon** layer.

- Click on the **Boolean Difference** command.
  - **Select first set of surfaces or polysurfaces** prompt: select the ring body and press "enter". **1**
  - **Select second set of surfaces or polysurfaces** prompt: select the extrusion and press "enter". **2**

accesses the **Solid Tools** toolbar

Boolean Difference command

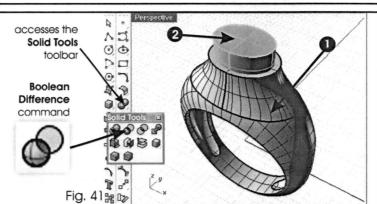

Fig. 41

- Turn off the **stone seat cutter** layer.

- Note the seat for the cabochon that has been cut out of the top of the ring with the boolean difference.

- Also note that the pipe command added some extra material for the stone seat.

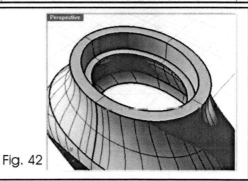

Fig. 42

- The finished ring

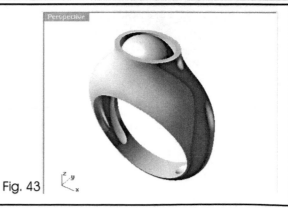

Fig. 43

277

Extruded Ring Bands
Extruding Planar and Non Planar Surfaces

- Create layers shown.

- Make **construction lines** layer current.

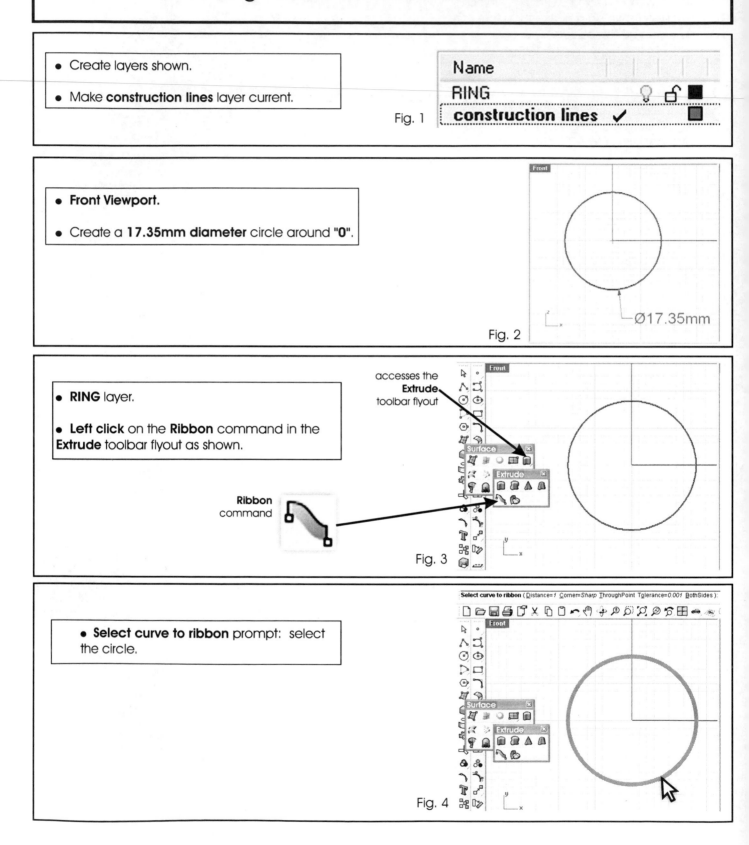

Fig. 1

Name		
RING		
construction lines ✓		

- **Front Viewport.**

- Create a **17.35mm diameter** circle around "**0**".

Ø17.35mm

Fig. 2

- **RING** layer.

- **Left click** on the **Ribbon** command in the **Extrude** toolbar flyout as shown.

accesses the **Extrude** toolbar flyout

Ribbon command

Fig. 3

- **Select curve to ribbon** prompt: select the circle.

Select curve to ribbon (Distance=1 Corner=Sharp ThroughPoint Tolerance=0.001 BothSides):

Fig. 4

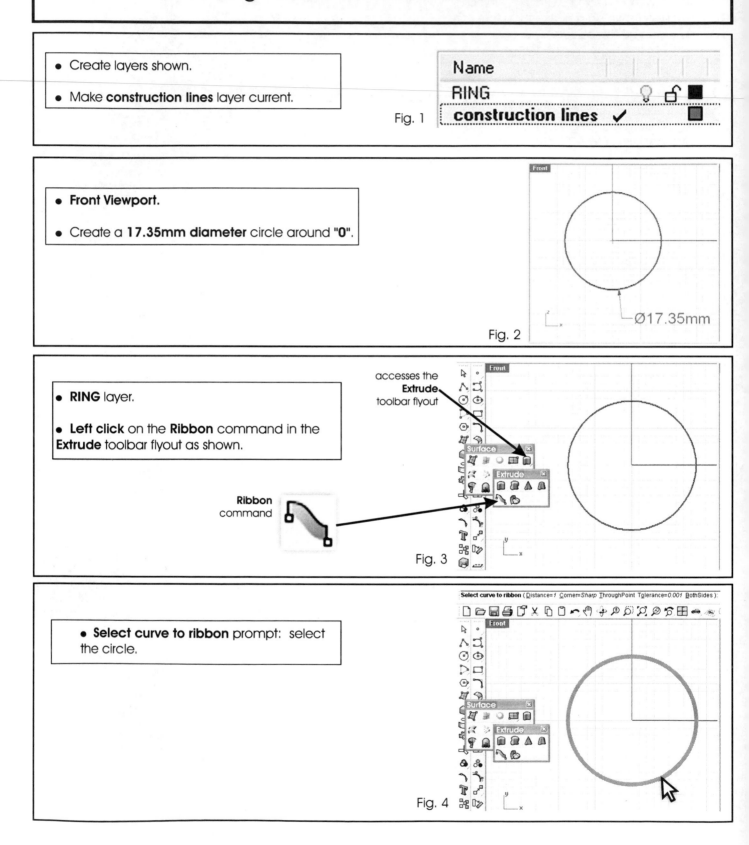

- **Side to offset** prompt: Type "**2**" and press "enter".

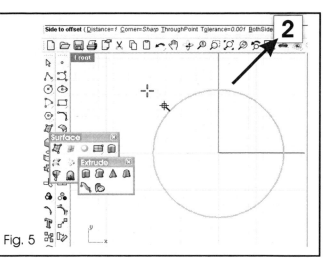

Fig. 5

- **Side to offset** prompt: Click to set the location of the offset as shown.
  - Make sure that the cursor is on the outside of the circle as shown.

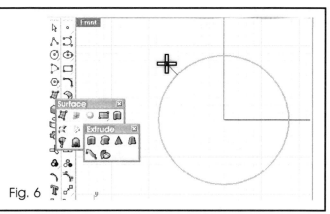

Fig. 6

- A new surface that is **2mm wide** has been created around the circle.

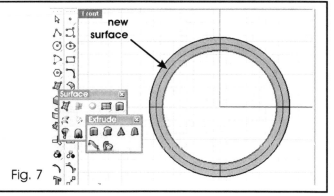

Fig. 7

- **Perspective TOP** viewport.

- Turn off the **construction lines** layer.

- Select the new surface and click on the **Extrude Surface** command in the **Solid** toolbar flyout as shown.

Extrude Surface
command

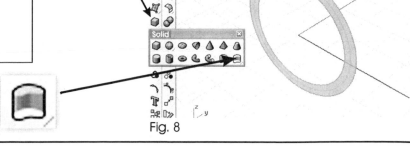

Fig. 8

- As you draw the cursor back along the X axis, notice that the surface extends ("extrudes") itself to become a solid object.
- **Extrusion distance** prompt: Type **"3"** and press "enter".

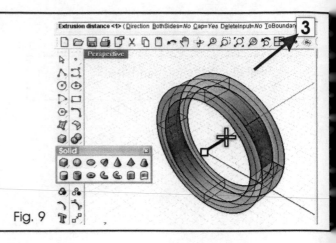

Fig. 9

- A simple band has been created from the extrusion of a planar (flat) surface.

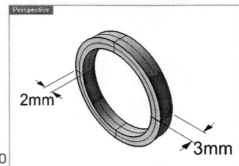

2mm

3mm

Fig. 10

- **Hide** the new extruded ring band, leaving the original surface as shown.

- Rebuild this original surface as shown.

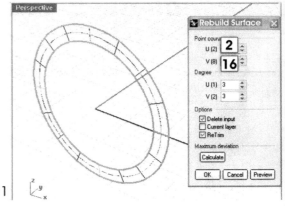

Fig. 11

- Turn on control points and select every other row of control points as shown.

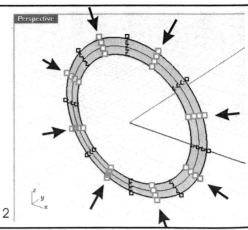

Fig. 12

- Use the **Move** command to move the selected control points straight back along the Y axis for a distance of **6mm**.
  - Notice the preview surface.

- Use **ortho**.

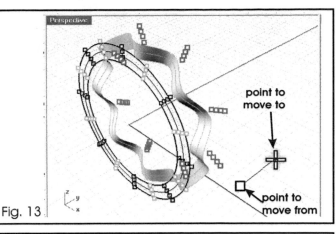

Fig. 13

point to move to

point to move from

- Select the surface and click on the **Extrude Surface** command in the **Solid** toolbar flyout.

- Notice that the surface is now being extruded vertically to the construction plane, rather than along the construction plane as before.

- This is because the surface to be extruded is now **non-planar** because of the previous control point editing. *It is not flat any more.*

Extrude Surface
command

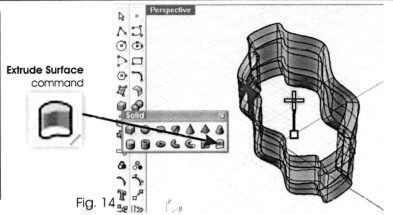

Fig. 14

- To set a correct extrusion direction, click on the **Direction** option in the **Command Line** as shown.

Fig. 15

Creating rendering   ncel
Extrusion distance   s=*No* Cap=*Yes* DeleteInput=*No* ToBoundary):

Direction

- **Base point for direction** prompt: click on the construction plane for a point of reference. ❶
  - **Second direction point** prompt: using **ortho**, draw the cursor straight up as shown and click to set direction.❷
- Press "enter" after setting these points to accept the default of **"3"** from the previous extrusion.

- The finished band's shape reflects the point editing of the surface.

- Even though this was a non-planar surface, the **Extrude Surface** command has still created a closed polysurface.

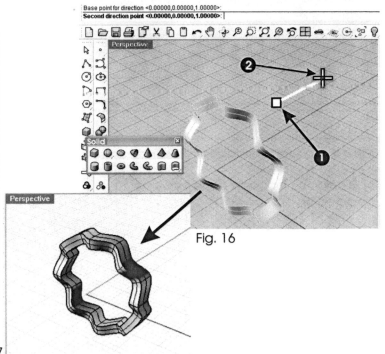

Fig. 16

Fig. 17

1mm Round Stone Maquette with Stone Seat/Hole Cutters

A simplified shape to use in place of a fully faceted stone model.

- Create the layers shown **and delete all extra unused layers.**

- **stone construction lines** layer current.

Name			
1MM RD STONE		💡 🔓 ⬛
stone construction lines	✓	⬛
stone reference geometry		💡 🔓 ⬜
stone seat cutter		💡 🔓 ⬜
stone seat cutter cons lines		💡 🔓 ⬛

Fig. 1

- **Perspective viewport.**

- Create a circle around "0" with a diameter of **.53mm** as shown.

- Create a second circle around "0" with a diameter of **1mm**.

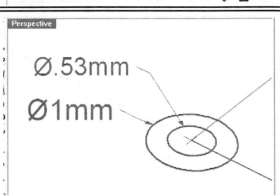

Ø.53mm
Ø1mm

Fig. 2

- **Front Perspective viewport.**

- **Move** the smaller circle up **.18mm**, using **ORTHO** for accuracy.

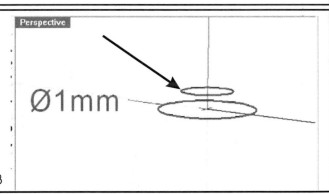

Ø1mm

Fig. 3

- **Still in the Front Perspective viewport.**

- Zoom in on the larger circle that is still centered on "0".

- Use the **Offset Curve** command with the **BothSides** option toggled on in the **Command Line**.
  - Offset distance: **.01mm**.

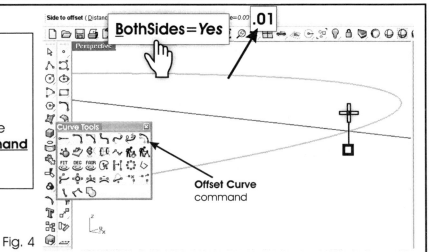

BothSides=Yes
.01

Offset Curve
command

Fig. 4

282

- The resulting offsets are on either side of the original curve.

- Change the original curve to the **stone reference geometry** layer.

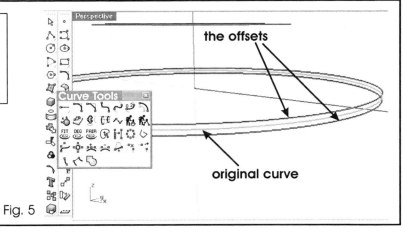

the offsets

original curve

Fig. 5

- Place a single **Point** on "0".

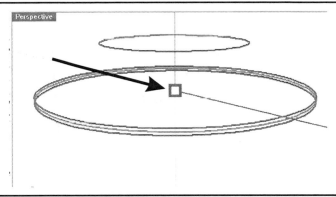

Fig. 6

- Using **ORTHO**, **Move** the new point down at a distance of **.43mm**.

- Turn off the **stone reference geometry** layer.

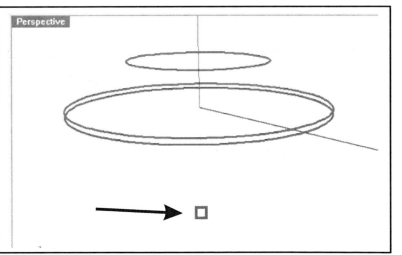

Fig. 7

- **Loft** the three circles and the point together.
  - Choose the **Straight Sections** option in the **Styles** drop-down menu as shown.

Loft
command

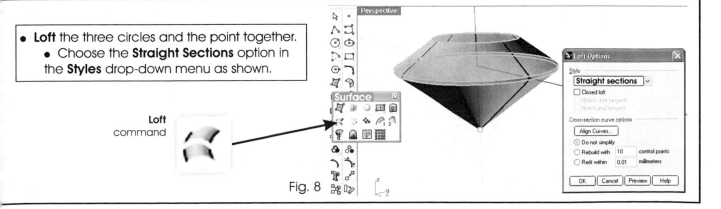

Fig. 8

- Select the lofted surfaces and click on the **Cap Planar Holes** command in the **Solid Tools** toolbar flyout to close the hole at the top of the stone as shown.

accesses the **Solid Tools** toolbar flyout

the cap

Cap Planar Holes command

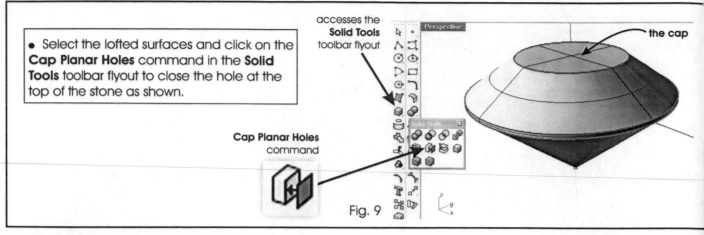

Fig. 9

- **Perspective** viewport.

- Turn off the **construction lines** layer.

- **stone reference geometry** layer current.

- Place a **Point** on "**0**" as shown.

- **Front viewport.**

- **Copy** the point up so that another point is placed slightly above the top of the stone as shown.

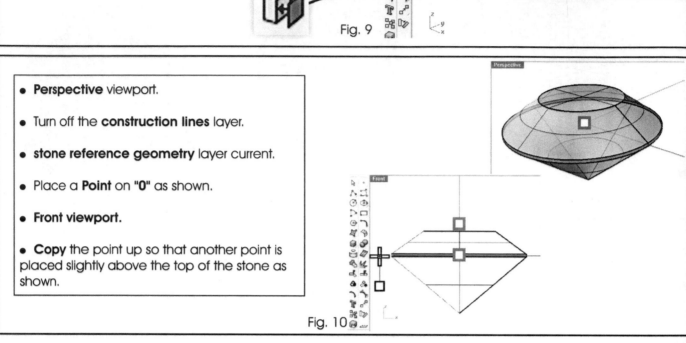

Fig. 10

- **Front viewport.**

- Turn off the **stone construction lines** layer.

- **stone seat construction lines** layer current.

- Create a polyline as shown, using **end osnap** to ensure that you touch the locations shown and **ortho** to set point ❸

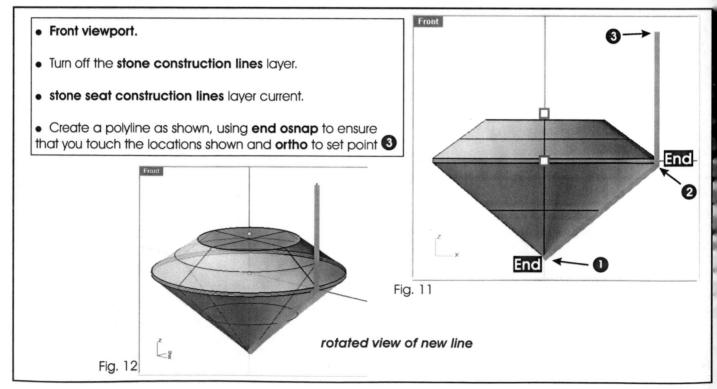

Fig. 11

rotated view of new line

Fig. 12

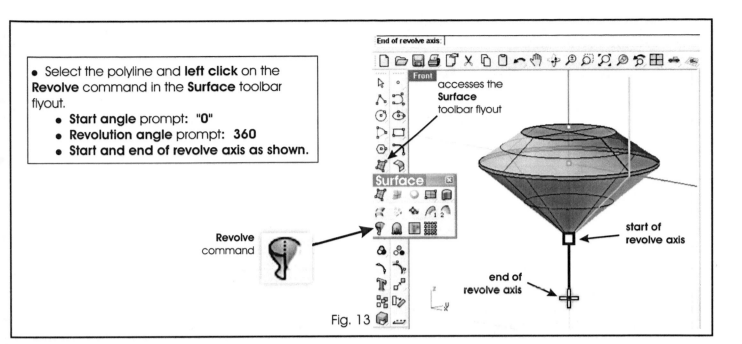

- Select the polyline and **left click** on the **Revolve** command in the **Surface** toolbar flyout.
  - **Start angle** prompt: **"0"**
  - **Revolution angle** prompt: **360**
  - **Start and end of revolve axis as shown.**

Revolve command

accesses the **Surface** toolbar flyout

start of revolve axis

end of revolve axis

Fig. 13

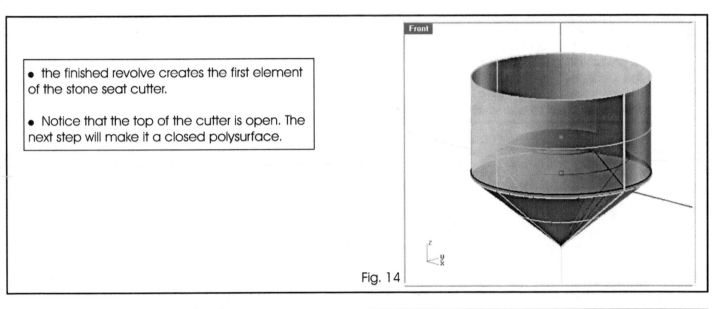

- the finished revolve creates the first element of the stone seat cutter.

- Notice that the top of the cutter is open. The next step will make it a closed polysurface.

Fig. 14

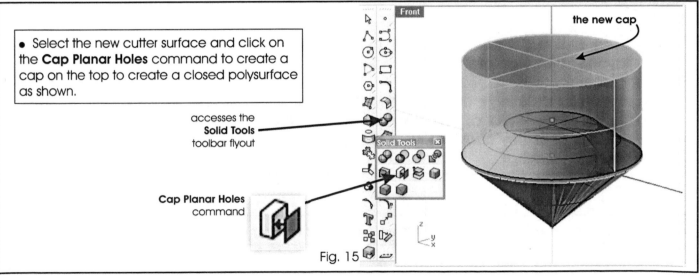

- Select the new cutter surface and click on the **Cap Planar Holes** command to create a cap on the top to create a closed polysurface as shown.

accesses the **Solid Tools** toolbar flyout

Cap Planar Holes command

the new cap

Fig. 15

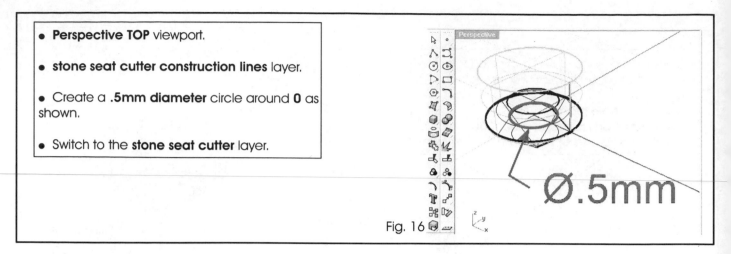

- **Perspective TOP** viewport.

- **stone seat cutter construction lines** layer.

- Create a **.5mm diameter** circle around **0** as shown.

- Switch to the **stone seat cutter** layer.

Fig. 16

Ø.5mm

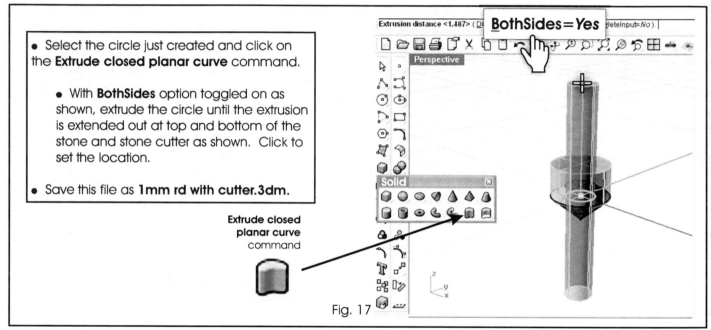

- Select the circle just created and click on the **Extrude closed planar curve** command.

  - With **BothSides** option toggled on as shown, extrude the circle until the extrusion is extended out at top and bottom of the stone and stone cutter as shown. Click to set the location.

- Save this file as **1mm rd with cutter.3dm**.

Extrude closed
planar curve
command

Extrusion distance <1.487> (D   eleteInput=No)

BothSides=Yes

Fig. 17

- **This stone and cutter model is meant to be imported into projects where a stone is needed.**

- **This stone and cutter can be scaled up to whatever size is required. Cutters (and cutter layers) can be deleted if not needed.**

- **The reason for deleting extra unused layers is that, when a file is imported into another Rhino file, all of the layers of the imported file are brought in as well.** *You don't need to have a bunch of empty unused layers being added to the layers box of the project on which you are working!*

Note: You can use this technique to create a cutter around a faceted stone model as well.

Prong Set Round Faceted Stone I
Straight perpendicular prongs

- Create layers as shown and delete unused layers.

- Make the **prong curves** layer current.

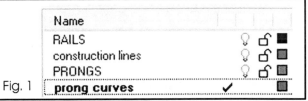

Name		
RAILS	💡 🔓 ◼
construction lines	💡 🔓 ◻
PRONGS	💡 🔓 ◻
prong curves	✓ ◼

Fig. 1

- **Right-click** on the **Import/Merge** command as shown.

- File to import: **1mm rd with cutter** from the previous exercise.

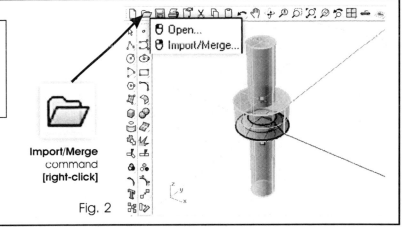

Import/Merge
command
[right-click]

Fig. 2

- The layers in the stone file have been imported along with the model, as you can see from the Layers dialog box.

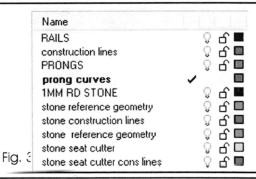

Name		
RAILS	💡 🔓 ◼
construction lines	💡 🔓 ◻
PRONGS	💡 🔓 ◻
prong curves	✓ ◼
1MM RD STONE	💡 🔓 ◼
stone reference geometry	💡 🔓 ◻
stone construction lines	💡 🔓 ◻
stone reference geometry	💡 🔓 ◻
stone seat cutter	💡 🔓 ◻
stone seat cutter cons lines	💡 🔓 ◻

Fig. 3

- **Delete** the following layers:
  - stone seat cutter
  - stone construction lines
  - stone seat cutter cons lines

- Remaining layers should be as shown.

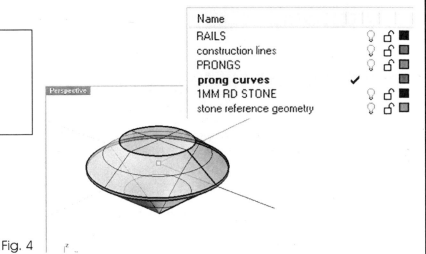

Perspective

Name		
RAILS	💡 🔓 ◼
construction lines	💡 🔓 ◻
PRONGS	💡 🔓 ◻
prong curves	✓ ◼
1MM RD STONE	💡 🔓 ◼
stone reference geometry	💡 🔓 ◻

Fig. 4

287

- Select the stone and its reference geometry and click on the **Scale 3-D** command in the **Scale** toolbar flyout.
  - **Origin point** prompt: type "**0**" and press "enter".
  - **Scale factor or first reference point** prompt: type "**6**" and press "enter".

Scale 3-D command

accesses the **Scale** toolbar flyout

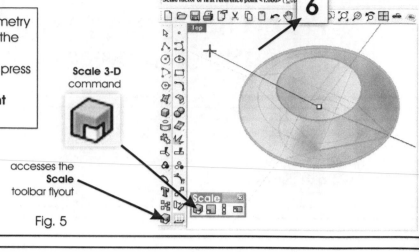

Fig. 5

- The stone has been scaled up so that it is now **6mm in diameter**.

- **The stone's reference geometry has also been scaled up.**

Ø6mm

Fig. 6

- **Top viewport.**

- **Offset** the circle (stone reference geometry) around the girdle of the stone to a distance of **.2mm**.

Offset command

the offset

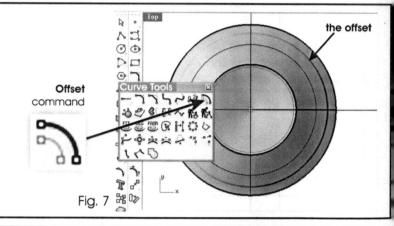

Fig. 7

- Using the **Circle: Diameter** command, create a circle that starts at the **quad** point of the offset circle you have just created.

- The diameter of this circle is **.9mm**.

- Use **quad** osnap to set the first location with accuracy and **ortho** when placing the second location.

Circle: Diameter command

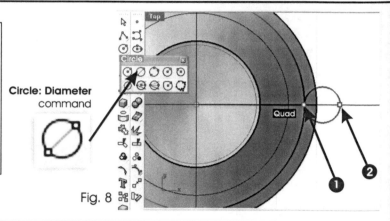

Fig. 8

- **Front viewport PERSPECTIVE.**

- **Construction lines** layer.

- Create a straight line down from the quad point of the circle around the girdle of the stone as shown. Make the line long enough to pass the bottom of the stone as shown.

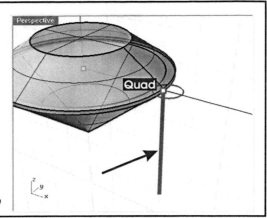

Fig. 9

- **Front viewport.**

- Create a perpendicular line **.75mm long** straight down from the bottom tip of the stone as shown. ❶

- Start a horizontal line from the lower end point of the perpendicular line just created and draw it to the right so that it intersects the vertical line drawn down from the stone as shown. ❷

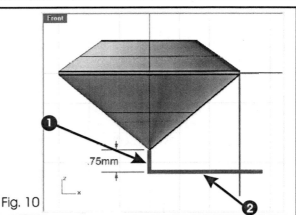

Fig. 10

- Click on the **Circle: Tangent, tangent, radius** command in the **Circle** toolbar flyout.
  - **First tangent curve** prompt: click on the perpendicular line at the approximate location shown. ❶
  - **Second tangent curve or radius** prompt: type ".4" and press "enter".
  - **Second tangent curve or radius** prompt: click on the horizontal line as shown. ❷

Circle: Tangent, Tangent, Radius command

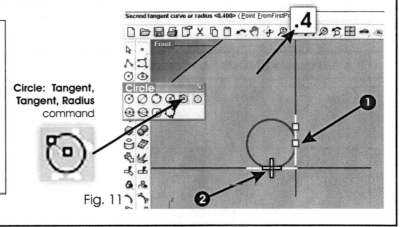

Fig. 11

- **Copy** the circle up so that it nestles under the stone but does not cross over to the right of the perpendicular line as shown.

Copy command

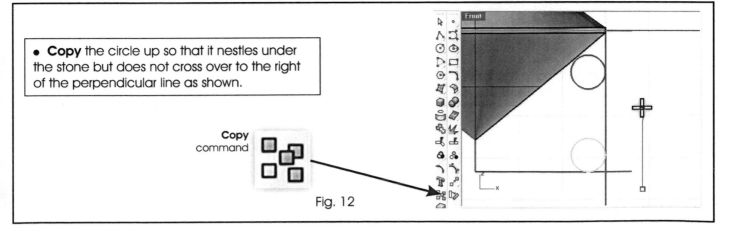

Fig. 12

289

- Switch to the **Front Perspective view** to see the lines and circles that have been created so far.

- Switch to the **RAILS** layer.

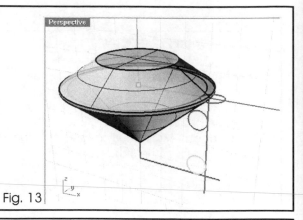

Fig. 13

- Select the two circles shown and click on the **Revolve** command in the **Surface** toolbar flyout.
    - **Start of revolve axis** prompt: click on an end point of the little .75mm line at the bottom of the stone. ❶
    - **End of revolve axis** prompt: click on the end point at the other end of the little line. ❷
    - **Start angle** prompt: press "enter" to accept the default value of **"0"**.
    - **Revolution angle** prompt: press "enter" to accept the default angle of 360-degrees.

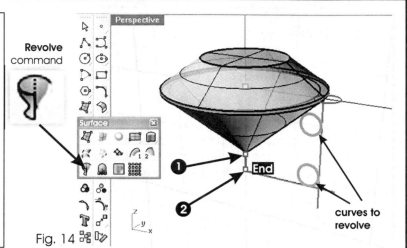

Revolve command

curves to revolve

Fig. 14

- The two bezel rails have been created.

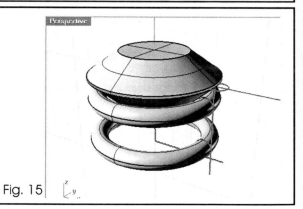

Fig. 15

- **Front viewport.**

- **Copy** the circle created in Fig. 8 up perpendicularly to a distance of **2mm**.

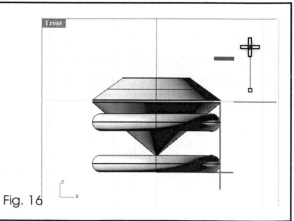

Fig. 16

290

- **Perspective TOP viewport.**

- **PRONGS** layer.

- Select the little prong circle that was copied up above the stone and click on the **Extend Closed Planar Curve** command in the **Solid** toolbar flyout.
  - Toggle to the **BothSides=No** option.
  - Draw the extrusion down and snap to the end point of the horizontal construction line at the bottom of the setting.
    - Snapping to this end point will ensure that the bottom of the prong will be at the same depth as the bottom of the lower bezel rail.

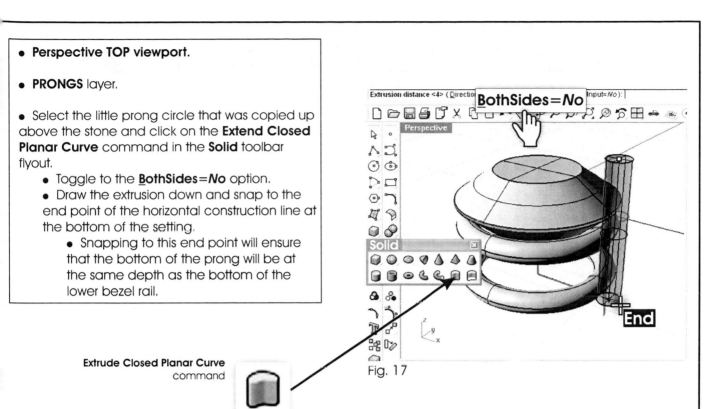

Extrude Closed Planar Curve
command

Fig. 17

- **Polar Array** the prong around the stone.

- In this example, 6 prongs have been created.

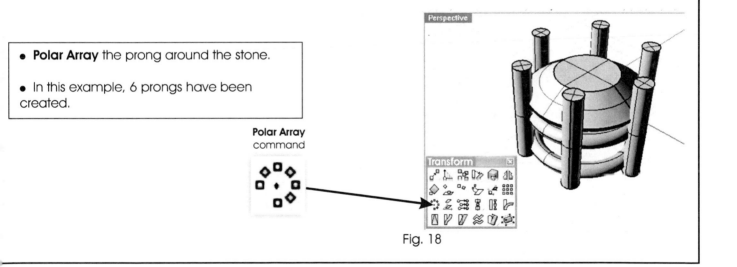

Polar Array
command

Fig. 18

Prong Set Round Faceted Stone II
Angled prongs

- Open Rhino and save the file as **6mm prong set round angled prongs.3dm**.

- Create layers as shown, **prong curves** layer current.

- **Delete all unassigned layers.**

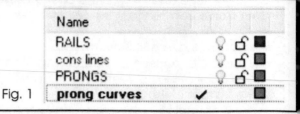

Name			
RAILS			
cons lines			
PRONGS			
prong curves	✓		

Fig. 1

- **Perspective viewport.**

- **Import** the file named **1mm round with seat cutter.3dm**.

- The stone and it's layers will be imported.

- Delete the cutters or turn off both cutter layers as well as the stone construction lines.

- Select the stone with all of its reference geometry and click on the **Scale 3D** command in the **Scale** toolbar flyout.

Import command [right click]

Scale 3D command

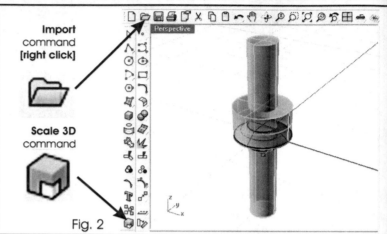

Fig. 2

- **Origin point:** type "**0**" and press "enter".
- **Scale factor or first reference point:** type "**6**" and press "enter".

- The stone and its curves will all be scaled up to a **6mm** diameter.

- Change the name of the stone's layer to **6MM RD STONE**.

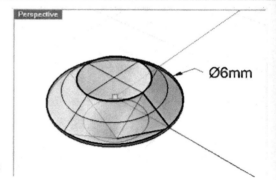

Ø6mm

Fig. 3

- **Top viewport.**

- Turn off all layers except for **stone placement geometry** and **prong curves**.

- **prong curves** layer current.

- **Offset** the circle around the girdle of the stone to a distance of **.3mm** to the **inside of the circle** to be offset as shown.

Offset command

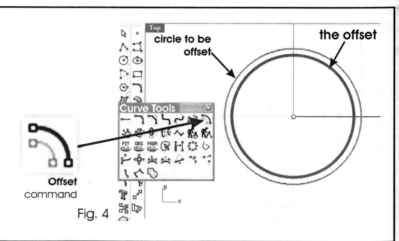

circle to be offset

the offset

Fig. 4

- Using the **Circle: Diameter** command, create a circle that starts at the **quad** point of the offset circle you just created.

- The diameter of this circle is **.9mm**.

- Use **ortho**.

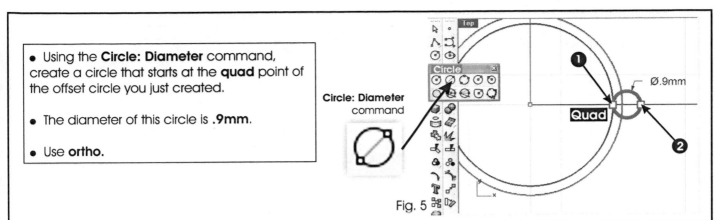

Circle: Diameter command

Ø.9mm

Quad

Fig. 5

- **Front viewport.**

- Turn on the **6MM RD STONE** layer.

- **Move** or **Drag** the circle just created straight up about **2mm** as shown.

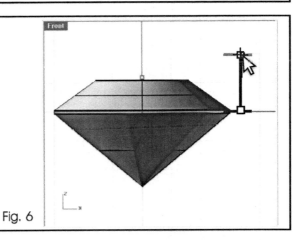

Fig. 6

- **Construction lines** layer.

- Create a **3mm** perpendicular line down from the bottom (culet) of the stone as shown.

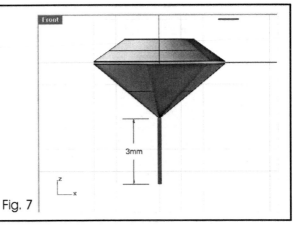

3mm

Fig. 7

- Create a perpendicular **8mm** line straight down from the inner quad point of the little circle that sits above the stone.

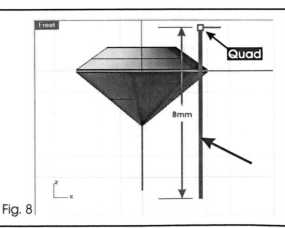

Quad

8mm

Fig. 8

293

- **Perspective FRONT viewport.**

- **Zoom** to view the intersection of the perpendicular line just created and the offset circle inside the stone.

- Place a **Point** at the intersection of the line and the circle as shown.

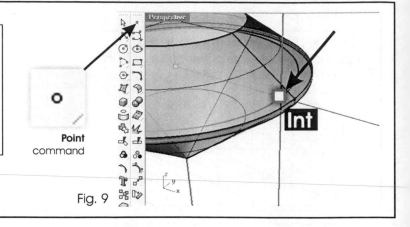

Point command

Fig. 9

- **Front viewport.**

- **Offset** the line created to the right side at a distance of **.3mm**

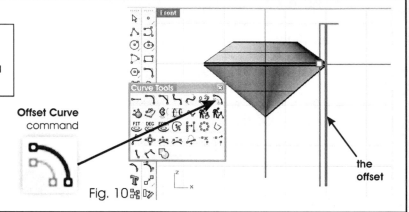

Offset Curve command

the offset

Fig. 10

- **Front perspective viewport.**

- **PRONGS** layer.

- In the perspective front viewport, you can see the project so far.

- Select the little prong curve circle at the top of the model and click on the **Extrude Curve Along Curve** command in the **Extrude Solid** toolbar flyout.

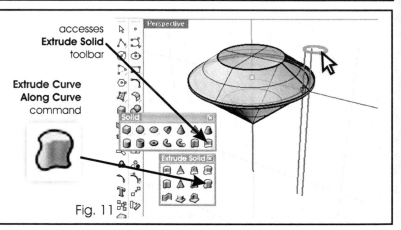

accesses **Extrude Solid** toolbar

Extrude Curve Along Curve command

Fig. 11

- **Select path curve near start** prompt: click on the top end of the perpendicular curve on the right of the two parallel curves as shown.

- *It is very important to click at this top end. Do not click at the other end!*

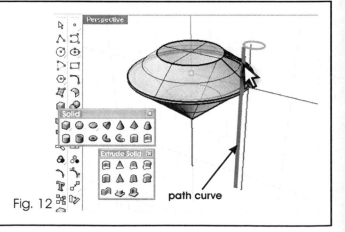

path curve

Fig. 12

294

- A solid extrusion will immediately be created along the designated line.

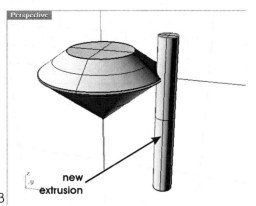

new extrusion

Fig. 13

- **Front viewport.**

- Use the **Circle: Diameter** command to create a **.8mm diameter** circle that touches the inner offset of the prong for its first point.

- Exact location along the prong will be determined later.

- Use **Near osnap** and **ortho.**

Circle: Diameter
command

Fig. 14

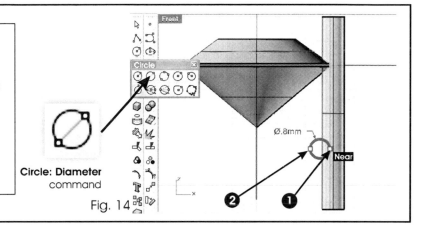

- Window select the prongs and all the curves and lines on and around it and click on the **Rotate** command.

Rotate
command

Fig. 15

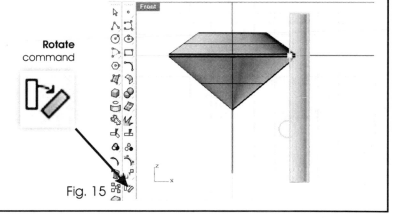

- **Center of rotation** prompt: snap to the point that was created earlier and click to set this location.

Fig. 16

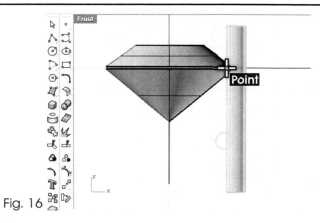

295

- **Angle or first reference point** prompt: draw the cursor out and click on the construction plane as shown.

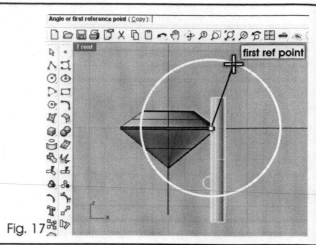

Fig. 17

- **Second reference point:** draw the cursor around and study the preview lines.
- Click to set the rotation when you like the angle of the prong.

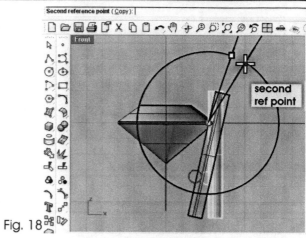

Fig. 18

- **Move** the small circle upward so that it nestles under the stone.

- Use **Near osnap** to maintain contact with the offset curve to control the direction of the move.

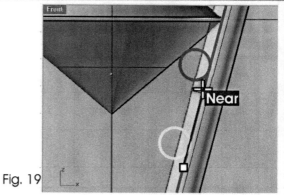

Fig. 19

- **Copy** the circle downward as shown.

- Use **near osnap** to guide the location.

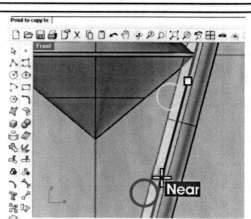

Fig. 20

- **Perspective FRONT viewport.**

- **RAILS** layer current.

- Select both of the little circles and click on the **Revolve** command.
  - **Start of revolve axis** prompt: click on one end of the 3mm line at the bottom of the stone. ❶
  - **End of revolve axis** prompt: click on the other end of the line. ❷

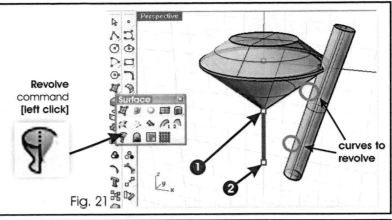

curves to revolve

Fig. 21

- **Start angle** prompt: press "enter" to accept "**0**" as default.
- **End angle** prompt: press "enter" to accept the default angle of 360-degrees.

- The two bezel rails will be created.

- The next step is to cut the angled prong so that it ends at the same depth as the lower rail.

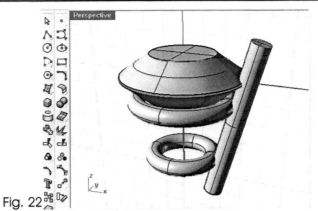

Fig. 22

- **Front viewport.**

- Select the prong and click on the **Cutting Plane** command in the **Plane** toolbar flyout.
  - **Start of cut plane** prompt: click on the lower quad point of the little circle shown.❶

accesses the **Plane** toolbar flyout

Cutting Plane command

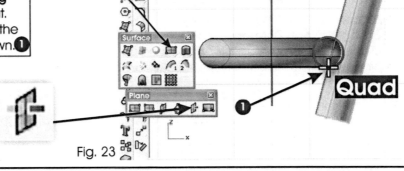

Quad

Fig. 23

- **End of cut plane** prompt: using **ortho**, draw the cursor out to the right and click to set the direction.❷
- Press "enter" to end the command.

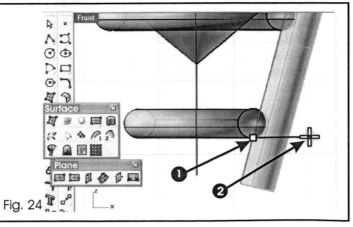

Fig. 24

- **Perspective FRONT viewport.**

- Turn off all layers with curves and lines.

- Before using the cutting plane, it is necessary to make sure that its surface normals, which indicate surface direction perpendicular to the surface, are oriented in the right direction.

- Select the cutting plane and click on the **Analyze Direction** command.

Analyze Direction command

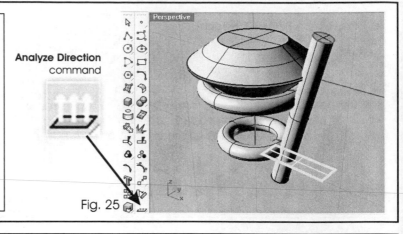

Fig. 25

- When the white direction arrows appear, they need to be pointing up, not down.
    - If they are pointing down, click on the **Flip** option in the **Command Line.**

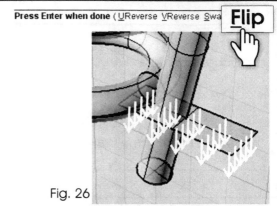

Fig. 26

- The direction of the arrows will change and be pointing up.

- Because this will be the cutting object in the upcoming **Boolean Difference** command, the arrows need to point up toward the part of the prong that you want to keep after cutting.

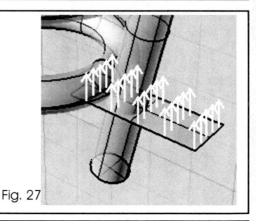

Fig. 27

- Click on the **Boolean Difference** command in the **Solid Tools** toolbar flyout:
    - **Select first set of surfaces or polysurfaces** prompt: select the prong and press "enter".

Boolean Difference command

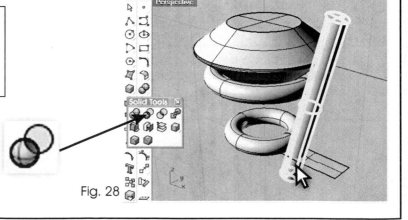

Fig. 28

298

- **Select second set of surfaces or polysurfaces** prompt: select the cutting plane and press "enter".

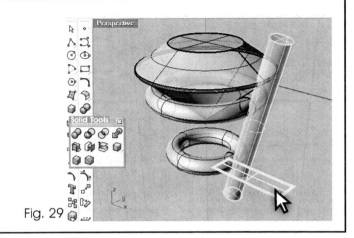

Fig. 29

- The lower part of the prong has been trimmed off. **Hide** or **Delete** the cutting plane.

- Switch to the **Perspective TOP viewport**.

- Select the prong and click on the **Polar Array** command in the **Transform** toolbar flyout.

Polar Array
command

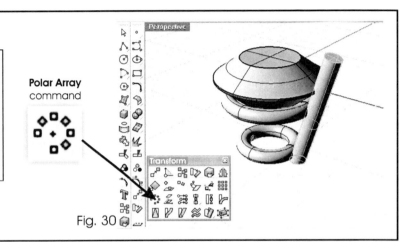

Fig. 30

- **Center of polar array** prompt: type **"0"** and press "enter".
- **Number of items** prompt: type **"6"** and press "enter".
- **Angle to fill or first reference point** prompt: press "enter" to accept the default of 360-degrees.

- The finished rails and prongs can be Booleaned together **(Boolean Union command)** if necessary for certain prototyping technologies that require one closed polysurface.

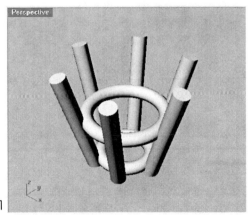

Fig. 31

Briolette Shapes
Using Surfaces to create faceted objects

- Create the layers shown and make the **construction lines** layer current.

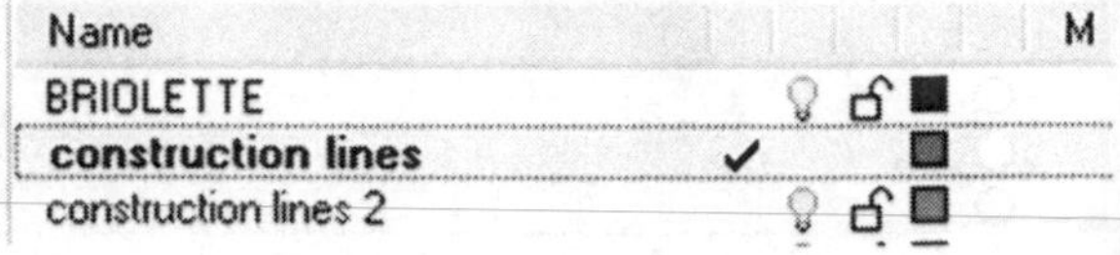

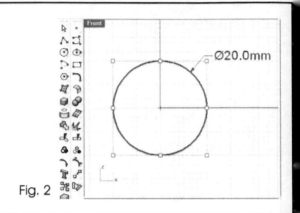

Fig. 1

- **Front viewport.**

- Create a **Circle** around **0** with a diameter of **20mm**.

- Turn on **control points**. **Do not rebuild.**

Ø20.0mm

Fig. 2

- Select the control point at the top of the circle and **Move** it upward **10mm**.

- Make sure to use **ORTHO** mode for perpendicular placement.

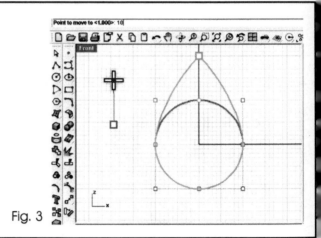

Fig. 3

- Create a line from the top end point of the pear shape down to the bottom quad point at shown.

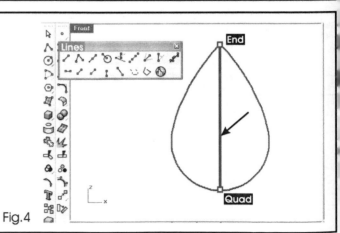

Fig.4

- Select the line and **Right-click** on the **Divide Curve by Number of Segments** command as shown.

accesses the **Point** toolbar flyout

Divide Curves by Number of Segments command

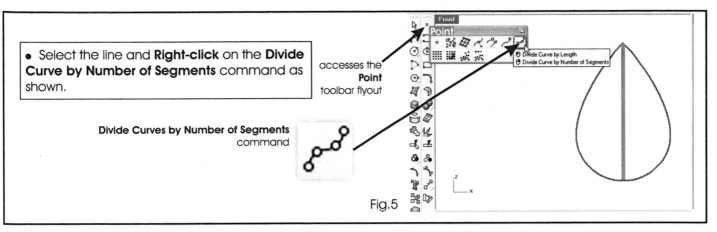

Fig. 5

- **Number of segments** prompt: type **"6"** and press "enter".

- The line will be divided in to 6 equal segments.

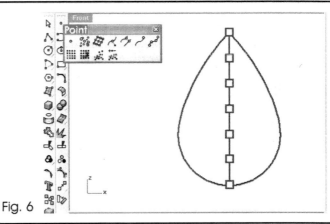

Fig. 6

- Use the **Line: from Midpoint** command to draw contour lines from each point object out to intersect the pear shaped outline as shown.

- Use **ortho** to make sure that these lines are perfectly horizontal.

Line: from Midpoint command

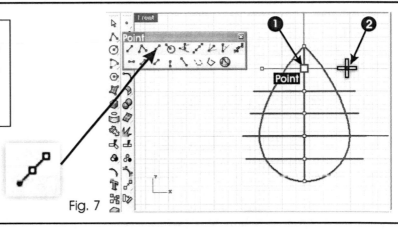

Fig. 7

- Drag the bottom line down with the **ALT KEY** pressed down to create a copy about halfway between the lowest line and bottom point as shown.

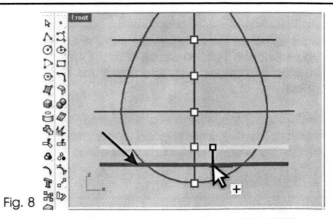

Fig. 8

- **Perspective viewport.**

- Notice that this piece is sitting up vertically on the Top construction plane. This is because it was created in the **Front** viewport.

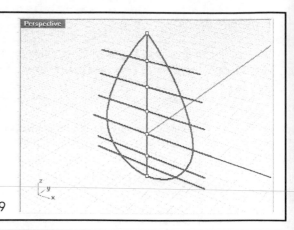

Fig.9

- Switch to the **construction lines 2** layer.

- Click on the **Polygon: Center, Radius** command.
  - **Center of inscribed polygon** prompt: snap to the point on the center line as shown. ❶

Polygon: Center, Radius command

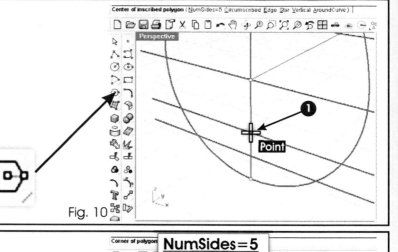

Fig. 10

- **Corner of polygon** prompt: click on the **NumSides=5** prompt.

- When prompted to enter a number, type **"12"** and press "enter".

Number of sides <5>: **12**

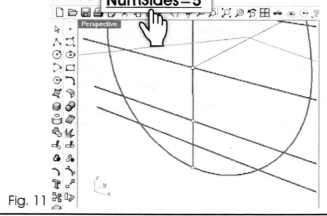

Fig. 11

- As you draw the polygon out with the cursor, you will notice that the shape of the polygon preview is changed because now it has 12 sides!

- Click on the intersection of the same contour line that you assigned for the center of the polygon and the pear shaped curve.

- Use **Intersection osnap**.

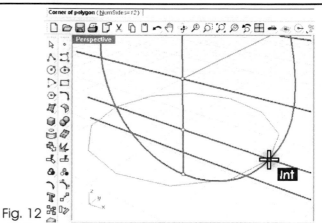

Fig. 12

- The finished polygon is resting on the second to lowest contour line.

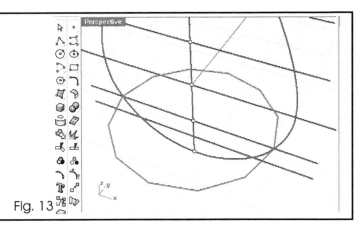

Fig. 13

- Create the same polygon on each contour curve as shown.

- Make sure that the corner of each polygon is located on the intersection of the line it is on and the outer pear-shaped curve.

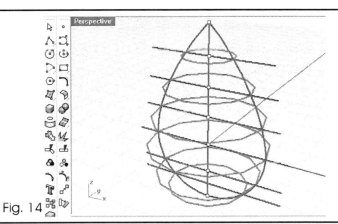

Fig. 14

- Place two **Points**, one at the very top and one at the very bottom. Use **End osnap.**

- There are already points at these locations but those points are on the **construction lines** layer which you are about to turn off.

- The new points you are adding now are on the **construction lines 2** layer which you will be now using.

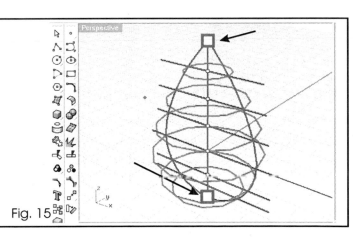

Fig. 15

- Turn off the **construction lines** layer.

- You will now see only the polygons and the top and bottom points, all on the **construction lines 2** layer.

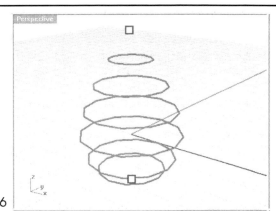

Fig. 16

- Switch to the **BRIOLETTE** layer.

- Click on the **Surface from 3 or 4 Corner Points** command.
  - **First, Second, Third, and Fourth corner of surface** prompts: Click on 4 polygon corners in the order shown. Use **end osnap!**

Surface from 3 or 4 Points
command

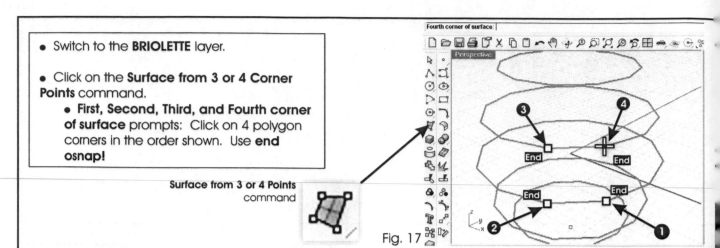

Fig. 17

- After the 4th corner is designated, a little surface will appear with its corners in the locations where you clicked.

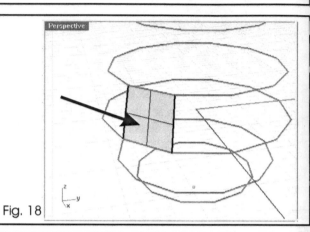

Fig. 18

- Pan to the bottom of the framework and create a surface that is bounded by two of the polygon corners and the bottom point as shown.

- When you have clicked on the 3rd location, press "enter" and a 3-sided triangular surface is created as shown.

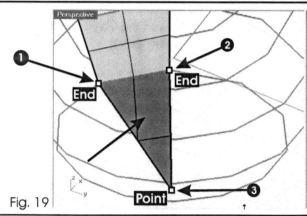

Fig. 19

- Continue up the row as shown until a line of surfaces is created from bottom to top.

- All surfaces will be 4-sided except the top and bottom ones that were snapped to the points at top and bottom.

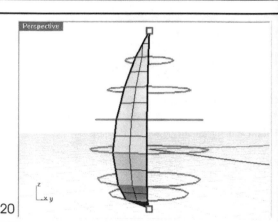

Fig. 20

- Select all pf the surfaces you just created and click on the **Polar Array** command.

Polar Array
command

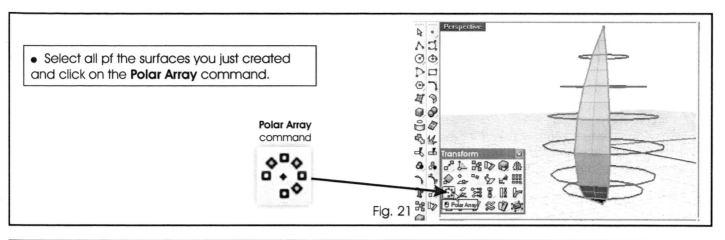

Fig. 21

- **Center of polar array** prompt: type **"0"** and press "enter".
- **Number of items** prompt: type **"12"** and press "enter".
- **Angle to fill or first reference point** prompt: press "enter" to accept the default value of 360-degrees.

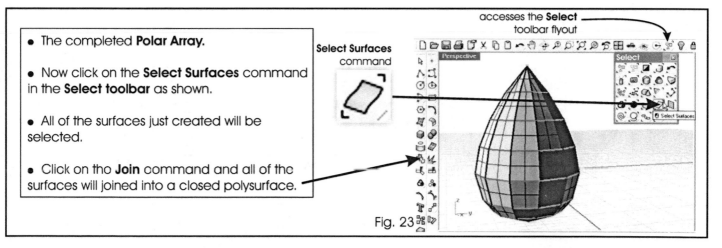

Fig. 22

- The completed **Polar Array**.

- Now click on the **Select Surfaces** command in the **Select toolbar** as shown.

- All of the surfaces just created will be selected.

- Click on tho **Join** command and all of tho surfaces will joined into a closed polysurface.

Select Surfaces
command

Fig. 23

- Switch to **Rendered Viewport** mode to view the finished briolette. Turn off the grid for a clear background.

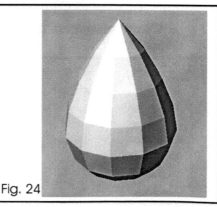

Fig. 24

- **Copy** the briolette and the **construction line 2** objects over to the side as shown.

- Turn off the **BRIOLETTE** layer and **Hide** the construction lines around it.

- Or, you can create a new layer for the constructions lines that you copied over with the completed briolette and then turn off that layer.

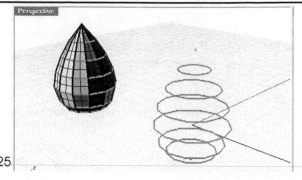

Fig. 25

- A new briolette shape will now be created with differently shaped surface facets.

- Select every other polygon as shown

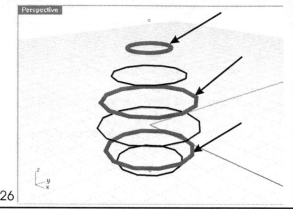

Fig. 26

- **Left click** on the **Rotate** command.

Rotate
command

Fig. 27

- **Center of rotation** prompt: type **"0"** and press "enter".

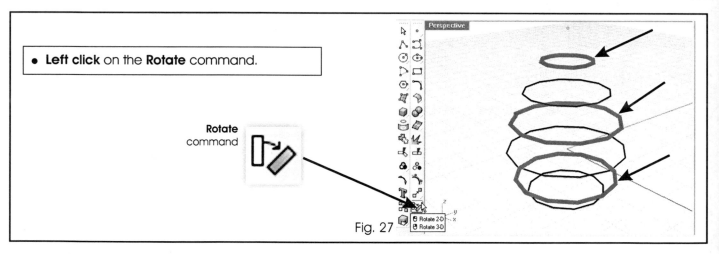

Fig. 28

306

- **Angle or first reference point** prompt: click on the midpoint of one of the lines as shown.**❶**
  - It does not matter which polygon you choose for this reference point but pick on one that you can see easily when you are zoomed in on your work.

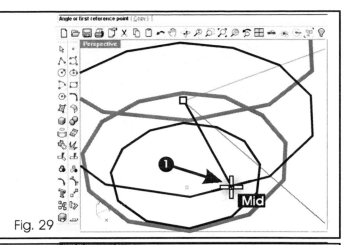

Fig. 29

- **Second reference point** prompt:
  - Snap to the nearest **end point** as shown.
  - Click to set location.

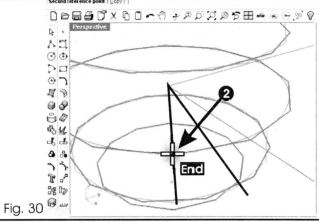

Fig. 30

- A quick look at the top view will show that all the selected polygons have been rotated so that their endpoints are shifted.

- They are now staggered with the other polygons and their endpoints are at vertical angles to each other.

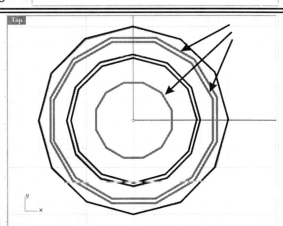

Fig. 31

- Create a new layer called **BRIOLETTE 2** and make it current.

- Use the **Surface from 3 or 4 Corner Points** to create a new surface. This surface will be triangular.

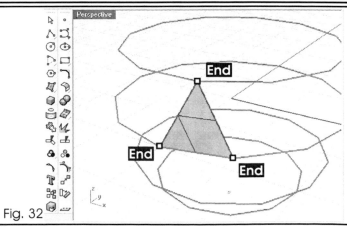

Fig. 32

- Create another surface next to the first surface as shown.

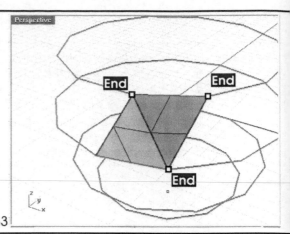
Fig. 33

- Because the position of every other polygon is shifted, it is now necessary to create two little triangular surfaces on each level as shown.

- Only one surface is needed at top and bottom as before.

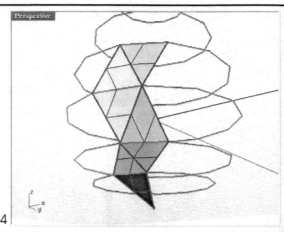
Fig. 34

- **Polar Array** and **Join** all surfaces as before.

Select Surfaces
command

Fig. 35

- Turn on the **BRIOLETTE** layer and view both briolette shapes in **Rendered Viewport** mode.

Fig. 36

Circular Filigree with Stone
Pipe Command with Filigree Polar Array

• Open the file **polar array filigree.3dm**.

• **Remember that your filigree design will not look exactly like this one as the original file is created according to the individual's own aesthetics.**

• The point object shown at top is the point that was placed on the **parent** curve to mark its position among the rest of the curves which are the **children**. The **parent and children** relationship is due to the fact that **History** was used when the Polar array was performed.

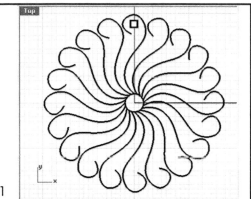

Fig. 1

• Create the layers shown.

• **construction lines** layer current.

• Change all objects - the curves and the point - to the **construction lines** layer.

Name			
FILIGREE		♀ ⌂ ■
construction lines	✓	■
BEZEL		♀ ⌂ ■
bezel crvs		♀ ⌂ ■
cab stone		♀ ⌂ ■
cab stone crvs		♀ ⌂ ■
cutter		♀ ⌂ ▢

Fig. 2

• Access the **History** toolbar flyout as shown.

• Click on the **Select objects with history** command in the **History** toolbar flyout as shown.

Select Objects with History command

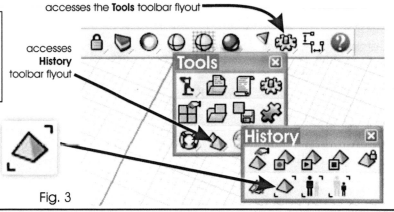

accesses the **Tools** toolbar flyout

accesses **History** toolbar flyout

Fig. 3

• All of the objects that are **children** will select as shown.

• It is easy to identify which object is the **parent** because it does not select.

• If you do not have a marker, like a point, on or near the parent object, put one there now to identify it. It may be hard to spot otherwise with all of the other curves in this design.

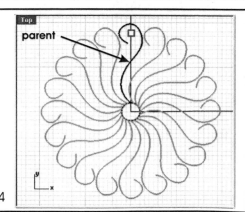

parent

Fig. 4

- **bezel crvs** layer.

- Create a **7mm** diameter circle around "0" as shown.

- **Offset** this circle *__to the outside__* at a distance of **.7mm**.

offset
command

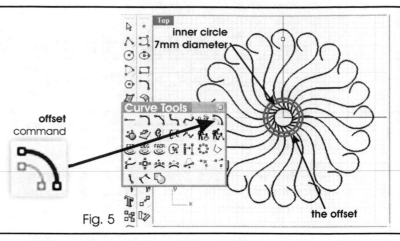

inner circle
7mm diameter

Curve Tools

the offset

Fig. 5

- **Drag** the **parent** object so that its end is between the two circles as shown.

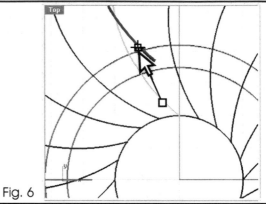

Fig. 6

- All of the other objects will update.

- Turn on the control points for the **parent** object.

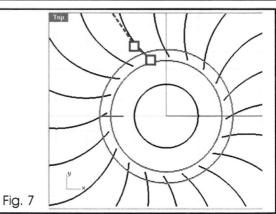

Fig. 7

- **Perspective viewport.**

- Select a single control point close to the inner circles but not at the end of the line as shown.

- Click on the **Move** command and, in the **Command Line,** click to toggle on the **Vertical=Yes!** option as shown.

Point to move from

Vertical=Yes

Perspective

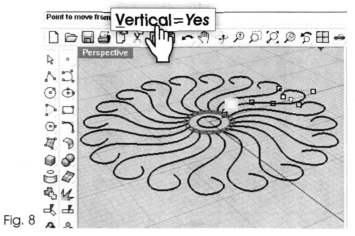

Fig. 8

- The movement of the control point is constrained in a vertical direction.

- The curve now has 3-dimensional characteristics and is no longer planar.

- Move the control point until the curve is similar to the one shown.

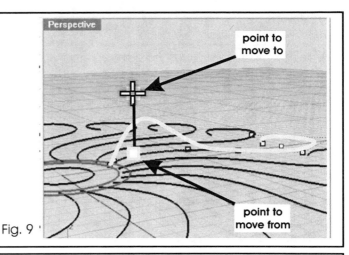

point to move to

point to move from

Fig. 9

- History will update the rest of the curves.

Fig. 10

- Continue to edit the parent object until you have your desired shape.

- Turn off control points.

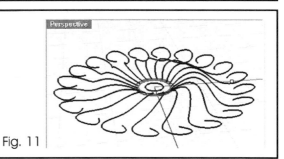

Fig. 11

- **FILIGREE** layer.

- Select the **parent curve**.

- Click on the **Pipe, Round Caps** command in the **Solid** toolbar.
  - **Start radius:** type".6" and press "enter".
  - **End radius:** type ".7" and press enter.
  - When prompted **again** for the **Point for next radius,** press "enter".

Pipe, Round Caps
command

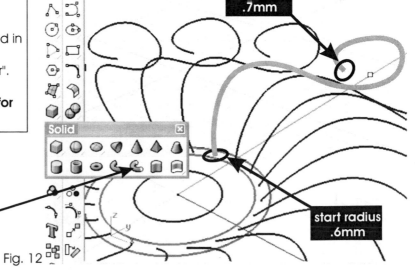

end radius .7mm

start radius .6mm

Fig. 12

- A new pipe-like polysurface with rounded ends will be created around the designated curve with a start radius of **.6mm** and an end radius of **.7mm**.

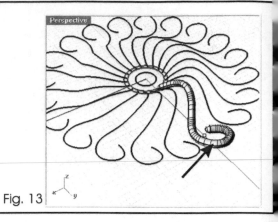

Fig. 13

- **Polar Array** the polysurface around **"0"**.

- Turn off the **FILIGREE** and the **construction lines** layers.

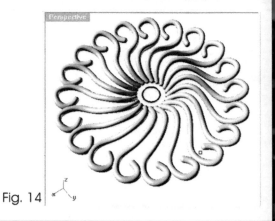

Fig. 14

- **Front perspective** viewport.

- **cab stone crvs** layer.

- Create a perpendicular **3mm line** from **"0"** upward, using **ORTHO** for accuracy.

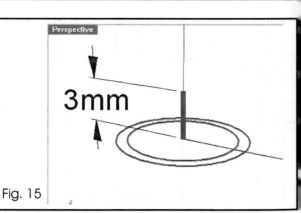

Fig. 15

- Use the **Arc: Start, End, Point on Arc** command to create an arc that connects two quad points of the inner circle to the end of the perpendicular line as shown.

Arc: Start, End, Point on Arc
command

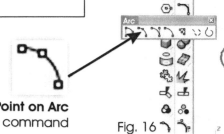

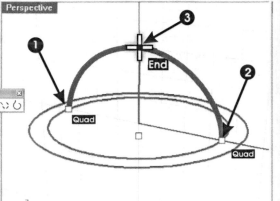

Fig. 16

- **Trim** the arc with the perpendicular line as shown.

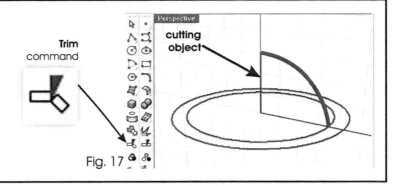

Trim command

Fig. 17

cutting object

- Select the arc and click on the **Revolve** command in the **Surface** toolbar flyout.
  - **Start of revolve axis** prompt: click on one end of the vertical line.
  - **End of revolve axis** prompt: click on the other end of the vertical line.
  - **Start angle** prompt: press "enter" to accept the default angle of **0**.
  - **Revolution angle** prompt: press "enter" to accept the default angle of 360-degrees.

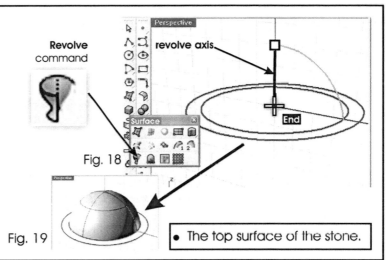

Revolve command

revolve axis

End

Fig. 18

Fig. 19

- The top surface of the stone.

- Close the opening at the bottom of the stone with the **Cap Planar Holes** command.

- Turn off the **cab stone** and the **cab stone curves** layers.

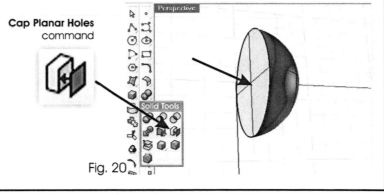

Cap Planar Holes command

Fig. 20

- **bezel crvs** layer.

- Use the **Rectangle: 3 Points** command to create a rectangle that touches the quad points of both circles as shown. ❶ & ❷
  - **Width** prompt: type **"1.5"** and press "enter".
  - **Choose rectangle** prompt: draw the rectangle upward using **ortho** and click to set the location.❸

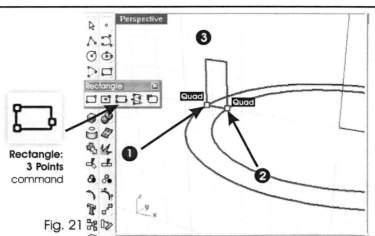

Rectangle: 3 Points command

Fig. 21

- Press "enter" to repeat the **Rectangle: 3 Points** command.

    - **Start of edge** prompt: snap to the lower end point of the first rectangle as shown. ❶
    - **End of edge** prompt: type ".7" and press "enter". Using **Ortho**, draw the cursor down and click to set this location. ❷
    - **Width** prompt: type "1.5" and press "enter". They draw the cursor to the right, using **ortho**, and click to set the location. ❸

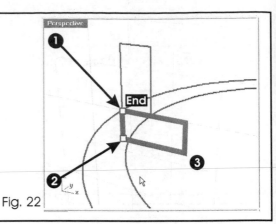

Fig. 22

- Repeat the command one more time to create a third rectangle below the second one.

- **Start of edge** prompt: snap to the lower end point of the first rectangle as shown. ❶
- **End of edge** prompt: type "2" and press "enter". Using **Ortho**, draw the cursor down and click to set this location. ❷
- **Width** prompt: type "1" and press "enter". They draw the cursor to the right, using **ortho**, and click to set the location. ❸

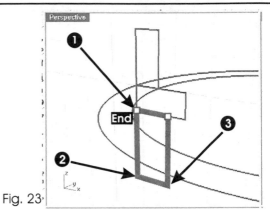

Fig. 23

- **Explode** all three rectangles.

- **Trim** them out so that they form the shape shown.

- **Join** all the lines back together to form a closed polyline

- The **Curve Boolean** command would work here as well.

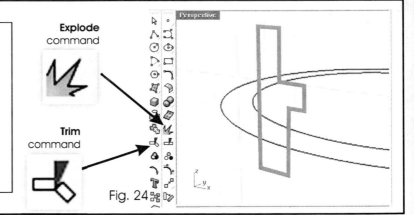

Explode command

Trim command

Fig. 24

- Toggle on the **Record History** function.

Record History

- **Revolve** the new polyline around the same revolve axis that was used to create the cabochon shape.

- Press "enter" to accept the default settings of the revolve command **[0** as start angle and **360** as the revolution angle].

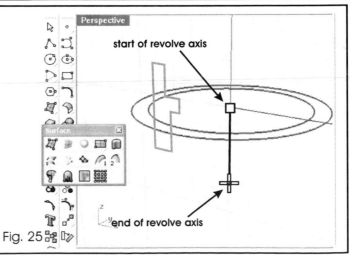

start of revolve axis

end of revolve axis

Fig. 25

314

- The bezel has been created.

- The shelf in the inner wall is the bearing upon which the stone will rest.

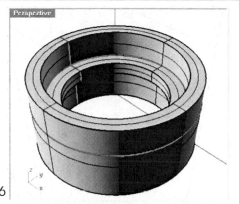

Fig. 26

- Turn on the **cab stone** and **FILIGREE** layers.

- Both stone and bezel need to be raised up as they are sitting too deeply into the piece.

- **Lock** the **FILIGREE** layer.

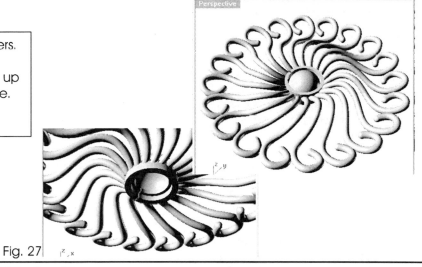

Fig. 27

- **SELECT ONLY THE CAB STONE AND THE POLYCURVE THAT WAS ROTATED TO MAKE THE BEZEL.**

- **DO NOT SELECT THE BEZEL!!** History will update It when the parent object (the curve that was revolved to create it) is moved.

Fig. 28

- **Front Viewport.**

- **Move** the selected objects up **.5mm**, or to the height you wish so that the stone and bezel are sitting high enough in the piece.

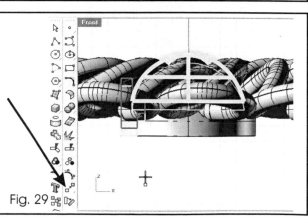

Fig. 29

- **Perspective** viewport.

- The bezel and stone are higher but the bottom of the bezel still needs to be adjusted as it sticks out at the bottom.

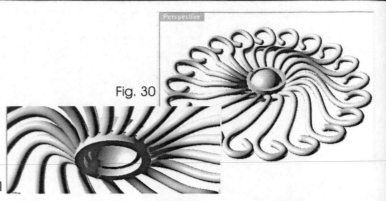

Fig. 30

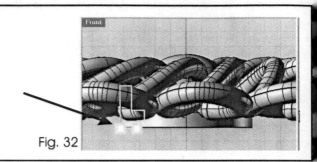

Fig. 31

- **Front viewrport.**

- Select the bezel curve that was revolved.

- Turn control points on and select the bottom two control points as shown.

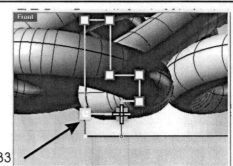

Fig. 32

- **Move** or **Drag** the control points upward until they pass the level of the filigree.

- History will cause the bezel to update the control point editing of the parent curve.

- This will shorten the bezel so that it does not stick out lower than the filigree.

Fig. 33

- The underside of the bezel has been shortened through history updating.

Fig. 34

- The finished model.

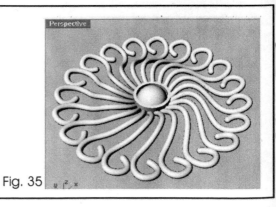

Fig. 35

Twisted Wire Look
Band Ring using History function

- Create layers as shown.

- Make **band ring construction lines** layer current.

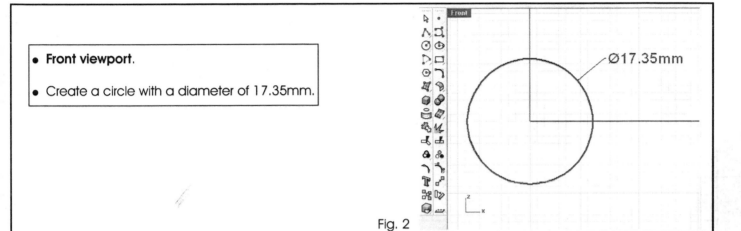

Fig. 1

- **Front viewport**.

- Create a circle with a diameter of 17.35mm.

Ø17.35mm

Fig. 2

- **Perspective TOP viewport.**

- Click on the **Length** command in the **Analyze** toolbar flyout.
  - **Select curves to measure** prompt: select the circle and press "enter".

Length command

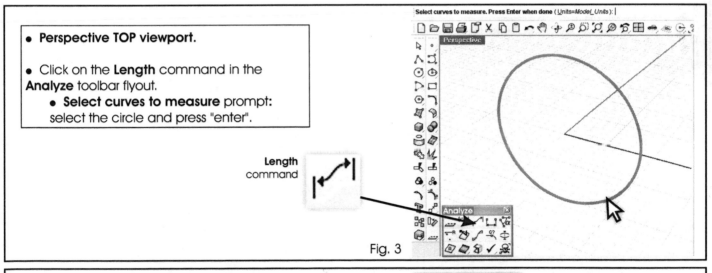

Fig. 3

- You can read the length of the curve of the circle in the History line as shown.

- In this example, the History line reads that the length of the measured curve is **54.507mm**.

Length = 54.507 millimeters

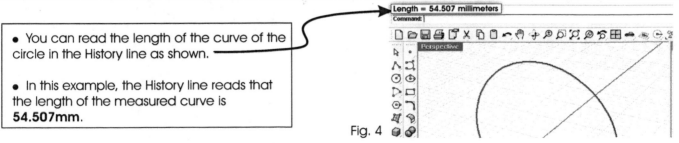

Fig. 4

- **flat layout curves** layer.

- Create a single line on the construction plane that measures **54.507mm** as shown, the same length as the circumference of the circle measured in Fig. 3 & 4.

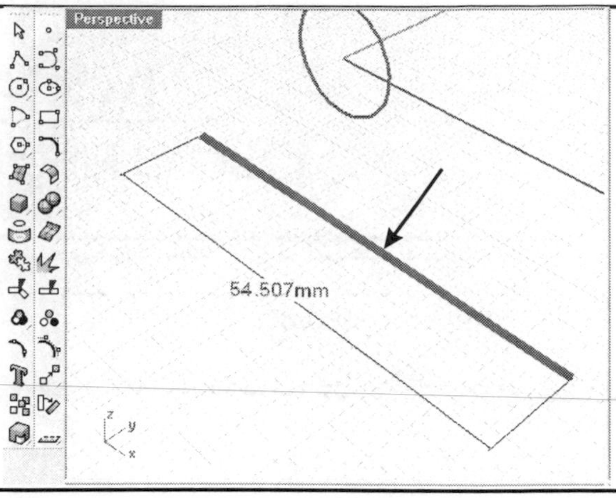

54.507mm

Fig. 5

- Place a **Point** on the left end of the new line as shown.

Point
command

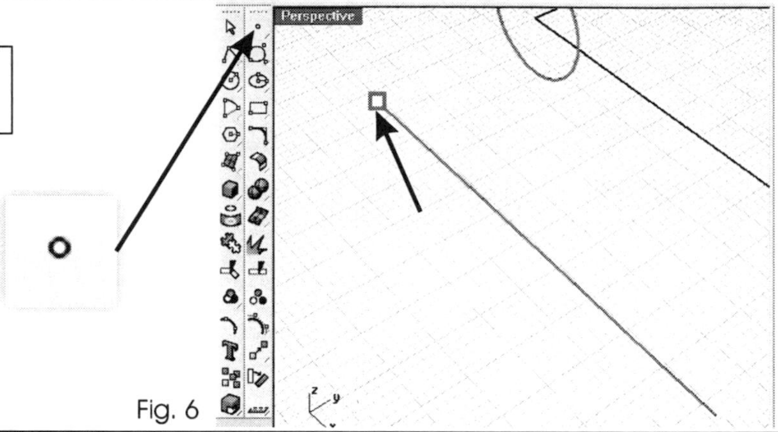

○

Fig. 6

- **Right viewport.**

- Create a line from the point just created straight up at a length of **.5mm**.

- Use **point osnap** for accuracy.

- Use **ortho.**

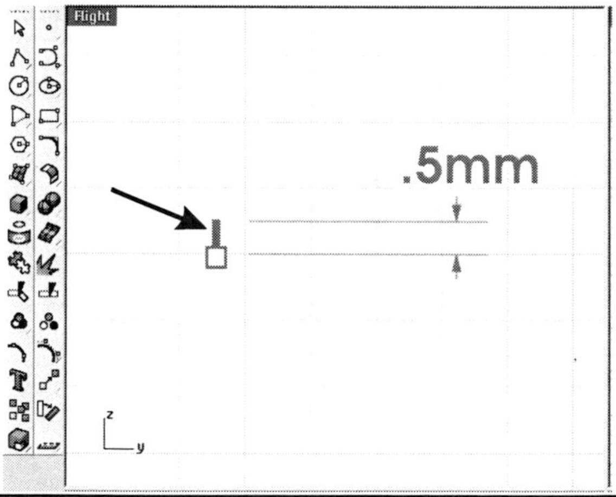

.5mm

Fig. 7

- Use the **Circle: Diameter** command to create a circle that touches the little line.

- Diameter of the circle: **1.5mm**

- Use **end osnap** and **ortho.**

Circle: Diameter
command

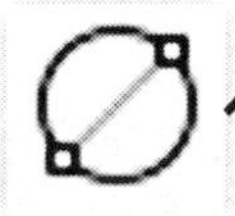

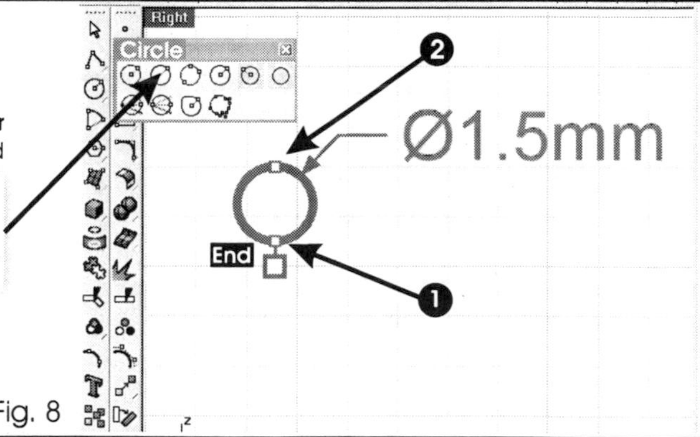

Ø1.5mm

End

❶

❷

Fig. 8

318

- **Polar array** the circle just created around the point object.
  - **Center of polar array** prompt: select the point object.
  - **Number of items** prompt: type "5" and press "enter".
  - **Angle to fill or first reference point** prompt: type "enter" to accept the default value of 360-degrees

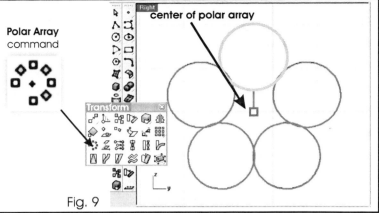

Polar Array command

center of polar array

Fig. 9

- Click on the **Fillet Curves** command.
  - **Select first curve to fillet** prompt: type ".15" and press "enter".
    - This sets the radius of the fillet to .15mm.
  - **Select first curve to fillet** and **Select second curve to fillet** prompts: select two circles at the points shown. ❶ ❷

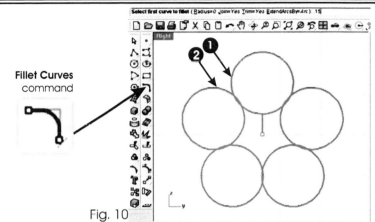

Fillet Curves command

Fig. 10

- A little fillet will appear.

- Go around the array and fillet the rest of the circles.

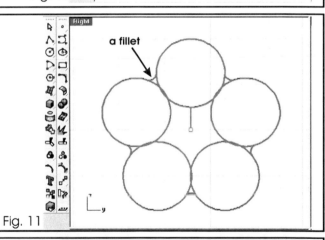

a fillet

Fig. 11

- Using the little fillets as cutting objects, use the **Trim** command to trim out the inside of the circles as shown.

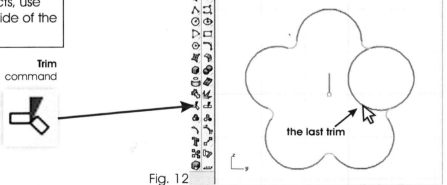

Trim command

the last trim

Fig. 12

- **Join** all curves together to achieve a closed polycurve.

- **Hide** or **Lock** the little line that extends upward from the point.

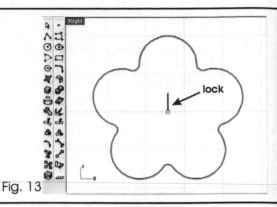
Fig. 13

- **Perspective TOP viewport.**

- Place a **Point** on the near end of the line as shown.

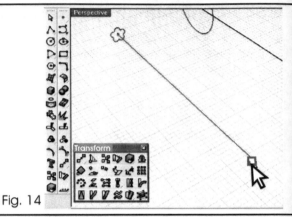
Fig. 14

- **flat layout for twisted wire** layer.

- Click on the **Extrude Straight** command in the **Surface** toolbar flyout..
  - **Select curves to extrude** prompt: select the polycurve as shown and press "enter".

accesses the **Surface** toolbar flyout

Extrude Straight command

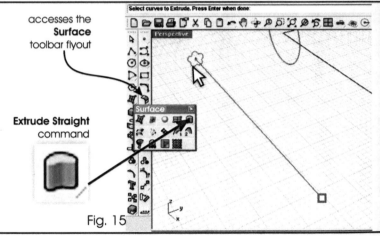
Fig. 15

- Draw out the extrusion until you **snap to the point** at the other end of the line.

- Click to set the extrusion length.

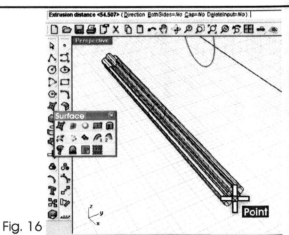
Fig. 16

320

- **Rebuild** the new extrusion.

- **60** points in both U and V directions.

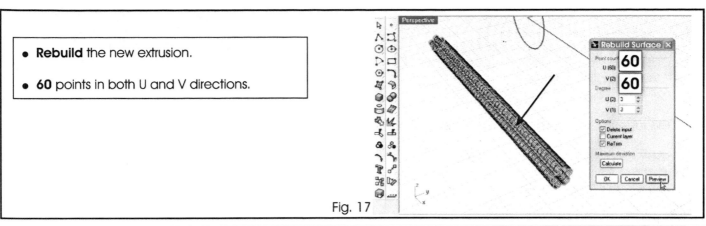

Fig. 17

- **Cap** the extrusion by selecting it and clicking on the **Cap Planar Holes** command as shown.

Cap Planar Holes command

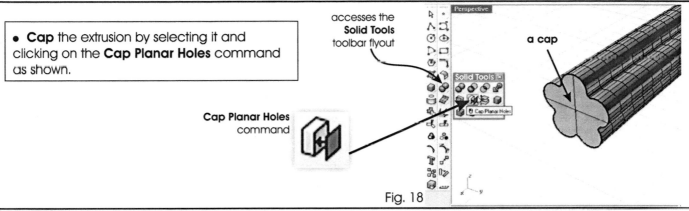

Fig. 18

- Click on the **Twist** command in the **Transform** toolbar flyout.
  - **Select objects to twist** prompt: select the capped the extrusion as shown.

Twist command

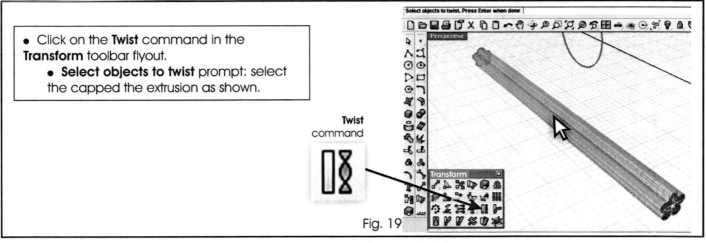

Fig. 19

- **Start of twist axis** and **End of twist axis** prompts: using **point osnap,** click on first one end of the line that runs through the middle of the extrusion and then the other as shown.

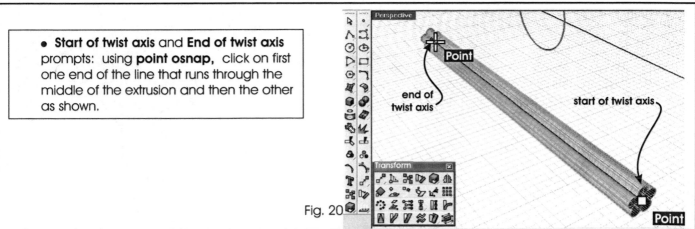

Fig. 20

- **Angle or first reference point** prompt: first toggle on the **Infinite=yes** option in the **Command Line.**
  - Then type **1800** and press "enter".

- This will achieve a **1800-degree twist**.

- *You can also drag the cursor around the end of the twist axis to twist this piece manually but in this case, it is done more easily by entering a value because of the number and density of the control points.*

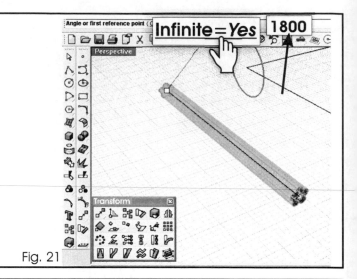

Fig. 21

- Click on **Shade** to see the finished twist.

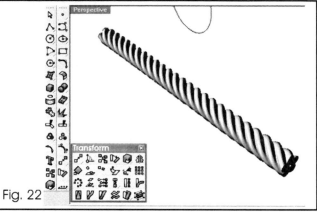

Fig. 22

- Incidentally, this is now the twist would look if you had left the **Infinite=No** option on in the **Command Line** shown in Fig. 21.

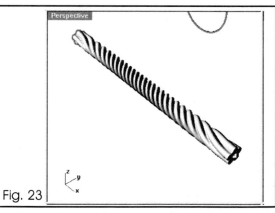

Fig. 23

- Up at the other end of the twist, create a line segment that connects to two bottom quad points of the original extruded curve as shown.

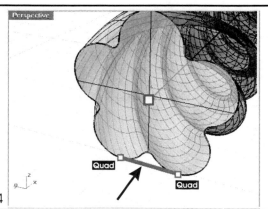

Fig. 24

- Carefully select and move the line that runs through the twisted element as well as the two points at each end down so that the end point snaps to the mid point of the line just created.

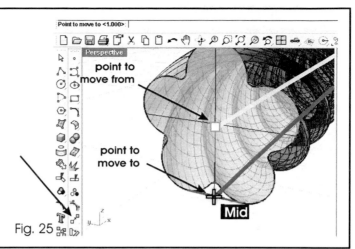

point to move from

point to move to

Mid

Fig. 25

- Turn off all layers except for the following:
  - **flat layout curves**
  - **band ring construction lines**

- Select the circle and the straight line shown.
  - Do not select the points or the profile curve for the twist.

- Click on the **Analyze Direction** command.

Analyze Direction
command

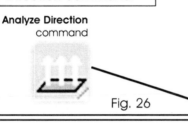

Fig. 26

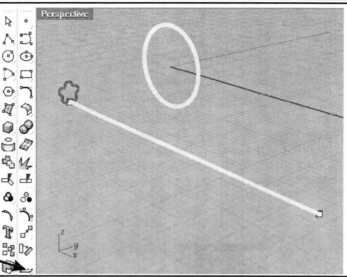

- Each selected object will show a single point and some white arrows.
  - The **points** indicate **curve seams**.
  - The **white arrows** indicate **curve direction**.

- In the next step in this exercise where you will be asked to designate a **Base Curve** and a **Target Curve** in turn.

- The straight line will be the **BASE CURVE** and the circle will be the **TARGET CURVE**.

- It is crucial for the desired effect to pick on the same respective ends of both curves because of the relation they will have to each other.

- Using **near osnap**, place a point at the starting end of both circle and line as shown.

Fig. 27

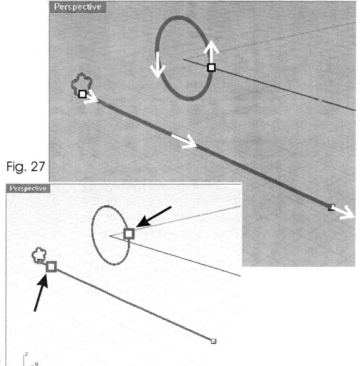

Fig. 28

- Select the line and circle and click on the **Analyze Direction** command to see how the placement of the two points is at the start of each curve.

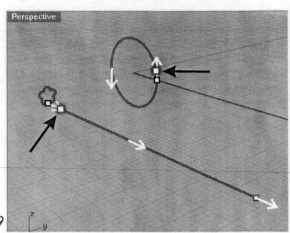

Fig. 29

- Down at the bottom of the workspace on the **Status Bar** click on the **Record History** button.

Snap   Ortho   **Planar   Osnap   Record History**

Fig. 30

- Click on the **Flow along Curve** command.
    - **Select objects to flow along a curve** prompt: select the twisted polysurface as shown and press "enter".

Flow along Curve command

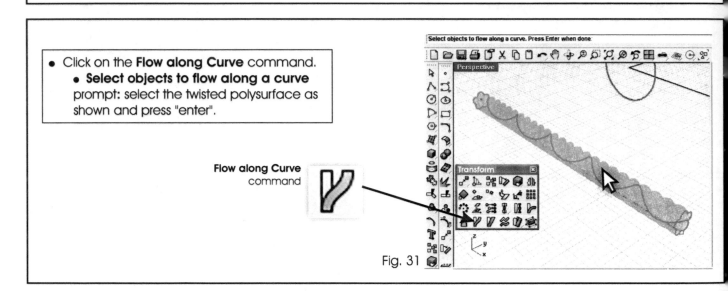

Fig. 31

- **Base curve - select near one end** prompt: select the curve that runs along the bottom of the extrusion at the far end as shown, where the point was placed earlier to mark the beginning direction of the line.

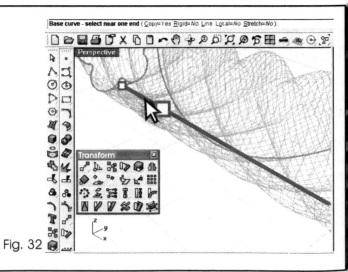

Fig. 32

- **Target curve - select near matching end** prompt: select the circle shown at the location of the start of the curve, indicated by the point applied earlier.

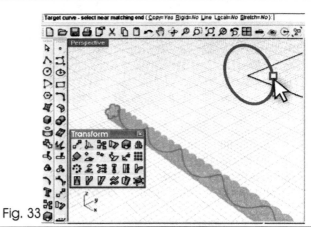

Fig. 33

- A copy of the twisted element will form itself around the outside of the circle as shown.

- The reason it forms around the outside of the circle is because of the location of the *base curve* which is *under the twisted element in the flat layout.*

target curve can just be seen here

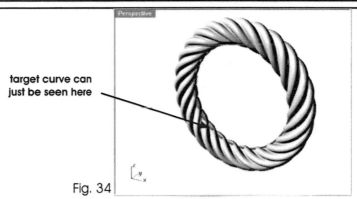

Fig. 34

- **Right viewport.**

- Change the twisted element around the circle to the **TWISTED WIRE - BAND RING** layer.

- Make the **construction lines** layer current.

- Turn off the **FLAT LAYOUT** and **flat layout curves** layers.

- Use the **Line: from Midpoint** command to create a line from the top quad point of the circle out so that the whole line measures **6mm long.**

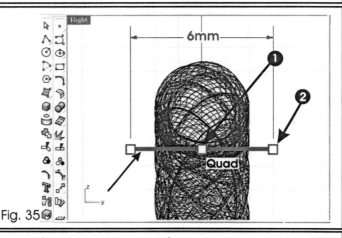

Fig. 35

- Use the **Rectangle: 3 Points** command to create a rectangle that touches both ends of the line just created. ❶ ❷

- Bring it up approximately to the location shown. ❸

Rectangle: 3 Points
command

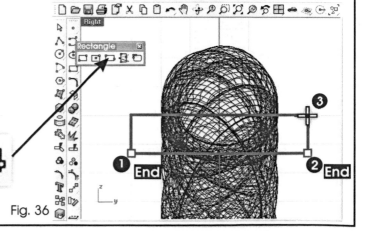

Fig. 36

325

- Use the **Arc: Start, End, Direction at Start** command to create the arc shown.
  - **Start of arc** prompt: snap to the end point of the top of the rectangle as shown. **①**
  - **End of arc** prompt, type 1 and press "enter".
    - The end point will be constrained so that the arc diameter will be 1mm as shown. **②**
  - **Direction at start** prompt: draw the cursor up and click to set, using **ortho.**

Arc: Start, End, Direction at Start command

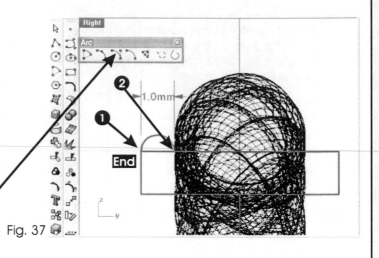

Fig. 37

- Use the **Arc: Start, End, Direction at Start** command again to create the additional arc shown.

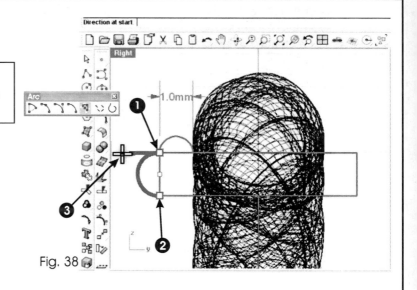

Fig. 38

- **Mirror** the two arcs over to the other side if the ring and trim the curves out as shown.

- **Join** the curves to create a closed polycurve.

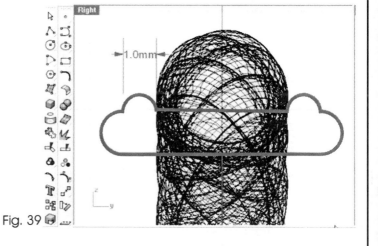

Fig. 39

- Down at the bottom of the workspace on the **Status Bar** click on the **Record History** button.

Snap   Ortho   **Planar   Osnap   Record History**
Fig. 40

- **Perspective - TOP viewport.**

- Turn off the **TWISTED WIRE - BAND RING** layer.

- **BAND RING** layer current.

- Select the polycurve and click on the **Revolve** command.
    - **Start of revolve axis** prompt: type **"0"** and press "enter". ❶
    - **End of revolve axis** prompt: draw the cursor up or down along the Y axis, **using ortho** and click along this direction to set the location. ❷

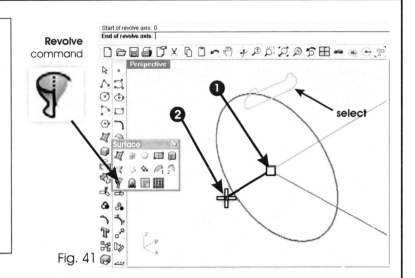

Start of revolve axis: 0
End of revolve axis:

Revolve command

select

Fig. 41

- **Start angle** prompt: press "enter" to accept the default value of **0**.
- **End angle** prompt: press "enter" to accept the default value of **360-degrees**.

- The finished revolve will be a closed polysurface that starts and ends at the designated curve to revolve as shown..

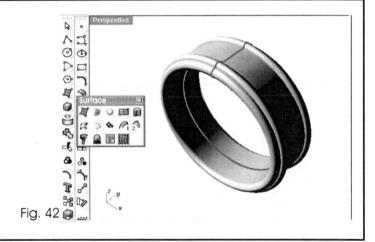

Fig. 42

- Turn on the **TWISTED WIRE - BAND RING** layer.

- Note that the twisted wire element is poking through on the inside of the band.

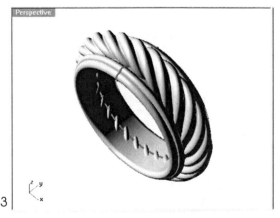

Fig. 43

- **Right viewport.**

- Turn on the **FLAT LAYOUT** and **layout curves** layers.

- Zoom in on the side view of the flat twisted wire as shown.

- Select the twisted element and click on the **Scale 1D** command:

Scale 1-D command

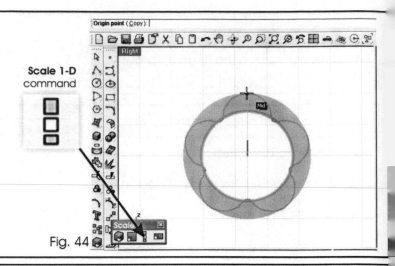

Fig. 44

- **Origin point** prompt: click on the top of the original twist curve. **1**
    - **Quad osnap** is a good snap to use to set this location.
- **First reference point** prompt: use **mid osnap** to snap to the midpoint of the horizontal line that connects the two flutes at the bottom of the twist curve as shown. **2**
- **Second reference point** prompt: draw the cursor upward a short distance upward and click to set the location. **3**

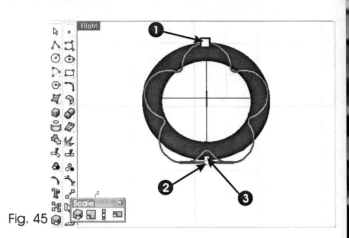

Fig. 45

- Turn the **TWISTED WIRE - BAND RING** layer back on.

- Now look at your ring band and notice that the twisted element no longer sticks through the inside of the band.

- **History** has updated the twisted element because its parent object was just edited in the **Scale 1D** command,

Fig. 46

- **Copy** the ring band up to one side.

the copy

Fig. 47

328

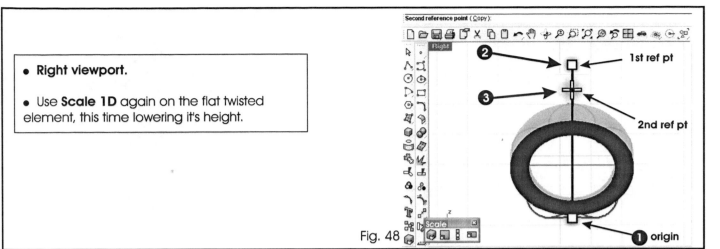

- **Right viewport.**

- Use **Scale 1D** again on the flat twisted element, this time lowering it's height.

Fig. 48

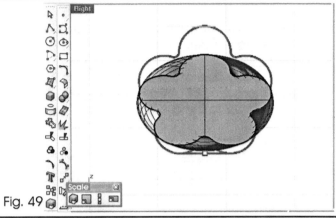

- Height has been significantly lowered.

Fig. 49

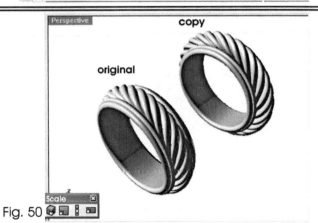

- **Perspective viewport.**

- Check out the original ring and see how **History** has updated the twisted element so that it is lower.

- The copy did not update because History was not enabled when the copy was made.

Fig. 50

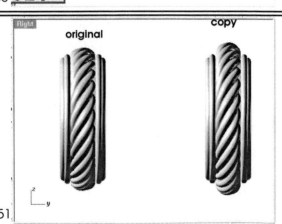

- **Right viewport.**

- Study this in the **right viewport** to see the difference in height between the copy and the original.

- The copy is not updated by the **Scale 1D,** just the original.

Fig. 51

- **Right viewport. Ghosted mode.**

- **Lock** the twisted element on the ring band with history.

- Turn on the **construction lines** layer.

- Turn control points on the cross section curve that was revolved to create the shank.

Lock command

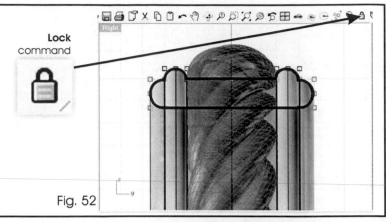

Fig. 52

- Since the band was revolved with the **History** option enabled, it is now possible to **edit the curve that was revolved so that the band can be updated** in order to further refine the design of the ring band.

- Select the two control points indicated by the arrows and drag them straight upward. Release the cursor at a location similar to the one shown.

- The band will update.

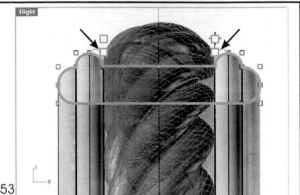

Fig. 53

- Select the two sets of control points shown.

- Click on the **Scale 1D** command.
  - **Origin point** prompt: snap to the point in the middle of the ring as shown. ❶

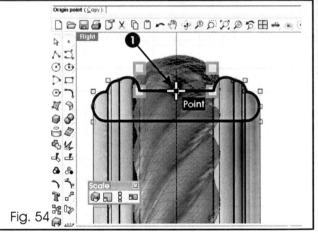

Fig. 54

- **First and Second reference point** prompts: draw the cursor outward and click on the locations similar to those shown. ❷ ❸

- The selected points are moved inward as shown.

- History will update the ring band.

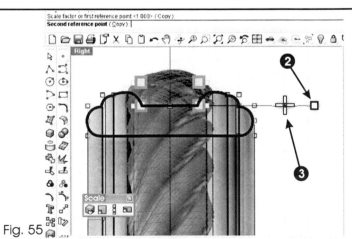

Fig. 55

- Switch to **Rendered Viewport** mode to view the updated band ring.

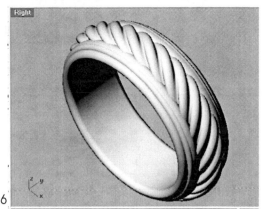

Fig. 56

- You can continue to modify the band by editing the curve until you are happy with the result.

- You can also continue to modify the twisted element.

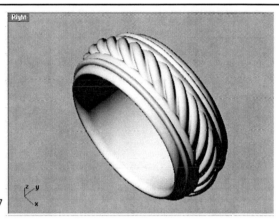

Fig. 57

Enameled Band Ring
Flow Along Surface command

- Create layers as shown.

- **ring body cons lines** layer currant.

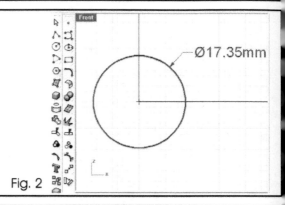

Name			
RING BODY		♀ ⌂ ■
ring body cons lines	✓	■
FLAT LAYOUT		♀ ⌂ ■
flat layout construction lines		♀ ⌂ ■
COLORED ENAMEL		♀ ⌂ ■
BASE SURFACE		♀ ⌂ ■
TARGET SURFACE		♀ ⌂ ■

Fig. 1

- **Front viewport.**

- Create a **17.35mm** diameter circle around **0.**

Ø17.35mm

Fig. 2

- **Perspective TOP viewport.**

- Select the circle the click on the **Length** command in the **Analyze** toolbar flyout.

- Notice that the length of the circle curve can be viewed as **54.507** in the history line.
  - A reading of "**54.51**" is OK. This simply means that the dimension settings in your Document Properties are not set to 3 decimal points ("**Precision**" line).

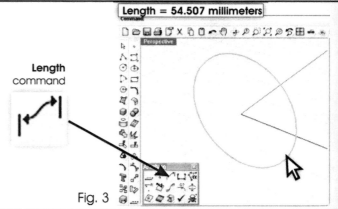

Length = 54.507 millimeters

Length command

Fig. 3

- **BASE SURFACE** layer.

- Click on the **Rectangular Plane: Corner to Corner** in the **Surface** toolbar flyout:
  - **First corner of plane** prompt: click on the construction plane. **❶**
  - **Other corner or length** prompt: type "**54.507**" and press "enter".
  - At the prompt for the **Width,** type "**8**" and press "enter".

- A rectangular surface measuring **54.507 x 8** will be created.

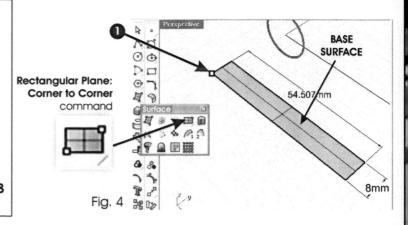

Rectangular Plane: Corner to Corner command

BASE SURFACE

54.507mm

8mm

Fig. 4

- **flat layout cons lines** layer.

- Place a **Point** at each corner of the base surface as shown, using **end osnap** for accuracy.

- You will now begin to create the profile of the band ring which will be created flat on the construction plane before being flowed in later steps onto an extruded surface created from the circle.

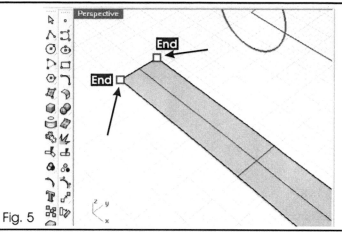

Fig. 5

- **Right perspective viewport.**

- Create a single line **2mm long** straight up from the midpoint of the edge of the base surface as shown.

- Be sure to use **ortho.**

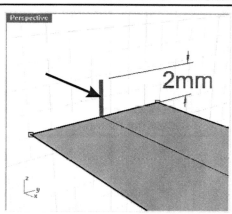

Fig. 6

- Create a **4mm** line straight up from the corner of the base surface as shown. Make sure that this line extends upward as shown.

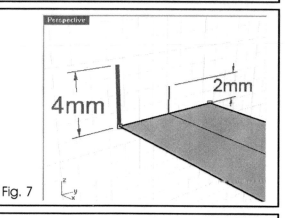

Fig. 7

- Click on the **Circle: Tangent, Tangent, Radius** command:
  - **First tangent curve** prompt: draw the cursor over the lower edge of the surface until a white constraint line appears. Click to set this edge as the first tangent curve. ❶
  - **Second tangent curve or radius** prompt: type ".5" and press "enter" to set the radius.
  - **Second tangent curve or radius** prompt: draw the cursor over the 4mm line and click to set this line as the second tangent curve when the white constraint line appears. ❷

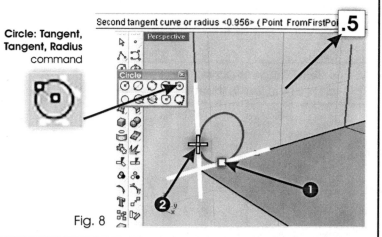

Fig. 8

333

- **Mirror** the circle over to the other side of the surface edge as shown.

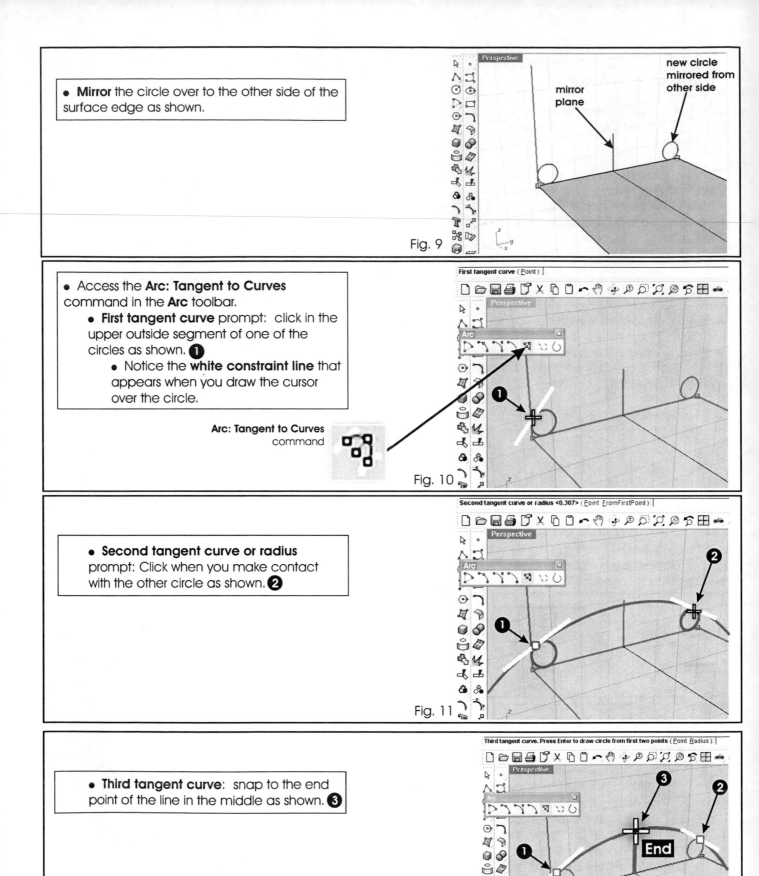

Fig. 9

- Access the **Arc: Tangent to Curves** command in the **Arc** toolbar.
  - **First tangent curve** prompt: click in the upper outside segment of one of the circles as shown. ❶
    - Notice the **white constraint line** that appears when you draw the cursor over the circle.

Arc: Tangent to Curves command

Fig. 10

- **Second tangent curve or radius** prompt: Click when you make contact with the other circle as shown. ❷

Fig. 11

- **Third tangent curve**: snap to the end point of the line in the middle as shown. ❸

Fig. 12

334

- **Choose arc** prompt, drag the cursor up above the arc as shown. This will set the final location and configuration of the arc as shown.
- Click to set this location.

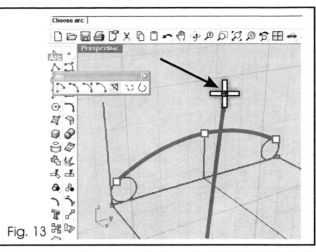

Fig. 13

- The finished arc is tangent to both circles and touches the top end point of the middle line.

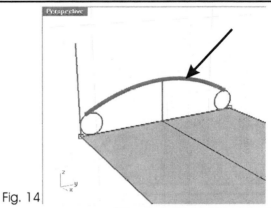

Fig. 14

- Select the new arc and click on the **Offset Curve** command.
  - **Side to offset** prompt: type "**1.3**" and press "enter".
  - **Side to offset** prompt: draw the cursor below the arc and click to set this location.

Offset Curve
command

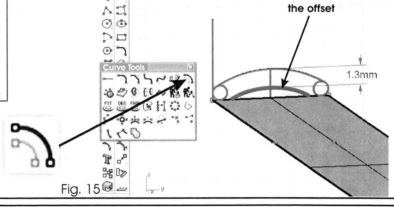

Fig. 15

- Turn off the **BASE SURFACE** layer.

- **Hide** or **Lock** the two points and perpendicular lines as shown.

- Create a **1mm** line starting from the lower quad point of the left circle as shown.

- Use **ortho.**

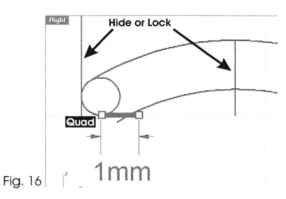

Fig. 16

- **Mirror** the new line over to the other side of the arcs as shown.

- It is now time to smooth out the ring's profile and create a graceful closed polyline.

Fig. 17

- Click on the **Fillet** command.
  - **Select first curve to fillet** prompt: Make sure that the **Join=Yes** option is toggled on.
  - **Select first curve to fillet** prompt: type ".5" and press "enter". This sets the radius of the fillet.

Fillet command

Select first curve to fillet (Radius

Join=Yes   ExtendArcsBy

.5

Right

Fig. 18

- **Select first curve to fillet** prompt: click on the offset curve at the location shown. **1**

Right

Fig. 19

- **Select second curve to fillet** prompt: click on the single line at the location shown. **2**

Right

Fig. 20

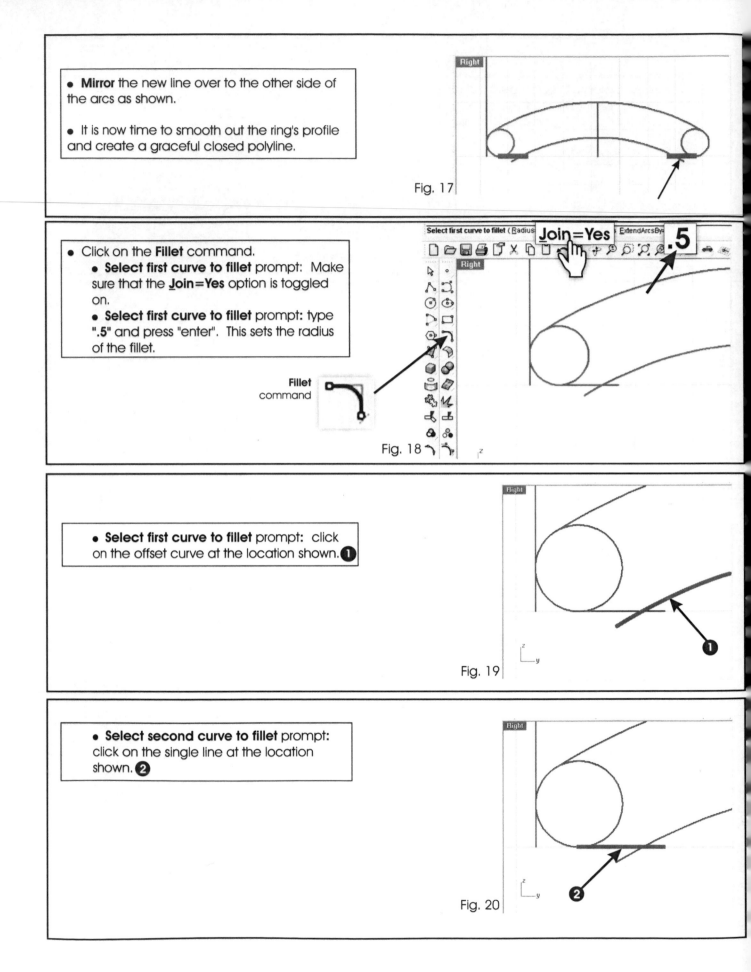

336

- A fillet has been made for a graceful transition between the two selected curves.

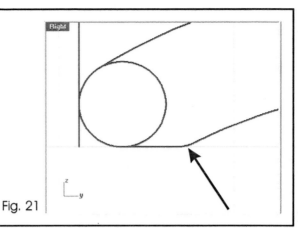

Fig. 21

- Repeat these steps on the other side as shown.

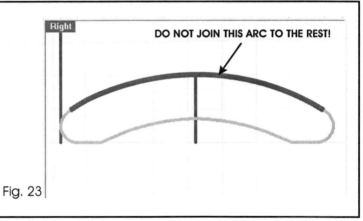

Fig. 22

- **Trim** out the curves as shown.

- **Join** the lower curves as shown.

- **DO NOT JOIN THE UPPER ARC - LEAVE IT SEPARATE.**

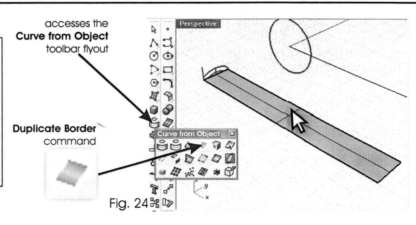

DO NOT JOIN THIS ARC TO THE REST!

Fig. 23

- **Perspective Top viewport.**

- Turn the **BASE SURFACE** layer back on.

- **flat layout cons curves** layer current.

- Select the base surface and click on the **Duplicate Border** command in the **Curve From Object** toolbar flyout.

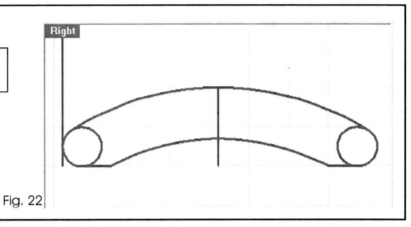

accesses the **Curve from Object** toolbar flyout

Duplicate Border command

Fig. 24

- A polyline with 4 segments appears exactly along the borders of the base surface. This is the duplicate border expressed as a polyline.

- Turn off the **BASE SURFACE** layer.

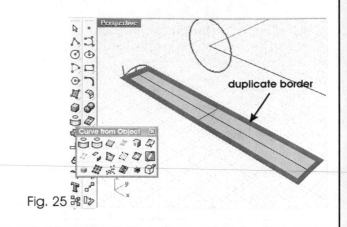

Fig. 25

- **FLAT LAYOUT** layer.

- Select the two previously created curves and click on the **Extrude Straight** command in the **Surface** toolbar flyout.
  - Make sure that the **BothSides=No** option is toggled on in the **Command Line.**
  - Draw the cursor out and snap to the other end of the polyline as shown.

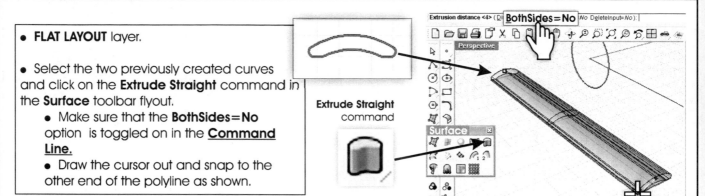

Extrude Straight command

Fig. 26

- The finished extrusion.

- Note that the top surface is not joined to the other bottom surface because the extruded curves were not joined together.

- Turn off the **FLAT LAYOUT** layer.

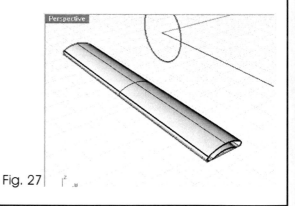

Fig. 27

- **flat layout cons lines** layer.

- **Top viewport.**

- Design or Import your enamel pattern.

- *Make sure that the curves or polylines that you use are closed.*

Fig. 28

- Lay your enamel pattern out within the boundaries of the base surface border as shown.

Fig. 29

- **Perspective TOP viewport.**

- Turn the **FLAT LAYOUT** layer back on and **Hide** the bottom surface.

- Select the surface and click on the **Split** command.
    - **Select cutting objects** prompt: select the design motifs which are lying on the construction planc and are visible through the ghosted surface.
    - Press "enter".

Spilt command

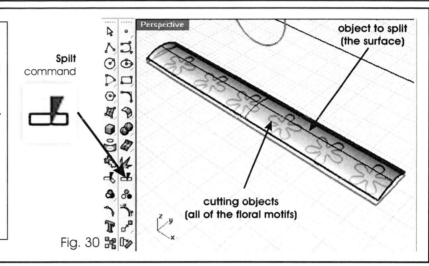

Fig. 30

- The finished splitting operation.

- The split parts of the surface will show as black edge curves of the little surfaces that have been split out of the larger surface.

- *Notice that even though the cutting objects do not touch the surface, they will split it.* They are lying on the Construction Plane under the surface and their outlines are "projected" onto the surface above to split that surface.

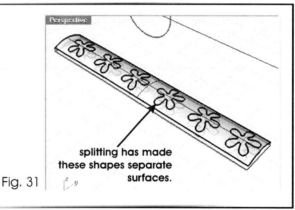

Fig. 31

splitting has made these shapes separate surfaces.

- Select one of the little split-off surfaces and click on the **Offset Surface** command in the **Surface Tools** toolbar flyout as shown.
    - Type **.5** to set the offset distance.
    - Click on the **Solid** option in the **Command Line.**
    - The white direction arrows must point in the direction of the intended offset which, in this case, is down.
        - If they are pointing up, click somewhere on the selected surfaces and they will change direction. Press "enter".

Offset Surface command

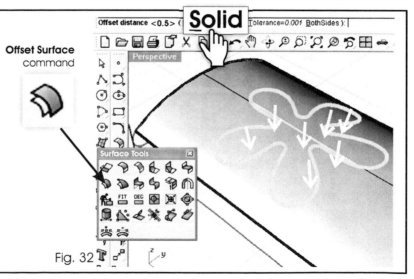

Fig. 32

- The finished solid extrude.

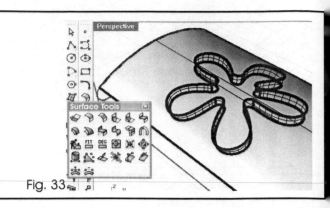

Fig. 33

- **Right-click** on the **Explode** button for the **Extract Surfaces** command..
  - **Select surfaces to extract** prompt: Select the top surface of the solid extrusion as shown.
    - Press "enter".

- The selected surface will be separated from the polysurface.

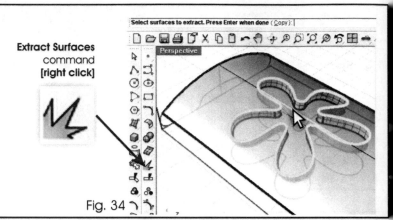

Extract Surfaces
command
[right click]

Fig. 34

- Select the extracted surface and change it to the **COLORED ENAMEL** layer.

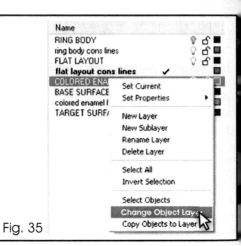

Fig. 35

- Switch to **Shaded Viewport** to see the enamel color in place.

- What you are seeing here is the default shade mode in which objects are shown in their layer colors.

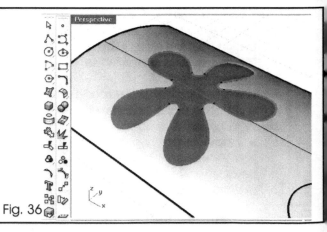

Fig. 36

- Create enamel cavities and layers with the other motifs, using the same strategy as in the first motif.

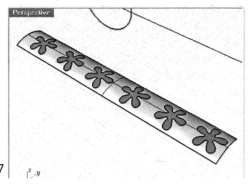

Fig. 37

- Turn off the **COLORED ENAMEL** layer to see the enamel cavities that have been created with the solid extrusions.

- **Join** these cavities to the large main surface.

- Test for **Naked Edges.** *The only Naked Edges should be the 4 edges that are the boundaries of the main surface as shown.*

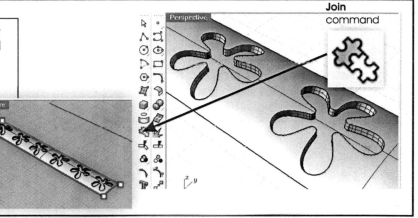

Fig. 38

- Click on the **Import/Merge** command to import the file named **1mm round w seat cutter** that has been previously created.

- All of the layers from the imported file will be imported into this new file.

- Delete the following layers:
    - **stone construction lines**
    - **stone seat cutter construction lines**

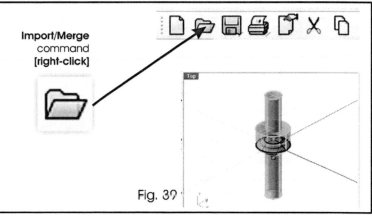

Fig. 39

- Before applying this stone to the surface of the flat layout, it is necessary to select the surface - *not the enamel surfaces* - and click on the **Analyze Direction** command.

- The white surface direction arrows should be pointing upward as shown.

- If they are pointing downward, click on the **Flip** option in the **Command Line.**

- The bunch of surface arrows over the floral motif are the arrows inside the enamel cavity. Ignore these arrows.

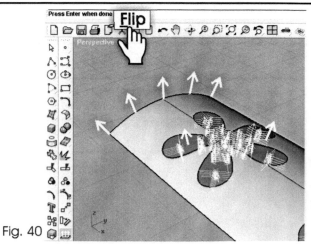

Fig. 40

- You can drag the stone and its cutters closer to the flat layout for better access when zooming in.

- Select the stone and its accompanying layers and click on the **Orient on Surface** command in the **Transform** toolbar flyout.

Orient on Surface
command

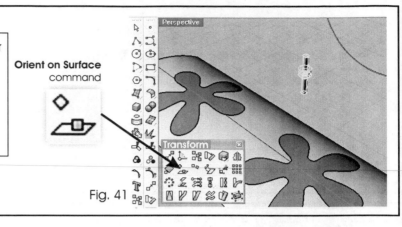

Fig. 41

- **Reference point 1** prompt: snap to the pont on top of the stone and click to set location.

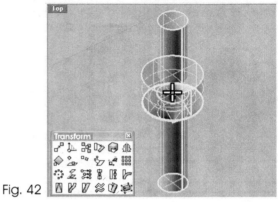

Fig. 42

- **Reference point 2** prompt: draw the cursor out and, using **ORTHO**, click somewhere nearby on the construction plane.
  - **ORTHO** must be used in this step as the point that you are snapping to is slightly above the construction plane.

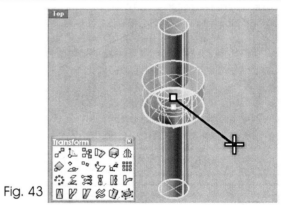

Fig. 43

- **Surface to orient on** prompt: click on the ring surface as shown.
  - *Do not click on the colored enamel.*

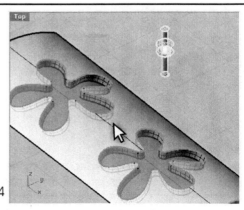

Fig. 44

342

- When the **Orient on Surface** dialog box appears, use the settings shown.

- Click the OK button.

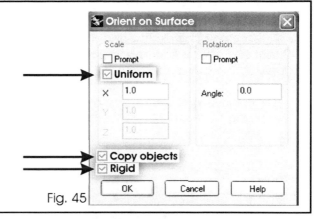

Fig. 45

- **Point on surface to orient to** prompt: as you draw the cursor over the surface, the selected objects will seem glide over the surface, always maintaining at a perpendicular position in relation to it.

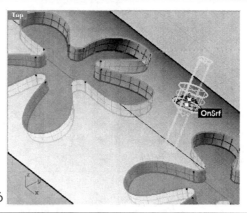

Fig. 46

- Click on a location and you leave a copy of the selected objects behind.

Fig. 47

- **Point on surface to orient to** prompt: you will continue to be prompted to click on the surface to make copies until you press "enter" to end the command.

- All of the copies will be perpendicular to the surface because that is the original object's orientation to the current construction plane.

- *This is why it is crucial in this command for the active construction plane to the one on which the object to be oriented sits upright.*

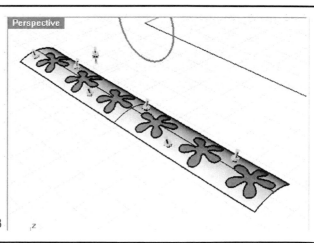

Fig. 48

343

- Select stone and cutters and click on the **Orient on Surface** command once again, applying the same reference points 1 and 2 as before.
  - In the **Orient on Surface** dialog box, change the scale from the default 1.0 to **"1.5"** as shown.
- Click the OK button.

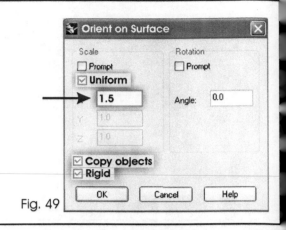

Fig. 49

- This time, when you click to make a copy on the surface, the copy will be a stone with a 1.5mm diameter.
  - Press "enter" to end the command when you are finished orienting stones to the surface.

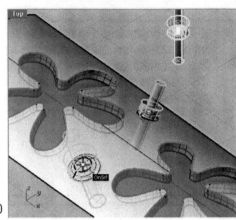

Fig. 50

- A couple of additional 1.5mm stones have been added to the surface.

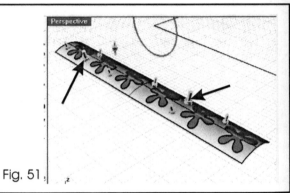

Fig. 51

- Select the stone and its cutters once again and click on the **Orient on Surface** command, setting **Reference points 1 and 2** as before.
  - **Select surface to orient on** prompt: click on the ring surface as before.
  - When the **Orient on Surface** dialog box appears, change the settings so that the **Prompt** option under the **Scale** category is checked.

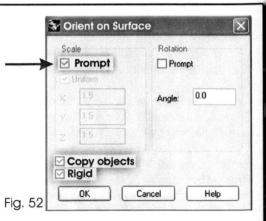

Fig. 52

- **Point on surface to orient to** prompt: click on the designated location for a stone.
- **Scale factor** prompt: type **"1.7"** and press "enter".

Scale factor <1.500>: **1.7**

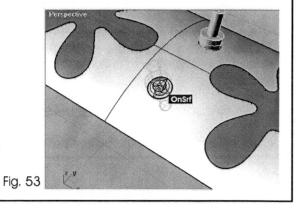

Fig. 53

- A **1.7mm** stone has been created on the surface.

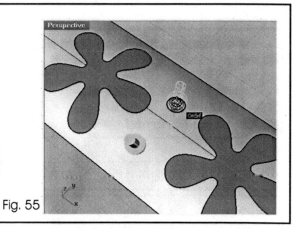

Fig. 54

- **Point on surface to orient to** prompt: click on another location.
- **Scale factor** prompt: type **"1.3"** and press "enter".

Scale factor <1.500>: **1.3**

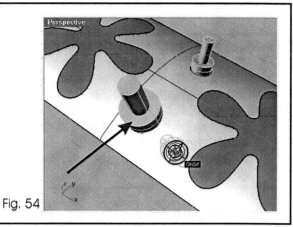

Fig. 55

- A new **1.3mm** stone has been created on the surface.

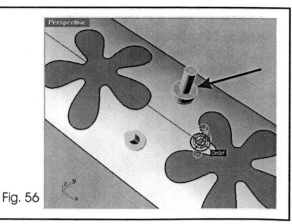

Fig. 56

- Orient more stones to the surface in different sizes of your choice and press "enter" when finished.

- **Unhide** the bottom surface of the band.

- **Join** the top surface to the bottom surface.

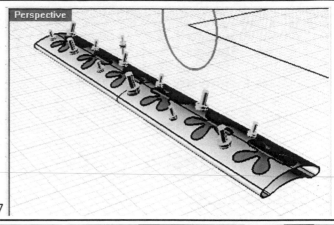

Fig. 57

- Make the **TARGET SURFACE** layer currant.

- Select the original circle and click on the **Extrude Straight** command in the **Surface** toolbar flyout.
    - Toggle on the **BothSides=Yes** option in the **Command Line.**
    - **Extrusion distance** prompt: type "4" and press "enter".

Extrude Straight
command

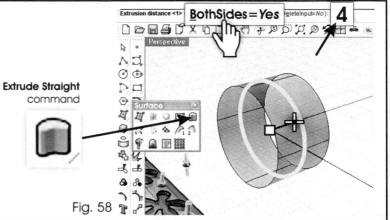

Fig. 58

- The extrusion will create an **8mm** wide band.

- Turn on the **BASE SURFACE** layer.

- Turn off the **flat layout cons lines** layer.

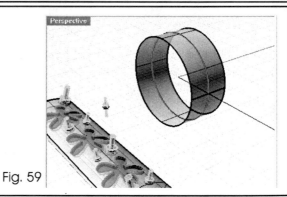

Fig. 59

- Select the new extrusion and click on the **Analyze Direction** command.
    - If the white arrows are pointing inward as shown, click on the **Flip** option in the **Command Line.**

Analyze Direction
command

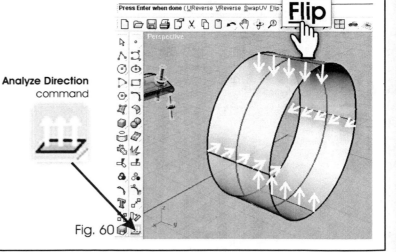

Fig. 60

346

- Run the cursor over the surface (the On Surf) icon will tell you that the cursor is making contact.

- Position the cursor as shown, in the corner near the seam and use the links in the **Command Line** to make the **U and V** arrows indicated line up as shown.

- The reason for doing all of this is that the base surface and target surfaces need to be in alignment with each other for the **Flow Along Surface** command in the next step.

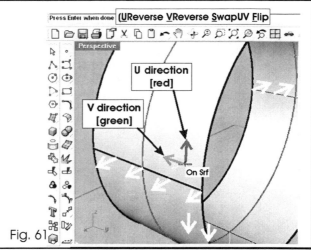

Fig. 61

- Place a **Point** on the edge by the corner of the surface as shown.

- Use **near osnap** to place this on the surface edge.

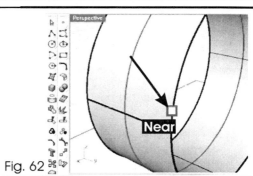

Fig. 62

- You can temporarily turn off the flat layout layers and turn on the **BASE SURFACE** layer.

- Use the **Analyze Direction** command to view the directions of this surface.

- Since this surface was done flat on the construction plane, it's directions should be aligned with those of the construction plane as shown.

- You can place a point at this lower edge if you wish.

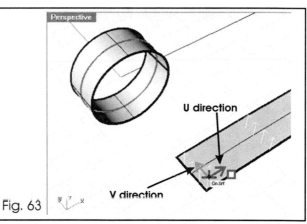

Fig. 63

- Turn on the flat layout and enamel layers. *Leave the stone layers off.*

- Click on the **Flow along surface** command in the **Transform** toolbar.
    - **Select objects to flow along a surface** prompt: select the closed polysurface and the little enamel color surfaces.
    - Press "enter".

Flow along surface
command

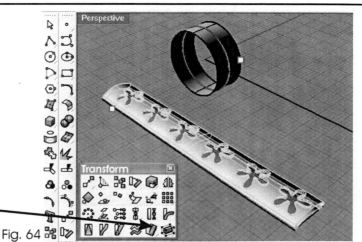

Fig. 64

347

- **Base surface - select near a corner**
prompt: click where indicated - near the
point that you positioned earlier.

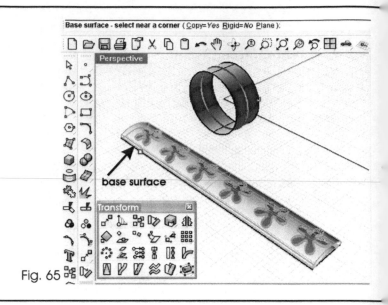

Fig. 65

- **Target surface - select near matching
corner** prompt: select where indicated -
near the point you positioned earlier as
shown.
  - The points that you click on for this
  step correspond to the surface
  directions you just set up.

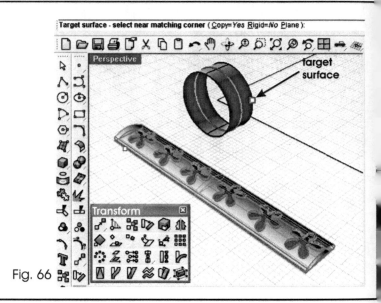

Fig. 66

- The flat layout has "flowed" on to the target
surface.

- Turn off the **TARGET SURFACE** layer to view
the inside of the ring band.

- The enamel color shown here is the color of
the layer it is on.

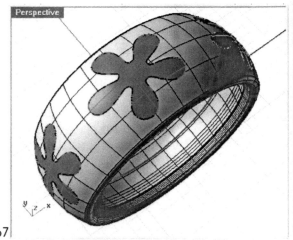

Fig. 67

- Create a new layer in the **Layer for Objects** dialog box and call it **colored enamel flat layout** and click OK.

- Select all of the little enamel surfaces on the flat layout and change them to this new layer.

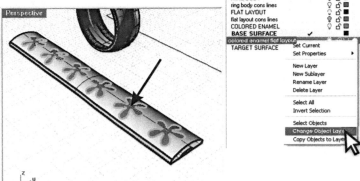

Fig. 68

- Select the new ring band - but not the little enamel surfaces - and change it to the **RING BODY** layer.

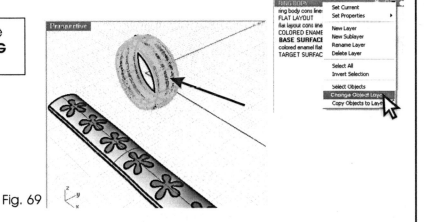

Fig. 69

- Turn off the ring and flat layout layers.

- Turn on the stone and stone seat cutter layers.

- **Hide** or **Delete** the original stone and its cutters.

- Notice how the stones seem to float above the base surface. This is because they were oriented to the flat layout of the ring which places them above the base surface in elevation.

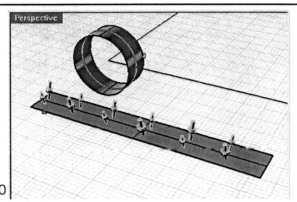

Fig. 70

- In the **Layers** box, **right-click** on the **stone seat cutter** layer to access the drop-down context menu.

- Click on the **Select Objects** option as shown.

Fig. 71

- All of the stone seat cutters will be selected.

- *The stones must not be selected for this step!*

- Click on the **Boolean Union** command.

Boolean Union
command

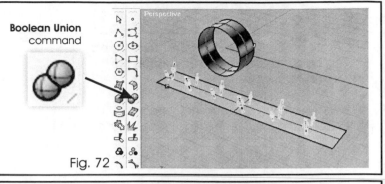

Fig. 72

- The stone seat cutters that were previously two objects - a seat cutter and a hole cutter - have been combined by the boolean union so that each one is now a single closed polysurface.

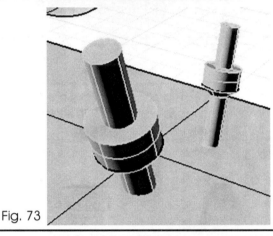

Fig. 73

- Select the stones and their cutters and click on the **Flow along surface** command in the **Transform** toolbar flyout.
  - Toggle on the **Rigid=Yes** option in the **Command Line.**
  - Select base and target surfaces as before.

Flow along surface
command

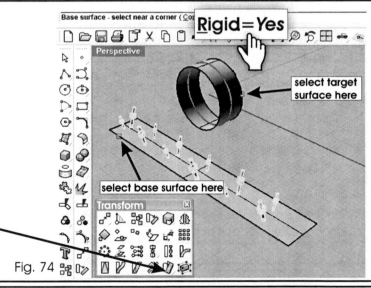

Rigid=Yes

select target surface here

select base surface here

Fig. 74

- The stones and cutters will be flowed to the target surface.

- The reason that the stones were not previously flowed on to the target surface with the rest of the ring is that, unlike the other ring components, the stones need to stay rigid - *you do not want them to become molded to the shape of the target surface.*

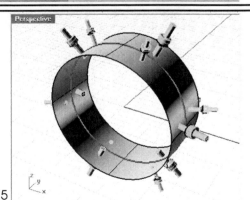

Fig. 75

- Turn on the layers for the ring band and enamel and you will see that the stones and their seat cutters are placed accurately on the surface of the ring.

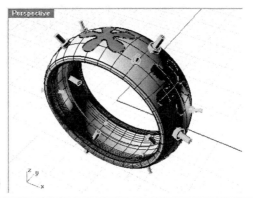

Fig. 76

- Select the ring body - but not the enamel surfaces - and click on the **Boolean Difference** command in the **Solid Tools** toolbar flyout.

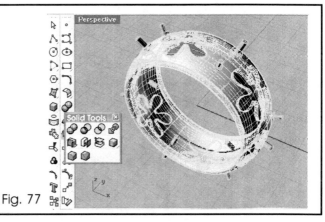

Fig. 77

- **Select second set of surfaces or polysurfaces** prompt: In the **Layers** box, **right-click** on the **stone seat cutter** layer to access the drop-down context menu.
- Click on the **Select Objects** option as shown.
- Press "enter".
- The boolean difference will be performed.

Fig. 78

- Turn off the **stone seat cutter** layer and see how the seat for the stone as well as the hole under it have been created.

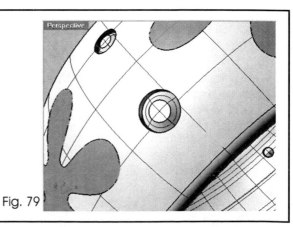

Fig. 79

Rendered Viewport Properties
Quick rendered viewport properties for the Enameled Band

- These **Rendered viewport** settings will give you the layer colors of objects. Otherwise, all surfaces will have a single white color in Rendered Viewport mode.

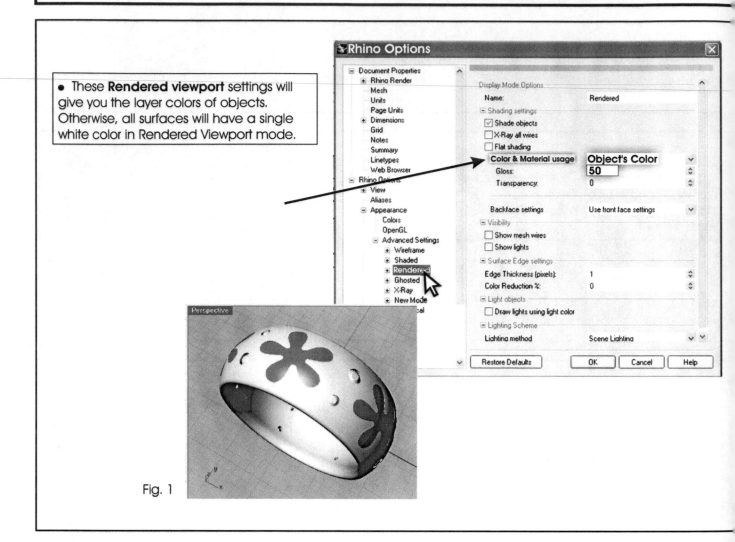

Fig. 1

- **Rendered viewport** mode.

- Turn off all layers except the **COLORED ENAMEL** layer.

- Now, select one of the little enamel surfaces and press the **F3 key.**
  - The **Properties** dialog box will appear.

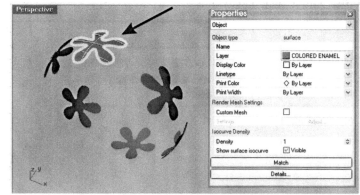

Fig. 2

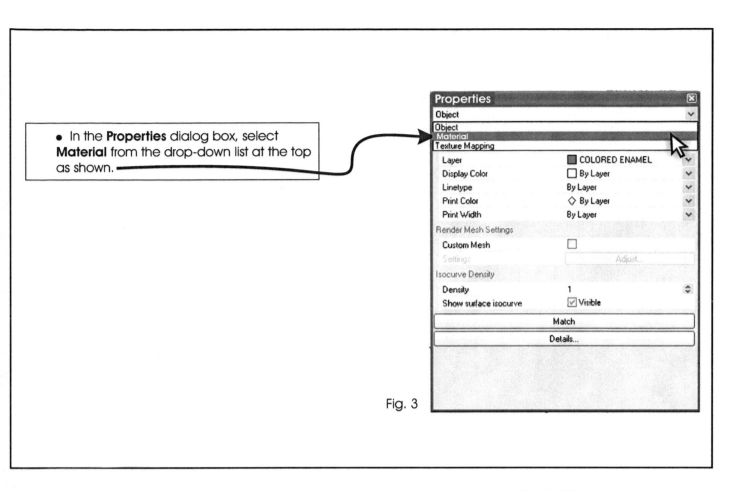

- In the **Properties** dialog box, select **Material** from the drop-down list at the top as shown.

Fig. 3

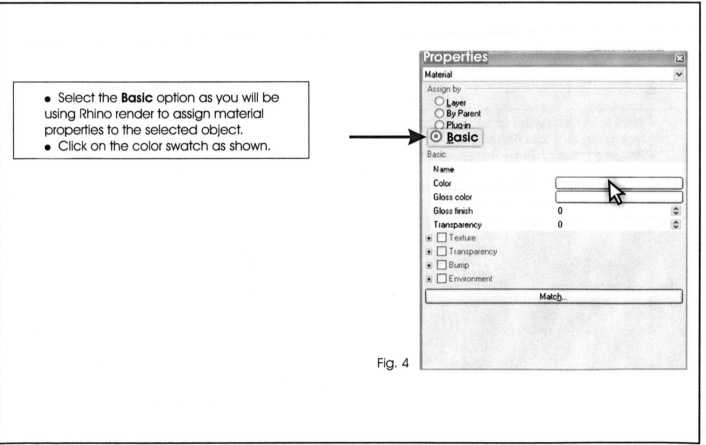

- Select the **Basic** option as you will be using Rhino render to assign material properties to the selected object.
- Click on the color swatch as shown.

Fig. 4

- Choose a color for the **enamel** in the **Select Color** dialog box and click OK.

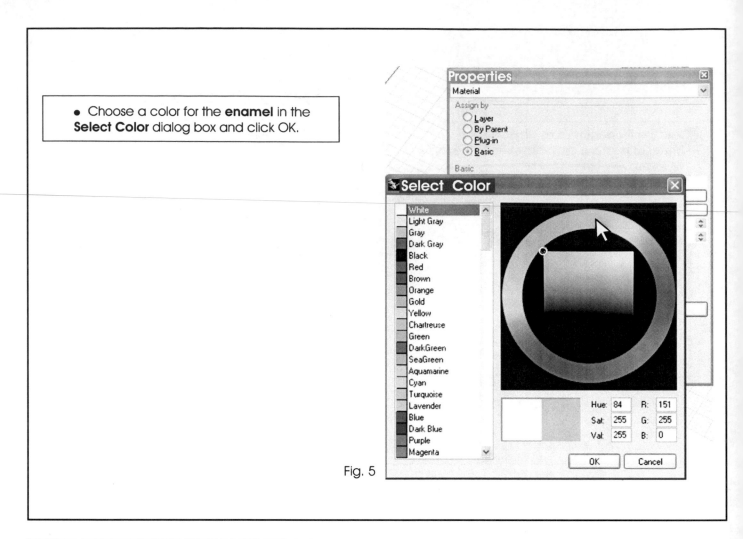

Fig. 5

- Back in the **Properties** dialog box, assign a high value for **Gloss Finish.**
- Assign a value of **35** for **Transparency.**
  - You can change these settings until you have achieved the desired look for the selected surface.

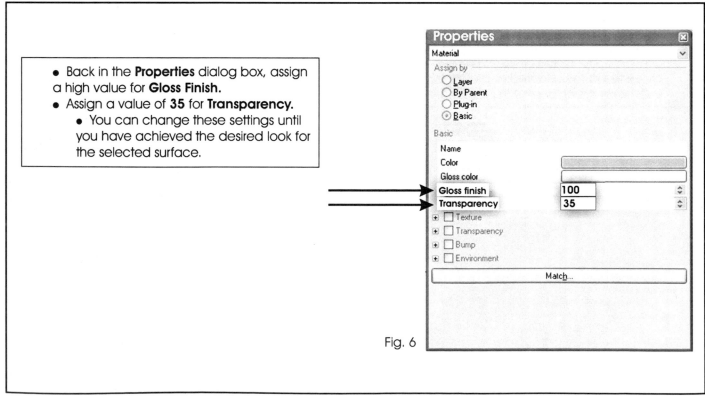

Fig. 6

- Turn on the **RING BODY** layer to view the color so far.

- You must be in **Rendered Viewport** to see the surfaces as shown.

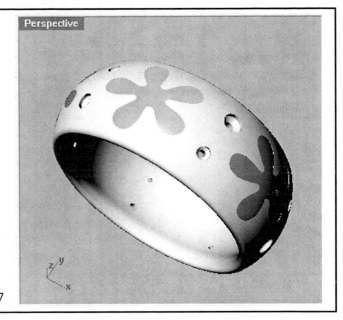

Fig. 7

- Turn off the **RING BODY** layer again.

- So far, you have only selected one element for the assignment of render materials.

- Now, multi-select some more - but not all - of the enamel pieces and press **F3** if you had previously closed the **Properties** dialog box.

- This time, while objects are still selected, click on the **Match** button at the bottom of the dialog box.

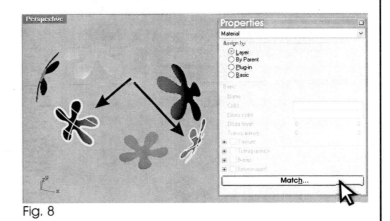

Fig. 8

- The little **Match** dialog box will open with all material boxes checked.

- Click on the OK button.

Fig. 9

- At the **Select object to match** prompt, *select the enamel surface that you had already assigned materials to previously.*

Fig. 10

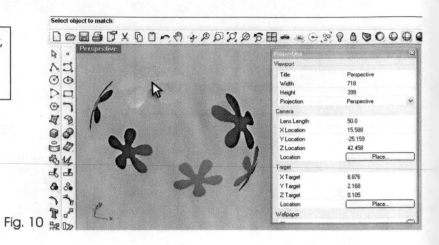

- All of the designated enamel surfaces will update to have the exact material/render properties as the original.

Fig. 11

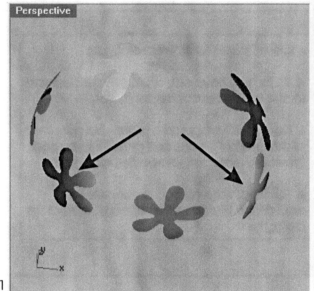

- Select the other floral surfaces that have not been assigned materials yet and press the **F3** key.

Fig. 12

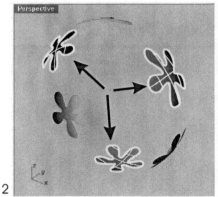

- When the **Materials** dialog box appears, assign a different color to the selected surfaces.
  - In this example, the Gloss Finish and the Transparency settings have been kept the same as before.

Fig. 13

- Turn on the **RING BODY** layer to view the enamel colors on the ring.

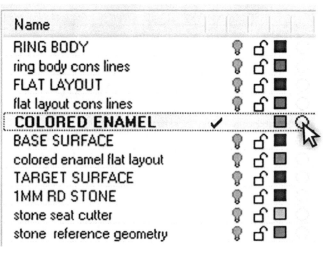

Fig. 14

- In the **Layers** box, click on the litlle circle on the **COLORED ENAMEL** line as shown.
  - This is the **Materials** column.

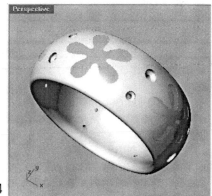

Fig. 15

Name			
RING BODY			
ring body cons lines			
FLAT LAYOUT			
flat layout cons lines			
COLORED ENAMEL	✓		
BASE SURFACE			
colored enamel flat layout			
TARGET SURFACE			
1MM RD STONE			
stone seat cutter			
stone reference geometry			

- When the **Material Editor** dialog box appears, change the color to black and the gloss finish to 100.
- Click the OK button.

- Note that there is no difference in the material properties of the enamel surfaces on the ring.

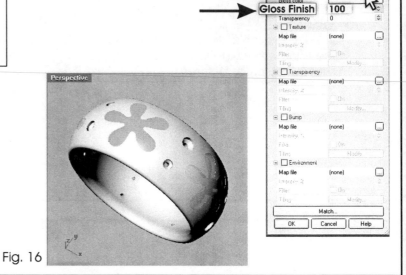

Fig. 16

- Select the enamel surfaces and press the **F3** key.

- Change the **Assign by** category setting from **Basic** to **Layer**.

- The enamel surfaces will immediately take the Black color assigned to the layer in the previous step.

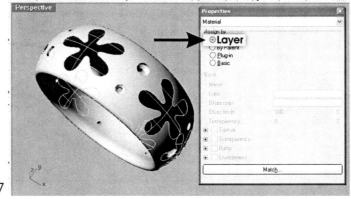

Fig. 17

- Click on the **Basic** option, and the first colors are restored.

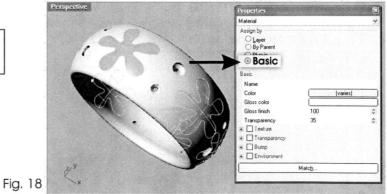

Fig. 18

- To obtain a simple "polished" gold surface on the metal ring band, select the ring band and press the **F3** key once again.

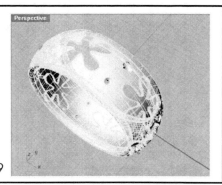

Fig.19

- Click on the color swatch as shown.

- When the **Select Color** dialog box opens, select the color **Gold** from the color list column on the left and, in the color selector box on the right, drag the marker horizontally to the position shown to lighten the color.

- Click OK.

- Type **"100"** in the **Gloss Finish** line and close the dialog box.

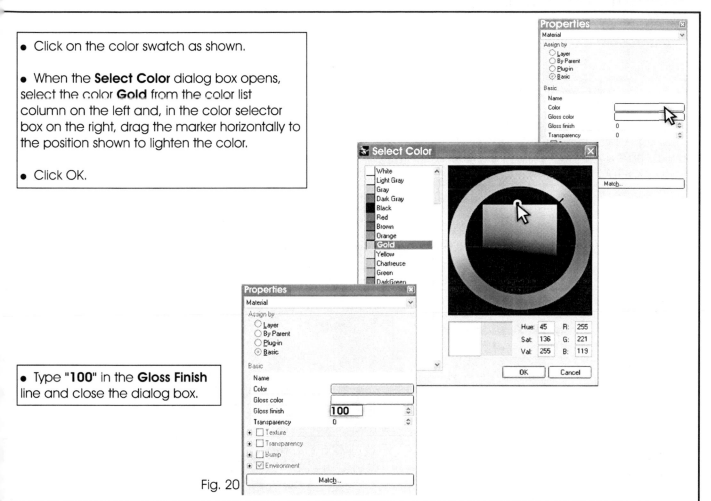

Fig. 20

- A reflective gold color will be assigned to the ring's surface.

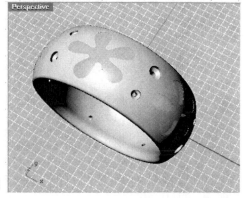

Fig. 21

- Turn off the layers for the ring and the enamel.

- Turn on the stone layer and select all the stones.

- Press the **F3** key and open the **Texture** category by clicking on the little plus sign by the word, **Texture**.

- Click on the little browse button to the far right of the **Map File** line as shown.

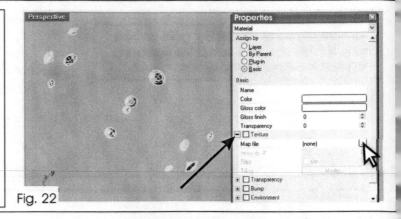

Fig. 22

- Browse for a bitmap of a diamond.

- With a window capture software like SnagIt ™, you can capture a good image of a faceted stone on the Internet. 200dpi is a good resolution for this purpose.

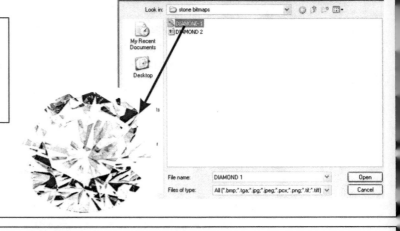

Fig. 23

- Assign **Gloss Finish** and **Transparency** as shown.

Fig. 24

- The diamonds will look sparkly enough but the gold color will remain looking more like plastic than metal.

- RhinoGold takes rendering to the photorealistic level with the help of Rendering programs such as Flamingo™, Hypershot™ and Brazil™.

- But, to get a quick shiny surface to the gold in Rhino, it is possible to put an **"Environment Map"** on the surface that will suffice for quick screen shots and layouts.

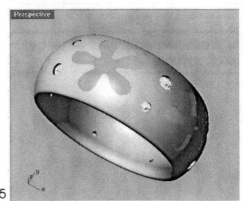

Fig. 25

- Select the ring's surface and press the **F3** key once again to get the **Properties** dialog box.

- This time, open up the **Environment** category and click on the little browse button on the far right of the **Map File** line.

- In this example a window capture was previously made of an image of modulating gold colors.

- Select this bitmap and click on the "open" button.

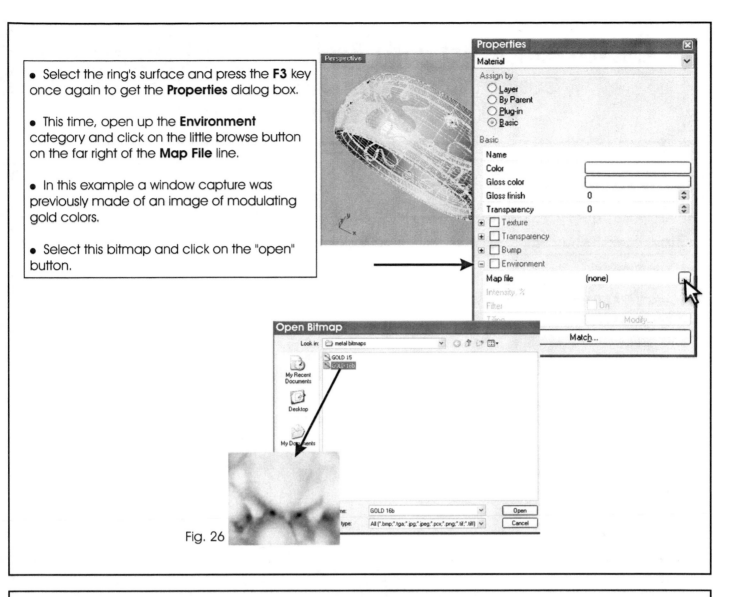

Fig. 26

- Although not exactly photorealistic, the ring has been assigned a shiny gold surface.

- If you type **"GradientView"** in the **Command Line,** you will get the background shown.
  - Press "enter" to repeat this command the Gradient is toggled off again.

  - If you type **"-GradientView",** the **Command Line** will display options that enable you to change the colors of the gradient.

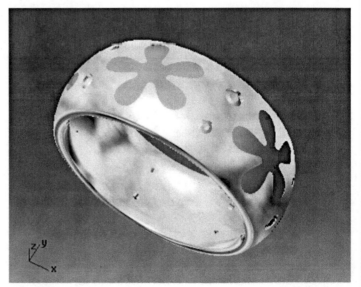

Fig. 27

Octagon Ring with Background Texture
- Custom Construction Plane Orientation
- Texture using Heightfield Bitmap

- Create layers as shown.

- **ring band reference geometry** layer current.

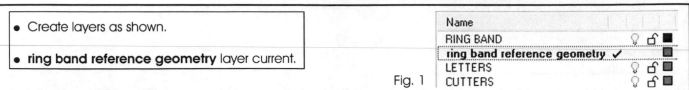

Fig. 1

Name		
RING BAND		
ring band reference geometry ✓		
LETTERS		
CUTTERS		

- **Front viewport.**

- Create a **17.35 diameter circle** around "0".

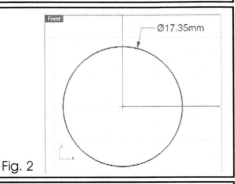

Ø17.35mm

Fig. 2

- Click on the **Circumscribed Polygon: Center, Radius** command in the **Polygon** toolbar flyout.
    - **Center of circumscribed polygon** prompt: click on the <u>Num</u>Sides=**5** option.

Circumscribed Polygon: Center, Radius
command

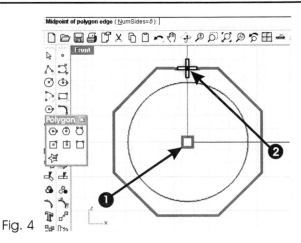

NumSides=5

Fig. 3

- **Number of sides** prompt: type "**8**" and press "enter".
- **Center of circumscribed polygon** prompt: type "**0**" and press "enter". ❶
- **Midpoint of polygon edge** prompt: type **"21.35/2"** and press "enter".
    - The "/2" that you typed means "**divided by 2**" as you are being prompted for the **radius** of the polygon.
    - Draw the cursor up and click to set, using **ortho.**❷

- A 21.35mm diameter polygon (at the midpoints of its flat sides) will surround the original circle.

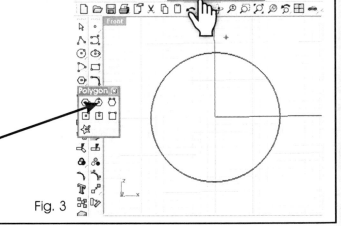

Fig. 4

- **Perspective TOP** viewport.

- Select the two closed curves and click on the **Extrude closed planar curve** command in the **Solid** toolbar flyout.

Extrude Closed Planar Curve
command

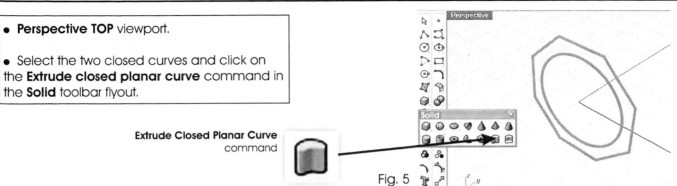

Fig. 5

- Make sure that the **BothSides=Yes** option is toggled on the **Command Line.**
- **Extrusion distance** prompt: type **"4"** and press "enter".

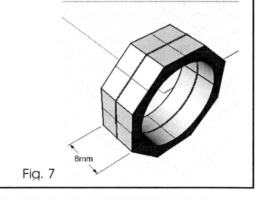

BothSides=Yes

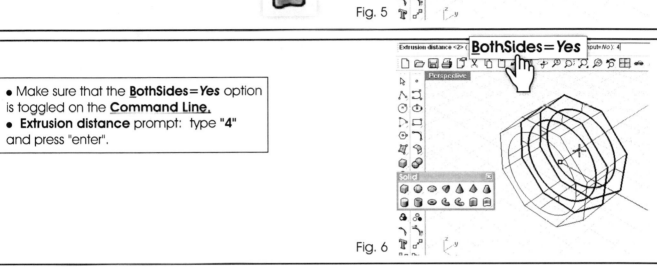

Fig. 6

- An **8mm wide** band has been created.

- Turn off the **ring band reference geometry** layer.

- **cutter reference geometry** layer current.

Fig. 7

- Use the **Rectangle: Corner to Corner** command to create a rectangle on the top of the ring, as shown.

- Use **End osnap** to snap to opposing corners as shown.

Rectangle: Corner to Corner
command

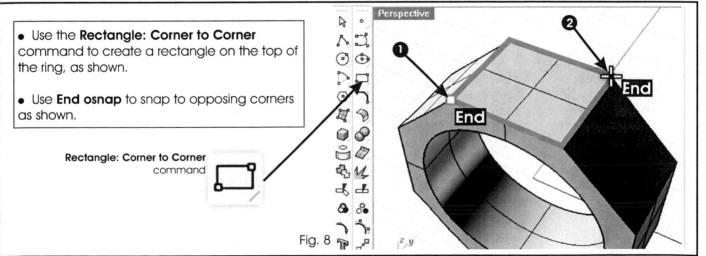

Fig. 8

363

- **Offset** the rectangle to the inside.
  - **Offset distance: .8mm**

Offset Curve
command

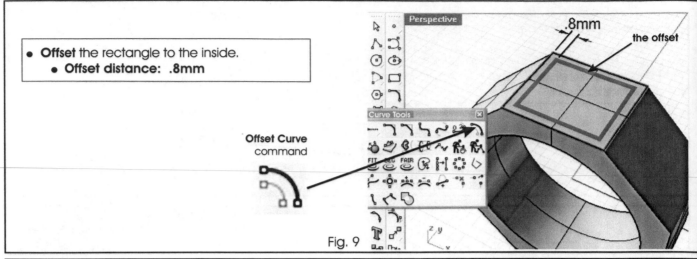

Fig. 9

- The next step will be to create a textured surface to use on the ring band.

- Scan this image of a cement surface.

- Save as a jpeg or bitmap and name it **"concrete texture"**

- **Desired size of image:** aprox 70mm x 50mm.

Fig. 10

- **CUTTERS** layer current.

- Click on the **Heightfield from Image** command in the **Surface** toolbar flyout.
  - When the **Open Bitmap** dialog box opens, find and highlight the file you named **"concrete texture"** and click the "open" button.

Heightfield from Image
command

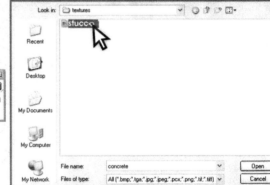

Fig. 11

- **First corner** prompt: click on the construction plane in the general area shown.
- **Second corner or length** prompt: type **"15"** and press "enter".

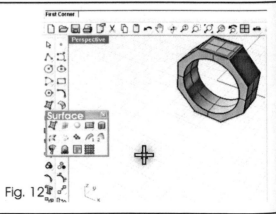

Fig. 12

- The **Heightfield** dialog box will open.

- Use the settings shown and click the OK button.

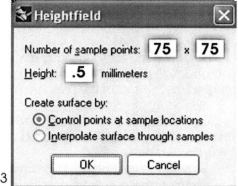

Fig. 13

- The **Heightfield from Image** command has created a dense surface whose modulation has been determined by the grayscale values of the selected bitmap image.

- The other settings in the **Heightfield** dialog box have also determined the height and density of the surface modulations.

- Experiment with these settings!

Fig. 14

- For example, this is what this same Heightfield command will produce with the same image and surface size but with settings changed as shown.

- The size of the texture detail may be good for visualization but may have detail too small for good reproduction on a prototyping machine which is usually limited in the size of recognizable images to aprox .25mm.

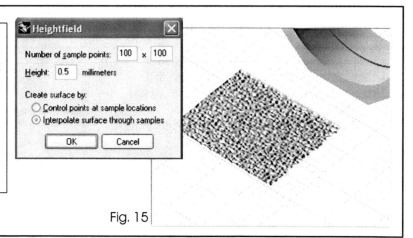

Fig. 15

- **Top viewport.**

- **Copy** the offset curve on the top of the ring over so that it sits over the new Heightfield surface as shown.

- Use the **Copy** command or drag with the **Alt** key held down to make a copy as shown.

- You may want to drag the new Heightfield surface closer to the ring for better availability.

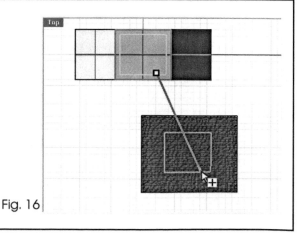

Fig. 16

- **Perspective TOP viewport.**

- The new copy is still hovering above the construction plane at the same height as the original on the top of the ring.

- Select the copied rectangle and click on the **Project to CPlane** command in the **Transform** toolbar flyout.
  - **Delete input objects?** prompt: click on the **Yes** option in the **Command Line** as shown.

Project to CPlane
command

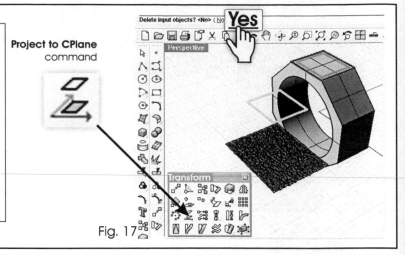

Delete input objects? <No> (No

Yes

Fig. 17

- The rectangle is now sitting on the construction plane.

Fig. 18

- Select the rectangle and click on the **Extrude Straight** command in the **Surface** toolbar flyout.
  - **BothSides=Yes** option toggled on as shown.
  - **Extrusion distance** prompt: type "**3**" and press "enter".

Extrude Straight
command

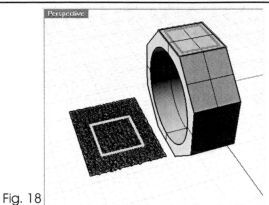

Extrusion distance <3> (Direction **BothSides=Yes** eleteInput=N **3**

Fig. 19

- Select the new extrusion and click on the **Trim** command.
  - **Select object to trim** prompt: click on the Heightfield surface *outside of the extrusion* as shown.

Trim
command

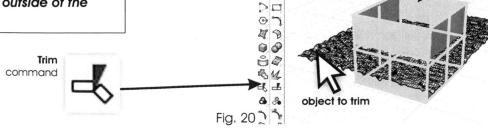

Select object to trim. Press Enter to clear selection and start over (ExtendLines=No Appar

cutting object

object to trim

Fig. 20

- the area of the Heightfield surface that was extending outside of the enclosure of the extrusion has been trimmed away.
- Press "enter" to end the command.

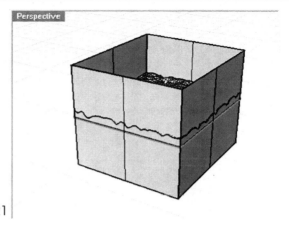

Fig. 21

- Select the remaining trimmed Heightfield surface and press "enter" to activate the **Trim** command once again.
  - **Select object to trim** prompt: click on the bottom of the extrusion, below the Heightfield surface in the general location shown.
  - Press "enter" to end the command.

Trim
command

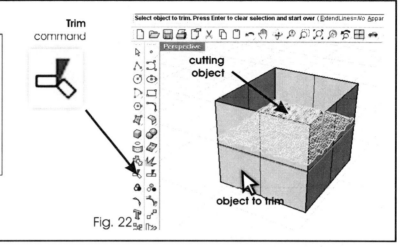

Fig. 22

- The Heightfield surface and the extrusion have trimmed each other.

- **Join** these two objects.

Join
command

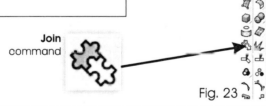

Fig. 23

- Select the new polysurface and click on the **Cap Planar Holes** command in the **Solid Tools** toolbar flyout.

- This is the finished cutter that will carve out cavities on the top three surfaces of the ring band.

Cap Planar Holes
command

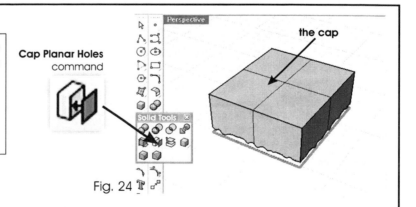

Fig. 24

- Select the cutter and click on the **Copy** command.
  - **Point to copy from** prompt: snap to the lower right corner of the cutter reference **geometry** rectangle just below the cutter as shown. Click to set location.

Copy command

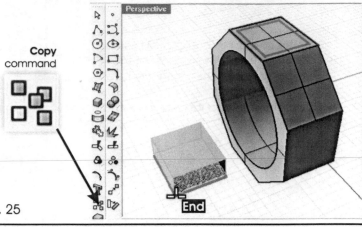

Fig. 25

- **Point to move to** prompt: snap to the lower right corner of the cutter reference geometry rectangle sitting on the top of the ring as shown.

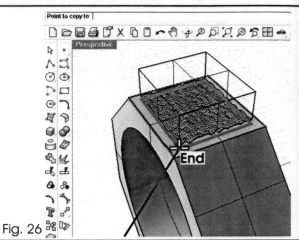

Fig. 26

- **Front viewport.**

- Turn on the **ring band reference geometry** layer and make it current.

- Turn off the **RING BAND** layer.

- Use the **Offset Curve** command to create an offset of the circle to the outside.
  - **Offset distance: .85mm**

Offset Curve command

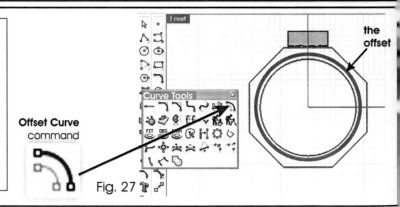

the offset

Fig. 27

- **Zoom** in on the top of the ring.

- **Drag** the cutter down to that it just touches the offset curve as shown.

- This is to ensure that, when the cutter cuts cavities out of the ring surfaces, that the wall thickness of the ring does not get thinner than .85mm.

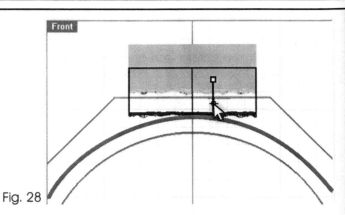

Fig. 28

- **Front perspective viewport.**

- Turn off the **ring band reference geometry** layer.

- Turn on the **RING BAND** layer.

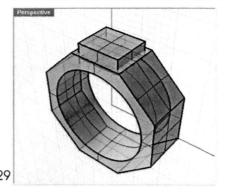

Fig. 29

- Select the cutter and click on the **Rotate** command.
  - **Center of rotation** prompt: click on the **Copy** option in the **Command Line.**
  - **Center of rotation** prompt: type **"0"** and press "enter".

Copy command

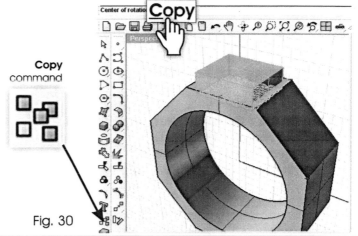

Fig. 30

- **Angle or first reference point** prompt: draw the cursor up and snap to the mid point of the back edge of the cutter as shown. Click to set location. **1**

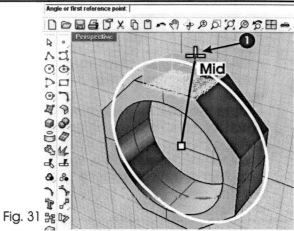

Fig. 31

- **Second reference point** prompt: swing the cursor to the right and snap to the mid point of the back edge of the ring surface as shown. Click to set location. **2**

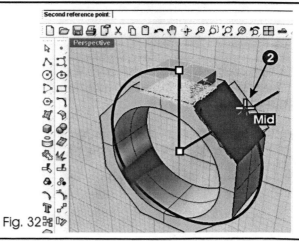

Fig. 32

- Swing the cursor around to the other side and snap to the corresponding midpoint. Click to set location.
- Press "enter" to end the command.

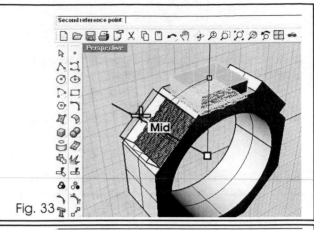

Fig. 33

- The cutter has been copied over to the sloping surfaces on either side of the top surface.

- Click on the **Boolean Difference** command in the **Solid Tools** toolbar flyout.
  - **Select first set of surfaces or polysurfaces** prompt: select the ring band.
  - Press "enter".

Boolean Difference
command

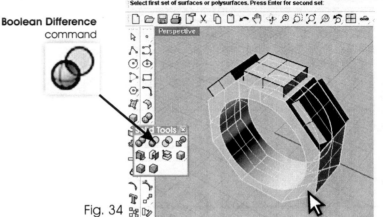

Fig. 34

- **Select second set of surfaces or polysurfaces** prompt: select the three cutters.
  - Make sure that the **DeleteInput=No** option is toggled on - you do not want this cutter to be deleted after this step as you spent too much trouble making it to say "goodbye" to it in one operation. You may use it again.
  - Press "enter".

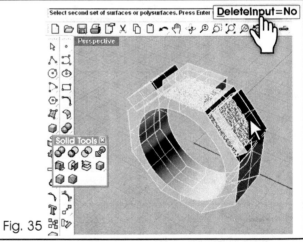

Fig. 35

- Turn off the **CUTTERS** layer and view the textured floors of the cavities that have been carved out.

- The textures will be a nice background for the letters or designs that will now be put into these spaces.

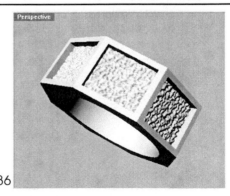

Fig. 36

The next step is to put letters in each of the three cavities that have been created.

The middle cavity is paralell to the construction plane but is not sitting on it so any letter/design elements that are created to sit inside it will have to be moved up on to it.

The two side cavities are not parallel to the construction plane which means that any letters/design elements that are created for them will have to be rotated into position.

The best way to accurately place letters in all three cavities is to use **custom construction planes**.

- **Right click** on the **Set Cplane** ("Construction Plane") **Mode** command in the **Construction Planes** toolbar flyout.

- This means that the new custom construction plane will only apply to the viewport in which you are working.
  - Left clicking on this command will activate **UPlane ("Universal Construction Plane") mode** which will involve all viewports which is not necessary here.

accesses the **Construction Planes** toolbar flyout

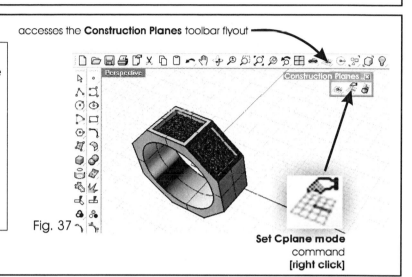

Fig. 37

Set Cplane mode
command
[right click]

- Click on the **Set CPlane Origin** command in the **Set CPlane** toolbar flyout.
  - Move the cursor and notice that the construction plane moves with the cursor at the origin point.
  - The **"Origin"** is another word for **"0"**, or **"0,0"**. This command will move the construction plane by its origin point.

Set CPlane Origin
command

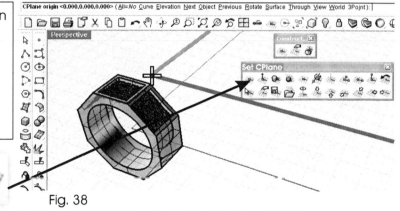

Fig. 38

- Snap to the end point of the front edge of the top surface. Click to set location.

Fig. 39

371

- The new construction plane is on the same level as the top of the ring band.

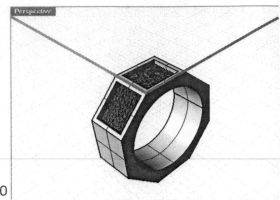

Fig. 40

- The lettering that will go into this cavity will be 1.5mm in height, enough to embed itself below the floor of the cavity and to have its top surface at the same elevation as the top of the ring band.

- Click on the **Set CPlane Elevation** command.
    - **Distance to move CPlane** prompt: type **"-1.5"** and press "enter".

Set CPlane elevation command

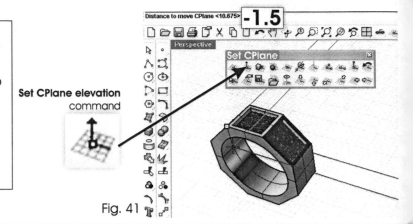

Fig. 41

- The construction plane has been lowered down 1.5mm because you typed a minus number.

- This is the construction plane upon which the letter on the top of the ring will sit.

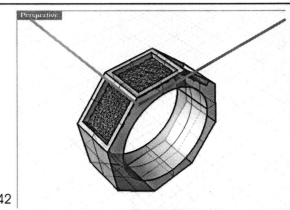

Fig. 42

- **Left click** on the **Save CPlane by Name** command.
    - **Name for the saved CPlane** prompt: press "enter" to accept the default name, **CPlane 1.**

Save CPlane by Name... command

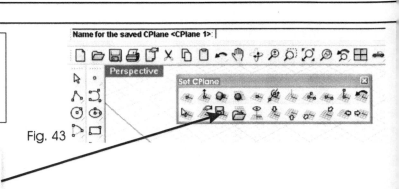

Fig. 43

- The next step is to create a custom construction plane for the sloping surface on the left side of the ring band.

- Click on the **Set CPlane by 3 Points** command.

Set CPlane by 3 Points command

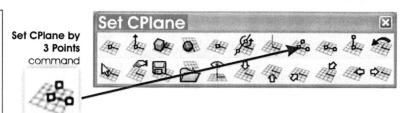

Fig. 44

- **CPlane origin** prompt: snap to the end point of the sloping surface on the left side of the ring as shown. Click to set location.

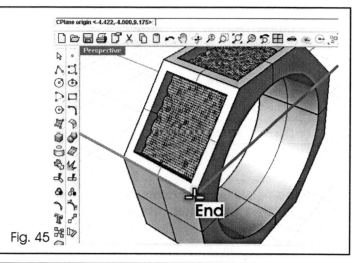

Fig. 45

- **X axis direction** prompt: snap to the end point to the right as shown. Click to set location.

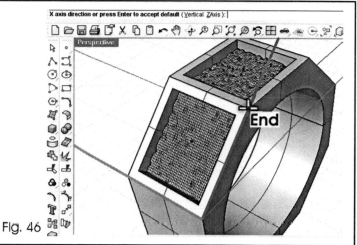

Fig. 46

- **CPlane orientation** prompt: snap the end point to the back of the sloping surface as shown. Click to set location.

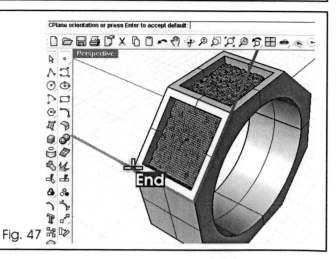

Fig. 47

Click on the **Set CPlane Elevation** command.
- **Distance to move CPlane** prompt: type "**-1.5**" and press "enter".

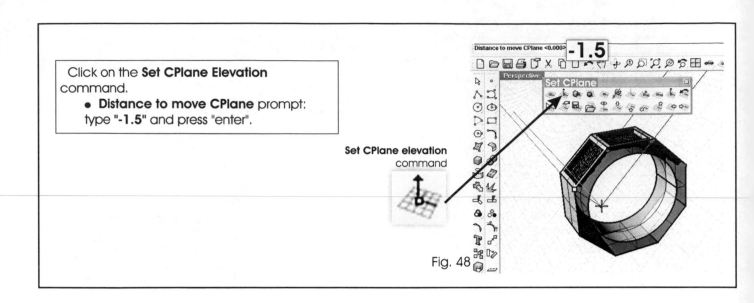

Set CPlane elevation command

Fig. 48

- The new construction plane has been lowered down 1.5mm because you typed a minus number.

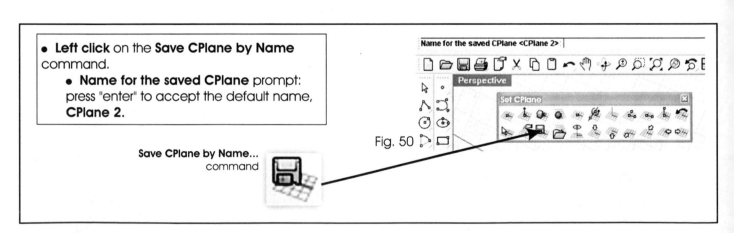

Fig. 49

- **Left click** on the **Save CPlane by Name** command.
    - **Name for the saved CPlane** prompt: press "enter" to accept the default name, **CPlane 2.**

Save CPlane by Name... command

Fig. 50

- Click on the **Set CPlane by 3 Points** command once again..

Set CPlane by 3 Points command

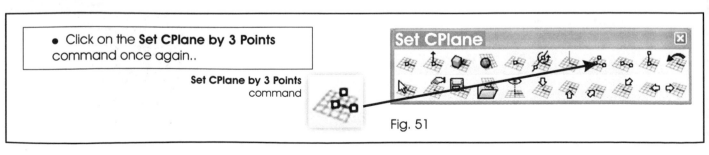

Fig. 51

- Snap to the three end points on the sloping surface on the other side of the ring in the order shown.

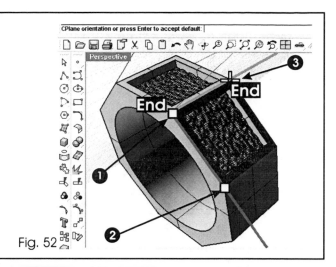

Fig. 52

- Click on the **Set CPlane Elevation** command.
    - **Distance to move CPlane** prompt: type "**-1.5**" and press "enter".

Set CPlane elevation
command

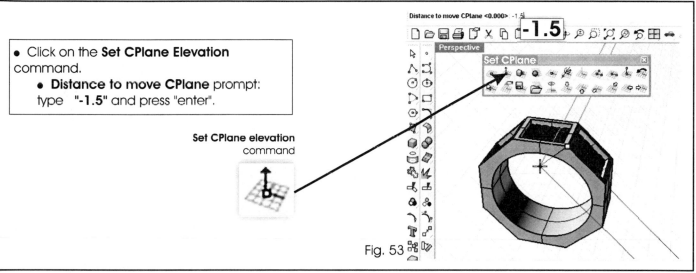

Fig. 53

- **Left click** on the **Save CPlane by Name** command.
    - **Name for the saved CPlane** prompt: press "enter" to accept the default name, **CPlane 3.**

Save CPlane by Name...
command

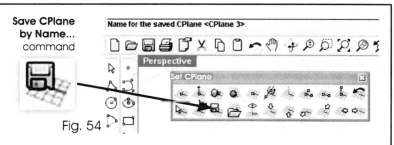

Fig. 54

- Click on the **Set CPlane World Top** command and you will return to the default "**World Top** construction plane.

Set CPlane World Top
command

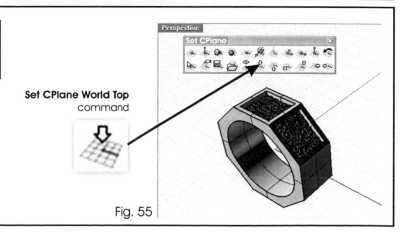

Fig. 55

- **Right clicking** on the **4 Default Viewports** command will return you to the 4 default viewports with their default construction planes.

Fig. 56

4 Default Viewports
command
[right click]

The next step is to put letters on each of the three textured surfaces.

- Click on the **Select saved Cplane** command.

- Three little X,Y,Z axis ikons will appear in the same positions of the three saved custom construction planes.
  - Note: The extra blue arrow represents the location of the **"Z axis",** which runs perpendicular to the construction plane and represents 3-D space.

Select Saved CPlane
command

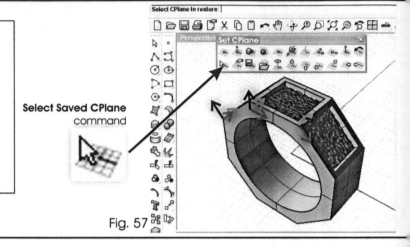

Fig. 57

- As the cursor is drawn across one of the little ikons, the ikon will select - it will turn yellow.

- Draw the cursor over the ikon at the top of the ring as shown. Click to select.

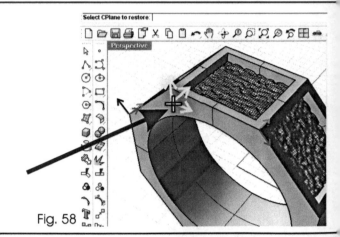

Fig. 58

- The construction plane is now the custom construction plane for the top of the ring, as selected.

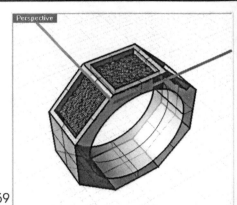

Fig. 59

- **Top viewport.**

- **LETTERS** layer current.

- Click on the **Text Object** command.
  - Type a letter in the **Text to Create** box and use settings shown.
  - Click OK.

Text Object command

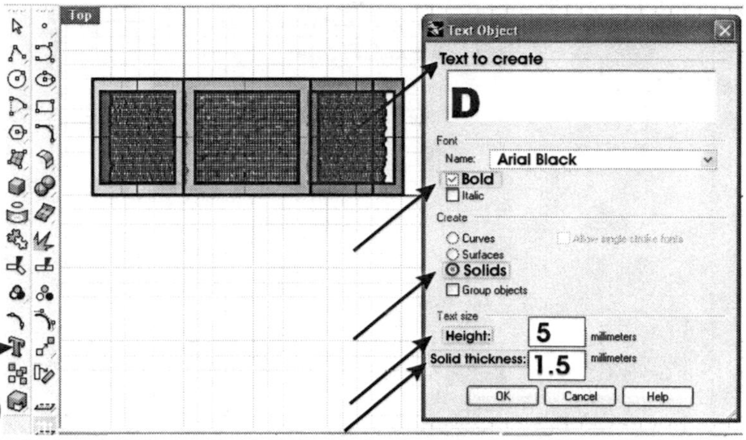

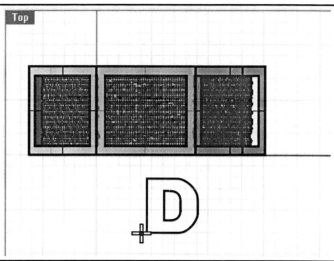

Fig. 60

- **Select insertion point** prompt: As you draw the cursor across the screen, a preview outline of the letter will move with it.

Fig. 61

- Draw the cursor over the ring until you like the position of the letter.
- Click to set the location.

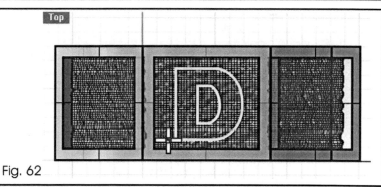

Fig. 62

- **Perspective TOP viewport.**

- The new letter is embedded in the textured floor of the cavity on the top of the band. Its top surface is on the same level as the top of the ring.

- It's bottom surface is resting on the custom construction plane.

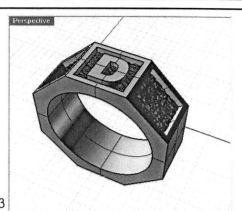

Fig. 63

- Click on the **Select Saved CPlane**
command.
  - Draw the cursor over to the custom
  CPlane ikon on the left and click to select.

Select Saved CPlane
command

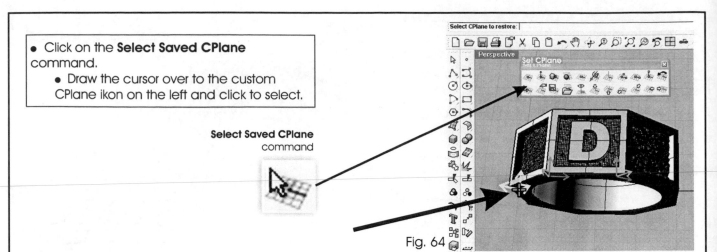

Fig. 64

- The custom construction plane that was
assigned to the left sloping surface of the ring
is now active.

- Navigation from this angle can be awkward.

- Click on the **Plan View of CPlane** command
in the **Set View** toolbar flyout.
  - The term **"Plan View"** means that the
  view is looking straight down on the
  construction plane.

accesses the **SetView** toolbar flyout

Plan View of CPlane
command

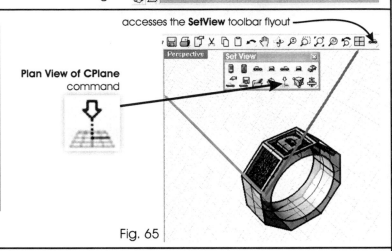

Fig. 65

- The view will now be looking straight down
on the custom construction plane for the left
sloping surface of the ring upon which you will
now place another letter.

- Click on the **Text Object** command once
again and create a letter of your choice, using
the same settings.

Text Object
command

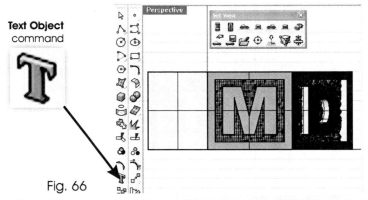

Fig. 66

- Using the same settings, create and place
the letter of your choice on the other side of
the ring as shown.

Fig. 67

Model of a Flower Component
Point Editing a Polysurface with the Cage Edit command

- Create layers as shown.

- **flower petal reference geometry** layer current.

Fig. 1

Name			
FLOWER PETALS		♀ ⌂ ■
flower petals reference geometry ✓		■
cage		♀ ⌂ ■

- **Top viewport.**

- Click on the **Ellipse: Diameter** command.
  - **Start of first axis** prompt: type "**0**" and press "enter". **❶**
  - **End of first axis** prompt: type "**20**" and press "enter".
    - Use **ortho** to draw the cursor upwards.
    - Click to set perpendicular location. **❷**
  - **End of second axis** prompt: type "**4**" and press "enter".
    - Use **ortho** to draw the cursor to the side.
    - Click to set location. **❸**

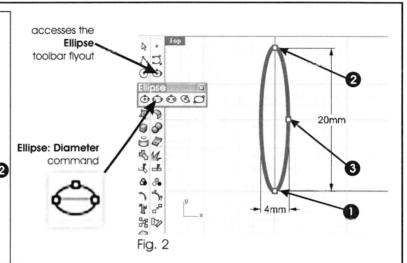

accesses the
Ellipse
toolbar flyout

Ellipse: Diameter
command

Fig. 2

- Select the ellipse and click on the **Extrude closed planar curve** command in the **Solid** toolbar flyout.
  - **Extrusion distance** prompt: type "**1**" and press "enter".

- The ellipse will be extruded upward 1mm as a solid object.

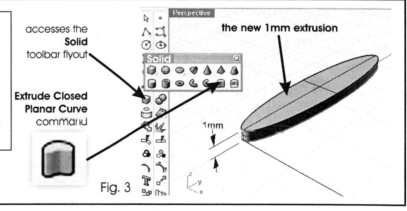

accesses the
Solid
toolbar flyout

the new 1mm extrusion

Extrude Closed Planar Curve command

Fig. 3

- Select the new polysurface and click on the **Explode** command.

- Delete the thin middle surface.

- You will be left with the top and bottom flat oval surfaces as shown.

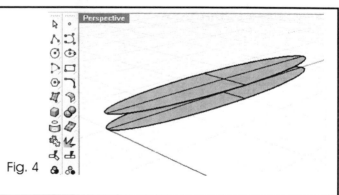

Fig. 4

- Click on the **Blend Surface** command in the **Surface Tools** toolbar flyout.
  - **Select segment for first edge** prompt: select the edge of one of the surfaces as shown and press "enter".

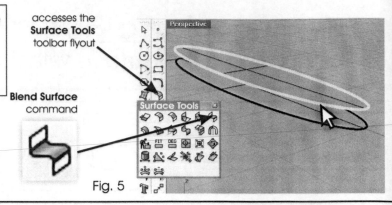

accesses the **Surface Tools** toolbar flyout

Blend Surface command

Fig. 5

- **Select segment for second edge** prompt: select the edge of the other surface.
- **Adjust closed curve seams** prompt: use **quad osnap** to move the seams so that they are lined up a the quad end of the ovals as shown and press "enter".

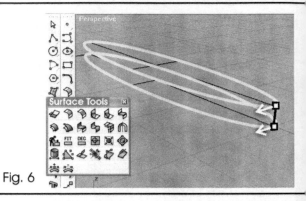

Fig. 6

- Click the OK button with the **Adjust End Bulge** dialog box opens up.

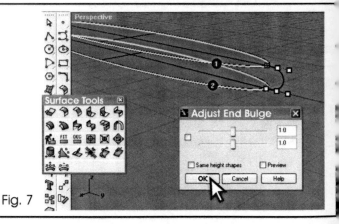

Fig. 7

- A surface will be created that smoothly blends the top and bottom surfaces.

- **Join** these three surfaces together to create a closed polysurface.

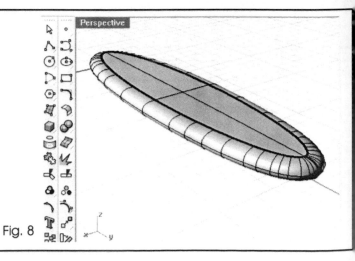

Fig. 8

- **cage** layer.

- Click on the **Cage Edit** command in the **Transform** toolbar flyout.
  - **Select captive objects** prompt: select the polysurface and press "enter".

Cage Edit command

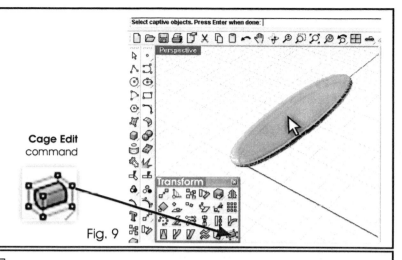

Fig. 9

- **Select control object** prompt: click on the **BoundongBox** option in the **Command Line. ❶**
  - **Coordinate system** prompt: press "enter" to accept the default of World. **❷**
  - **Cage points** prompt: click on the **XPointCount=4** option in the **Command Line. ❸**
  - **X point count** prompt: type **"7"** and press "enter". **❹**
  - **Cage points** prompt: type "enter" to accept the values now shown which include the new value that you typed for the **X** point count.

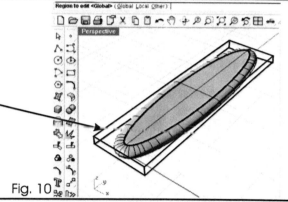

❶ Select control object **BoundingBox** angle Bo

❷ Coordinate system <World> (CPlane World):

❸ Cage point **XPointCount=4** nt=4 ZPointCount=4

❹ X point count <4>: **7**

- Notice that a preview outline of the bounding box has now appeared.

- **Region to edit** prompt: press "enter" to enter the default **Global** option.

Fig. 10

- The command is ended and the Cage's control points are now showing.

- This cage now controls the movements and deformation of the polysurface.

- The control points in the X direction are more numerous to allow for more detailed editing in this direction.

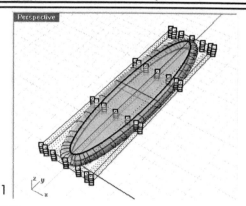

Fig. 11

- **Top viewport.**

- Press **F11** or the **Esc** key to turn off the control point s of the cage.

- Select the Cage and move it up **2mm** as shown. **Do not move the polysurface.**

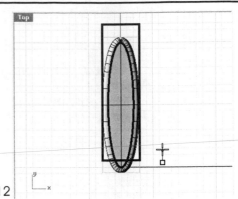

Fig. 12

- As soon as the move is over, the polysurface will move up to the same location as the polysurface because it is now controlled by the cage object.

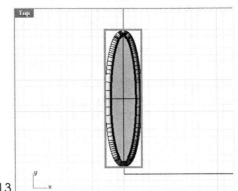

Fig. 13

- Click on the **Record History** button at the bottom of the Rhino workspace as shown.

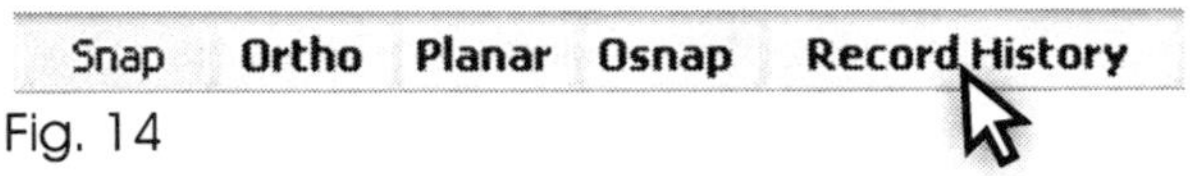

Snap   **Ortho**   **Planar**   **Osnap**   **Record History**

Fig. 14

- **Polar Array** the polysurface around **0.**
  - **Number of items: 6**

- *Do not array the cage objects.*

- **Lock** the new flower petals but do not lock the original one.
  - You will be point editing the cage object to sculpt the polysurface it controls and it is easier to lock the other objects so that you can not select them.

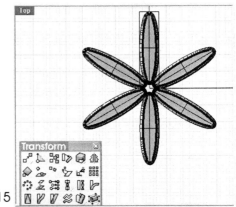

Fig. 15

- **Perspective top** viewport.

- Turn on the control points for the cage.

- Select the first two sets of control points of the middle row as shown.

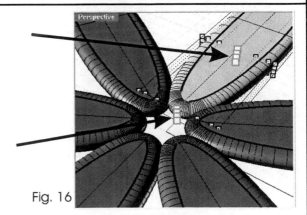

Fig. 16

382

- To make a groove down the petal, drag the selected points downward to a distance of approximately **2mm**.
  - *Remember to keep the Ctrl key pressed down so that you drag vertically downward instead of the default parallel to the construction plane.*

Fig. 17

- Even though the other petals are locked, they still update when the parent object is edited.

Fig. 18

- Window select the next row of control points as shown.

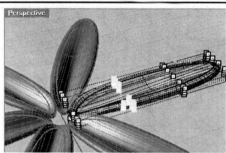

Fig. 19

- Press the **Ctrl** key down so that you can drag the selected control points straight up as shown.

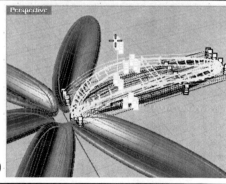

Fig. 20

- After the control points are released, the rest of the petals update as before.

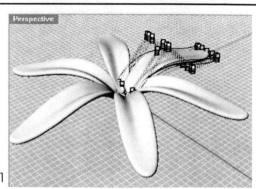

Fig. 21

- The next row of control points has been lifted and the flower petals have updated.

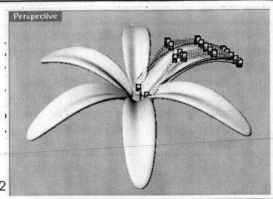

Fig. 22

- **Top viewport**.

- Window select the bottom row of control points as shown and click on the **Scale 1-D** command in the **Scale** toolbar flyout.
    - **Origin point** prompt: snap to the center point and click to set location.

Scale 1-D
command

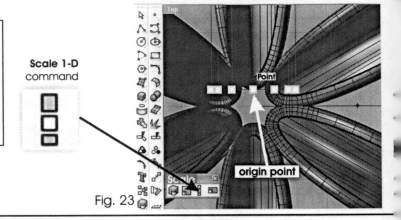

origin point

Fig. 23

- **First and second reference point** prompts: draw the cursor out and click in approximate locations shown.

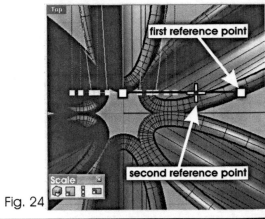

first reference point

second reference point

Fig. 24

- Point editing has made the inner end of the petal more pointy. The other petals update.

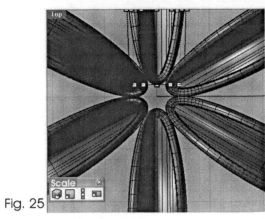

Fig. 25

- Select the outer two rows of control points and **right-click** on the **Rotate** button to activate the **Rotate 3-D** command.
  - This command is used to designate a rotation axis that does not have to be perpendicular to any construction plane.
  - **Start of rotation axis** prompt: snap to one of the points at the tip of the petal as shown. Left-click to set location.

Rotate 3-D command [right-click]

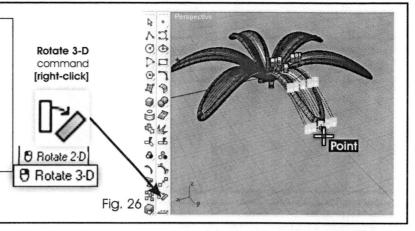

Fig. 26

- **End of rotation axis** prompt: draw the cursor upward along the Y axis and click to set the direction of this rotation axis.

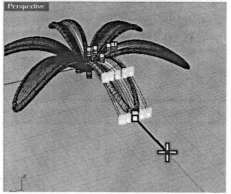

Fig. 27

- **Angle or first reference point** prompt: when the round preview circle appears, click on a location like the one shown to set the first reference point.

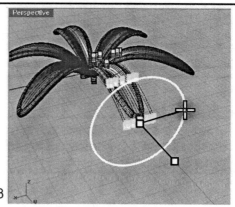

Fig. 28

- **Second reference point** prompt: Draw the cursor around to rotate the selected control points and click to set the location.

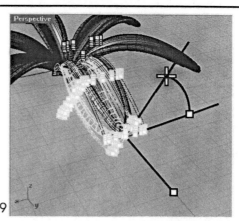

Fig. 29

- The other petals update and now all of the petals have a slight twist to their shapes.

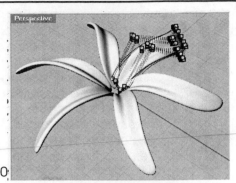

Fig. 30

- **Top viewport.**

- Window select the top row of control points and drag them downward to the left as shown.

Fig. 31

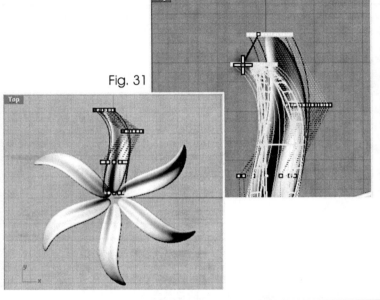

- The rest of the petals have updated.

Fig. 32

- Select the row on control points shown and use the **Scale 1-D** command to widen the petal at this point.

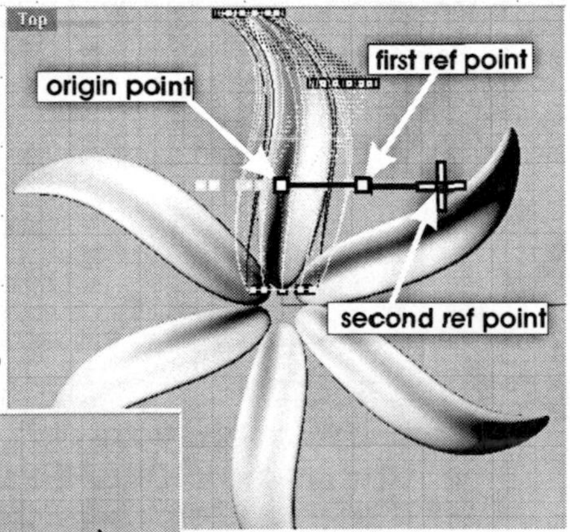

origin point   first ref point

second ref point

Fig. 33

- The updated petals.

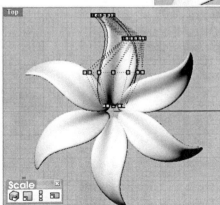

Fig. 34

• Carefully window select the bottom left three rows of control points shown.

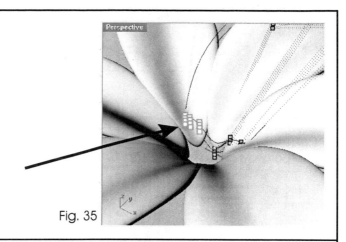

Fig. 35

• Drag the selected control points up a short distance.

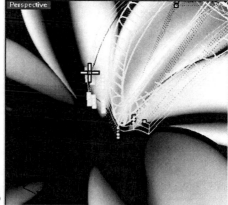

Fig. 36

• The updated flower petals now look like they are slightly overlapping.

Fig. 37

• The floral component you have just created can be further edited or saved off and used in other models.

• In this illustration prong setting has been imported into the file.

Fig. 38

Ring Band with Bead Set and Flush Set Stones

- Create layers as shown.

- **ring curves** layer current.

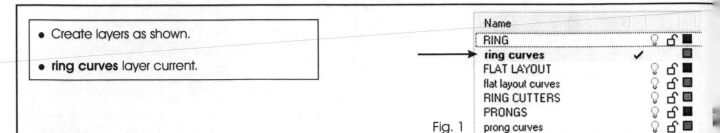

Fig. 1

- **Import** the file, **1mm round w seat cutter** that was created in a previous chapter.

- You may import a faceted stone model if desired.
  - A faceted stone can be imported and used along with the simpler maquette so that when the model is rendered, the faceted stones can give a better display.

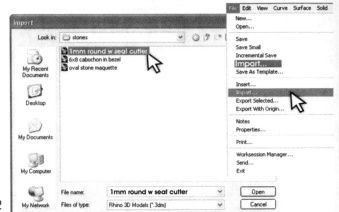

Fig. 2

- **Perspective TOP viewport.**

- A round stone, 1mm in diameter, will be imported with seat and hole cutters.

- Select the two objects on the **stone seat cutter** layer and click on the **Boolean Union** command.
  - The two cutters will now be one closed polysurface.

Boolean Union command

select for boolean union

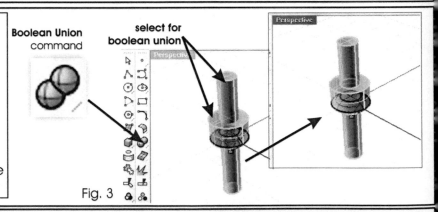

Fig. 3

- Delete the **stone construction lines** layer and the **stone seat cutters construction lines** layer. They will not be needed.

- **Copy** the stone, its geometry and its seat cutters over to the side as shown.

- Window select the original stone with its geometry and cutters and click on the **Scale 3-D** command.

Scale 3-D command

original

copy

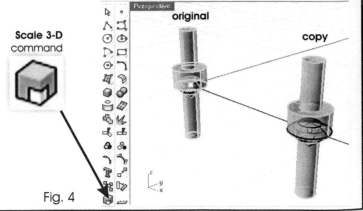

Fig. 4

- Follow prompts for the **Scale 3-D** command:
  - **Origin point** prompt: snap to the point in the middle of the stone as shown. **Point osnap is essential for accuracy.**
  - **Scale factor or first reference point** prompt: type **"2"** and press "enter".

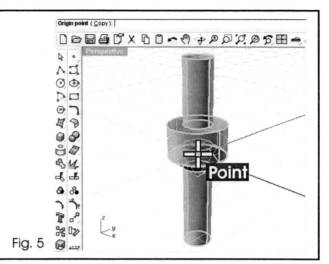

Fig. 5

- The stone is scaled up and now measures **2mm** in diameter.

- Create 3 new layers:
  - **2mm stone**
  - **2mm stone placement geometry**
  - **2mm stone seat cutters**

- Change the layers of all three of the above elements of the stone that you just scaled up to these new layers.

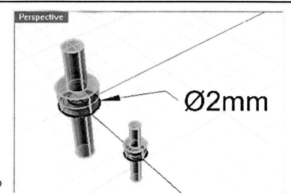

Ø2mm

Fig. 6

- Window select the remaining smaller stone, its geometry, and its stone seat cutters.

- Click on the **Scale 3-D** command.
  - **Origin point** prompt: snap to the point in the middle of the stone as shown. Use **point osnap** as before.
  - **Scale factor or first reference point** prompt: type **"1.8"** and press "enter".

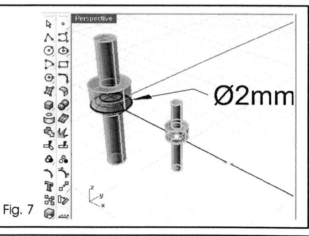

Ø2mm

Fig. 7

- The second stone is now 1.8mm in diameter.

- Create 3 new layers:
  - **1.8mm stone**
  - **1.8mm stone placement geometry**
  - **1.8mm stone seat cutters**

- Change the layers of the 1.8mm stone, its geometry, and its cutters on to the new layers.

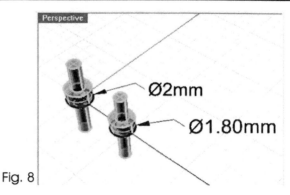

Ø2mm

Ø1.80mm

Fig. 8

- Window select the 2mm stone with its geometry and cutters and click on the **Group** command.

- *This is not a join command.* Grouping will enable all grouped objects to be selected as one unit.

- Any elements of this group that are on layers that are turned off will still update when other visible elements are moved, edited, or copied.

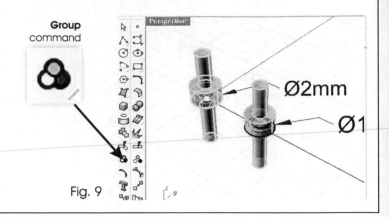

Group command

Fig. 9

- Window select the 1.8mm stone with its geometry and cutters and click on the **Group** command once again.

- **Delete** the following layers:
  - **1mm round stone**
  - **stone placement geometry**
  - **stone seat cutters**

- These layers are now empty and are no longer necessary.

- Turn off all stone and stone associated layers.

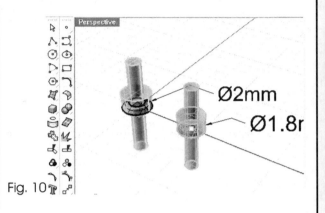

Fig. 10

- **Front viewport.**

- **ring curves** layer.

- Create a circle around "**0**" with a diameter of **17.35mm**.

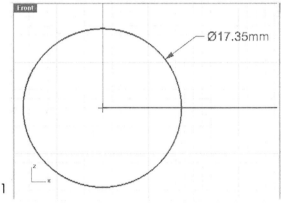

Fig. 11

- **Right perspective viewport.**

- Use the **Line: from Midpoint** command to create a line on the top quad of the circle.
  - **Quad osnap** is essential for placing the **Middle of the line**.
  - Total length of line: **8mm** as shown.

Line: from Midpoint command

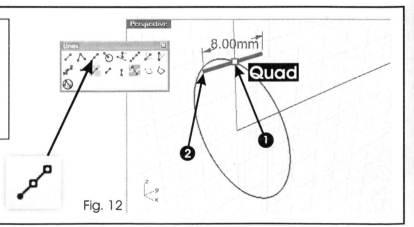

Fig. 12

- Create a line straight up from the midpoint of the line just created.

- Length of this new line: 2mm as shown.

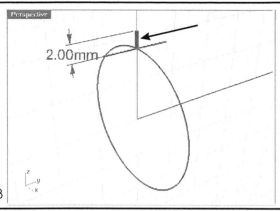

Fig. 13

- Use the **Arc: Start, End, Point on Arc** command to create a arc that passes through the three end points of the straight lines as shown.

- The next step will be to make the ends of the arc and line less sharp and to add more fullness to the ends of the arc.

Arc: Start, End, Point on Arc
command

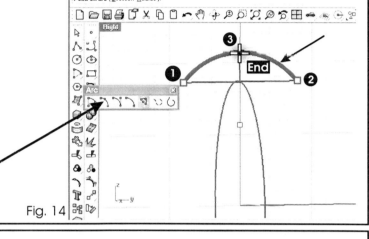

Fig. 14

- Turn on the control points for the new arc.

- Select the second point in from the left and click on the **Move** command. ❶
  - Draw the cursor over to the left, using **ortho**. ❷
  - **Tap the TAB key** once and the direction of the move will be constrained.
  - Move the cursor down and snap to the end point of the arc below. ❸
  - The point you are moving will be moved to a point directly above it.

- Repeat this step on the other side for symmetry.

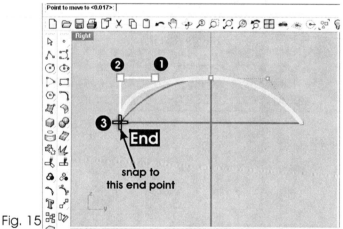

Fig. 15

- **Fillet** the lower corners of the arc and straight line with a fillet radius of **.5mm** as shown.

Fillet
command

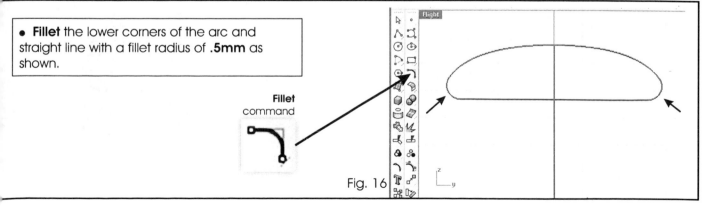

Fig. 16

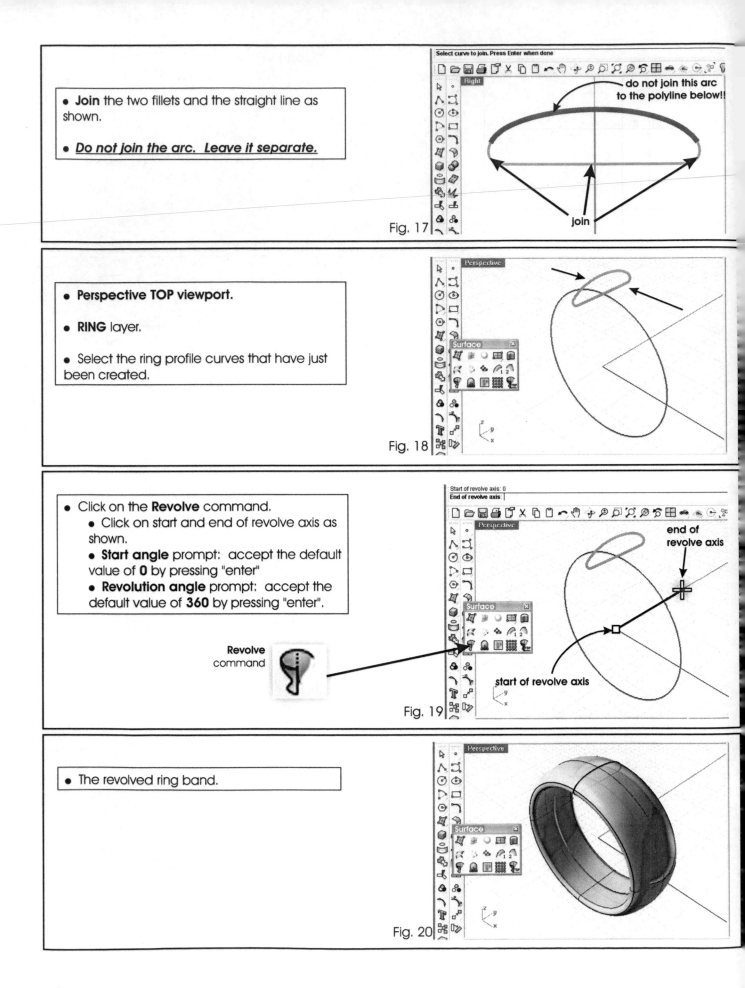

- **Join** the two fillets and the straight line as shown.

- *Do not join the arc. Leave it separate.*

Fig. 17

do not join this arc to the polyline below!!

join

- **Perspective TOP** viewport.

- **RING** layer.

- Select the ring profile curves that have just been created.

Fig. 18

- Click on the **Revolve** command.
    - Click on start and end of revolve axis as shown.
    - **Start angle** prompt: accept the default value of **0** by pressing "enter"
    - **Revolution angle** prompt: accept the default value of **360** by pressing "enter".

Revolve command

end of revolve axis

start of revolve axis

Fig. 19

- The revolved ring band.

Fig. 20

392

- **Hide** the inside surface of the ring band as shown.

- Notice that it is not joined to the outside of the band because the original ring profile curves were not joined.

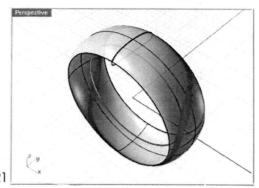

Fig. 21

- **Perspective TOP viewport.**

- Turn off the **ring curves** layer.

- **flat layout curves** layer.

- Select the ring band surface and click on the **Create UV Curves** command in the **Curve from Object** toolbar flyout.
  - **Select curves on surface to create UV curves** prompt: press "enter".

Create UV Curves
command

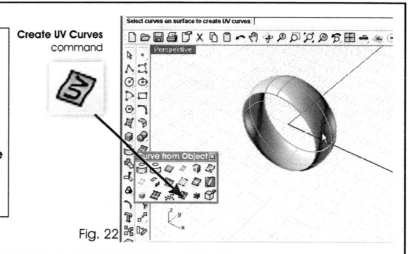

Fig. 22

- A rectangle that represents the surface area of the ring band will appear on the construction plane.

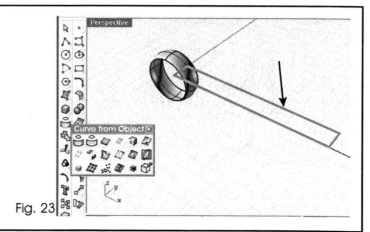

Fig. 23

- Drag the rectangle down for better visibility and **explode** it so that it is now 4 separate line segments.

Explode
command

Fig. 24

- **Top viewport.**

- **Offset** the top and bottom lines of the rectangle.
  - Offset distance: **3mm.**

Offset Curve
command

lines to offset

3mm
3mm

the offsets

Fig. 25

- Select the two offsets and **right click** on the **Divide Number of Segments** command.
  - **Number of segments** prompt: type **"8"** and press "enter".
  - Points will appear along the lines, dividing each into 8 equal segments.

Divide Curve by Number of Segments
command
[right click]

Fig. 26

- Select 2 sets of points and copy them out so that they extend beyond the original lines. Do this on both sides as shown.

- Use **Point osnap** for accuracy.

copies

objects selected to be copied

copy to

copy from

Fig. 27

- **FLAT LAYOUT** layer.

- Using the **Curve: Interpolate Points** command, create the wavy line shown.

- **Point osnap** is essential here.

Curve: Interpolate Points
command

Next point. Press Enter when done (Degree=3 Knots=Chord EndTangent Close Sharp=No Undo):

Point

Fig. 28

- The finished curve.

Fig. 29

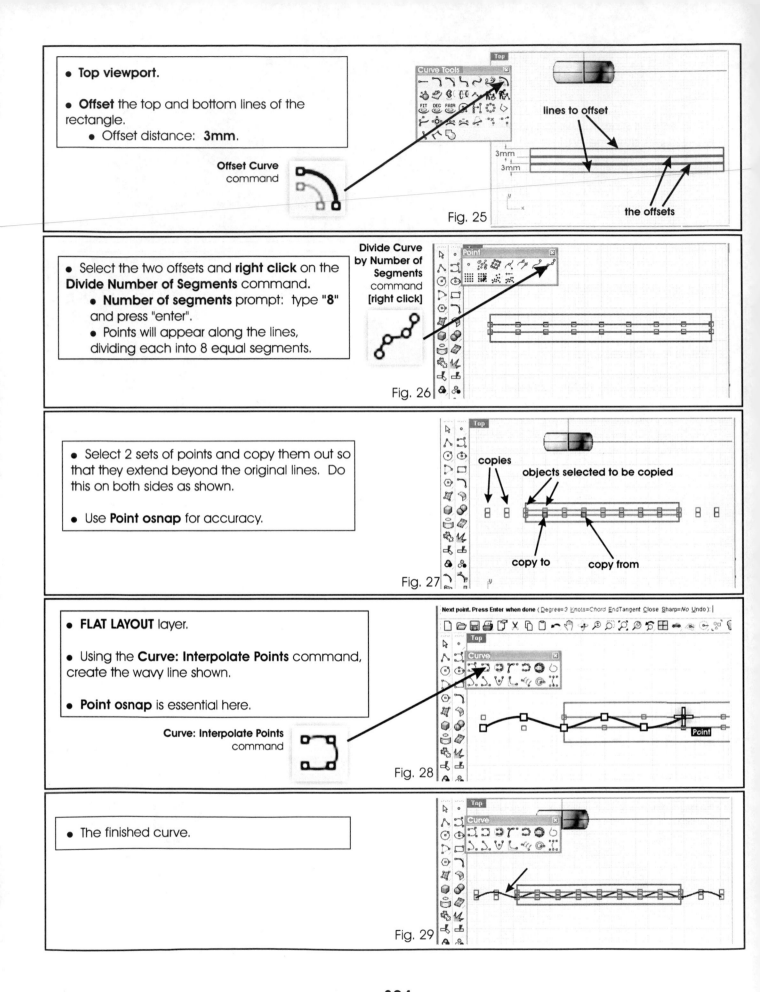

394

- Use the two perpendicular line segments on the ends of the rectangle to trim away the wavy curve on each side as shown.

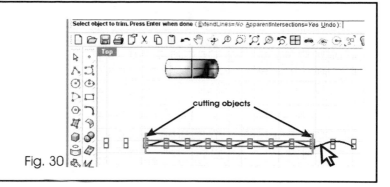

Fig. 30

- The trimmed wavy curve is now within the bounds of the rectangle.

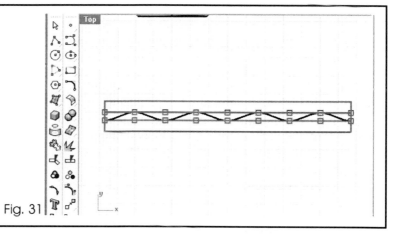

Fig. 31

- Carefully select and **Hide** both offset curves and all of the points so that only the wavy line and rectangle are visible.

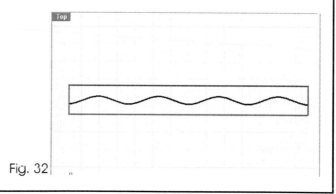

Fig. 32

- Use the **Rectangular Plane: Corner to Corner** command to create a rectangular surface within the bounds of the polyline rectangle as shown.

- Use **end osnap**. Pick the lower left and then the upper right corners of the rectangle to create this rectangular surface.

Rectangular Plane: Corner to Corner
command

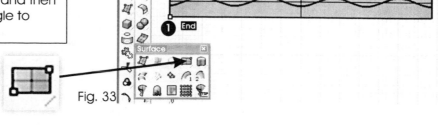

Fig. 33

- **Perspective TOP viewport.**

- Select the base surface and click on the **Analyze Direction** command.
  - Note the direction of the U and V arrows.
  - If the U and V are not in this orientation, use the options in the **Command Line** to bring them into the alignment shown.
  - Note the white arrows pointing up.
  - Press "enter"
- Place a point on the edge as shown to indicate the location of this corner.

Analyze Direction command

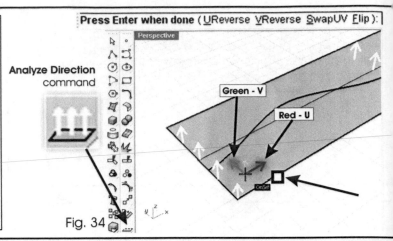

Green - V
Red - U
OnSrf

Fig. 34

- Select the ring surface and click on the **Analyze Direction** command.

- In this example, the U and V directions are correct for the accurate flow of the wavy line because the direction of the layout surface has the same UV orientation. The white arrows are pointing outward.

- If the U and V were not in this orientation, use the options in the **Command Line** to bring them into the alignment shown.

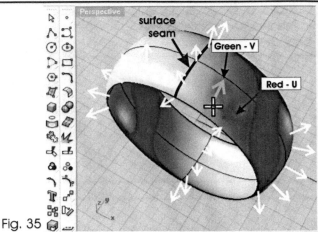

surface seam
Green - V
Red - U

Fig. 35

- You can turn off the **ring curves** layer.

- Using **near osnap,** place a point along the edge of the ring surface to mark the location shown.

- This point marks where the corner of the ring's surface corresponds with the lower left corner of the flat layout surface.

- This is crucial in the next step.

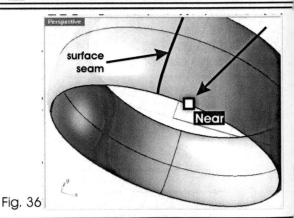

surface seam
Near

Fig. 36

- Select the wavy line and click on the **Flow along surface** command in the **Transform** toolbar flyout.
  - **Base surface** prompt: click on the lower left corner of the base surface where indicated.

Flow Along Surface command

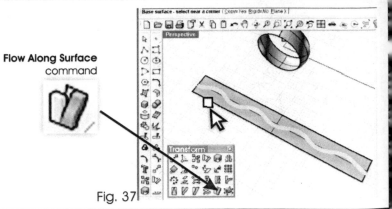

Base surface - select near a corner (Copy=Yes Rigid=No Plane)
Transform

Fig. 37

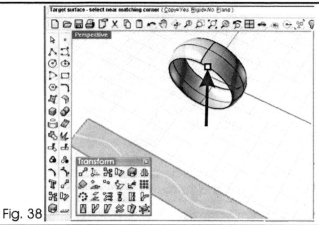

- **Target surface** prompt: click on a location near where you placed the point on the ring band as shown.

- You do not need to snap to the point. Clicking in the general location is sufficient.

Fig. 38

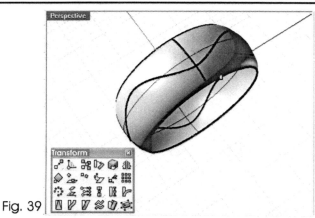

- The wavy curve has been "flowed" onto the surface where it molds itself to it's surface contours as shown.

- Switch this newly flowed curve to the **RING CUTTERS** layer.

- Turn off the **FLAT LAYOUT** and the **flat layout curves** layers.

Fig. 39

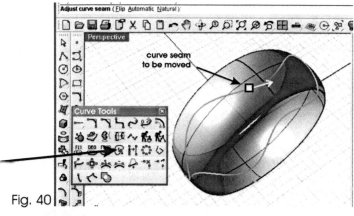

- Select the wavy line and click on the **Adjust Closed Curve Seam** command.

- Drag the curve seam of the wavy line so that it is snapped directly on the seam of the ring surface.

Adjust Closed Curve Seam
command

Fig. 40

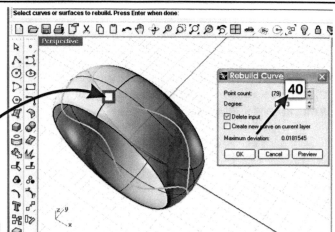

- **Rebuild** the wavy curve with **40** control points.

- Change this wavy line to the **RING CUTTERS** layer.

- Turn off the **FLAT LAYOUT** and the **flat layout curves** layers.

curve seam has
been moved to sit on
the surface seam

Fig. 41

- **RING CUTTERS** layer.

- Select the wavy line that is flowed on the surface and click on the **Pipe, Flat Caps** command in the **Solid** toolbar flyout.
  - **Radius for closed pipe** prompt: click on the **Diameter** option.
  - **Diameter for closed pipe** prompt: type "**2.9**" and press "enter".
- A pipe surface will be created around the wavy line with a diameter of **2.9mm**

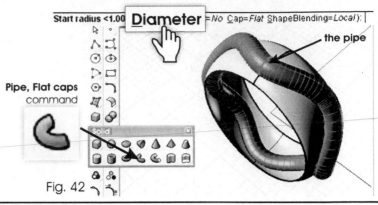

Pipe, Flat caps command

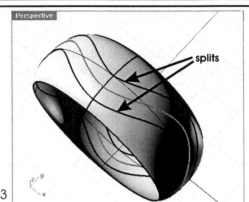

Fig. 42

- Select the ring band surface and click on the **Split** command.
  - **Select cutting objects** prompt: select the pipe and press "enter".

- **Hide** the pipe.

- The two heavy lines on each side of the wavy line indicate where the surface has been split.

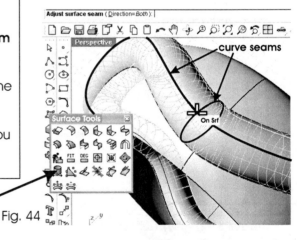

Fig. 43

- If the split is not successful, the problem may be that the seam of the pipe is resting on the seam of the ring band surface.

- Select the pipe and click on the **Adjust Closed Surface Seam** command in the **Surface Tools** toolbar flyout.
  - **Adjust surface seam** prompt: draw the cursor over the surface of the pipe and click when the seam that girdles the pipe has been moved to the left or right.

- Both U and V seams may move at once which is OK but if you want to just move one seam, click on the **Directions** option in the command line and opt for one specific direction.

Adjust Closed Curve Seam command

Fig. 44

- Create another pipe with a **diameter of 2.25mm** and use it to **Split** the small inner surface that it touches.

- Turn off the **RING CUTTERS** layer.

- Make the **RING** layer current.

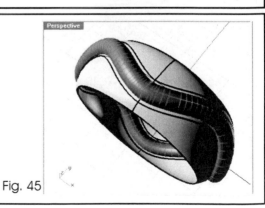

Fig. 45

- Note how the two pipes have split the ring surface.

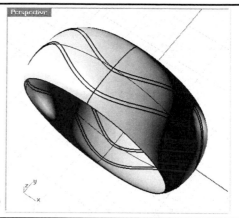

Fig. 46

- Carefully select and delete the two skinny surfaces on each side of the wider center surface as shown.

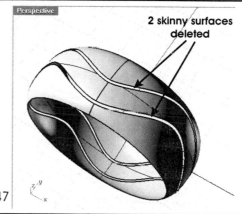

2 skinny surfaces deleted

Fig. 47

- **Perspective TOP** viewport.

- Select the inner surface shown and click on the **Offset Surface** command. to offset the center wavy surface as shown.
    - White surface direction arrows must point inward as shown.
    - **Offset distance** prompt: type "**.35**" and press "enter".

Offset Surface
command

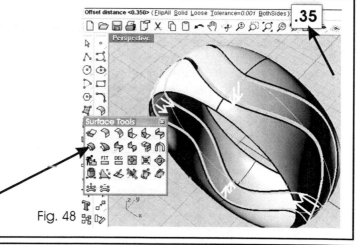

Offset distance <0.350> (FlipAll Solid Loose Tolerance=0.001 BothSides) .35

Fig. 48

- Delete the original surface and view the new offset surface that has been offset toward the inside fo the ring.

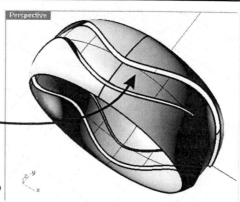

Fig. 49

- **ring curves** layer current.

- Create a little line between the two edges, snapping to the **end points** of the surface seams as shown.

- Repeat this on the other side of the ring.

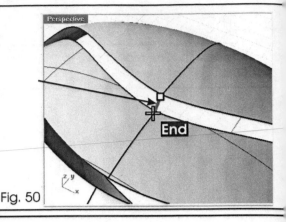

Fig. 50

- Click on the **Sweep 2 Rails** command.
  - Select the two rails and the one cross section curve as shown.
  - Press "enter".
  - Use the options shown in the **Sweep 2 Rails Options** dialog box and click OK.
    - A thin surface will appear between the two rail edges as shown.

- Repeat this process on the other side of the ring.

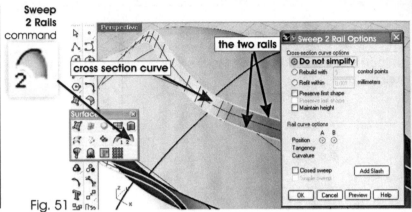

Fig. 51

- if, when you are prompted for the **first or second rails,** you are only able to select a segment of the surface edge as shown, you need to proceed to the step after this one.

- You need to use the **Merge Edge** command to repair this "broken edge".

- Trimming and splitting operations can sometimes cause "broken edges".

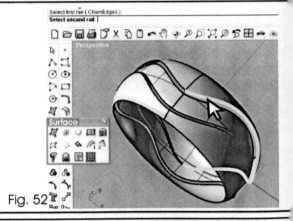

Fig. 52

- **Right click** on the **Merge Edge** command to mend any of these edges that have been broken into smaller edges.
  - **Select edge to merge** prompt: select one of the wavy surface edges that were caused by the splitting operation.
  - Click on the **Edge** option in the little context menu that appears as shown.
  - The selected edge, if broken into segments, will repair itself to become one edge again.
  - Select all 4 wavy edges in turn.

Merge Edge command [right click]

accesses the **Edge Tools** toolbar flyout

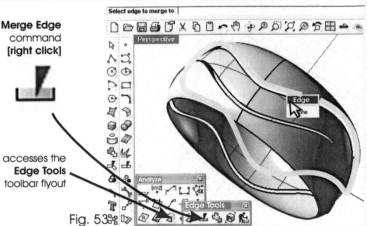

Fig. 53

400

- **Delete** the central wavy surface and create a line between the endpoints of the two seams as shown.

- Use **2-Rail Sweep** to create a flat surface between the two edges connected by the profile curve.

- **Join** all surfaces.

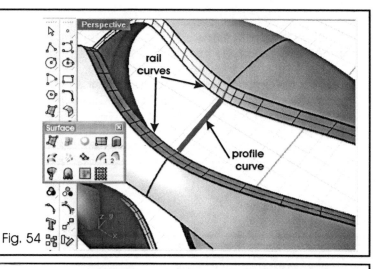

Fig. 54

- Click on the **Show edges** command in the **Analyze** toolbar flyout.
  - **Select surfaces, polysurfaces or meshes for edge display** prompt: Select the ring band and press "enter"
  - The **Edge Analysis** dialog box will appear.
    - Make sure that the radio button for **Naked Edges** is selected.
  - The two outside unconnected edges will light up with a pink color, indicating that they are "*naked edges*".
  - Only the outside edges shown should be lit up as the center wavy surfaces should all be joined with no gaps.
  - **Naked Edges** are surface edges that are not joined to other surface edges. A **closed polysurface (necessary for prototyping models)** has no naked edges
  - Close the **Edge Analysis** dialog box to end this command.

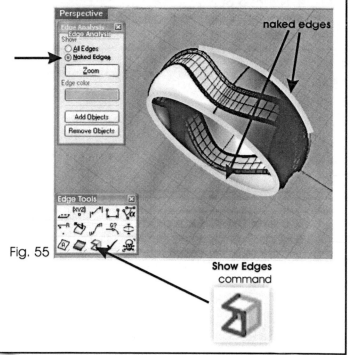

Fig. 55

Show Edges command

- Click on the **Extract Isocurve** command in the **Curve From Object** toolbar flyout.
  - **Select surface for isocurve extraction** prompt: click on the central wavy surface.
  - Make sure that the **Direction=U** option is toggled on.
  - Draw the cursor over the selected surface and note that a preview line moves with the cursor.
  - Snap to the **mid point** of the profile curve and click to set the location of a new curve on the surface.

accesses **Curve from Object** toolbar flyout

Select isocurve to extract | **Direction=U**

Extract Isocurve command

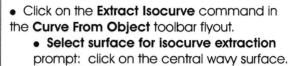

Fig. 56

401

- Turn on the **2mm stone** and the **2mm stone placement geometry** layers.

- Select the 2mm stone and its placement geometry and click on the **Array along Curve on Surface** command in the **Array** toolbar which is in the **Transform** toolbar.
  - **Base point** prompt: snap to the point object in the center of the stone as shown.

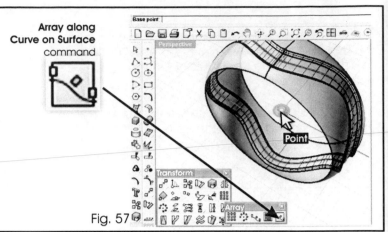

Array along
Curve on Surface
command

Fig. 57

- **Select a curve on a surface** prompt: select the newly created curve from an isocurve.

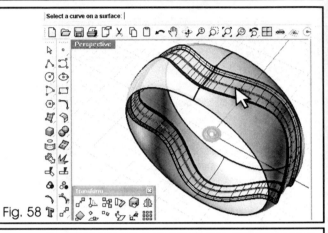

Fig. 58

- **Select the surface** prompt: select the surface that the wavy line runs upon.

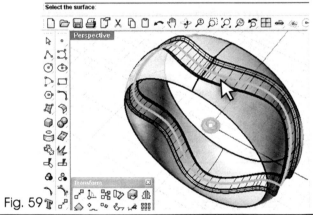

Fig. 59

- **Position objects or distance from last** prompt, click on the **Divide** option in the **Command Line.**

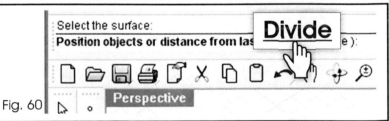

Fig. 60

- At the **Number of objects** prompt, type **"32"** and press "enter".

- Press "enter" again to end the command.

Fig. 61

402

- The stones are evenly arrayed along the wavy curve.

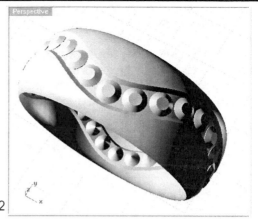

Fig. 62

- Turn on the **2mm stone seat cutters** layer and notice that they have been arrayed along with the 2mm stones.

- This is because they were previously grouped with the 2mm stone and will update along with objects in their groups, even when their layer is turned off.

- Turn off the **2mm stones**, the **2mm stone seat cutters** layer and the **ring curves** layer.

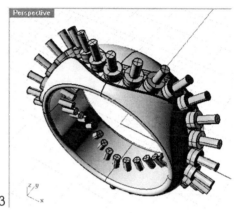

Fig. 63

- **prong curves** layer.

- Zoom in on the wavy surface.

- Notice that the stone placement circles and points are showing on the surface.

- Use the **Circle: Tangent to 3 curves** command to create the little circle shown.

Circle: Tangent to 3 Curves command

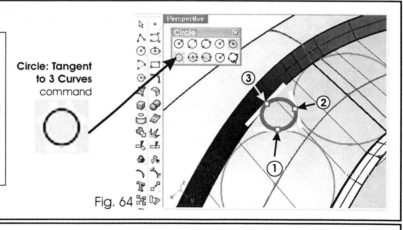

Fig. 64

- Use the **Circle: Tangent to 3 curves** command to create more circles in the 4 rows shown.

4 rows of prong curves

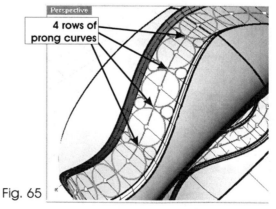

Fig. 65

- **Front viewport.**

- Use the **Line: from Midpoint** command, snap to a grid point (use **Grid snap)** on the X axis and click to set the midpoint of the line.
  - **End of line** prompt: type ".25" and press "enter"

- Place a point on the midpoint of this line (use **Mid osnap).**

Line: from Midpoint
command

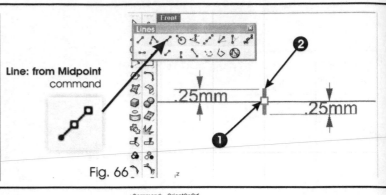

Fig. 66

- **Perspective TOP viewport.**

- Select the line and point created in the previous step and click on the **Orient on Surface** command in the **Transform** toolbar flyout.
  - **Reference point 1** prompt: snap to the point in the middle of the line and click to set this location.

Orient on Surface
command

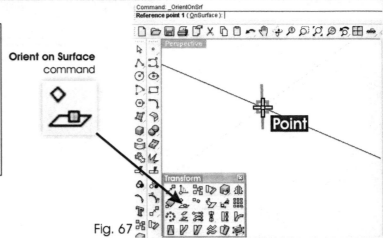

Fig. 67

- **Reference point 2** prompt: Draw the cursor out, using ortho, and click to set direction.

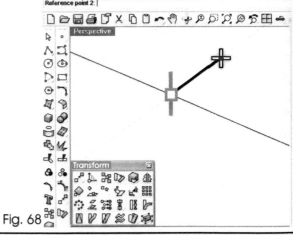

Fig. 68

- **Surface to orient on** prompt: click on the wavy surface upon which the stone curves and prongs are resting.

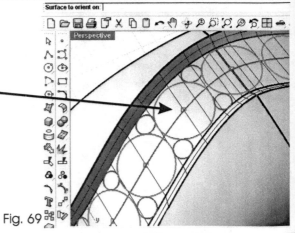

Fig. 69

- When the **Orient on Surface** dialog box appears, make sure that the settings are as shown and click the OK button.

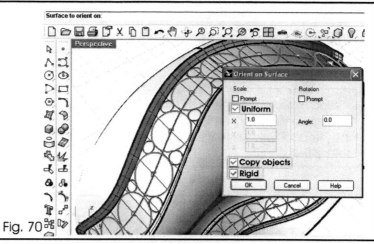

Fig. 70

- Draw the cursor over the designated surface and notice that the little line travels with it.
- Snap to the **center** of one of the prong curves as shown.
- Click and a copy of the little line is left in the center of the circle, perpendicular to the surface upon which it now rests.

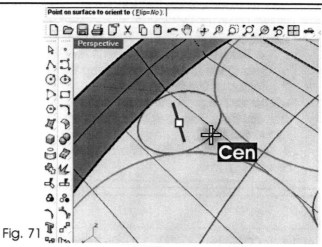

Fig. 71

- Snap to the rest of the little prong circles in turn, leaving a copy of the little line in the center of each.
- Press "enter" to end the command.
- All of the little lines are now in the center of the prong circles and are perpendicular to the surface.
- All of these lines are half buried below the surface because the first point of reference was in the middle of the line to be oriented on the surface.

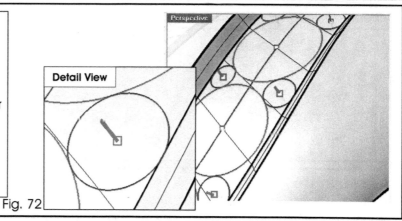

Detail View

Fig. 72

- *Important note: It is necessary to be in the top construction plane for this command to work properly.*

- This illustration shows what happens if you are in the front viewport when you perform the **Orient on Surface** command.

- The line is lying on the surface because that is it's orientation to the front construction plane. The selected object will sit on the target surface with the same orientation as it has to the active construction plane.

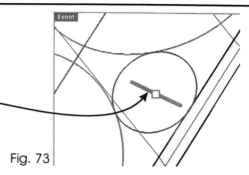

Fig. 73

405

- Turn off all layers so that you can see only the **RING** and **prong curves** layers.

- **PRONGS** layer current.

- Select one of the little lines that were just oriented to the wavy surface and click on the **Pipe, Round Caps** command in the **Solid** toolbar flyout.

Pipe, Round Caps
command

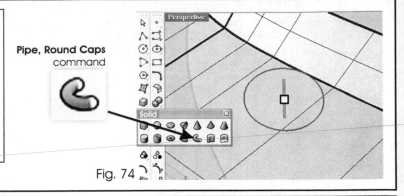

Fig. 74

- **Start radius** prompt: draw the cursor over to the circle and snap to one of the **quad** points of that circle. Click to set location.
    - This will determine the radius of the prong to be exactly matching the radius of the prong circle.
- **End radius** prompt: press "enter" to accept the same radius for the other end of the pipe.
- **Point for next radius** prompt: press "enter" again.

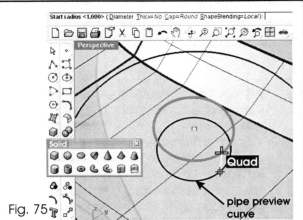

Quad

pipe preview curve

Fig. 75

- A little prong (or "bead") has been created on the exact location and radius of the prong circle.

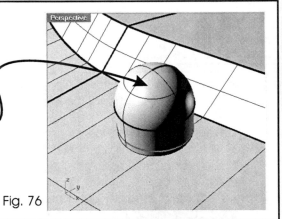

Fig. 76

- Create beads in the remaining prong circles as shown.

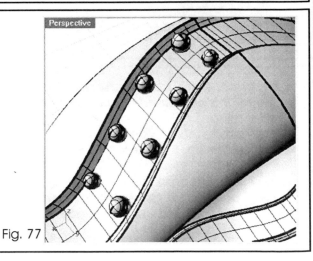

Fig. 77

406

- **Mirror** the beads over to the other side of the ring band.

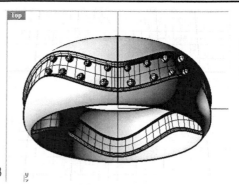

Fig. 78

- **Front perspective viewport.**

- Select all of the beads and click on the **Polar Array** command in the **Transform** toolbar flyout..
    - **Center of polar array** prompt: type "0" and press "enter".
    - **Number of items** prompt: type "4" and press "enter".
    - **Anger to fill** prompt: press "enter" to accept the default 360-degrees.

Polar Array command

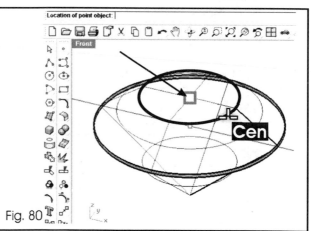

Fig. 79

- **Front viewport perspective.**

- Turn off the **PRONGS** layer.

- Turn on the following layers:
    - **1.8mm stone.**
    - **1.8mm stone placement geometry.**

- **1.8mm stone placement geometry layer** current.

- Place a point on the top of the stone, if there was not point already, snapping to the **center** of the top seam as shown.

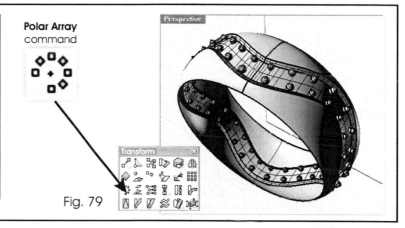

Fig. 80

- **Front viewport.**

- **Move** the point in the center of the stone upward at a distance of **.05mm.**

Move command

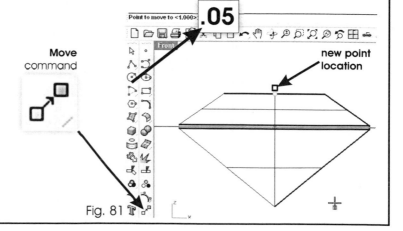

new point location

Fig. 81

- Select the new point and click on the **Add to Group** command in the **Grouping** toolbar flyout.
  - **Select group** prompt: select the stone.

accesses the **Grouping** toolbar flyout

Add to Group command

Fig. 82

- The History Line will now read "**Added object to group**".

Fig. 83

- **Perspective TOP viewport.**

- Select the stone and its reference curves and click on the **Orient on Surface** command.
  - **Reference point 1** prompt: snap to the new point at the top of the 1.8mm stone and click. ❶

Orient on Surface command

Fig. 84

- **Reference point 2** prompt: draw the cursor out as shown and **left click** to set location, **making sure to use ORTHO.** ❷

Fig. 85

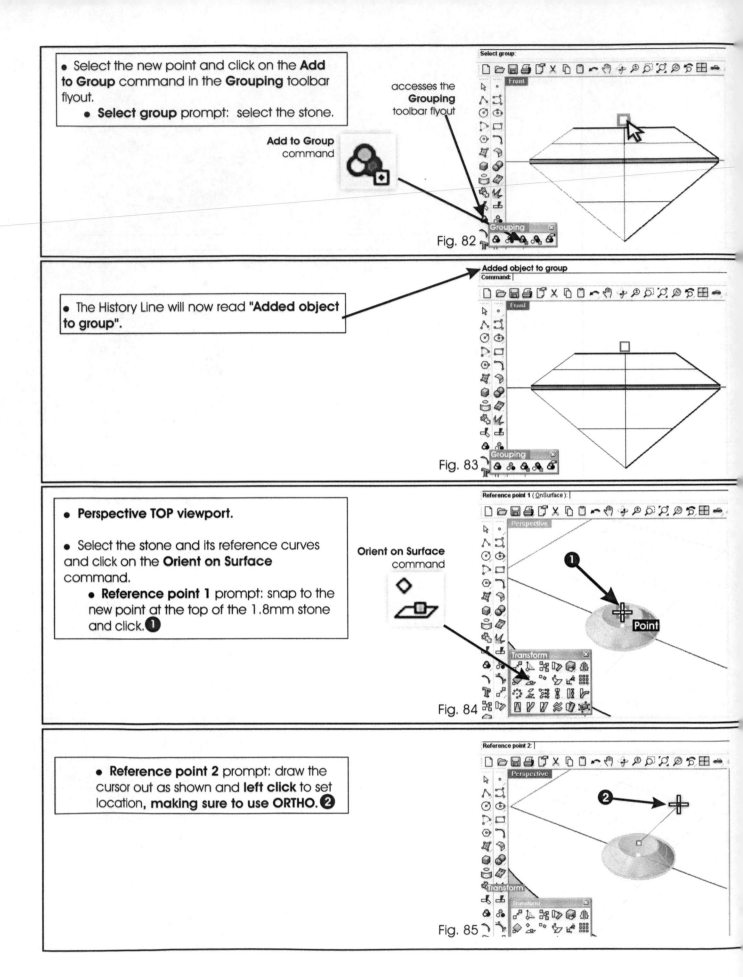

- **Surface to orient on** prompt: select the surface indicated.

- Assign the options shown in the **Orient on Surface** dialog box and click on the OK button.

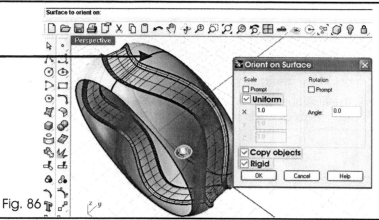

Fig. 86

- **Point on surface to orient to** prompt: Move the selected object over the surface, using **near osnap** to snap to the surface seam as shown.

- Click to set a location on this seam.

- Notice that the stone seat cutters are moving with the stone, even though they are on layers that are turned off. This is because they are **grouped** with the stone and reference geometry.

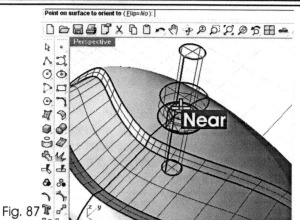
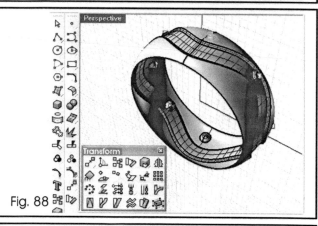

Fig. 87

- **Front perspective viewport.**

- Select the stone and curves that were just oriented and click on the **Polar Array** command in the **Transform** toolbar flyout.
  - **Center of polar array** prompt: type **"0"** and press "enter".
  - **Number of items** prompt: type **"8"** and press "enter".
  - **Angle to fill** prompt: press "enter" to accept the default 360-degrees.

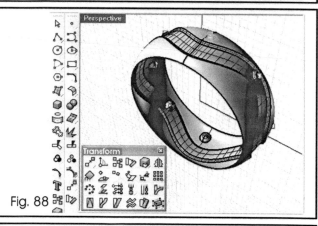

Fig. 88

- **Perspective TOP viewport.**

- Turn on the 1.8mm stone seat cutters layer.

- Notice that every other stone is not correctly placed. Select these mis-placed stones and curves and mirror them over to the other side of the ring, across the X axis..

- The pre-selected stones for the mirror command will still be selected.

- Press the **Delete** key to delete these stones.

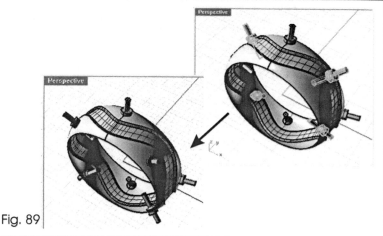

Fig. 89

- **Unhide** the inside of the ring and join outside and inside surfaces together to achieve a *closed polysurface*.

- There should be no naked edges on this polysurface at this stage.

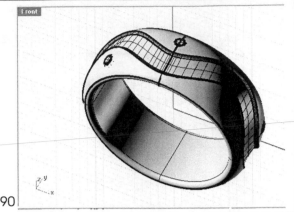

Fig. 90

- Turn on both stone seat cutter layers.

- Select all cutters and click on the **Ungroup** button.

- This is necessary because you need to select the cutters separately from other objects when using them in the Boolean Difference command.

Ungroup
command

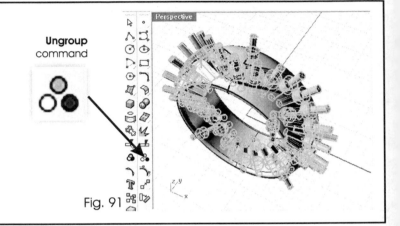

Fig. 91

- Click on the **Boolean Difference** command.
    - **First set of surfaces or polysurfaces** prompt: select the ring band and press "enter".
    - **Second set of surfaces or polysurfaces** prompt: select the stone seat cutters and press "enter".
    - Turn off the **1.8mm stone seat cutter** layer.

- **Note: With this many cutters, try selecting a few cutters at a time, repeating the Boolean Difference command until all the cutting is done.**

Boolean Difference
command

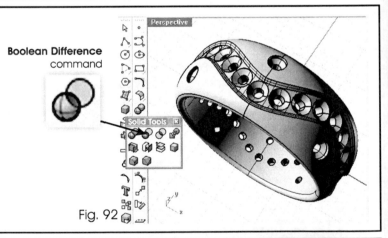

Fig. 92

- Turn on prongs and stones.

- You can use the **Boolean Union** command to boolean the prongs to the ring band.

- Finally, the finished piece.

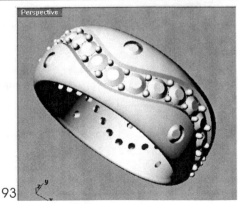

Fig. 93

Generating Technical Drawings
from 3-dimensional Models
Make 2-D Drawing command

- Sometimes, when making a technical drawing, it is easier to make a model and then generate a technical drawing from it. The accuracy that is achieved is at a higher level than just doing a drawing.

- This can also be useful when communicating with clients who want to see the actual dimensions of a proposed model as well as a rendered image.

- The **Make 2-D Drawing** command generates a technical drawing, in actual size, of a designated 3D object, except for the perspective view which can be scaled.

- This exercise uses the file created from the previous chapter, **Ring Band with Bead Set and Flush Set Stones.**

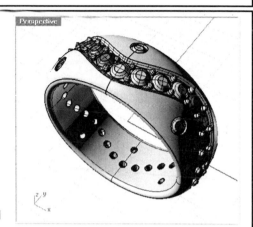

Fig. 1

- **Top Viewport.**

- Select the ring, stones, and prongs.

- Click on the **Make 2-D Drawing** command in the **Dimension** toolbar flyout.

Make 2-D Drawing command

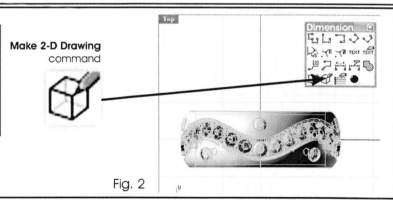

Fig. 2

- The **2-D Drawing Options** dialog box will open up.
- Click OK to accept the default setting of **4-View (USA).**

Fig. 3

411

- *You may have to wait several minutes or more for the drawing to be created, depending on the number of surfaces in your model.*
- The finished drawing appears on the top construction plane, nestled in the angle of the X and Y axes.

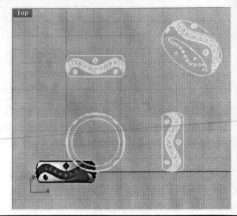

Fig. 4

- With the help of **Grid Snap** mode and **Center osnap,** you can use the **Move** command to center the new technical drawing on the Y axis as shown.

- Note that the perspective drawing is not to scale.

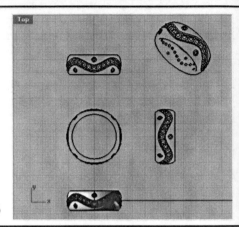

Fig. 5

- Tap the up arrow on your keyboard 3 or 4 times to get a tipped front view of the ring.

- Window select as before and click on the **Make 2-D Drawing** command.

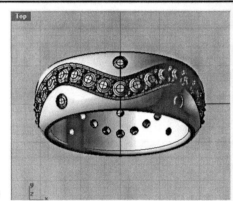

Fig. 6

- Click on the **Current View** option in the **2-D Drawing Options** dialog box and click OK.

Fig. 7

412

- A new technical is created, reflecting the new tipped view of the ring.

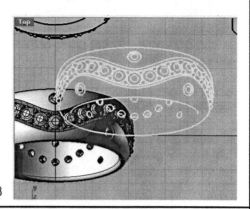

Fig. 8

- The new technical is in place with the other views.

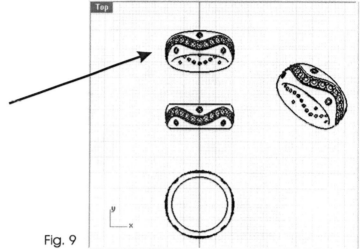

Fig. 9

- Zoom in on one of the views and note how the prongs lack some lines.

- The line that is missing is the intersection of the prong and the surface on which it sits.

- This is because the prongs have not been booleaned to the surface and so there are no seams to indicate intersections with the ring's surface.

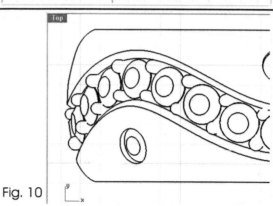

Fig. 10

- Select the ring and the prongs and click on the **Object Intersection** command in the **Curve from Object** toolbar flyout.
    - *Note: do not select the stones for this command!*

- A curve will appear at each intersection of stone and ring.

Object Intersection command

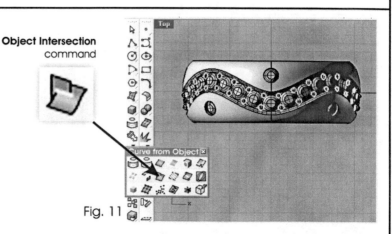

Fig. 11

413

- You can now see the point of intersection between prong and ring.

- Some gaps remain where some of the stones appear slightly in front of the prongs.

- **Make 2-D Drawing** is an excellent command but it is not perfect and you can get gaps such as the ones shown here.

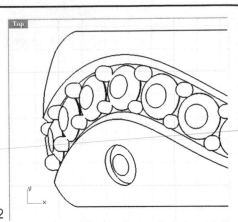

Fig. 12

- The **Extend by Arc to Point** is being used here to accurately close a gap.

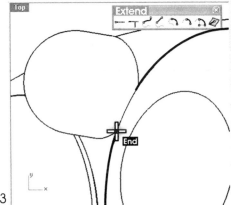

Fig. 13

- The gaps have been corrected.

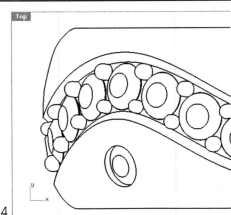

Fig. 14

- Here the **Bombe Ring with Blended Bezel** is going to generate a technical drawing.

- In this example, notice that the **Show hidden lines** option is toggled on.

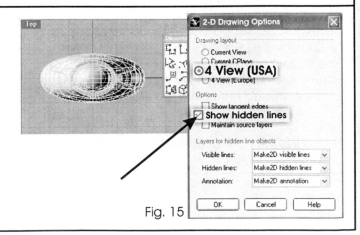

Fig. 15

• The resulting drawing shows the "hidden lines" in white, some of which you will want to delete.

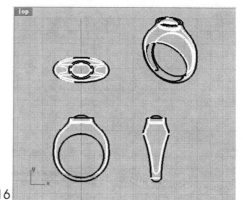

Fig. 16

• The finished drawing has dimensions and the hidden lines have been given a dotted linetype.

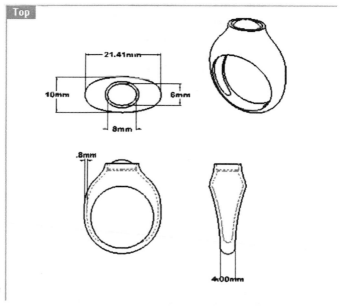

Fig. 17

Making Objects Planar (Flat)
Project to CPlane - Set XYZ Coordinates commands

When Trim or Fillet commands do not work.
When objects do not extrude as expected.
Other problems may arise when objects are not planar in themselves or in relation to other objects.

Project to CPlane command

When objects need to be planar (flat) and need to rest directly on the construction plane.

- These rectangles can not trim each other - the **Trim** command does not work.

- They are both planar objects.

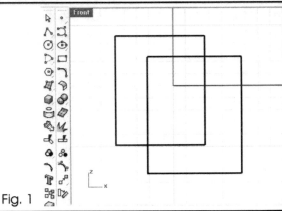

Fig. 1

- A perspective view shows that only one of the rectangles is resting on the X axis while the other one is behind it. They are not on the same plane - These two planar objects are not planar to each other.

- **The Goal:** To place the back rectangle on the X axis but in the same position looking at it from the front view, as in Fig. 1.

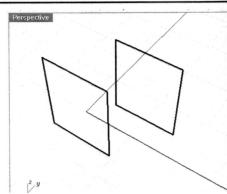

Fig. 2

- **Front perspective** viewport.

- The rectangle at the back is selected.

- The **Project to CPlane** command button in the **Transform** toolbar flyout is clicked.
    - **Delete input objects?** prompt: the **Yes** option is toggled in the **Command Line.**

Project to CPlane
command

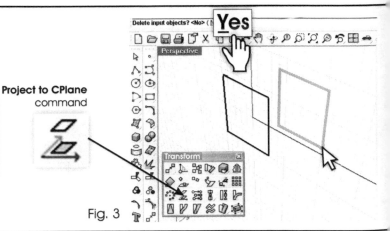

Fig. 3

416

• The selected rectangle will immediately "project" itself on to the construction plane where the other rectangle lies.

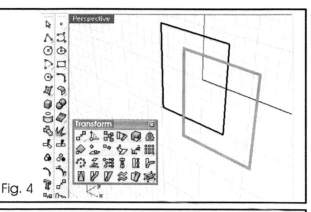

Fig. 4

• The two rectangles are now on the same plane and the Trim command now works.

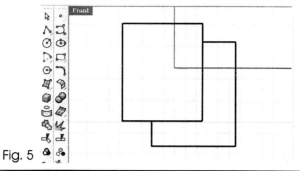

Fig. 5

Set XYZ Coordinates (or "Set Points") command
When all objects need to be planar to each other but not on the construction plane.

• **Perspective TOP viewport.**

• Back to the two rectangles that are not planar to each other as in Fig. 1.

• **The Goal:** to make the two rectangles planar to each other but this time, *they will end up on the plane on which the back rectangle resides*.

• The two rectangles are selected and the **Set XYZ Coordinates (or Set Point)** command in the **Transform** toolbar flyout is clicked.

Set XYZ Coordinates
(or Set Points)
command

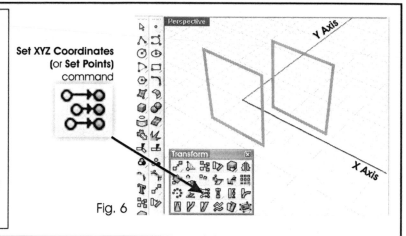

Fig. 6

• When the **Set Points** dialog box opens, use the settings shown.
   • The **Set Y** option is the only one chosen because these objects are crossing the Y axis and their orientation will be as such.
   • **Align to World** refers to the construction plane that is active, which is default World top.
   • Click OK.

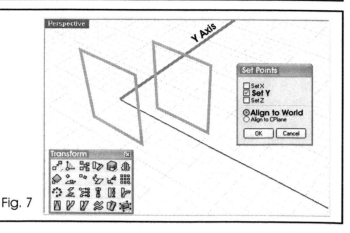

Fig. 7

- **Location for points** prompt: both rectangles are together on the same plane but they are traveling with the cursor, which is constrained to moving up and down the Y axis only.
- Notice that the original placement of the rectangles is still selected visible for reference.

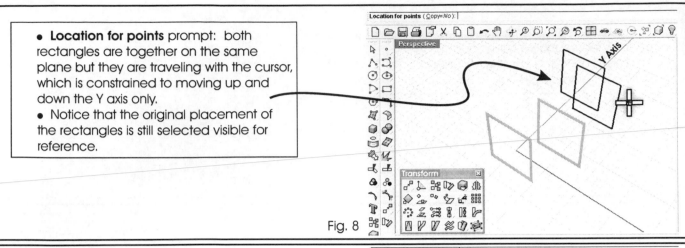

Fig. 8

- Snap to one of the **end points** of the original rear rectangle which is still selected and visible for reference.

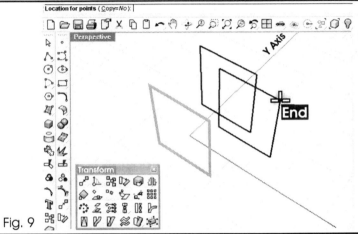

Fig. 9

- Both rectangles are now planar to each other at the original location of the back rectangle.

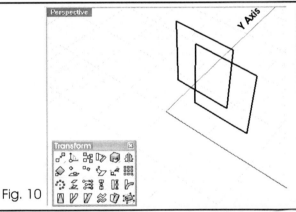

Fig. 10

- If the two rectangles had been in this position, *perpendicular to the X axis,* the settings in the **Set Point** dialog box would be as shown.

- If the two rectangles had been on another construction plane, such as Front or Right, the selected option at the bottom of the dialog box would be **Align to CPlane.**

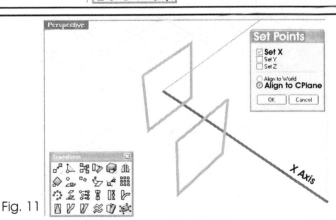

Fig. 11

- This time, the two rectangles are together on the same plane, *constrained to move along the X axis*.

- Snap to the end point of one of the original rectangles and click to set location as before.

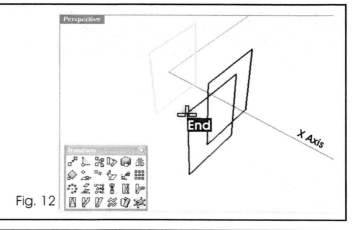

Fig. 12

Set XYZ Coordinates (or "Set Points") command
When the objects themselves are not planar.

- The circle being extruded here looks planar but small shifts in some of its control points caused it to become non planar.

- As a result, when the extrude command was attempted, the direction of the extrusion, rather than being in a direction planar to the circle, reverted to a direction perpendicular to the construction plane.

- Extrusion direction can be changed but in this instance it is important for the desired result that the ends of the extrusion be planar.

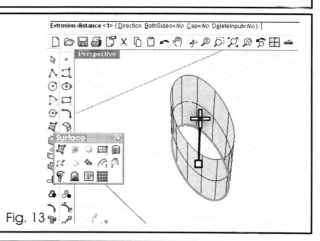

Fig. 13

- The circle is selected and the **Set XYZ Coordinates** command is clicked.

- Dialog box settings are as shown.

Set XYZ Coordinates (or Set Points) command

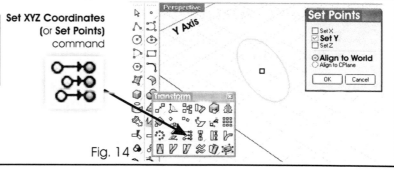

Fig. 14

- The flattened, now planar, circle will travel with the cursor along the Y axis. In this case, the cursor snaps to the desired point that marks the center of the circle.

- The extrude command can now be performed with the proper orientation and expected result.

Fig. 15

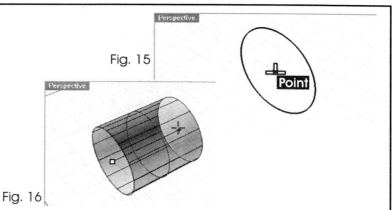

Fig. 16

Setting Up Your Workspace
for Modeling of Small Objects

- There are a number of settings that will enhance your workspace for basic jewelry modeling - or the modeling of other types of small items.

- The following examples will go through some of the various ways that you can set up your workspace. They are basic settings that will get you started. As you study the various options, eventually you may want to experiment and customize further.

Opening Rhino

- Double click on the Rhino ikon to open up Rhino.

- Before the Rhino workspace opens, you will see the **Startup Template** dialog box.

- You will see a list of templates. These are the default templates that come with Rhino. Their settings are default settings.

- Later, we will be creating a custom template that will be added to this list of template options when you open Rhino.

- Highlight the **Small Objects - Millimeters** option in the list. This directs Rhino to open this file with **millimeters** as the unit of measurement. Notice that when you highlight this option, a brief explanation appears in the window below.

- Press the **Open** button. The Rhino workspace will open.

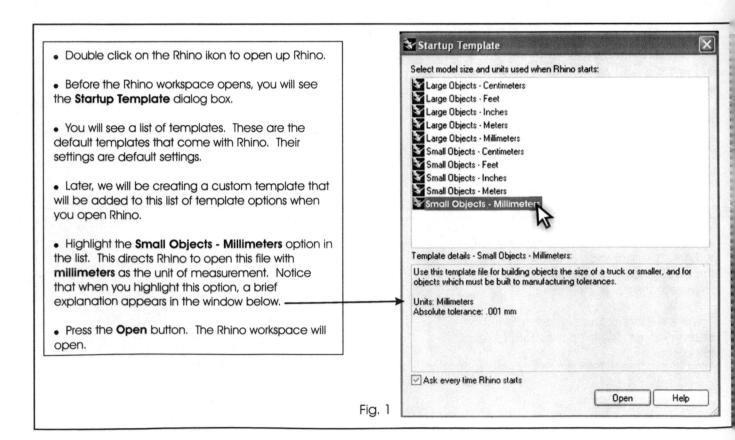

Fig. 1

Your Workspace
Settings for Document Properties

- **Left click** on the **Options** command to access the **Rhino Options** dialog box.

- This dialog box has a list of different categories. Highlighting the various links will take you to different setting options.

- Click on the **Units** category in the list to the left of the **Rhino Options** dialog box.
  - Notice that **Millimeters** are the model units because you chose the **Small Objects - Millimeters** template option when opening Rhino.
  - Notice that **Absolute Tolerance** is already set to .001mm as this is another characteristic of the chosen template.
    - This value refers to the smallest unit of measurement that Rhino will recognize.

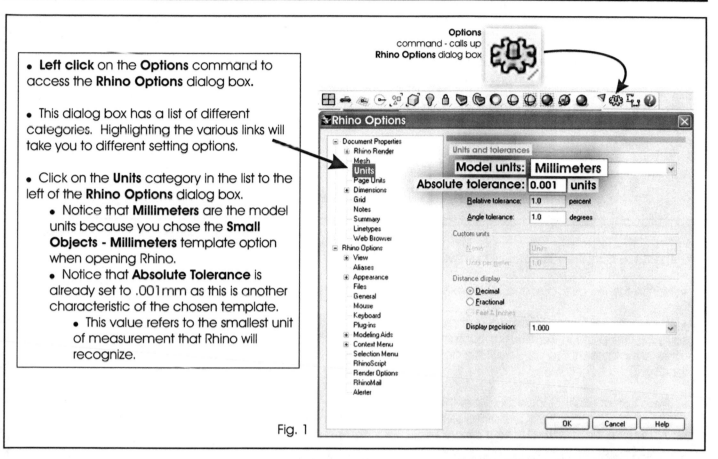

Fig. 1

- Click on the **Grid** category. The grid setting options will appear.
  - Change the **Minor Grid Lines** setting to every **1** grid line.
  - Change the **Major Grid Lines** setting to every **5** grid lines.
  - Type 0.5 in the **Snap Spacing** box. This will constrain Grid Snap to .5mm intervals.

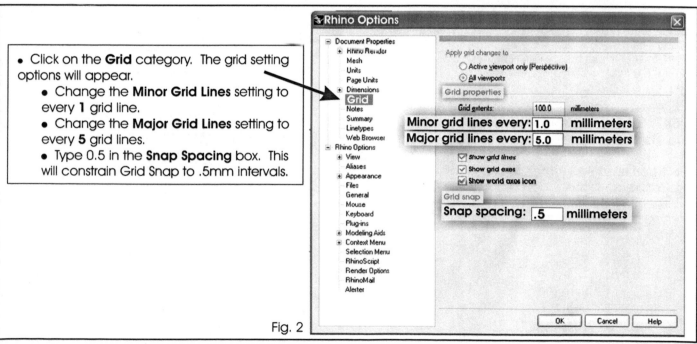

Fig. 2

Saving Your Document Properties Settings as a Template

- Save the **Document Properties** settings by creating a new Rhino template file that you can choose when you open Rhino again.

- From the **File** drop-down menu, click on the **Save as template** option as shown.

Fig. 1

- The **Save template file** dialog box will open.

- Name the file as suggested in this example.

- If you are working on your own computer, save this template in the file that contains the other templates as shown. This is the default location.

- If you are at another location, save this to a CD or other portable storage device so that you can take it home and load it onto your own computer.

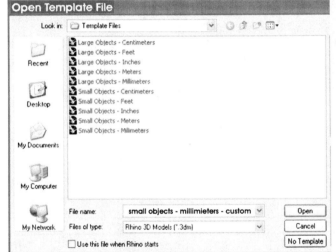

Fig. 2

- When you open Rhino again to start a new file, your new custom template will be added to the list of other available templates.

- If you have your template in another location, go to that location and open the template file itself.

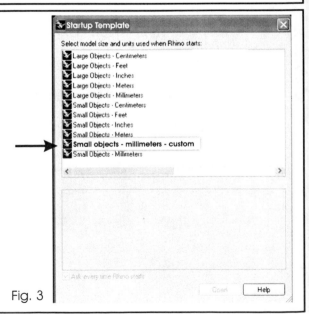

Fig. 3

Rhino Options: Basic Settings
Settings that will remain each time Rhino is opened

- Highlight the **View** category.

- Check the **Single-click Maximize** box under **Viewport Properties.**

- This allows you to maximize and minimize viewports with a single click on the viewport label instead of a double-click. You may appreciate the ease of this new setting.

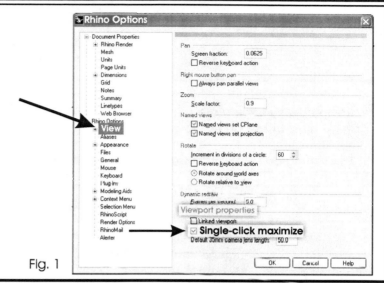

Fig. 1

- Highlight the **Mouse** category.

- Check the box that says **Drag selected objects only.** This means that in order to drag an object, you first have to select it.

- This helps to prevent the accidental dragging of objects when they are being selected. **This is a very good option.**

Fig. 2

- Highlight the **Files** category.

- **Autosave** automatically saves your work every 20 minutes, a time segment that can be adjusted.

- *WARNING: If you are using the EVALUATION VERSION OF RHINO, this feature will use up the 25 saves allowed on this trial version.*
  - Click on the green check mark to disable this feature if you wish.

- Otherwise, if you are using your own Rhino seat, this is a good feature to have enabled.

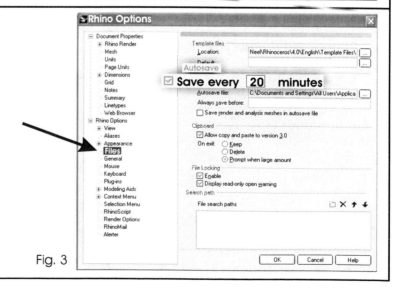

Fig. 3

Rhino Options: Adjusting Display Settings
- Line Width
- Point Size
- Surface Seam Width

- Rhino's default line width on the screen is a hairline, 1 pixel. The default point is very small, 2 pixels. This can be hard to see on the screen.

- The setting adjustments described here will afford better screen visibility.

- Click on the **Appearance** page and then open the drop-down for **Advanced Settings** and then the drop-down for **Wireframe** objects.

- In the **Surface Edge Settings** box, make the edge thickness **3 pixels** as shown.

- When modeling with surfaces, it is a tremendous help to be able to see the edges of surfaces as thicker lines.

Fig. 1

- Click on the **Objects** category.

- Change the **Control Point** size to **4 pixels**.

- This will make control points larger and easier to see on the workspace.

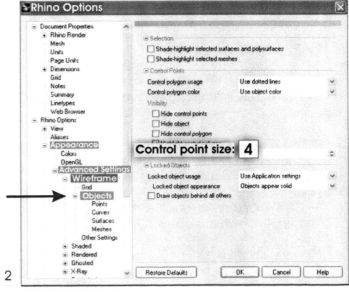

Fig. 2

- Click on the **Points** category.

- Change the **Point Object** size to **4 pixels**.

- This will make your point objects easier to see on the workspace.

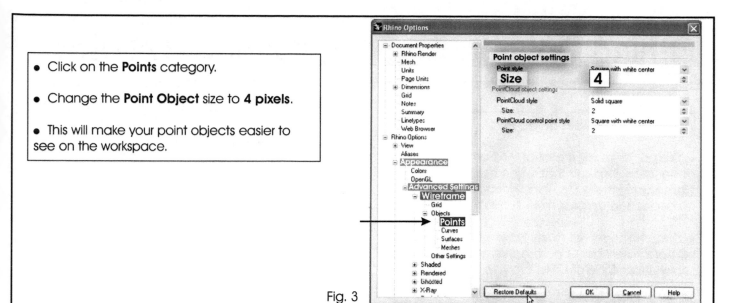

Fig. 3

- Click on **Curves** in the drop-down list.

- In the **Curve width (pixels)** category, assign the value of **3** in the box shown.

- This will widen your curves and lines for easier viewing while working on them but will not influence their actual print width.

- Adjust the settings for the other display modes in this same manner.

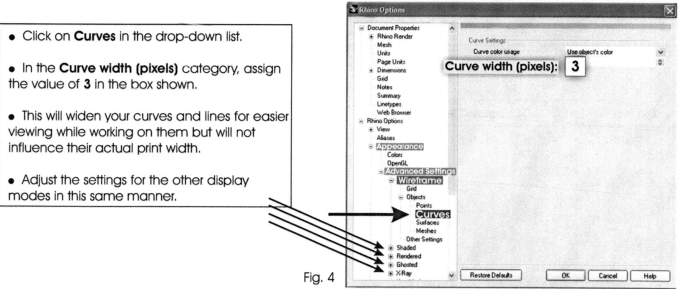

Fig. 4

- Highlight the **Rendered** page.

- In the **Color & Material Usage** drop-down list, select the **Single Color for all objects**.

- This will make all rendered objects the white color that you see on the **Single object color swatch**.

- This can be changed by clicking on the color swatch but this present setting is useful for now and is used in these tutorials.

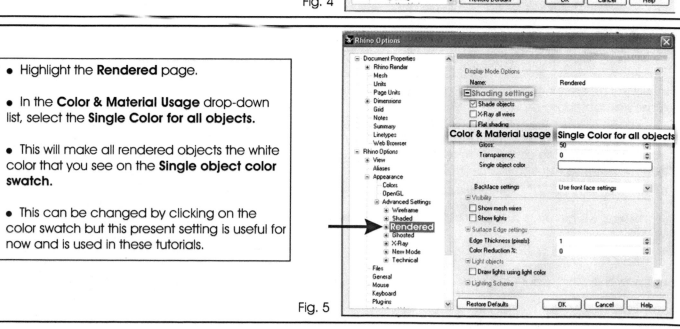

Fig. 5

425

Rhino Options: Creating Keyboard Aliases

- Highlight the **Aliases** category.

- This page will show a list of "Aliases", little designated shortcuts that, when typed into the **Command Line** in the Rhino workspace, call up often used commands.

- Since Rhino serves many types of users, you will note a number of commands in the list shown that will be of no use to you.

- Highlight the **Advanced Display** alias shown. Click on the **Delete** key at the bottom of the box as shown.

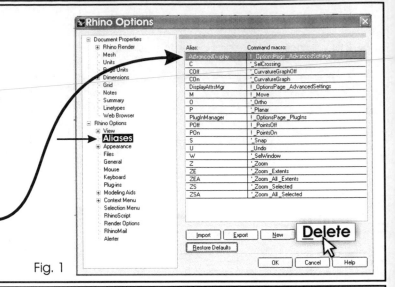

Fig. 1

- The highlighted Alias has been deleted.

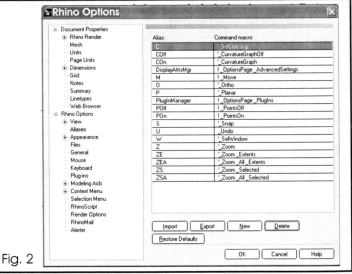

Fig. 2

- Use this delete function to delete all the Aliases except those shown.

- Don't be afraid of inadvertently deleting the wrong alias. You can always click on the **Restore Defaults** key and the original Aliases will be restored.

- Now you will create a series of useful Aliases.

- Click on the **New** button.

- A new line will appear as shown.

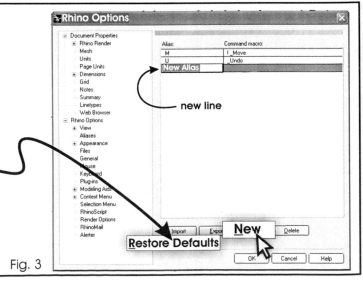

Fig. 3

- Type a new Alias in the new line. Repeat this function until you have a list like the one shown.

- Note: Before each "command macro" in the right column, type an **exclamation mar**k and then an **underscore**: !_

- The **exclamation mark** cancels whatever command you are in before using this alias and the **underscore** means that the command will run the as an English command name.

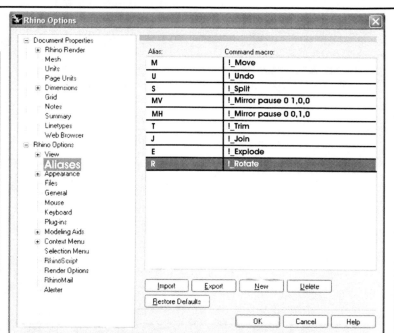

Fig. 4

- The final step is to save these Aliases so that you can import them into Rhino in other locations or if you re-install Rhino which will bring back the defaults.

- Click on the **Export** button.

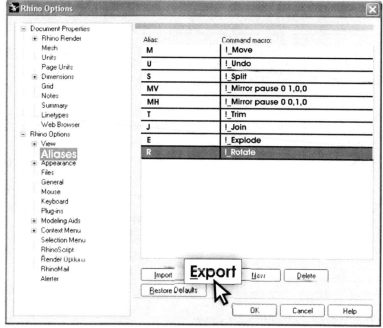

Fig. 5

- A **Save text file** dialog box will open up. Save this file in the computer location of your choice. In this case, a separate folder has been created for alias text files.

- Name this file "alias text file - your name".

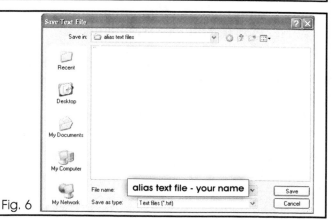

Fig. 6

- For practice importing the new Alias text file into rhino, click on the **Restore Defaults** button.

- All of the default aliases will appear again.

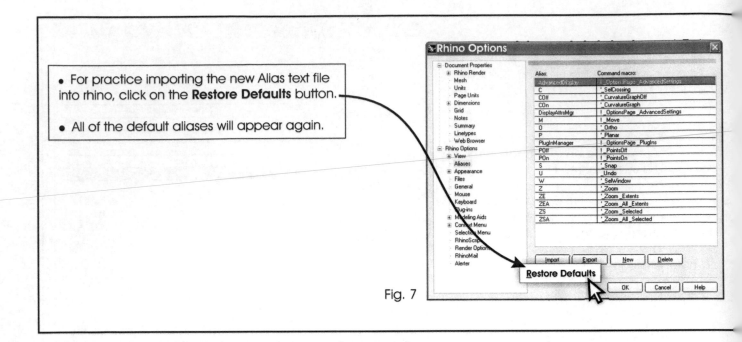

Fig. 7

- Click on the **Delete** button repeatedly to delete all of the aliases. The last alias will have to be clicked on with the mouse before the delete button will remove it.

- The reason for this is that when the new Alias text file that you created is imported into this box, you don't want the default ones to remain there too!

- Click on the **Import** button.

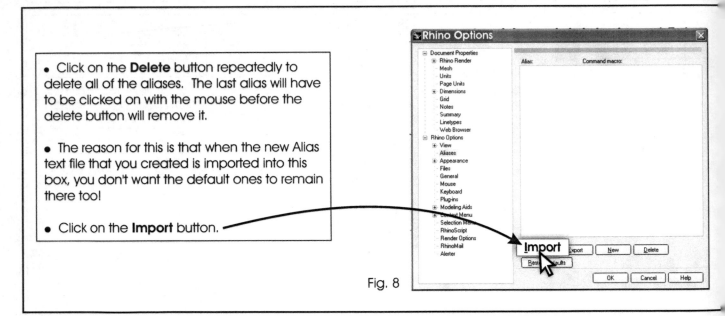

Fig. 8

- The **Open text file** dialog box will open.

- Select the alias text file you just created and click open.

- Notice in this example that there are a number of alias text files created for different purposes.

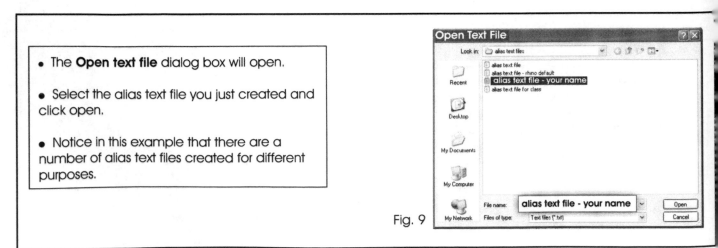

Fig. 9

- The empty page will fill up with the aliases you just imported.

- Click OK in the little **Rhinoceros 4.0 Import Command Aliases** dialog box that appears.

Fig. 10

- The new aliases in place and ready for use.

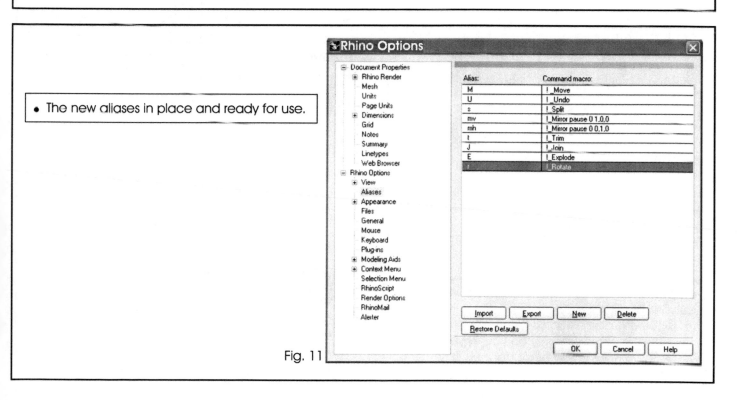

Fig. 11

Rhino Options: Hotkeys
Useful hotkey assignments to favorite commands

• Highlight the **Keyboard** option.

• These are keyboard shortcuts.

• Press one of the hotkeys shown and the command that it accesses will be called up.

• Clicking in one of the macro lines will highlight the macro, either to be deleted or to be re-written to a command of your choice.

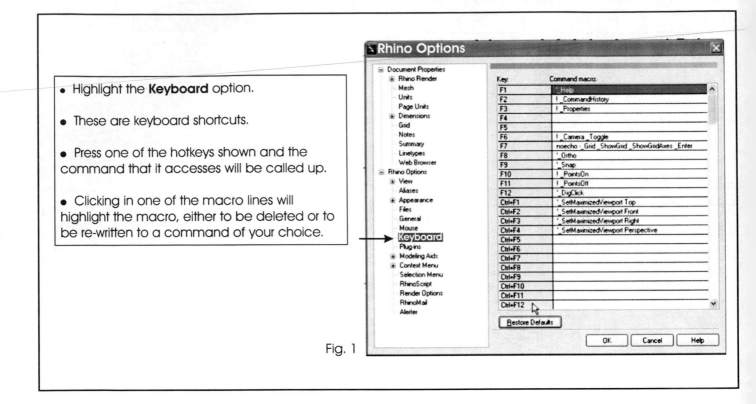

Fig. 1

• Type commands in the **Command Macro** column as shown.
  • Delete other macros by highlighting and pressing the **delete** key on your keyboard.
  • The **exclamation point** cancels any previous command.
  • The **underscore** runs the command in English.
  • The **apostrophe** allows for a "nested" command which means that one can toggle it on and off within another command. Grid snap and Ortho need to nested so that you can toggle them off and on while you are working.

• Be sure to click the OK button to set these settings.

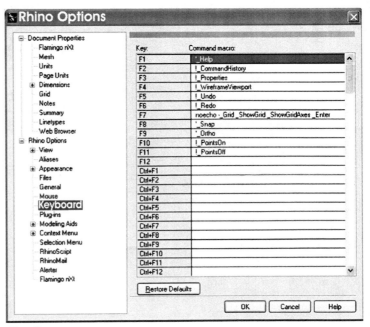

Fig. 2

Exporting & Importing Rhino Options

Loading your options into another computer.

- Your Rhino Options settings can be saved as a file and imported into Rhino when you open it in a different computer.

- **Left click** on the **Export Options** command in the **Utilities** toolbar flyout as shown.

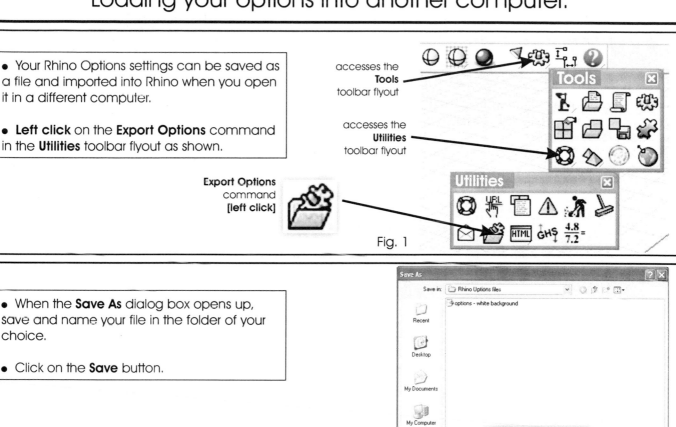

accesses the **Tools** toolbar flyout

accesses the **Utilities** toolbar flyout

Export Options command **[left click]**

Fig. 1

- When the **Save As** dialog box opens up, save and name your file in the folder of your choice.

- Click on the **Save** button.

options file name

Fig. 2

- To import your settings, **right-click** on the **Import Settings** command.

Import Options command **[right click]**

Fig. 3

- The **Import Options** dialog box will open.

- Click on the little browse button.

- Locate the Options settings file with the **Open** dialog box, highlight it, and click the **Open** button.

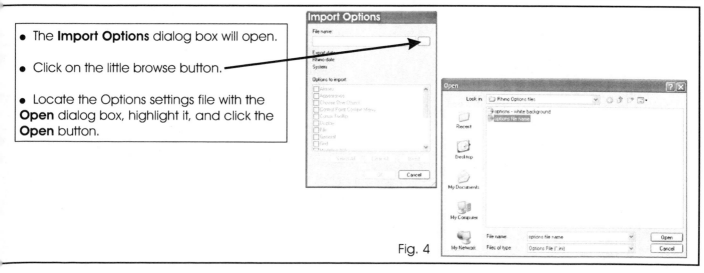

Fig. 4

- The name of the file and other information will appear in the **Import Options** dialog box.

- Click on the **Select All** button to import all options in the file.

- Click OK.

- All of your Rhino Options settings will be imported except for Advanced Settings.

- Advanced Settings will import as well in Rhino 5.0.

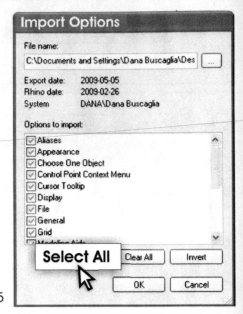

Fig. 5

Creating a Custom Toolbar Collection
Customizing your workspace

- The term, "Toolbar Collection" refers to the grouping and configuration of toolbars in the workspace. When Rhino is opened up for the first time, the toolbars that you see are called the "default" toolbar collection.

- Not every command, toolbar or toolbar button that is in the default collection is something that you will need. Rhino is used by so many people and industries, that it is natural that a user will not need everything that is in the default collection.

- In this exercise, you will create your own custom toolbar collection that will be saved as its own ".tb" file and which can be carried to another computer and opened in Rhino there.

- **Left click** on the **Edit Toolbar Layout** command button in the **Tools** toolbar flyout as shown.

Edit Toolbar Layout command

accesses the **Tools** toolbar flyout

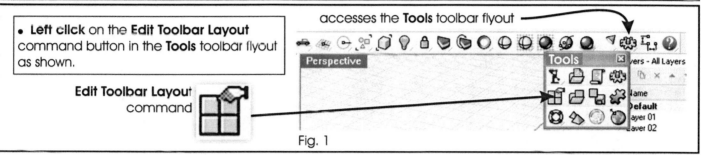

Fig. 1

- the **Toolbars** dialog box will appear.

- Toolbar collections are all named. The default toolbar collection is what Rhino will open up with when first installed.

- Notice the scroll-down window below. This is a list of all of the toolbars available.

- Some toolbars have check marks beside them. These are the toolbars that are presently visible in the workspace as components of the default toolbar collection.

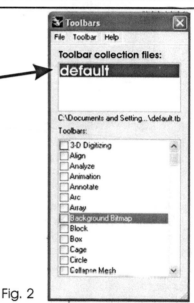

Fig. 2

- For experimentation, check the box by the **Arc** toolbar in the list as shown.

- Notice that when you do this, the **Arc** toolbar appears.

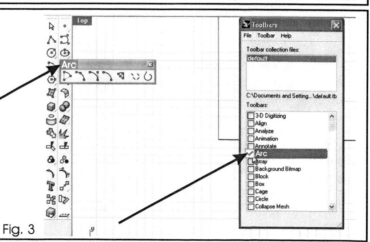

Fig. 3

- Click again to un-check the box and the **Arc** toolbar goes away.

- Scroll down the list and check and un-check to see different toolbars. *This is a good way to discover new and interesting features.*

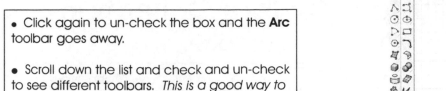

Fig. 4

- This is still the **default** toolbar collection and it is important not to change it.

- For this reason, you need to save this toolbar collection off with a another name.

- From the **File** drop-down menu in the **Toolbars** dialog box, click on **Save as...** as shown.

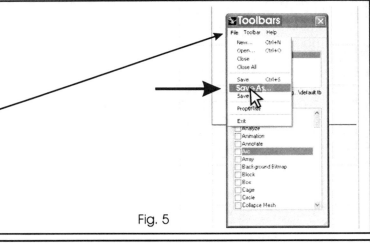

Fig. 5

- The **Save Toolbar Collection** dialog box will open up and ask you to name the new toolbar collection. Save it as with a name of your own choosing.

- If you are on a school computer, not on your own home computer, save this toolbar collection on your CD or other portable storage media so that you can take it home. You can also email it to yourself as an attachment!

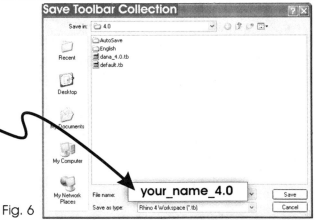

Fig. 6

- Notice in the **Toolbars** dialog box that the open toolbar collection now has the name you assigned to it.

- The **default** toolbar collection still exists and can be used again with all toolbars and buttons intact as they came with the Rhino software.

Fig. 7

Deleting a Toolbar Button when creating your custom toolbar collection.

- Start the new toolbar collection's configuration by deleting unwanted buttons.

- With the **Shift key held down, left click** on the button to be deleted and drag it down on to the construction plane.

- A "**Move**" tooltip will appear.

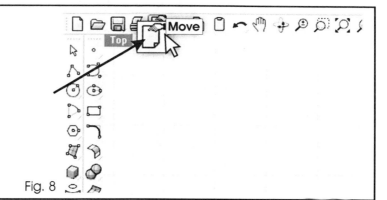

Fig. 8

- When the button is dragged on to the construction plane, the ikon will change to a red "**X**" and a "**Delete**" tooltip.

- Release the button and the shift key.

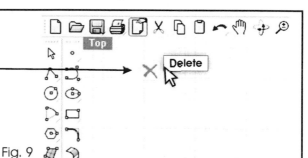

Fig. 9

- A **Rhinoceros 4.0 Toolbars** box will open asking if it is OK to delete the button. Click on the OK button if you are sure you want to delete it.

- **VERY IMPORTANT: ONCE YOU DELETE A BUTTON, YOU CAN NOT GET IT BACK!! UNDO WILL NOT WORK HERE! MAKE SURE YOU WANT TO DELETE IT.**

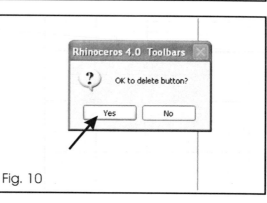

Fig. 10

- The button is now gone.

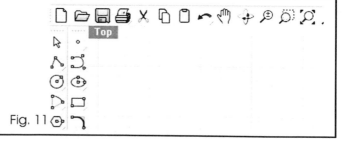

Fig. 11

- In this example, more buttons have been deleted.

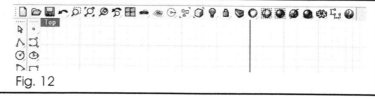

Fig. 12

- The next step will be to create a new toolbar so that commands can be copied to it.

- Open the **Lines** toolbar flyout and drag it out on to the construction plane.

Fig. 13

- **Right click** on the blue title bar.

- From the drop-down menu that appears, click on **New Toolbar** option as shown.

Fig. 14

- In the **Toolbar Properties** dialog box that appears, type in a new name for the toolbar as shown.

- Accept the default button size as shown.

- Click OK.

Fig. 15

- A new toolbar with just one button has been created and will appear on the construction plane.

right click here

Fig. 16

- **Right click** on the blue title bar of the new toolbar and select **Properties** from the drop-down menu.

Fig. 17

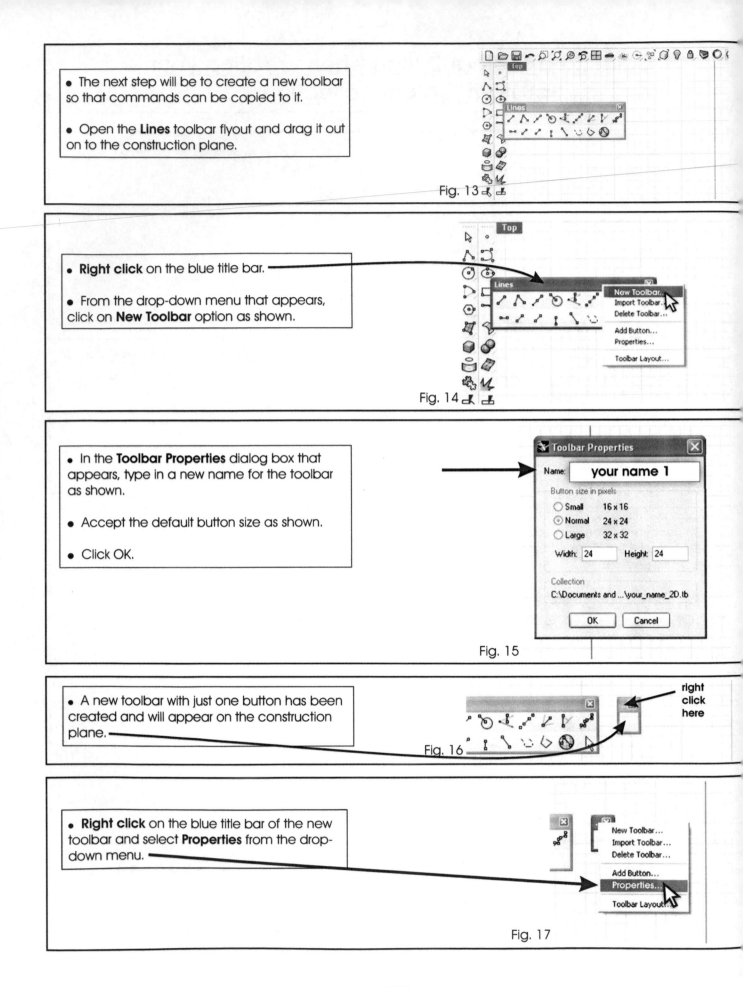

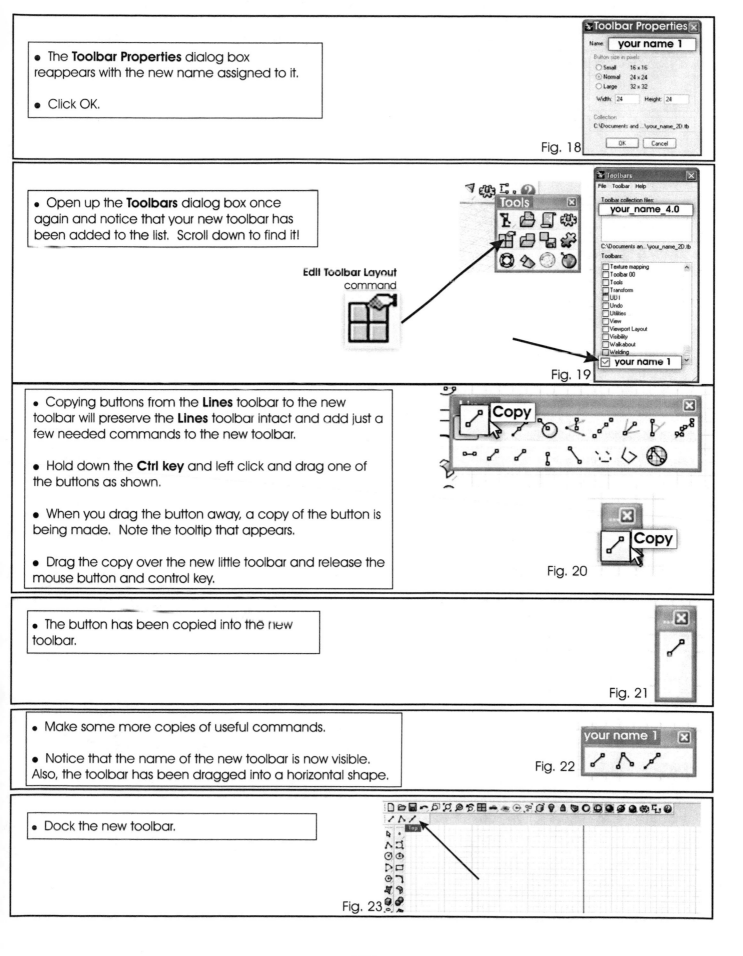

- The **Toolbar Properties** dialog box reappears with the new name assigned to it.

- Click OK.

Fig. 18

- Open up the **Toolbars** dialog box once again and notice that your new toolbar has been added to the list. Scroll down to find it!

Edit Toolbar Layout
command

Fig. 19

- Copying buttons from the **Lines** toolbar to the new toolbar will preserve the **Lines** toolbar intact and add just a few needed commands to the new toolbar.

- Hold down the **Ctrl key** and left click and drag one of the buttons as shown.

- When you drag the button away, a copy of the button is being made. Note the tooltip that appears.

- Drag the copy over the new little toolbar and release the mouse button and control key.

Fig. 20

- The button has been copied into the new toolbar.

Fig. 21

- Make some more copies of useful commands.

- Notice that the name of the new toolbar is now visible. Also, the toolbar has been dragged into a horizontal shape.

Fig. 22

- Dock the new toolbar.

Fig. 23

- Open the **Curve** toolbar flyout.

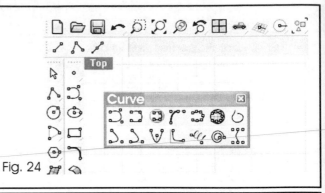

Fig. 24

- Copy a couple of buttons from the **Curve** toolbar onto the Your Name 1 toolbar.

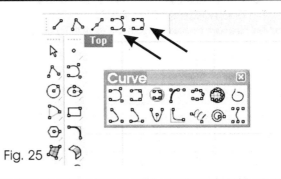

Fig. 25

- Repeat with other toolbars, such as the **Circle** toolbar.

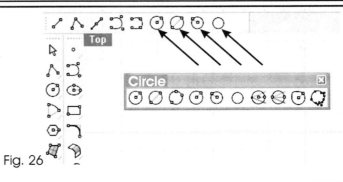

Fig. 26

- In this example, the buttons are not in the order desired. It is necessary to **Move** one button over.

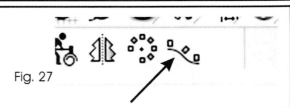

Fig. 27

- Hold down the **Shift key** and left click and drag the button to be moved.

- When it is positioned as desired, release the mouse button and **Shift** key.

- If you drag this button on to the construction plane, the **Delete** function will take over which you do not want here.

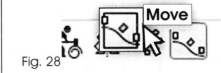

Fig. 28

- The button has been moved.

Fig. 29

- Notice that a couple of buttons from the circle toolbar are hard to read because their colors do not have enough contrast.

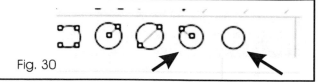

Fig. 30

- Hold the **Shift key down and right click** on one of the buttons that are hard to read.

- The **Edit Toolbar Button** dialog box will open.

- In this dialog box, things can be changed and added, such as macros, tooltips and flyouts.

- You want to edit the image on the button. Click on the **Edit Bitmap** button.

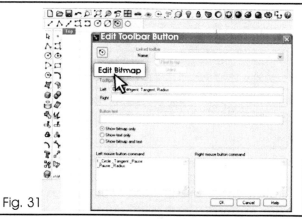

Fig. 31

- The **Edit Bitmap** dialog box will open.

- Click on the gray swatch at the lower left of the colors as shown.

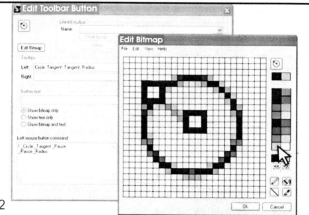

Fig. 32

- This gray will become the **current color** as shown in the left of the little color swatches at the top.

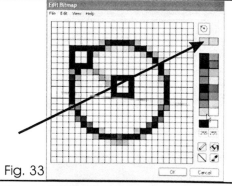

Fig. 33

- Click on the **Flood Fill** function as shown.

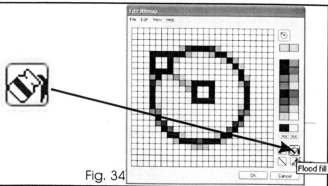

Fig. 34

439

- The cursor will now look like a little paint bucket.

- Drag this cursor into a corner of the image where you know that all the colors are the same and click.

- The entire color block in the bitmap will be transformed into the gray color.

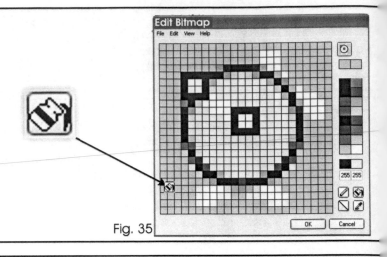

Fig. 35

- Click again on the inside of the circle and the images is now easier to read.

- Click OK.

- Click OK to exit the **Edit Toolbar Button** dialog box.

- If you do not want to save the changes in the bitmap, just click on the Cancel button and you will return to the **Edit Toolbar Button** dialog box.

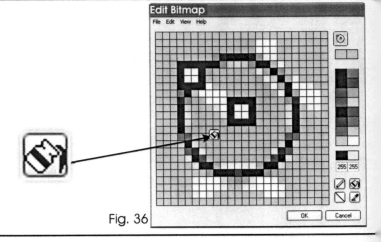

Fig. 36

- Repeat this with the other button and see how easy they now are to read!

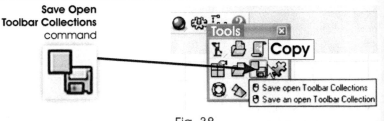

Fig. 37

- Open the **Tools** toolbar flyout and copy the **Save Open Toolbr Collections** button over to the new toolbar.

Save Open Toolbar Collections command

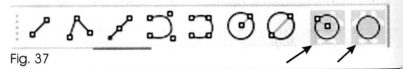

Fig. 38

- The copied button in place.

- Click on this button often, Each time you make a change to your toolbar collection, the change will only be preserved for subsequent Rhino projects if you same the open toolbar collection. Every time you copy, move, or delete a button, make it a habit to click on this button.

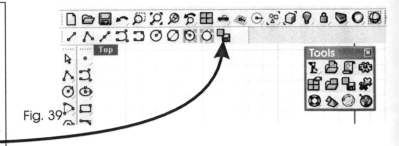

Fig. 39

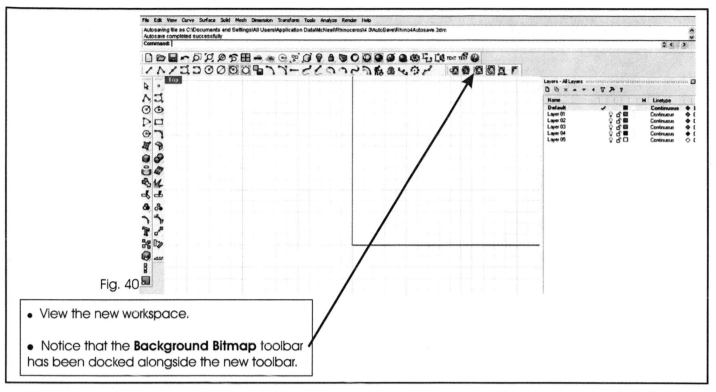

Fig. 40

- View the new workspace.

- Notice that the **Background Bitmap** toolbar has been docked alongside the new toolbar.

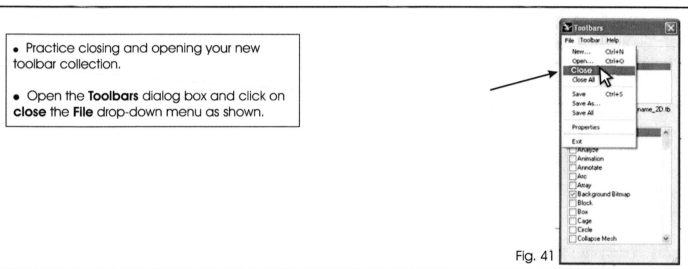

- Practice closing and opening your new toolbar collection.

- Open the **Toolbars** dialog box and click on **close** the **File** drop-down menu as shown.

Fig. 41

- Click on the "Yes" button when prompted if you want to save the changes to your toolbar collection.

Fig. 42

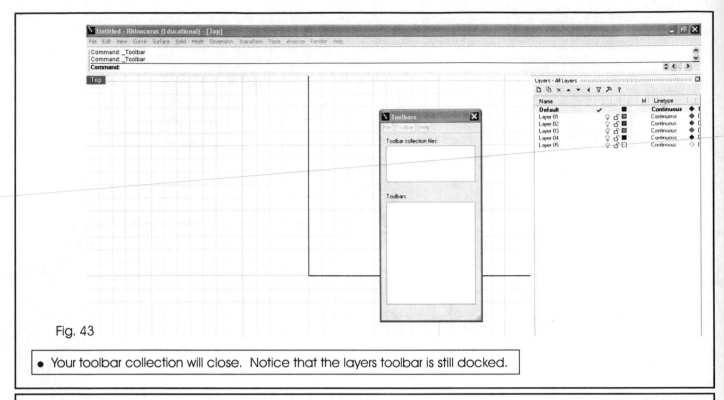

Fig. 43

- Your toolbar collection will close. Notice that the layers toolbar is still docked.

- Click on the **Open** option in the **File** drop-down menu in the **Toolbars** dialog box.

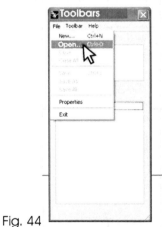

Fig. 44

- Choose your toolbar collection in the **Open Toolbar Collection** dialog box and click on the **Open** button.

Fig. 45

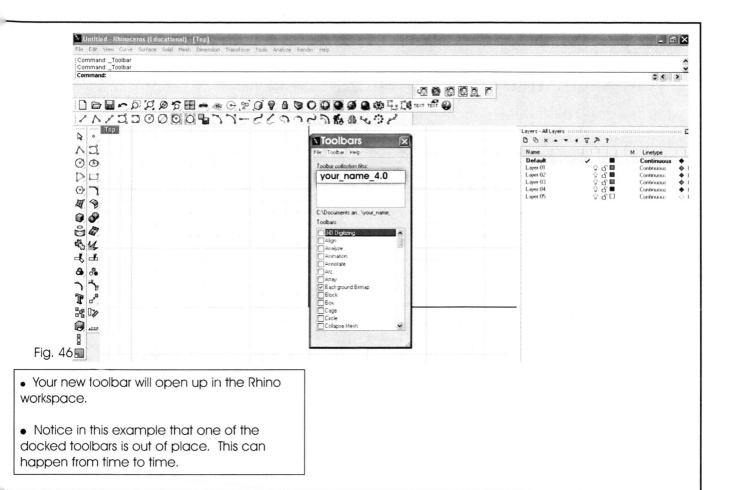

Fig. 46

- Your new toolbar will open up in the Rhino workspace.

- Notice in this example that one of the docked toolbars is out of place. This can happen from time to time.

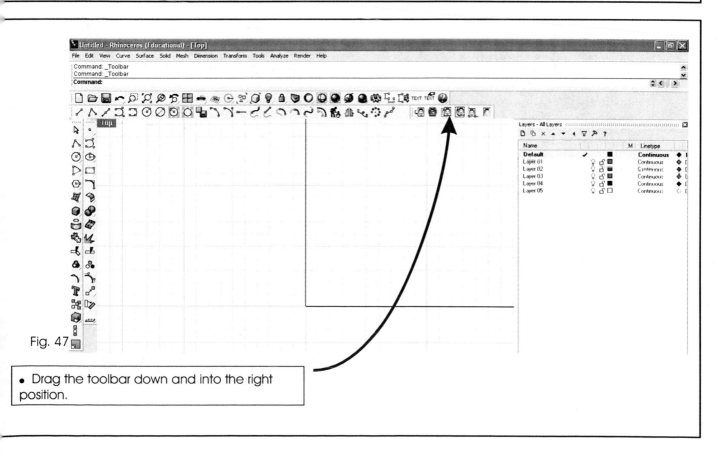

Fig. 47

- Drag the toolbar down and into the right position.

INDEX

Dana Buscaglia has had many years of experience as a designer for the jewelry industry, both in-house and freelance.

In the late 1990's, she became interested in the possibilities of CAD for jewelry design and product development. Since then she has worked in Rhinoceros™ software, both as a designer doing technical drawings and as a model maker, creating models for prototyping.

Dana has been teaching CAD for jewelry privately and at the Fashion Institute of Technology since 2004.

CPSIA information can be obtained at www.ICGtesting.com
Printed in the USA
LVOW091934191012

303643LV00004B/85/P